Syntactic Analysis
An HPSG-Based Approach

In syntactic analysis, as in linguistics generally, the skills required to first identify, and then make sense of, complex patterns in linguistic data involve a certain specific kind of reasoning, where various alternatives are entertained and modified in light of progressively broader empirical coverage. Rather than focus on transmitting the details of complex theoretical superstructures, this textbook takes a practical, analytical approach, starting from a small set of powerful analytic tools, applied first to simple phenomena and then to the passive, complement, and raising/control constructions. The analytic tools are then applied to unbounded dependences, via detailed argumentation. What emerges is that syntactic structure and intricate networks of dependencies linking different parts of those structures are straightforward projections of lexical valence, in tandem with very general rules regulating the sharing of feature values. Featuring integrated exercises and problems throughout each chapter, this book equips students with the analytical tools for recognizing and assessing linguistic patterns.

ROBERT D. LEVINE is Professor of Linguistics at Ohio State University. He is the co-author of *The Unity of Unbounded Dependency Constructions* (with Thomas E. Hukari, 2015) and the editor of *Formal Grammar* (1992) and *Studies in Contemporary Phrase Structure Grammar* (with Georgia M. Green, Cambridge, 2010). He has also published many articles in journals such as *Natural Language and Linguistic Theory*, *Language*, *Linguistic Inquiry*, *Linguistics and Philosophy* and *Journal of Linguistics*.

CAMBRIDGE TEXTBOOKS IN LINGUISTICS

General editors: P. AUSTIN, J. BRESNAN, B. COMRIE, S. CRAIN,
W. DRESSLER, C. EWEN, R. LASS, D. LIGHTFOOT, K. RICE, I. ROBERTS,
S. ROMAINE, N.V. SMITH.

Syntactic Analysis
An HPSG-Based Approach

Syntactic Analysis
An HPSG-Based Approach

ROBERT D. LEVINE

Ohio State University

CAMBRIDGE
UNIVERSITY PRESS

University Printing House, Cambridge CB2 8BS, United Kingdom

One Liberty Plaza, 20th Floor, New York, NY 10006, USA

477 Williamstown Road, Port Melbourne, VIC 3207, Australia

484324, 2nd Floor, Ansari Road, Daryaganj, Delhi – 110002, India

79 Anson Road, #06–0406, Singapore 079906

Cambridge University Press is part of the University of Cambridge.

It furthers the University's mission by disseminating knowledge in the pursuit of
education, learning and research at the highest international levels of excellence.

www.cambridge.org
Information on this title: www.cambridge.org/9781107018884
10.10179781139093521

© Cambridge University Press 2017

First published 2017

Printed in the United States of America by Sheridan Books, Inc.

A catalogue record for this publication is available from the British Library

Library of Congress Cataloging-in-Publication data
Names: Levine, Robert, 1947– author.
Title: Syntactic analysis : an HPSG-based approach / Robert D. Levine.
Description: Cambridge ; New York, NY : Cambridge University Press, [2016] |
Series: Cambridge textbooks in linguistics | Includes bibliographical references and index.
Identifiers: LCCN 2016022602 | ISBN 9781107018884 (Hardback)
Subjects: LCSH: Grammar, Comparative and general–Syntax. |
Head-driven phrase structure grammar. | Generative grammar. | Linguistic analysis (Linguistics) |
BISAC: LANGUAGE ARTS & DISCIPLINES / General.
Classification: LCC P158.4 .L384 2016 | DDC 415.01/823–dc23 LC record
available at https://lccn.loc.gov/2016022602

ISBN 978-1-107-01888-4 Hardback
ISBN 978-1-107-61412-3 Paperback

Contents

Preface

There is a long tradition in syntax textbooks whereby the early sections (or chapters) present a particular 'take' on the key properties of human language (e.g., its unboundedness, the fact that speakers can pass intuitive and more or less definitive judgments on the well-formedness as stand-alone sentences of arbitrary strings of words, and so on), followed by an overview of fundamental data structure that are said to best capture these properties, followed by a series of chapters applying those data structures to a range of natural language data. Along the way, technical refinements are introduced, attempts are made to formalize the often informal statements of descriptive machinery given at the outset to jump-start the discussion, and the discussion increasingly becomes focused on the content of the theoretical framework, with natural language data used as points of departure for exploring that content. Every such framework seems to have its own 'set piece' examples which demonstrate its explanatory reach, its ability to capture apparently profound generalizations with a minimal number of additional assumptions. The virtues of this narrative organization are obvious: the point of any science is to capture the behavior of its objects of interest as parsimoniously as possible, which in turn requires an analytic toolkit to capture the generalizations that represent that science's *discoveries* about its domain of inquiry. In order to say anything useful about that domain, students must first acquire a basic working familiarity with those conceptual tools by applying them to simpler phenomena (typically using optimally simple or idealized data sets) and progressively refine and expand their mastery of the framework by tackling increasingly challenging or even open-ended problems. So far, so good.

But this kind of storyline faces a certain kind of risk: the text becomes in effect a kind of recipe book of stock analyses, with large chunks of the thinking that went into these analyses presented as faits accomplis, which students are expected to internalize and extend to new data. The result is a heavily 'top-down' presentation of syntax, making it a matter of mastering a typically complex set of technical tools, specialized notations, and axioms. But anyone who has spent much time doing syntax is well aware that, in practice, research in the field has more the quality of a series of difficult challenges, counterexamples, analytic directions that go nowhere, and novel data that force investigators to backtrack and modify their thinking continuously. What makes syntax so attractive and exciting as a field of study are the demands it places on its practitioners for flexibility, lateral thinking, and persistence. These aspects of the field are, I think, inherent in the nature of the kind of data that syntacticians try to make sense of, and in order to teach syntax, we need to focus on eliciting from students just this kind of flexible thinking and skill in finding analyses that work. Many modern textbooks, regardless of theoretical stance, seem to me to favor detailed presentations of a preferred system, but what students need to master in order to pursue syntax successfully is the ability to construct well-thought-out arguments for specific proposals. Ideally, the details of a particular framework emerge incrementally as a body of successful analyses is built up, with new problems leading to extensions or revisions of the original proposals.

A near-perfect example of what I have in mind here is the great Soames/Perlmutter textbook *Syntactic Argumentation and the Structure of English*, and while the following chapters are arranged in a quite different, more traditional format, I've tried to follow as much as possible Soames and Perlmutter's expository practice in two respects:

- emphasizing the burden on the investigator not only to propose an analysis which accounts for the data in question, but also to experiment with a few plausible alternatives and push them as far as possible before pronouncing them untenable;
- relying on a small, powerful set of analytic tools, and trying to get as much mileage out of their use as possible before going on to introduce elaborations, and then only the most conservative innovations that are needed to capture the observed regularities.

To equip students with the argumentation skills necessary for making sense of a range of syntactic dependencies, Soames and Perlmutter took the ordered trans-formational rule cycle as their conceptual workhorse. In the following chapters, I use instead the satisfaction of lexically specified valence specifications, with the formal platform of Head-driven Phrase Structure Grammar's (HPSG) feature logic, as per Pollard and Sag (1994), assumed in the background, as the central explanatory key to a wide range of local dependencies, incorporating analytic insights that originated in the paradigm-transforming work of the pioneers of Generalized Phrase Structure Grammar, HPSG's direct ancestor. From a pedagogical standpoint, the lexically based version of HPSG employed here (as vs the version of HPSG which has evolved over the past two decades, via increasing reliance on hierarchies of often very elaborate syntactic types, into a version of construction grammar) is particularly user-friendly; phenomena which were treated by cyclic 'relation-changing' rules in the 'Standard Theory' era – passive, extraposition, *there* insertion, Raising and similar operations – are all simply statable in terms of valence specifications, and identity between the values of valence features, using the logic of path identities that the 1994 avatar of HPSG was based on.

But I want to emphasize that this book is *not* intended to be an introduction to strongly lexicalist HPSG; rather, as its title suggests, it's an introduction to the art of reasoning about the phrase structure of natural language sentences

and their subparts, *grounded in* the formally explicit and consistent technology
of feature structures and their description logics (with these formalisms hidden
from the user), and guided by what I take to be the fundamental insight of HPSG:
that syntactic structure is nothing but a reflection of the steps mandated by
the grammars of individual languages through which the valence requirements
of lexical items are satisfied. It's important that the conceptual resources of a
framework have explicit denotations – something which is unfortunately not the
case in a good deal of contemporary syntactic theorizing – but formally secure
foundations are nothing more than a necessary condition on saying something
that actually corresponds to a well-defined object. Arguing for the superiority of
a particular analysis requires that one not only recognizes the pattern or regularity
that needs to be captured, and how a given proposal duly captures that pattern, but
also that other possibly quite plausible alternatives be ruled out by confronting
them with contradictory data. And there is no simple procedure for determining
what such data might be. The narrative thread in the rest of this book therefore
consistently follows the mindset of the analyst confronting a range of possible
solutions to an increasingly wide-ranging set of interlocking problems. This is,
in fact, pretty much the permanent situation of syntacticians. As Paul Postal put
it, in perhaps the most eloquent passage in the whole literature of grammatical
theory:

> we remain with hardly a single reasonably articulated analysis of any
> component of the grammar which even approaches relative stability or
> unchallengeability. Proposal after proposal ... has collapsed or slid into the
> murk of competing claims and contradictory evidence ... as the documen-
> tation of the factual enormity of, for example, English grammar continues
> and expands ... we can ... see with increasing clarity the quite incredible
> scope of human grammar and correspondingly the limitations of any set of
> principles that can be posited today to reconstruct this system. Even the best
> theory is none too good. One must, I think, be led to an increased respect
> for the subject under study and, ultimately, for the unknown forces which
> brought it into existence.   (Postal 1972: 160–162)

What Postal wrote in 1972 is as true today as ever. And it holds even with respect
to the framework that this volume is couched in. HPSG, like all other phrase-
structure based approaches, has significant lacunæ in its coverage, particularly
in the areas of coordination and ellipsis, two vast domains of phenomena
which raise serious questions about the ultimate viability of phrase structure
configuration as the appropriate representational language for expressions in
natural languages, and which I therefore have had nothing to say about in this
book. So far as semantics is concerned, the somewhat different problem is one
of intrinsic difficulty: the only formally explicit framework mapping HPSG
syntactic representations to actual truth-conditional representations, Lexical
Resource Semantics, is technically far too difficult to include in a source with
this book's intended audience. Rather than substituting one of the various markup
languages which have, for most of HPSG's evolution, been used as a substitute

for a genuine semantics, I've used very informal characterizations of relevant truth conditions where necessary, in the expectation that instructors using this text will supplement the text with their own favorite syntax/semantics translation mechanisms.

Despite these shortcomings, the approach taken in HPSG to both local and nonlocal dependencies gives students the critical analytic means not only to understand individual syntactic dependencies but also to see how they can be chained together in arbitrarily complex ways. Thus, the lexicon and a very small number of lexical and structural combinatory rules will license sentences such as *It seems to have already been decided that John was guilty*, where the independent analyses of extraposition, passive, and 'raising' properties of both *seems* and the auxiliaries jointly entail the well-formedness of such sentences as a straightforward consequence of the feature path identities imposed by the HPSG constraint system. Following the first chapter laying the basic arguments for, and the most perspicuous representation of, the internal hierarchical structure of sentences, the next four chapters develop a set of interconnected arguments about the organization of the auxiliary complex in English sentences and the consequent basic picture of clause structure, relatedness between constructions as an epiphenomenon of systematic relations between the valence properties of morphologically related lexical items, and the propagation of information in nonfinite clauses. The addition of nonlocal dependencies requires an additional mechanism beyond the simple valence saturation which is sufficient to handle the example just given, for reasons that I've taken some pains to lay out in detail in Chapter 6.

But I think it's also important for students studying syntax at even a fairly basic level to appreciate that much of the data which we've taken to reflect something about syntactic combinatorics is in fact a reflection of interacting functional factors – working memory, processing routines and their inherent bottlenecks, pragmatic coherence (or lack of coherence), prosodic requirements, and so on. For this reason, I've included a final chapter, part of which looks at what were regarded for a long time as syntactic island phenomena, and summarizes some of what has been learned over the past extremely productive two decades about the extragrammatical sources of island effects. These findings are of compelling interest in their own right, I think, but for students there is a particularly important message: on the one hand, syntax may actually be, not easier, but *simpler* than we thought it was – but on the other, the lesson of this research is that one can't do syntax in isolation from psycholinguistics, pragmatics and semantics, and prosody, at least if one wishes to avoid what I believe are the problematic assumptions of the past.

I am enormously indebted to a number of people for the conversations, arguments, and collaborations which have shaped my thinking about the content of framework which serves as the platform for the material in this book: Carl Pollard, Robert Borsley, Detmar Meurers, Manfred Sailer, Frank Richter, Gert Webelhuth, Stefan Müller, Tibor Kiss, Erhard Hinrichs, Geoff Pullum, the late Ivan Sag and, most especially, my long-time friend and collaborator Thomas Hukari, none of whom bear the slightest responsibility for any shortcomings in what I've written. Thanks also to Hoskuldur Thrainsson for some very useful information about Icelandic, and to Bob Borsley for discussing with me data from Welsh which show that it belongs to the class of languages which mark extraction pathways. A special debt to the almost thirty years of my graduate and undergraduate syntax students at Ohio State University, who shaped my thinking about both syntax and the teaching of syntax.

Finally, my sincere thanks to Gert Webelhuth, who gave me invaluable detailed comments on an early draft, to Helen Barton, my unfailingly patient and encouraging editor at CUP, and to Daphne and Adrian.

1 Syntactic Data, Patterns, and Structure

1.1 Introduction: The Problem, and a Possible Solution

1.1.1 Natural Language Data

Linguists appear to be in an enviable position among scientific disciplines. The lifeblood of science is data, and unlike, say, glaciologists, who can only collect primary material for their research in remote and generally rather inhospitable parts of the planet, or particle physicists, who require access to massive, extremely expensive, and sometimes erratic machines – with demand for access to such machines far exceeding supply – linguists are literally surrounded by the kind of data that make up the target of their investigations. It's true that field linguists need informants at a considerable distance from where they themselves live, and experimental linguists often need laboratories with elaborate and sophisticated equipment. But for syntacticians – linguists who investigate the structure of sentences, a large fraction of whom (possibly a majority) study sentences in their own respective languages – matters are as convenient as they could possibly be. Syntacticians have intuitive access to all of the sentences made available by their own knowledge of their language, as well as the speech (and reactions) of their fellows in constant use around them, and ready-made corpora in the form of written materials and electronic records, many of which are available for searches based on word sequences (Google, for example, is a valuable source of data for both syntacticians and morphologists). Learning how to take advantage of this vast pool of readily available data is a major component of syntacticians' training.

In a sense, of course, the true data of syntax are not strings of words themselves, but *judgments* about the status of those strings of words. The syntactician's primary responsibility is to give an account of how it is that certain strings of words have the status of sentences, while other do not, and still others have a kind of shadowy intermediate status – not bad enough to be outright rubbish, but not good enough to pass completely unnoticed in conversation as utterly and tediously normal. For example, consider the status of the three word strings in (1):

(1) a. I asked Robin to leave the room.

    b. I requested Robin to leave the room.

    c. I inquired (of) Robin to leave the room.

Many speakers appear to rank (1)a as completely unexceptionable, (1)b as 'off'
in some noticeable way but not totally unacceptable, and (1)c to be altogether
wrong, something that a native speaker of English would simply never say.
A complete account of what gives a particular string of words the status of a
sentence should, ideally, provide an explanation for the peculiar nature of the
deviance of (1)b and the altogether ill-formed status of (1)c. In constructing such
an explanation, the linguist will bear very much in mind that *ask* and *inquire* can
substitute for each other quite acceptably in the sentences in (2).

(2) a.   I $\left\{\begin{array}{l} \text{asked} \\ \text{inquired} \end{array}\right\}$ about Robin's health.

   b.   I $\left\{\begin{array}{l} \text{asked} \\ \text{inquired} \end{array}\right\}$ whether Robin would be home later.

What is going on in (1) to produce the striking disparity between the first and
third examples?

One obvious approach we might start with is that on one of its senses, *ask*
points to a relationship between (i) a speaker, (ii) a potential actor, and (iii) an
action, of the same general type as *command* or *ordered*, but much weaker. In
all of these cases, the speaker has expressed a solicitation for Robin to carry
out a certain action, one whose precise nature is made clear by the sequence
of words *to leave the room*. That preference may have relatively little force to
back it up, or, in the case of *command*, quite a bit of force. *Inquire*, on the other
hand, does not seem to correspond to this sense of *ask*, but only to a solicitation
of information. So one might assume that the contrast between the first and
third examples in (1) – which itself is conspicuously at variance with the verbs'
overlapping distribution in (2) – reflects the fact that only verbs which correspond
to some solicitation of action can appear in a context, such as (1), where action,
rather than information, is sought.

This kind of account is intuitively satisfying, because it seems to correspond
to common sense: using a word which is dedicated to one meaning in a context
reserved for quite a different meaning is very likely to result in nonsense, and
little more needs to be said. But there are problems with this purely meaning-
based account. *Request*, for example, *does* correspond to a solicitation of action:

(3) a.   I requested assistance from the police.
   b.   I will request that the police provide me with an escort.

Moreover, in (4), it seems clear that *inquire* is actually being used to solicit a
kind of action, rather than information alone:

(4)   I inquired whether Robin would be so good as to close the window.

Yet, as noted, for many speakers who find the examples in (3) fine, (1)b is still
less than perfect. And while the effect of using *inquire* in (4) in this way is a
degree of politeness that borders on unfriendliness in its formality, it is clear
that on the most natural interpretation, the speaker is asking Robin to close the

window, rather than any far-fetched alternative meaning involving Robin's self-assessment of his or her potential 'goodness.' In effect, one might take the verb *inquire* to be 'coerced,' by certain kind of assumptions about implicit meanings in ordinary discourse, into taking on the sense of a verb of command. For English speakers who display the kind of judgments of the data in (1) already noted, then, something other than simple 'overt' meanings seem to be involved.

Similar observations could be made with respect to *demand*: *I demanded him to leave the room* is judged as awful by virtually all native speakers, in spite of the fact that *demanded* is a solicitation of action roughly comparable in force with *order*, which works perfectly here: *I ordered him to leave the room*. Note, finally, that there is no problem with *demand* as a verb. Again, something besides the notion of meaning seems to be called for.

Examples leading to the same conclusion can be found with little effort in all human languages which have been examined in sufficient detail. A particularly nice illustration for English is given in (5):

(5) a.   They charged Robin with perjury.
    b.   They accused Robin of perjury.
    c.   They indicted Robin for perjury.

Charge, accuse, *indict*, and similar words, which can be characterized as verbs of judicial sanction, are extremely close in meaning. Yet in each of these cases, replacing the preposition in the example with one of the other two will yield a bad result (notated henceforth with a preceding asterisk): **They charged Robin of perjury* is universally regarded as unacceptable, even though, in judicial or quasi-judicial contexts, *charge* and *accuse* are virtually identical in meaning. Another example of this sort is shown in (6):

(6) a.   Robin $\left\{ \begin{array}{c} \text{grew} \\ \text{became} \end{array} \right\}$ belligerent.

    b.   Robin $\left\{ \begin{array}{c} \text{grew} \\ \text{*became} \end{array} \right\}$ to hate mathematics.

    c.   Robin $\left\{ \begin{array}{c} \text{*grew} \\ \text{became} \end{array} \right\}$ a skeptic about the usefulness of standardized tests.

The property of being belligerent, and the property of being a skeptic, that is, skeptical, both seem to be the same sort of thing; just as being belligerent and hating mathematics both seem to refer to mental/emotional attitudes. So why do the facts sort the way they do in (6)? Indeed, if we replace *a skeptic* with *skeptical* in (6)c, *grew* becomes just as acceptable as in (6)a. Once again, meaning does not appear to be a particularly promising angle from which to attack the problem posed by (6).

Still another instance of the same mismatch between syntactic form and semantic interpretation is afforded by cases such as

(7)   We $\left\{ \begin{array}{c} \text{solved} \\ \text{resolved} \end{array} \right\}$ the problem.

(8) a.   We arrived at a solution $\left\{ \begin{array}{c} \text{to} \\ \text{??*of} \end{array} \right\}$ the problem.

   b.   We arrived at a resolution $\left\{ \begin{array}{c} \text{of} \\ \text{??*to} \end{array} \right\}$ the problem.

The notation * indicates outright ill-formedness, and ??* a highly marginal status at best. Yet given that we often use *solve* and *resolve* to mean exactly the same thing with respect to problems (particularly of the human conflict sort), a meaning-based view of the conditions under which the prepositions *to* and *of* can appear makes the facts in (8) quite mysterious.

A somewhat more complex example of the same difficulty is afforded by cases like the following:

(9) a.   That jail sentence confused the twins.
   b.   The twins were confused by that jail sentence.

The formal connection between such sentences, which we will investigate in some detail in Chapter 4, is referred to by linguists as the active/passive relationship, and (9) is completely representative of the fact that passives invariably mean the same thing as their corresponding active forms. One very clear pointer to this identity in meaning is that if an active sentence is true, the passive analogue is true and vice versa; we say that the active and passive forms are *truth-conditionally equivalent*. What changes going from the active to the passive is, very roughly speaking, which of two different roles – the initiator of an action vs the target of that action, to take a very common kind of active/passive relationship – gets assigned to which element in the sentence (*the twins* follows the verb in (9)a, but precedes it in (9)b. But the situation depicted by the active and passive is invariably the same.

But things appear to be very different in the case of (10).

(10) a.   The twin's imprisonment confused them.
    b.   They were confused by the twin's imprisonment.
    c.   In spite of their legal sophistication, the twins were confused at being sentenced to imprisonment.
    d.   Friends of theirs were confused by the twin's imprisonment.

Native speakers of English are unanimous in their judgment that in sentences such as (10)a, the third person plural pronoun can be taken to refer to the same two people as *the twins*, while in (10)b the pronoun *cannot* refer to those people. In the latter case, *they* must be someone other than the twins. Since, as we have already observed, active and passive sentences have the same meaning, what is responsible for the restriction on who it is that *they* can refer to in (10)b?

Again, there is a seemingly obvious answer based on meaning considerations. Pronouns such as *they* are, after all, pointers to individuals, objects or other types of entity which typically have already been mentioned in the sentence or the discourse, whereas in (10)b, the intended referent – the thing(s) the pronoun is pointing to – is mentioned only *after* the pronoun. How can a linguistic expression intended to refer to some preceding element be successfully used in a sentence to point to an entity which has not yet occurred in that sentence? Hence, the story goes, it makes sense that reference to the twins is ruled out for *they* in this example: one should not be able to use a form to point back to something which has not yet appeared.

But while this answer is plausible, and appealing in its simplicity, it is shown to be incorrect by the data in (10)c–d. We see that while the possessive pronouns *their/theirs* precedes *the twins*, we have no problem interpreting the two expressions as referring to the same individuals in either of these examples. Grasping at straws, one might try to explain the difference in the cases as a reflection of the difference between possessive forms of pronouns, which one might assume can find their referent in a following linguistic expression, versus nonpossessive pronouns which can only share a referent with a preceding expression. But this rather contrived explanation cannot be maintained, as examples such as the following show:

(11) a.   Those stories about them are not what the twins wanted to hear.
     b.   After they were taken to the dean, the twins received a stern lecture about plagiarism and intellectual honesty.
     c.   Which stories about them do you think the twins would least like to have repeated?

In all cases, *they/them* can refer to the twins.

So it turns out that the simple account of (10) in terms of the relative linear order of the pronoun and its referent fails in the face of quite ordinary and straightforward facts about English, a few of which are given in (10)–(11). For our present purposes, this result means that we cannot take the position either that there is some semantic reason why the possible meanings of the pronouns in (10)a and b respectively are different (after all, actives and their corresponding passive mean the same thing) or that these different possibilities can be accounted for in terms of simple linear order of words within sentences (since whether or not a pronoun can refer to the same thing as an expression such as *the twins* does not seem to be determined by which of these precedes the other).

A final example will help set the stage for the next step in the development of a practical approach to identifying the factors which determine what is and is not possible in the form of any given sentence. Consider:

(12) a.   You may want to laugh at them, but you should not laugh at them.
     b.   You may want to laugh at them, but you should not.

Following the negative marker *not*, we can omit the word string *laugh at them* with no loss of acceptability; in fact, unless fairly heavy stress falls on *not* in (12)a, the latter seems a bit stilted and artificial. Compare (12) with:

(13) a.   You may want to laugh at them, but you should try to not laugh at them.
     b.   *You may want to laugh at them, but you should try to not.

For some reason, the result of omitting *laugh at them* after *to* here yields a very ill-formed example, one which most English speakers find distinctly anomalous. One response to this discrepancy between (12) and (13) is to suppose that the existence of an alternative order which *is* acceptable – *You may want to laugh at them, but you should try not to* – has the effect of making the first ordering of words bad. But this explanation lacks credibility, given that we have the same alternative order available for the well-formed (13)a – *You may want to laugh at them, but you should try not to laugh at them* – with no resulting ill-effects. Both this ordering and the ordering in (13)a are fine. And in general, variant word orders which correspond to identical meanings are not exactly rare in natural languages; note, for example,

(14) a.   That Robin is a spy seems strange.

    b.   It seems strange that Robin is a spy.

(15) a.   Robin strode fearlessly into the room.

    b.   Into the room strode Robin fearlessly.

(16) a.   I'm fairly sure that everyone likes ice cream.

    b.   Ice cream, I'm fairly sure that everyone likes.

In the first of these examples, the only difference in the collection of words used in the two sentences is a meaningless *it*, commonly referred to as a 'dummy' pronoun, which adds precisely nothing to the meaning, since the first sentence conveys exactly the same information without this *it* being present. In the second and third examples, the inventory of words in the two sentences is exactly the same, but the order in the a and b versions is significantly different in both cases. Yet in all three examples, both of the orders displayed in a and b are perfectly acceptable. The rhetorical effect might be slightly different, but the meanings are – in the truth-conditional sense referred to earlier – identical. So whatever the problem with (13)b is, it's very unlikely to be the existence of an alternative order in and of itself.

Such facts, and scores of similar ones that can be easily discovered once one starts looking for them, make it seem reasonable to be very skeptical about the possibility of using either word meanings or the simple linear arrangement of words to explain the somewhat mysterious behavior of English sentences; and investigation of any other well-studied language would lead to the same conclusion. On the other hand, it's important not to go so far as to assume that neither meaning nor linear order *ever* play important roles in determining the status of strings of words in the judgment of native speakers – nothing about the preceding discussion would support that position, and it turns out that it too must be rejected on empirical grounds. The right conclusion is that meaning and linear order cannot account for the behavior of word strings in English – that is, the *syntax* of English – *in general*; and the same holds across the board for all other human languages whose syntax we know something about. Clearly, we have to look in a different direction if we want to make sense of syntactic patterns.

1.1.2   A Possible Line of Solution

The data reviewed in the preceding section suggest that there are other properties of sentences, involving neither meaning nor simple observations about word order, which have important consequences for the possible form of English sentences. But this result requires us to attribute properties to sentences that we have no immediate evidence for. We know how sentences are pronounced, obviously. We know what they mean. And we know what order the words they comprise appear in. But apparently there are properties of sentences which bear strongly on their possible form, but which involve none of the obvious characteristics just mentioned. Something else is necessary, which we have no direct information about at this point. Nonetheless, we can hazard some reasonable guesses. The fact that meaning seems to be largely irrelevant to the behavior we've observed points to the likelihood that some aspect of sentence *form* is responsible for this behavior.

One avenue worth exploring is that words enter into relations with other words, or other groups of words, and these relations are independent of meaning. And since the simple order of words also appears to be irrelevant in the crucial cases where we might want to invoke it, it seems a good bet that at least one of the formal properties we're searching for will have to involve relationships among words which are not immediately 'visible'. This line of reasoning leads to the possibility that what is relevant for solutions to the kinds of problems pointed out earlier may be covert arrangements of lexical items. Earlier, we sought to explain the behavior of pronouns on the basis of certain kinds of overt arrangements – an hypothesis which, as we observed, fails empirically. But we can still entertain the possibility that there are hidden, or more abstract, relations, inaccessible to direct observation, which give rise to the observed behavior.

This kind of reasoning is not unusual in any scientific study of particular phenomena; many people can recall high school physics classes in which a large metal tin, the kind commonly used for olive oil, is filled with water and then has the water siphoned out, with the can collapsing into a crushed heap as the water is removed. If this experiment were conducted in a vacuum, the can would remain intact under the same conditions, yet there would be no visible differences in the two situations that would account for the different effects. We would then be inclined to posit some invisible factor responsible, and look for further evidence to challenge or corroborate this hypothesis, eventually leading us to conclude that an invisible medium is indeed present in the context in which the can is crushed, that that same medium allows a flame to be struck from a match (as opposed to the situation in which the can remains intact, and where no match would ignite regardless of how many times it was struck), and so on. Since we're looking at sequences of words, rather than physical objects, however, it's not immediately apparent what linguistic analogue would correspond to the presence vs absence of the invisible gas we call air.

A more specific sort of analogy which may help make this possibility more concrete can be found instead by comparing the sentences in the examples given above with strings of beads that make up different necklaces or bracelets, with each bead corresponding to a word. Imagine being in the position of someone looking at a necklace consisting of a line of beads on a string and wondering if there were any properties of that necklace which couldn't be explained by the simple linear order in which the beads had been set. An obvious candidate for such a concealed property would be in the way the beads are grouped: is there any possibility that what looks like a single uninterrupted strand actually has small knots separating certain groups of beads from others? If there are knots between the fifth bead and the sixth, and betweeth the fifteenth and the sixteenth, then the effect of cutting the string in the exact middle of the necklace is going to have a rather different effect when the two separate halves are picked up by the uncut ends than a necklace with no internal partitions. The same may well be true for two otherwise identical necklaces with knot partitions established in different places respectively.

These examples suggest a way in which seemingly identical strings of elements of the same kind can indirectly reflect hidden differences which are strictly independent of the overt order of the elements that the string comprises. Without actually proving that human language sentences necessarily incorporate structural differences of just this kind, they offer a kind of existence proof that where systematic differences exist in the patterns of behavior manifested by different-looking sentences, the divergence could in principle reflect distinct ways that the words in the two sentences 'cluster,' in some sense still to be made more specific. But since deductive reasoning can only take us so far, we need to turn to some actual data, some phenomenon or set of phenomena which might shed light on the questions we've posed.

1.2   Structure: Some Clues

Our chief tool, here and in the following chapters, will turn out to be the relatively simple idea that where we have sets of sentences which seem to be related to each other in a systematic way, the precise form of the relationship must – wherever a simple account in terms of meaning cannot be given – be accounted for in terms of some *formal* property of the sentences involved.

1.2.1   Displacement: A Basic Natural Language Pattern

We've already mentioned, in passing, one of the key components of the data we need to use as a basis for probing the possibility of hidden linguistic structure: the existence of sentences which mean the same thing, use identical or nearly identical vocabulary, but manifest significant differences in word order. Consider for example sentences of the form in (17):

(17) a.   That Robin turned out to be a spy $\left\{\begin{array}{c} \text{worries} \\ \text{troubles} \\ \text{encourages} \\ \text{annoys} \\ \text{enrages} \\ \text{impresses} \end{array}\right\}$ me.

b.   It $\left\{\begin{array}{c} \text{worries} \\ \text{troubles} \\ \text{encourages} \\ \text{annoys} \\ \text{enrages} \\ \text{impresses} \end{array}\right\}$ me that Robin turned out to be a spy.

c.   I'm $\left\{\begin{array}{c} \text{worried} \\ \text{troubled} \\ \text{encouraged} \\ \text{annoyed} \\ \text{enraged} \\ \text{impressed} \end{array}\right\}$ that Robin turned out to be a spy.

Not only are these sententences truth-conditionally identical in meaning, but they reflect an orderly and systematic pattern involving near-identical vocabulary arranged in three distinct word-order patterns which relate to each other in a completely regular manner. Furthermore, the same relationship holds if we replace *That Robin turned out to be a spy* with *That my cousin's wife won a Nobel Prize in physics*, or with *That the Dean of the Medical School never pays any taxes*, and so on, and replace *me/I* with *them/they*, or with *the trustees*, or with *an old friend of mine from school*, etc. We can almost always do this sort of thing: record a number of English sentences at random, and then on the basis of these sentences, construct other sentences using almost exactly the same words, which mean exactly the same thing as the original sentences, but nonetheless differ noticeably so far as word order is concerned. We might note, for example, that forms of sentences such as (18)a are systematically matched with sentences such as (18)b:

(18) a.   If Terry SAID you have made a mistake, then you HAVE **made a mistake**.

     b.   If Terry SAID you have made a mistake, then **made a mistake** you (definitely) HAVE __.

In the second of these, the string of words *made a mistake* appears to be missing from what we believe its normal place to be as reflected in the first example; it appears instead at the front of the second part of the larger sentence, directly following *then*. The meanings of the two sentences in (18) are identical, and exactly the same words are present in (18)a and b; all that has changed between the two is the order of a particular substring shared by both sentences.

It is not difficult to find any number of completely parallel examples, for example:

(19) a.   Terry SAID she may go to the movies, and indeed, she MAY **go to the movies**.

b.   Terry SAID she may go to the movies, and indeed, **go to the movies** she MAY __.

(20) a.   If Terry SAID that Robin has been giving Leslie a hard time, then Robin definitely HAS been **giving Leslie a hard time**.

b.   If Terry SAID that Robin has been giving Leslie a hard time, then **giving Leslie a hard time** Robin definitely HAS been __.

What are we to make of such examples? The very simplest assumption is that, where we have a series of words that we recognize as a sentence, we also expect to find a different series of words, related to the first by repositioning *any* substring *X* so that *X* appears at the front of the sentence. But this summary of the pattern exhibited in (18)–(20) fares badly in the face of examples such as the following:

(21) a.   Terry says she is putting the book on the table, and **putting the book on the table** she is __.

b.   *Terry said she is putting the book on the table, and **putting** she is __the book on the table.

c.   *Terry said she is putting the book on the table, and **putting the book** she is __on the table.

d.   *Terry said she is putting the book on the table, and **putting the book on** she is __the table.

Apparently, not all subsequences of words within a sentence are created equal. There is a clear difference in status between *putting the book on the table* in (21)a and *putting, putting the book*, and *putting the book on*. *X* cannot be any arbitrary substring, and to advance our current line of analysis, we need a way to mark the subsequences of words within any give sentence which are displaceable, in contrast to those which are not.

We might start by using some fairly transparent notation, such as brackets ([ ]) around the sequences we've been able to relocate, indicating that these sequences constitute some kind of covert unit. For the sentence *She is putting the book on the table*, we could use this notation to capture the pattern exhibited in (21) as follows:

(22)   she is [putting the book on the table]

We further assume that only such unitary strings are able to appear at the front of the sentence, leaving an apparent gap corresponding to the position they occupy in (22). Simple as this move appears to be, it leads immediately to some interesting problems which help us to clarify just what kind of solution it is we're considering.

(23) a.   Terry said she would leave, and [leave] she did.
     b.   *Terry said she would leave us, and leave she did __us.

On the basis of our provisional approach to the problem posed by such apparent displacement, we have to regard *leave* as a displaceable unit, since, given (23)a, it obviously does appear in the displaced position at the left of the sentence. Yet in (23)b it is *not* displaceable. There seems to be a contradiction here which we can find in other examples as well. Consider:

(24) a.   Terry said she would leave us, and [leave us] she did __.
     b.   *Terry said she would leave us the keys, and leave us she did __the keys.
     c.   Terry said she would leave us the keys, and leave us the keys she did.

Before reading on, stop for a moment and try to think through what's going on in these examples. Do you see the parallel between the pattern in (24)a vs (24)b and (23)a vs (23)b? What is the general lesson that such pairs of example have for us? Think carefully about this last question, and make sure you see clearly how it amounts to a question about whether or not the fact that a certain string of words combine to form a unit in one sentence means that in any other sentence that same string of words will *necessarily* also be a unit.

You should be able to see from the examples in (23) and (24) that, while it might be true that some particular substring of words will be a unit in a given sentence, it does not follow that in a different sentence the same string of words necessarily constitutes a displaceable unit. We need to keep this fact in mind, because it will keep emerging in the course of our investigations. Other examples are:

(25) a.   I had argued with the guy.
     b.   ... and [argued with the guy] I had __.

(26) a.   I had argued with the guy from Tucson.
     b.   ... and [argued with the guy from Tucson] I had __.
     c.   *... and [argued with the guy] I had __from Tucson.

You should find it fairly easy to construct your own examples along these lines. But what are we to make of them?

Let's use (26) as a test case. We have evidence from (25) that, following the verb *had*, the string *argued with the guy* behaves as a unit – if this string appears displaced on the left, the result is impeccable (and receives the same interpretation as (26)a. And we have evidence from (26)b, where it also follows *had*, the string *argued with the guy from Tucson* behaves as a unit. But what (26)c shows us is that the string *argued with the guy*, which is an uncontroversial unit in (25), is NOT a unit in (26)a, since it fails the displacement test which it passes with no trouble in (25)b. So, very roughly speaking, what we are looking for is an account of the fact that in the context depicted in (27)a, when X = ∅, that is, silence, the string can show up in the displacement context, whereas when X = *from Tucson*, the string *argued with the guy* is nondisplaceable:

(27) a.   Robin had argued with the guy X.

    b.   Robin had [argued with the guy X]

If we assume that there is a bracketed structure [argued with the guy X] as per (27)b, and that only bracketed structures can displace, then we predict (28) exactly:

(28) a.   Robin had [argued with the guy]

    b.   Robin [argued with the guy from Tucson]

    c.   [Argued with the guy], Robin had.

    d.   *[Argued with the guy] Robin had [from Tucson]

In the first example, *argued with the guy* is surrounded by brackets which include no other material. In the second, this string is not immediately bordered by brackets, meaning, according to our conventions, that it does *not* constitute a unit with respect to the displacement test. This, of course, is exactly the result we want to implement, so we have some reason to take our notation here seriously as a formal expression of structural relationships revealed by English data.

But even so, the situation is far from satisfactory. We really have no idea what the bracketing notation actually means – at this point, it's just a series of symbols on a page. Things will become clearer as the discussion proceeds, but for the moment, we simply acknowledge that the use of the bracket notation introduced earlier to capture some notion of unithood with respect to displaceability is versatile enough to be compatible with the fact that some given substring of words may be a displaceable unit in one sentence and a nonunit in other sentences. The notational issue can (and will) be addressed in depth, but a logically prior question involves the status of the notion 'unit' as we've used it here. Exactly what does this notion of unithood actually buy us, in the way of descriptive depth?

The possibly surprising answer at this point is, not very much. The problem is that there is a kind of implicit circularity in our approach which deprives our arguments for syntactic structure based on displaceability of any logical force. In a nutshell, we are using the displacement criterion to identify an abstract unit, while at the same time appealing to the unithood of the string so identified to motivate its displaceability. Clearly, as long as we have no *independent* evidence except for displacement for identifying certain substrings as units, the claim that we can displace just those substrings which are syntactic units amounts to the fairly uninteresting claim that we can displace just those substrings of the sentence that are displaceable.

The solution is to show that there are other distributional facts about substrings in sentences – facts which cannot be reduced to any kind of variation of displacement – and that a general account of these facts must appeal to exactly the same notion of unithood as displacement. The two phenomena which appeal to unithood must, in other words, be fundamentally independent. Normal methodological considerations then make it highly unlikely that the joint appeal to syntactic unithood from two independent sources envisioned here arose from coincidence. Rather, such a state of affairs would strongly support the existence of a class of subunits within any sentence to which the principles regulating the distributional facts in question had to appeal. And as it turns out, such a class of independent facts indeed exists.

1.2.2 VP Proform Replacement

Consider the data presented in (29)–(33):

(29) a. If Terry SAID she would go to the movies, then she WILL go to the movies.
  b. If Terry SAID she would go to the movies, then go to the movies she WILL.
  c. If Terry SAID she would go to the movies, then she will DO SO.

We have in a simple structure (29)a which is matched by an instance of displacement (29)b on the one hand, and on the other, by a version (29)c in which a sequence *do so* appears to have replaced just that string of words which is displaced in the preceding sentence. And such examples are hardly isolated cases:

(30) a. If Terry SAID she was putting the book on the table, then she WAS putting the book on the table.
  b. If Terry said she was putting the book on the table, then she was DOING so.
  c. If Terry said she was putting the book on the table, then putting the book on the table she was.

(31) a. *If Terry SAID she was putting the book on the table, then she was DOING so the book on the table.
  b. *If Terry SAID she was putting the book on the table, then putting she was the book on the table.

(32) a. *If Terry SAID she was putting the book on the table, then she was DOING so on the table.
  b. *If Terry SAID she was putting the book on the table, then putting the book she was on the table.

Note in addition the following data:

(33) a. *If Terry SAID she was putting the book on the table, then she was DOING so the table.
  b. *If Terry SAID she was putting the book on the table, then putting the book on she was the table.

There is a striking pattern suggested in this sequence of examples: wherever replacement by some form of *do so* is possible, displacement of the replaced substring is possible, and wherever such replacement is blocked, so is the corresponding displacement. Naturally, the data exhibited are only a small sampling of the possibilities, and it would be an instructive exercise for the reader to take various substrings at random and see whether any of them that are replaceable by *do so* if the morphologically appropriate variant are not displaceable. The goodness of fit between the *do so* replacement facts and the displaceability facts is significant, because displacement and replacement are quite independent phenomena, as we require. Below we will see that there are several subtypes of displacement, so that showing a given substring undergoing several of these subtypes wouldn't really count as an array of independent bases for positing syntactic units: if all of these cases are instances of displacement, then even though they represent different manifestations of displacement, the case can easily be made that it's only a single criterion being satisfied. But the existence of *do so* in an example which neatly lines up with the presence of a gap, where the substring matching that gap is exactly the substring whose denotation *do so* points to in the replacement case, is an instance of truly independent lines of evidence converging on a single class of substrings.

On the basis of data sets such as (29)–(33), therefore, we can formulate a preliminary conclusion: the word sequences *go to the movies* and *putting the book on the table* have the status of syntactic units, and hence can be (i) displaced and (ii) replaced. The general pattern we have is that where we find a string of words matching the template in (34)a – roughly formulated but useful as a point of departure for further investigation – we will find both (34)b and (34)c, as illustrated in (35) and (36). This pattern suggests that the structural basis for both of these logically independent distributional phenomena is some common property of the displaced and replaced strings – a property which does *not* hold of substrings blocked from appearing in at least one of the contexts summarized in (34).

(34) a.   Noun aux **Verb W** (where W ranges over word sequences, and 'aux' identifies the class of morphemes called auxiliaries that includes various forms of *be*, *have*, *can*, *will*, and so on, to which Chapter 3 is devoted.)

    b.   **Verb W** Noun aux __

    c.   ... Noun aux [**do so**]

(35) a.   Robin has eaten breakfast.

    b.   ... and eaten breakfast, Robin has __.

    c.   Terry has eaten breakfast, and Robin has $\left\{ \begin{matrix} \text{eaten breakfast} \\ \text{done so} \end{matrix} \right\}$ as well.

(36) a.   Robin will talk to Terry about this problem.

    b.   ... and talk to Terry about this problem, Robin (certainly)will __.

    c.   ... and Bill will (certainly) do so as well.

We therefore provisionally assume that there are certain word groupings which have a kind of unitary status, forming a single larger whole, and that word groupings which have this status enjoy distributional possibilities unavailable to those which do not have that status. Any word-grouping which has this unitary property will be said to form a *constituent*. Before proceeding, however, we need to revisit some of our earlier observations to more clearly understand what it means for some sequence of words to be a constituent.

Consider again the data in (23). When we first looked at this kind of example, we concluded that in some cases, *leave* constituted a syntactic unit, or in our current terminology, a constituent, while in others it didn't. But it is clearly the case that *leave* is a word of English, which seems to run at cross-purposes to our notion of a constituent as a word *group*. Is there a conceptual problem here?

The answer becomes clear if we consider cases such as the English singular indefinite determiner *a*. On the one hand, this undisputed *word* is a single sound, written [ʌ] in the International Phonetic Alphabet symbol set. On the other hand, it is a dictionary entry – an item in the mental lexicon – which is not just a separate morpheme but a syntactically independent element. Obviously, not all instances of the sound [ʌ] are words; but this particular word can be phonetically manifested as a single sound. There are, in short, two different aspects to *a*: it corresponds to a single sound, in terms of its phonetic description, and a syntactic unit at the same time.

Another way of seeing the same point is to consider the case of a small academic department with five faculty members, where two members retire in the same year, and two accept job offers elsewhere. There is now an entire academic unit 'manifested' by a single individual. Clearly there is a distinction between an abstract organizational entity, a department, and a concrete biological object, the person who is the sole remaining faculty member in that department. Nonetheless, the person in question in a sense *is* the department. If the university hires another faculty member in the same department, however, the correspondence between the biological individual and the institutional unit breaks down.

The point of such examples is that a single entity of one type can play the role corresponding to a structural unit of a qualitatively different type, but – crucially – will not *always* do so. As we will see directly, a simple formal system is available which will in effect determine when a single unit of one level can take on the role of a unit defined at a higher structural level. For the time being, the important point is that a single word may well take up the structural space occupied by such a more complex unit.

Practice Exercises

1. All syntactic analysis of any given sentence begins with a string of words which bear labels corresponding to their parts of speech. Thus, in the sentence *Robin wrote a book*, *wrote* is written [v *wrote*], *book* is written [N *book*] and so on, with V abbreviating 'verb' and N abbreviating 'noun'. Carry out this exercise for the following sentences. (In some cases, you may not find it obvious just how to label a particular word – in which case you may need to do some background research on English lexical items and the categories that they are usually assigned to.)
   a. Robin dropped the parcel.
   b. The signs direct you to the nearest exit.

c.   Three of the students stayed after class to argue with their instructor.

d.   Terry works independently better than the rest of the class.

2.   For any substring of words in a sentence, there are four possible ways that the tests introduced above will sort out: (i) both displacement and replacement will apply; (ii) displacement will apply, but not replacement; (iii) replacement will apply, but not displacement; (iv) neither test will apply. Only in case (iv) is the burden of proof on someone who claims that the string in question is a constituent. (And even in such cases, we may have good reason to treat the string as a constituent, though this is somewhat unusual.) In each of the following sentences, a sequence of words is underlined. Use the tests introduced to decide in each case whether we have sufficient reason to treat the underlined sequence as a constituent or not.

a.   Pat took a <u>very strong position on the academic misconduct issue</u>.

b.   Leslie carelessly dropped <u>that book</u> of poems onto the shelf.

c.   You can tell them <u>this story</u>, though they won't believe you.

d.   You have to invite <u>Robin and Terry</u>, but they may not accept.

e.   Robin definitely is <u>extremely versatile</u>.

f.   Robin definitely is an <u>extremely versatile</u> player.

g.   The new instructor had possibly <u>given too much homework</u>. [**Note:** in carrying out the displacement test, do *not* introduce a very different intonation pattern from what would be used normally in the undisplaced version given.]

1.3   Labeling Phrasal Categories: Why VP?

We've now established convergent lines of evidence supporting the claim that in a sentence such as *We will speak of this to Robin tomorrow*, the substring *speak of this to Robin tomorrow*, displaceable (*. . . and speak of this to Robin tomorrow, we will!*) and replaceable (*. . . and we will do so*) as it is, is a syntactic unit, a constituent. But while this demonstration is an important step in understanding the structure of the sentence, we can go further. One of the places where the 'beads on a string' analogy breaks down in the case of natural language sentences is that it implies a kind of equality among the words of a phrase, similar to that which one finds with identical beads in a necklace. Even if some beads are relatively large or small, there's unlikely to be any kind of structural dependence in the necklace itself on one particular bead. In the case of sentences, however, there is a clear asymmetry among the subparts of the sentence. Consider the following data:

(37) a.   We will speak of this to Robin tomorrow.

b.   We will speak to Robin tomorrow.

    c.   We will speak of this tomorrow.

    d.   We will speak tomorrow.

    e.   *We will of this to Robin tomorrow.

    f.   *We will to Robin tomorrow.

A perfectly parallel set of data can be produced in which the word *tomorrow* is missing from every example. There is thus a very clear distinction between the distribution of the word *speak* and the substrings *of this*, *to Robin* and *tomorrow*: any or all of the latter can be omitted, with the well-formedness of the original sentence (37)a preserved. But if *speak* is omitted, the sentence becomes unacceptable. We can summarize these facts by observing that within the constituent *speak of this to Robin tomorrow*, the verb *speak* is obligatory, while various other substrings within the phrase are optional. This formulation is not quite literally true; thus, if *of* is present, *this* must also be present. But the critical point is that the sequence *of this* can itself be omitted, just as *to Robin* and *tomorrow* can be, whereas *speak* cannot be.

    This observation is linked in an important way with another: the position following a word such as *will* in (37)a is pretty much restricted to verbs, possibly followed by other material. Thus we have

(38) a.   We will leave.

      b.   *We will horses.

      c.   *We will from.

      d.   *We will trendy.

The only form in this (quite representative) data set which is permitted following *will* is a verb; the noun (*horses*), the preposition (*from*), and the adjective (*trendy*) are all unacceptable in this position. (This is not quite accurate; words such as *too* and (not) can as well. But in these cases, there is good reason to believe that something quite different from (38) is involved structurally. This point will be clarified further below.) The same result holds regardless of which noun, preposition or adjective we try to substitute for *leave* here. Such facts strongly suggest that verbs are the only major part of speech which can appear in this position following an auxiliary form such as *will*. But clearly it is not only solitary verbs which appear here; we've seen that a constituent containing a verb can as well. If a constituent is a structural unit, and the verb is just one element contained *within* that unit, then based on what has just been said, we must conclude that there is something about the phrase which reflects the fact that it contains a verb. The fact that certain strings of words we've identified as constituents can appear following *will* and similar lexical items then suggests that such constituents have a strongly verb-like quality which entitles them to appear in syntactic contexts ruled out for nonverbs. In a sense, from this point of view, we would want to say that the whole syntactic unit acts as a kind of 'superverb', a verb-plus-other-elements, so that even with the various added material, the constituent really is a scaled-up verb.

We will, in the material covered in the rest of this text, find ways to make this notion precise. But even at this point, we can make explicit the verb-based properties of the kinds of units in question by identifying them not merely as constituents, but also as constituents of a certain kind, which we shall call *verb phrases*. The term 'phrase' is standardly used to define a constituent of a certain (maximum) structural complexity; the description of a string of words as a *verb phrase*, abbreviated VP, explicitly marks a constituent as different in its distribution and syntactic behavior from other phrases which do not embody something we might think of as 'verbiness'. A string of words W which reflects the properties we have identified as diagnostic for VP – the verb is obligatory, and X's distribution is essentially parallel to that of one or another verb's, as vs all other parts of speech – will be notated as $[_{VP}$ W], and we will say that the verb is the *head* of that string. For the time being, we can regard the notation VP as just a label calling attention to a kind of property that whole phrases can share with one of their component words; later on we will be able to characterize the meaning of such symbols much more exactly.

1.4   Subconstituents of VP

Phrases, as we have defined them, may be constituents of sentences. The claim that a given string of words is a constituent of some larger structure requires us to demonstrate that the words belonging to that string have a mutual syntactic closeness which identifies them as a syntactic unit which, as we have already seen in the case of VPs, belong to one or another kind of phrase of the language under study. It might seem, therefore, that the notions 'phrase' and 'constituent' are interchangeable, but this is in fact not quite the case. A given string of words can be identified as a phrase in some language if it is licensed as a multiword syntactic unit by the grammar of that language, where we use 'grammar' in a technical sense which will be defined more precisely below. For example, *that book on the table* is, as we'll see directly, an English phrase, because the rules of English syntactic structure define a certain kind of grammatical unit in a way that yields *that book on the table* as a possible instance of that structure. But there is no guarantee in general that *the book on the table* will be a constituent of any given sentence of English. In *Robin put that book on the table*, we can (and will) show that *that book on the table* is not a constituent of the sentence, because it does not constitute a syntactic unit. If a given string of words is a constituent in even one sentence, it will be a phrase according to any empirically adequate set of structural rules for the language in question, but the converse does not hold: the fact that a given string is a phrase of English does not guarantee that it will be a constituent in any arbitrary sentence. Constituency, unlike phrasehood, is always defined with respect to some particular sentence. In contrast, a string of words which is identified by the grammar of English as a syntactic unit in *some* context is thereby identified as a phrase of

English, even if that same string is not a constituent (and thus not a phrase) in a particular sentence.

1.4.1   Evidence for NPs

We can employ precisely the same reasoning already used to identify VP constituents as a method of identifying subconstituents *within* the VP itself. The crucial fact that gives us confidence in positing an abstract structural grouping labeled VP – the convergence of two different and logically independent lines of evidence (displacement and replacement) which both require appeal to the same notion of phrasal unit – is also relevant to certain other subsequences of the sentence. To begin with, consider the data in (39):

(39) a.   Robin put this book on that table.
  b.   [₅ Robin [ᵥₚ put this book on that table]]

At this point, we have a solid basis for taking the substring *put this book on that table* to be a VP – the *do so* test (*Robin did so*). It is also true that strings of the form displayed in the bracketed string here are displaceable (*... and put this book on that table Robin did*) – a suggestive fact, but in view of what has been said in §1.2.1 about the status of a given string in two different sentences, not decisive. Notice, now, the possibilities available to certain of the substrings contained within this VP:

(40) a.   That table, Robin put this book on __.
  b.   This book, Robin put __ on that table.

The word sequences *that table* and *this book* are both clearly displaceable from the positions indicated in (40)a and b respectively. Not all word sequences enjoy these possibilities, however:

(41) a.   Robin put a book on the table.
  b.   *Table, Robin put a book on the __.
  c.   *The, Robin put a book on __ table.
  d.   *Book, Robin put a __ on the table.
  e.   *A, Robin put __ book on the table.
  f.   *A book on the table, Robin put __.
  g.   *On the, Robin put a book __ table.
  h.   *Book on, Robin put a __ the table.
  i.   *On the, Robin put a book __ table.

Compare the facts in (41) with those in (40) and imagine yourself trying to make the case that there are special relationships which set certain subparts of a sentence off from others. In looking for support for this position, what kind of use could we make of the contrast between these two sets of examples?

In fact, the reasoning involved here is exactly the same as that which we employed in justifying the existence of VPs. And we can provide a backup argument, based on proform replacement, to the argument just suggested based on displacement.

Practice Exercise

Work out a fully explicit argument, based on data such as the contrast between (40) and (41), showing that the simplest, and therefore most highly valued hypothesis is that the displaced substrings in (40) constitute constituents in exactly the sense already discussed in connection with VPs in the preceding section. In constructing your argument, make explicit reference to relevant data of the following sort:

(42) a.   Robin put it on the table.
    b.   Robin put the book on it.

Be careful to construct the details of your argument along the same lines as that already given for the constituency of the word strings we are calling VPs.

It should be obvious, at this point, that the constituents for which you've just constructed an argument cannot be VPs. We've labeled phrases on the basis of the obligatory element they contain, and in the case of *that table* and *this book*, no verb is present. In fact, if we change the singular form of the noun in this example to the plural, and replace the determiners *this*, *that* with *the*, we find that it is the nouns that are the essential elements in such data sets:

(43) a.   Robin put the books on the tables.
    b.   The BOOKS, Robin put __ on the tables.
    c.   The TABLES, Robin put the books on __.

(44) a.   *Robin put the on the tables.
    b.   *Robin put the books on the.

(45) a.   Robin put books on the tables.
    b.   Robin put the books on tables.
    c.   Robin put books on tables.

The upshot of (43)–(45) then is that, given a phrasal element of the general form Det N, it is the N which is the indispensable component of such phrases, or, using the terminology introduced above, that N is the head of the phrase. Based on our previous logic, we take such sequences to be *Noun* Phrases (NPs), so that the constituent structure of (39)a can now be given in the finer-grained bracketing in (46):

(46)   [s Robin [VP put [NP this book] [P on] [NP that table]]]

In spite of this advance, however, we still have no analysis for the nominal element preceding the VP, the name *Robin*. How should we treat the name *Robin* syntactically? The following kind of example provides an important clue:

(47) $\left\{\begin{array}{c}\text{Robin}\\ \text{The librarian}\\ \text{*The Robin}\\ \text{*The the librarian}\end{array}\right\}$ put a book on the table.

The distribution of *Robin* appears to be parallel to that of *the librarian*, which we already have reason to believe is a phrasal constituent of a certain kind; it therefore seems most reasonable to treat *Robin* as being the same kind of constituent, that is, an NP. The logic here is that, if both *Robin* and *the librarian* are NPs, the same rules which allow the latter to appear in the context __*put a book on the table* will also allow the former to do so. Furthermore, the same rules which block the appearance of *the librarian* following *the* will also block the appearance of *Robin* in that context. We shall therefore identify so-called proper nouns, such as names, as NPs, subject to the same conditions as multiword structural units of that description.

1.4.2   Versions of the Displacement Test

So far, the displacement test has been presented as though it consisted of a single distributional possibility: some NP or VP can appear at the leftmost position, as well as its normal place within the sentence. There are, however, a considerable number of different constructions which all involve displacement in some form or other. The following are examples of different kinds of phenomena in which a constituent, called the *filler*, is linked to a gap site – a part of the structure, that is, which normally requires a sequence of words with specific properties that the filler must match to appear in it. This part of the structure is, as in our earlier examples of displacement, indicated with an underline.

- **Topicalization:** JOAN's picture of Robin, I really like __.
- **Cleft:** It's JOAN's pictures of Robin that I really like __.
- *Wh* **question:** Whose pictures of Robin do you really like __?
- *Wh* **relative:** The person whose pictures of Robin I really like __is JOAN.

All of these different versions of the displacement phenomenon are valid tests for constituency. When using displacement to argue for constituent structure, you only need to provide data based on *one* of these tests. The reason you need to be aware of the variety of possibilities in displacement phenomena is that, in different contexts, different tests may provide relatively more and less 'natural-sounding' examples, so it's a good idea to experiment to see which of these yields the best results. If a certain string of words is NOT a constituent, none of the tests shown will yield a well-formed example.

1.4.3   Evidence for PP

We now have parallel strands of evidence for VP and NP constituents, and the obvious question is, are there other types of phrase as well? The following data strongly suggest that there are, and contains a significant hint as to their description:

(48) a.   On that table, Robin put the book __.
      b.   Robin put the book there.
      c.   *Robin put the book the table.

(49) a.   I gave a book to Robin.
      b.   *I gave a book Robin.
      c.   It was to Robin that I gave a book.
      d.   ??It was Robin that I gave a book.

Clearly, in (48), *on that table* is a constituent: it is displaceable in (48)a, and replaceable in (48)b by *there*. But what kind of a constituent is it? If it were an NP, we would expect that we could omit the preposition *on* and still have a legal form, but (48)c shows that the result of this omission is ill-formed. Should we then conclude that *on* is the head of this phrase? Similar considerations apply to the data in (49).

It is nonetheless also true that omission of the NP in the phrase *on the table* also yields an unacceptable result: certainly *Robin put the book on*, where *put X on* has the same sense as in *Robin put the book on the table* (i.e., where the book is not treated as a garment), is not a meaningful English sentence. We've used the criterion of omissibility to determine phrasal type, but here it appears that neither the P nor the NP that this kind of phrase can be divided into are omissible. Are there any clues as to what the correct description of such phrases is in other data?

The following data should suggest an answer to you:

(50) a.   Robin went out the door.
      b.   It was out the door that Robin went.
      c.   Robin went out.
      d.   *Robin went the door.
      e.   Leslie went out the door, and Robin did so as well.

(51) a.   The twins strode along the road.
      b.   It was along the road that the twins strode.
      c.   The twins strode along.
      d.   *The twins strode the road.
      e.   The triplets first strode along the road, and then the twins did so.

(52) a.   Leslie scampered through the passageway.
      b.   It was through the passageway that Leslie scampered.
      c.   Leslie scampered through.

d.   *Leslie scampered the passageway.

e.   Robin scampered through the passageway today, and Leslie will do so tomorrow.

The point should be clear by now: there are abundant examples of constituents (as attested by the b examples) which, when occurring as part of a VP (as attested by the e examples), can apparently dispense with the NPs they contain but not the Ps. By our criterion of nonoptionality, this fact strongly supports the description of these constituents as prepositional phrases (PPs).

What about the cases where neither the P nor the NP in such constituents can be omitted: *Robin slipped the letter into the envelope/*Robin slipped the letter into/*Robin slipped the letter the envelope* and so on? As we know, the same problem arises in the case of verbs which cannot appear without associated phrasal constituents of certain kinds. The verb *put*, for example, which we've seen in many examples, requires both an associated NP and an associated PP; neither can be omitted:

(53) a.   Robin put the book on the table.

b.   *Robin put the book.

c.   *Robin put on the table.

d.   *Robin put.

This extremely strict requirement is a lexical property of *put*, one that it doesn't share with many verbs. The verb *placed*, which in *John placed the book on the table* seems essentially synonymous with *put*, has quite different requirements; thus one can say *Robin placed the book carefully*, without a locational PP specified, but this doesn't work for *put* at all: *Robin put the book carefully*. There are other verbs which appear to require an NP and a PP, such as *give*, but with these verbs one can sometimes omit one or the other of these constituents (*I give at the office*), and often can replace the PP with an NP *I gave a book to Robin/I gave Robin a book*), unlike *put* (*Robin put the table a book*). We therefore have to accept the fact that while it is a general property of phrasal types that an instance of a certain lexical category must be present within them – thus constituting an important part of identifying that particular item as the head of phrases belonging to that type – there may also be other required categories within these phrases, depending on the particular word serving as the head of the category. The case of prepositions heading a category PP which do not merely allow, but actually require, a following NP (or some other category), is no different in this respect from what we find with many Vs within the VPs built around them.

Problem

Consider the following sentences.

i.   Robin definitely is proud of herself.

ii.   Robin is proud of herself, and Dana is even more proud of herself.

Apply the displacement test to i, and the replacement test to ii, to show that there is evidence to support *proud of herself* as a constituent. For the latter test, you need to find a proform that seems to replace adjectives, possibly including additional material, but that preserves the meaning of what it replaces; in particular, pay attention to what could replace *proud of herself* in ii that preserves exactly the meaning of ii. Present an argument that the form you propose to use in the replacement test really is a proform, parallel to *her* for NPs or *do so* for VPs. Use the omissibility criterion to determine what kind of phrase this constituent should be described as.

1.5   Tree Representation of Constituent Structure

At this point, we have good reason to assume that there is sufficient evidence for the following syntactic phrasal units: S, NP, VP, and PP, along the lines argued above. In view of the preceding discussion of PP constituents, the structure of (54)a may be given, using our bracket notation, in (54)b:

(54) a.   The twins put the book on the table.

b.   [$_S$ [$_{NP}$ [$_{DET}$ the][$_N$ twins]][$_{VP}$ [$_V$ put][$_{NP}$ [$_{DET}$ the][$_N$ book]][$_{PP}$ [$_P$ on][$_{NP}$ [$_{DET}$ the][$_N$ table]]]]]]

As emphasized earlier, (54) represents a specific set of claims. The credibility of such structural analyses hinges entirely on whether or not all of the bracketings are justified by our various tests, and that all of the category labels for words and phrases are correct. Each phrasal bracketing implies that either displacement or replacement is possible, and each choice of label depends on our being able to show that the kind of phrase receiving that label really does require an element of the indicated part of speech as its non-omissible element. And these results are perfectly encoded in the bracket notation in (54). Labeled brackets are completely explicit about the clustering relations among the subparts of the string of words that the sentence comprises: they tell us that the string of words beginning with the first *the* and ending with *table* is indeed a syntactic unit of type S, that within this string, the initial *the* and *twins* cluster more closely than either does with any of the other words in the sentence, while the words within the substrings labeled with the VP bracket cluster more closely within this VP than any of them do with those in the NP bracketing *the twins*. But while all of this information, and a good deal more, is available in (54)b, it's not at all easy to retrieve, given the graphic encoding which the bracket notation makes available. Is it possible to remedy this situation at all?

We can best approach this question by rethinking the nature of the bracketing notation in terms of the key relationships we are using it to express. Suppose we have a bracketing of the form

(55)   [$_A$ [$_X$...] [$_Y$...]]

The symbols diplayed in (55) effectively convey the fact that word sequences within the outermost brackets constitute a phrase of type A, and that this particular instance of A can be broken down into a sequence of two substrings of words, of type X and Y respectively, each of which represents an internal clustering (justified, as always, by appeal to various tests for constituency, some of which we have already examined in this chapter). It is clear from this description of (55) that there is a special asymmetrical relationship between A and X (or Y): a particular string (describable as an instance of X) is a subsequence of a larger string (describable as an instance of A), whereas the A string is not a substring of the X string. Simply put, the string labeled A *contains* the string labeled X, but not vice versa, because containment is not a symmetrical relationship. We would like to depict this asymmetry between the strings themselves in the relationship between the categories that label these strings. But the asymmetry between A and X, Y is different from that between the string which belongs to category A and those which belong to X and Y, because strings and the labels which we assign to them are fundamentally different kinds of entities. Strings are objects, while labels are descriptions of those objects. The first step in making the representation of structure more accessible than the notion in (54) is to work out exactly what it is that we want to see represented.

Suppose we say that the relation which holds between the labels A and X (or Y) in this case is called the DOMINATION relation, to emphasize its inherently asymmetrical character (this is oversimplifying a bit, as we'll see quite shortly, but it will get the discussion started). Suppose we have two sequences of words, one contained within the other. Then the category describing the larger string is said to DOMINATE the category describing the string it contains. For example, in (56), the category of the larger string, S, dominates the category of the bracketed string it contains, NP:

(56)   [$_s$ John read [$_{NP}$ the book]]

There is an extremely important subvariety of domination which it's useful to define at this point. Intuitively, we have cases in which a certain string Str_0 belonging to a category A is decomposed into a number of substrings, each of which belongs to some syntactic category and – crucially – no two of which themselves form a constituent. Putting it naively, each of the category labels Cat_1, Cat_2, ... belonging to these respective substrings Str_1, Str_2, ... respectively is dominated 'directly' by A. If there is no constituent string smaller than Str_0 to which any of S_1, S_2, ... belong, then Str_1, Str_2, ... are, intuitively, the 'biggest' subparts of Str_0 which have the status of independent syntactic units. Such 'biggest subparts' of a string which have phrasal status are called the *immediate constituents* of the string, and there is a corresponding relationship between the category label of Str_0, that is, A, and the labels of S's immediate constituents: we say that A *immediately dominates* each of X_1, X_2, ...

A clear example of immediate constituency is found in (54)a. From the analysis in (54)b, we can see that the immediate constituents of the whole sentence are *the twins*, for which the description NP is justified, and *put the book on the table*, for which the description VP is justified. Although there are other substrings in the sentence which are constituents of S – in the sense that they represent substrings of S as just defined which have the status of phrasal constituents – they are not *immediate* constituents, since they also are parts of larger constituents which themselves are subparts of S. So, for example, the PP *on the table* is a substring of the whole sentence, but it combines with *put* and *the book* to form the string *put the book on the table* which, by the *do so* replacement probe, is a VP constituent. Thus, while *on the table* is a constituent of S, it is not an immediate constituent – a 'biggest part' – of the sentence in (54)a, since there is a phrasal unit smaller than S but bigger than *on the table* which contains the latter. It follows that the label for the whole sentence, that is, S, dominates the label PP for *on the table*, but does not *immediately* dominate it.

One of the advantages of using the domination relation to think about syntactic structure is that it enables us to generalize over individual containment relations and find constant structural relations between classes of strings over many different particular cases. Consider the relationships reflected in the bracketing in the following sentences:

(57) a.   [$_S$ [$_{NP}$ the twins][$_{VP}$ ran around the block five times]]
      b.   [$_S$ [$_{NP}$ my cat][$_{VP}$ asks for food several times an hour]]
      c.   [$_S$ [$_{NP}$ the other scholars at the meeting][$_{VP}$ complained about the attention the company-sponsored events were getting]]

In each case, we have unique strings which contain unique substrings. But in terms of the domination relation, we have three different instances of a single pattern: an S dominates an NP and VP, in that order. Domination relations thus give us a way of expressing a single structural relationship which may be exhibited by any number of different strings and their respective substrings. In particular, we can say that the structure of sentences reflected by an S dominating an NP and a VP is a general property of English sentences. (This is an oversimplification because, in some cases, S immediately dominates a PP (or some other nonnominal phrase) and a VP, but the point is the same.)

What we now need is a notation which directly, and transparently, displays the immediate constituents of some phrase, the immediate constituents of those constituents, the immediate constituents of those immediate constituents, and so on down to the individual words – that is, the chains of immediate domination among the various substrings of the original sentence – and at the same time expresses the domination relations among the labels of these various constituents. The bracket notation expresses these grouping relations, but in a form that is quite difficult to read, even for simple sentences, as shown by (54). A little bit of thinking about the problems posed by the bracketing notation will suggest a simple, effective way to highlight these relationships.

The difficulty with an even moderately complex bracketing of a string is that it requires us to pair left and right brackets – something which gets difficult to do

quite quickly, as the number of brackets increases. Consider the specific bracketing of the string *abcdefghijklmn* which we write as [*ab*[[*c*[*d*[[*efg*]*hij*]]*k*]*lm*]*n*]
and ask yourself which substrings corresponding to constituents contain *k* and
which do not. It's far from easy at first (or even second) glance to answer this
question. Try it and you'll find yourself having to actually *count* pairs of left- and
right-hand brackets in tandem, working from the outside inwards from the ends
of the string – a tedious and error-filled process for which we have no special
visual gift.

These considerations suggest the use of a notation in which left-to-right order
is displayed in a completely distinct manner from domination relations. Since
linear order is most naturally portrayed in terms of the horizontal dimension,
we can safely keep that aspect of bracket notation. But we can also add the
visually independent vertical dimension to represent domination relations, a
natural and straightforward way of exploiting two dimensional space, with nodes
corresponding to greater inclusiveness shown higher in the picture. Compare the
bracketed string in the previous paragraph with that in (58), which represents the
same relationships but uses vertical connections to indicate domination relations
among various constituents:

(58)

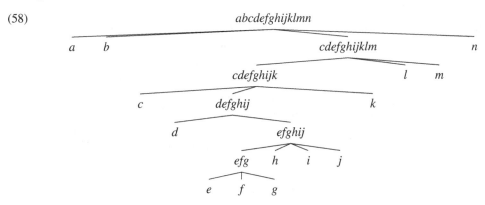

The reader will see that it is now completely transparent what the smallest
constituent substring containing *k* is: one simply finds *k* in the structure and
observes all the other letters which can be linked to the point from which
k branches off. The substring *cdefghijk* is graphically accessible in such a
diagram in a way that the bracketed representation of the same subgroupings
cannot possibly be, for the reasons indicated. Clearly if we want a visually
'legible' method of representing the kinds of subgroupings within word strings
that we evidently need, an upside-down tree-like object as in (58) is a marked
improvement over the labeled bracketings we've used so far. We could use this
visual method of representation to identify the parts of the sentence in (57), at a
certain level of detail, as

(59)   S
          ⌒
        NP   VP

What (59) tells us is that we have a single object, which has properties that entitle us to call it a sentence (S), which constitutes a unit whose largest subunits are two adjacent substrings, the first of which justifies the description NP and the second of which justifies the description VP. Even at this simple level, the clarity of (59) contrasts with the bracketed notation $[_s [_{NP} \ldots][_{VP} \ldots]]$, simply because the bracket-counting we have to do with the latter is missing from (59).

But an important caveat is in order: there is an implicit danger in using tree notation that, in practical terms, doesn't exist in the case of labeled bracketing. The price of using a tree rather than brackets to represent grouping relationships within word strings is that we run the risk of making it possible to illustrate a situation which we have no reason to believe exists: a case where, within the string *acbd*, *ab* and *cd* are actually the syntactic units which in turn are combined to make up a string – but where the linear order of elements is such that *c* occurs *between a and b*.

(60)

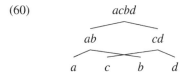

Here, parts of different syntactic units are shuffled together, so to speak, producing what are sometimes referred to as tangled trees. But there is no data we will encounter in this textbook which calls for this kind of analysis, and we therefore exclude it from our formal framework as a matter of principle.

Let's take a concrete instance of trees as an alternative to labeled bracketing, which, for a sentence such as (39)a, we understand quite well, at this point. On the basis of displacement and replacement, we arrived at the representation of structure given in (46), to which we now add the representation of PP constituents that we omitted earlier. The result is the bracketing in (61):

(61) $[_s [_{NP} \text{Robin}] [_{VP} \text{put} [_{NP} \text{this book}] [_{PP} \text{on} [_{NP} \text{that table}]]]]$

This kind of labeled bracket notation highlights containment relations, with domination relations somewhat obscured, though still retrievable – but only with considerable visual effort. We will eventually be able to see that the description 'S' immediately dominates the descriptions 'NP' and 'VP' with the latter dominating a V, two NPs and a PP; but what really strikes us is the set of string containment relations – though these too are hard to read, for the reasons given above. It turns out that if we simply translate the linear portrayal of domination relations into the vertical dimension made possible by tree graphs, both domination and containment relations become immediately transparent.

Since S immediately dominates NP and VP, we can start at the top of the tree with the root node – that is, the topmost node in any tree – labeled S, and write underneath it two nodes NP and VP, connected by edges to the root node. The result is given in (62):

(62)

Since the brackets labeled NP here contain the word *Robin*, we seem to have to say that this NP *dominates* the word *Robin*, apparently contradicting the earlier point that domination is a relationship between descriptions, not strings. The problem is only apparent, however, for in such cases the notation exhibited in (63) does not express the domination of the word *Robin* by NP, but rather the fact that the NP labels a string containing no other word than *Robin*.

(63)   NP
              |
            Robin

Later on, we'll be able to paint a more informative picture of the relationship between labels and the words themselves, but for the time being, no harm is done by having category labels such as NP depicted in trees as dominating individual words.

We continue the translation of (61) by observing that the VP node is shown by the bracketing to immediately dominate two nodes: NP and PP. In the tree, we represent these immediate domination relations directly:

(64)

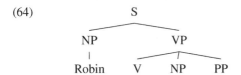

By continuing in this same fashion through the rest of the relations depicted in (61), we arrive at (65):

(65)

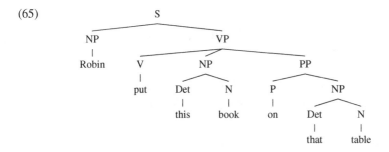

Practice Exercise

Provide all the intermediate steps that will take you from (64) to (65). Explain your reasoning clearly at each step.

This general approach is a good way to get started in working out tree diagrams. But fairly soon the intermediate steps depicted will not be necessary, and you will be able to work out the tree(s) corresponding to any given sentences without using the bracket notation at all.

The reader should be clear on just what is required in order to have a defensible description of the syntactic structure of a sentence. In general, justification of constituent structure must include an explicit chain of reasoning appealing to *all* applicable constituency tests. The following model 'worked example' illustrates the kind of justification necessary to ensure that your analysis is plausible.

1.6   A Worked Example: Solution Procedure

Before you present your solution formally, carry out the following procedure to arrive at your analysis:

i.   Read the data set *carefully* and get it straight in your mind.

ii.   Identify all substrings of the datum which can undergo displacement successfully (i.e., yield a well-formed result which is recognized by native speakers as a sentence of the language). *Provide the relevant examples of this successful displacement for each of the substrings which can undergo it.*

iii.   Put brackets around the substrings you have identified to this point.

iv.   Check each of the bracketed expressions for replaceability by a proform.

After having carried out these steps, you'll be ready to write up your answers to the kind of syntax questions you're going to encounter on assignments and exams.

v.   Present your complete analysis of each datum in the form of a tree. Remember, each node in the tree corresponds to a single constituent – either a lexical item or a phrase – and that the appearance of a node which marks a phrasal constituent is a hypothesis, one you must be able to defend. *Label each node in the tree with a number.*

vi.   For each label corresponding to a node in the tree, provide evidence from both displacement and proform replacement, whenever possible, or else appealing to some special motivated assumption(s), defending your decision to group the descendents of that node as a single constituent.

To see how this procedure works in practice, let's look at an example typical of the sort of data you'll be asked to analyze:

Datum

(66)   That weary courier had shown an ominous message to those terrified
           villagers.

Application of structural probes

It is useful to have a general format for presenting the results of your analysis and
your justification for the latter.

Tree

(67)

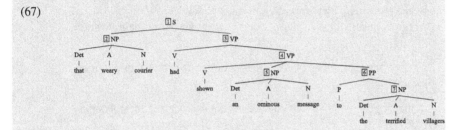

Justification

[1] The S node identifies a clause, taken by methodological assumption to be a basic
syntactic unit, hence (as a multiword expression) a phrasal constituent.
[2] This NP node can be justified by both displacement and replacement effects, as
shown by the following data (where in the first example, the original sentence has
been embedded within a larger sentence *I doubt that weary courier had shown an
ominous message to those terrified villagers*:

(68) a.   THAT weary courier I very much DOUBT __ had shown an ominous
           message to those terrified villagers.
     b.   S/he had shown an ominous message to the terrified villagers.

The string *that weary courier* is both displaceable and replaceable (by proforms
s/he), hence warrants analysis as a constituent The presence of the determiner, and
its replaceability by a pronoun, identifies this constituent as an NP.
[3] This VP node will be defended in Chapter 3 on the basis of certain constructional
patterns which definitively identify the material it dominates as a constituent; for the
moment it is justified by special assumption.
[4] This VP node can be justified by both displacement and replacement effects, as
shown in the following data:

(69) a.   ... and shown an ominous message to those terrified villagers, that weary
           messenger (definitely) had __.
     b.   ... and that weary messenger had (definitely) done so.

The string *shown an ominous message to the terrified villagers* is both displaceable and replaceable (by the proform *done so*), hence warrants analysis as a constituent. The presence of the verb at the left edge of the string, and the string's replaceability by a form of *do so*, identifies this constituent as a VP.

⑤ This NP node can be justified by both displacement and replacement effects, as shown by the following data:

(70) a.   Which ominous message had that weary courier shown __ to those terrified villagers?

b.   That weary courier had shown it to the terrified villagers.

The string *which ominous message*, where *which* is a *wh* question determiner corresponding closely to *an*, is displaceable, and *an ominous message* is itself replaceable, hence warrants analysis as a constituent. The presence of the determiner, and its replaceability by the pronoun *it*, identifies this constituent as an NP.

⑥ This PP node can be justified by displacement effects, as shown in the following data:

(71)   To THOSE terrified villagers, that weary courier had shown an ominous message __.

The presence of the preposition at the left edge of the displaced string identifies this constituent as a PP.

⑦ This NP node can be justified by both displacement and replacement effects, as shown by the following data:

(72) a.   THOSE terrified villagers, that weary courier had shown the ominous message to __.

b.   That weary courier had shown an ominous message to them.

The foregoing is what in math or physics textbooks is called a 'worked example'. *You can use it as a model for answering any assignment or exam question which asks you to provide a phrase structure tree of a natural language sentence.*

Some essential rules for drawing trees are the following:

- Trees are to be drawn with the root node for any constituent *above* the nodes which correspond to its descendents, *never below*. More generally, a node corresponding to the category labeling a larger string are always above the nodes corresponding to the categories labeling the constituent subparts of that string, never below. The former node is called the *mother* of the nodes which label the immediate constituents of the string labeled by the mother; the latter nodes are referred to as the *daughters* of that mother. Domination is top-down, not bottom up. The model here is of a genealogical, not a botanical, tree.
- Every node except the root node is to be connected to its mother node by a single edge line.
- Above all: do not 'make up' a structure for which you cannot give justification along the lines just detailed.

Practice Exercise

Use the various techniques and results discussed previously to provide labeled bracketings for the following sentences:

a.   Some old villagers gathered in the square.
b.   The twins have lived next to that ruined windmill for forty years.
c.   Robin might dislike that kind of problem.

Next, present the results of your syntactic analysis for a–c in the form of a tree diagram.

1.7   Trees and Grammars: A Preview

The fact that we have defined a reliable general procedure for determining the hierarchical structure of sentences in some language L, and settled on a reasonably clear format for presenting that structure, is itself only the first step in formulating a compact set of statements that identify what is and is not a sentence of L. Tree representations in themselves do not explain why a given string of words taken from L's vocabulary is (or is not) well-formed. That task belongs to the *grammar*, the linguist's description of the set of rules, principles, and other formal devices which operate jointly to allow only certain structures to be identified as possibilities corresponding to the speakers' knowledge of L. We can therefore think of a grammar as a device which inspects an arbitrarily large set of candidate trees and determines whether or not any given tree in that set is legal. If it is, then the string of words corresponding to the bottom level of the tree read left to right is a sentence of L. As we will see in the following chapters, it's entirely possible that two or more different trees, corresponding to the same string of words, are admitted (or, as is sometimes said, *licensed*) by the grammar. In such cases, we have a situation called *structural ambiguity*: multiple structural representations of the same sentence. Since the meaning of a sentence is typically dependent on the formal organization of that sentence, it's usual for structurally ambiguous sentences to be semantically ambiguous as well. As a typical example, consider

(73)   Robin saw the student with a telescope.

We can easily identify at least two distinct meanings for this sentence, and can show that each of these meanings is associated with a specific phrase structure representation. One of the tasks the grammar must accomplish is to show how such multiple structures are admitted and how different respective meanings are determined.

The picture just outlined is one in which the grammar is responsible for admitting (or blocking) tree representations, leading to an identification of the corresponding word strings as well-formed or ill-formed. The grammatical principles which achieve this effect must therefore make reference to the relationships among different parts of tree structures – and this in turn means that we need a vocabulary for talking about such relationships.

The following definitions of tree node relations will provide most of what we'll need in the remainder of this textbook to state the necessary restrictions that allow all and only well-formed sentences to be admitted by the grammar. In certain cases, they provide explicit illustrations of tree-structure relationships introduced earlier in this chapter. We take (74) as an illustration of a general format for using trees in syntactic representations.

(74)

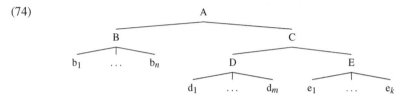

With respect to (74), the following definitions hold:

- As already noted, the topmost node in any tree is the *root* node; thus in (74), A is the root node.
- When two nodes are connected by a line, that line is called an *edge*, the upper node is called the *mother* and the lower the *daughter*. Thus A is the *mother* of B and C; B is the mother of b_i (for all i); C is the mother of D and E, D is the mother of d_i (for all i), and E is the mother of e_i (for all i).
- If nodes L and M are the daughters of N, then they are *sisters*; hence B and C are sisters; for all i, the b_i are sisters, etc.
- A mother node is said to *immediately dominate* its daughter nodes; thus A immediately dominates B and C, for all i; B immediately dominates b_i; etc.
- In a tree, A dominates X if there is a downward path from mother nodes to daughter nodes which begins with A and terminates in X. We can define domination inductively: if A immediately dominates X, then A dominates X, and if A immediately dominates Y, and Y dominates X, then A dominates X.
- All nodes dominate themselves.

Practice Exercise

Identify, in the tree in (74), which nodes dominate which other nodes. Prove your claims in each case by showing how the nodes you say are in the domination relation satisfy the definition of *dominates* just given.

Practice Exercise

Carry out exactly the same assignment for the tree in (67).

- If a node A occurs to the left of node B, then A *precedes B*. If two nodes A and B have the same mother and A occurs to the left of B, and there is no node C such that C is to the left of B but to the right of A, then A *immediately precedes* B.
- No node may precede itself.
- If (i) A precedes B, and (ii) A dominates *x* and B dominates *y*, then *x* precedes *y*.

Practice Exercise

Given the definitions above, identify which nodes in (74) precede which other nodes. Prove your claims in each case by showing how the nodes you say are in the precedence relation satisfy the definition of *precedes* just given.

Practice Exercise

Carry out exactly the same assignment for the tree in (45).

Problem

Show, by formal reasoning from the definitions and conditions given, how the 'tangled tree' structure shown in (60) is ruled out by the definitions and conditions just stated.

Problem

On the basis of the foregoing definitions, say whether it is possible for a phrase structure tree to conform to the following partial description: 'Node A dominates and precedes node B.' Defend your conclusion by explicit reasoning from the preceding system of definitions.

These last parts of the assignment are not exercises, but rather problems to be solved: on the basis of the definitions given, it is possible to answer both questions, by strictly logical arguments amounting to a formal proof. What is at issue is (i) whether or not parts of a single constituent may be split by members of a different constituent, and (ii) whether or not domination and precedence are mutually exclusive relationships within a tree. Don't attempt to answer these questions by drawing trees and arguing from such drawings; the graph that a tree consists of is only a visual aid in picturing the more abstract relationships of domination and precedence, and is intended to make easier the identification of phrase structural relationships among the components of a sentence. It is therefore not possible to establish such structural relationships on the basis of what you think a tree might or might not look like. It is, however, possible to answer both questions by supplying a formal proof based on what the definitions and conditions tell you explicitly.

1.8   What Comes Next?

Our inquiries into the form of natural language sentences began by investigating the possibility that the overt form of such sentences reflects a concealed set of structural properties and relationships, and the phenomena of displacement and replacement makes it clear that we indeed need to posit hidden structure, along the lines made explicit in tree representations. But this outcome itself demands an account: what determines what structures are possible? In other words, where do tree structures come from? There must be some restrictions on what trees are admissible, because otherwise all possible sequences of words would be licensed as sentences of English (or any other human language). Since the facts are quite different, it is necessary to formulate principles which rule out the ill-formed cases. In the next chapter, we begin the task of laying out the precise form of the grammar and making explicit the restrictions which hold on the form of phrase structure trees in English.

2 Syntactic Rules and Lexical Valence

2.1 The Setting

In the previous chapter, we reviewed some of the evidence for a specific kind of structural relationship as the basis for the form of English sentences. The fact that neither meaning nor simple linear order can account for certain well-attested syntactic patterns led us to consider a more abstract relationship – structural constituency – as a possible source for these patterns. Displacement and replacement emerged as 'gold standard' probes for what turns out to be a hierarchical structure, in which words combine into syntactic units and such units in turn combine into still larger units, corresponding ultimately to the whole sentence. Phrase structure trees were introduced as a convenient graphic representation of this hierarchical mode of organization, and a systematic and workmanlike procedure was demonstrated to guide the reader in constructing arguments for structural analyses of any given sentence.

Having argued for the existence of phrase structure, we now turn to the question of its origins. What determines the class of trees that correspond in English (or in any other human language) to exactly the set of sentences constituting that language? One often sees arguments to the effect that the familiar fact of speakers being able to distinguish sentences of their languages, regardless of length, from nonsentences using the same set of vocabulary, means that whatever it is that corresponds to that knowledge must be finite (since it models a cognitive ability which is itself necessarily finite) but with no specified upper limit on the number of separate structures, and therefore word strings, that it can define as well-formed. Putting it quite roughly, our knowledge of language points to some kind of formal system with a finite set of components but no inherent limit on the size of its output. But this line of reasoning asserts an identity between a theory of the sentences of a language and our *knowledge* of those sentences, which is quite problematic (after all, a theory of the integers is going to look quite different from a psychologically plausible theory of our ability to count and carry out arithmetic operations). The best argument for taking a grammar to be finite is methodological: an infinite grammar would be no better, in principle, than a simple listing of the sentences of the language, which we have no reason to believe to be finite in number, so if one is going to try to construct a grammar, it had better be a finite object!

There is in fact a variety of such finite systems licensing outputs of unbounded size. But the linguist demands something more of them than just making available a correct phrase structure for every sentence. Languages are full of patterns and *dependencies* – linkages between two separate (and possibly quite distant) parts of a phrase structure representation. A typical example is given in (1):

(1) a.   There $\left\{ \begin{array}{c} \text{continues} \\ \text{*continue} \end{array} \right\}$ [to [appear [to [be [a problem] [with this committee]]]]].

   b.   There $\left\{ \begin{array}{c} \text{continue} \\ \text{*continues} \end{array} \right\}$ [to [appear [to [be [problems][with this committee]]]]].

Strong justification exists for the bracketings in (1), creating an interesting and perhaps unexpected state of affairs: the finite verb must be the third person singular form *continues* when the NP after *be* is singular, but the plural form *continue* when that NP is plural – a surprising linkage, given the syntactic distance/depth between the finite verb and the deeply buried post-copula NP. Such examples are, however, typical of human languages, and we want the formal devices which make up our grammars of natural languages to be capable of expressing these dependencies in a concise fashion, both accurately and comprehensively. But what kind of formal devices are available for this purpose?

2.2   Where Do Syntactic Structures Come From?

We noted in Chapter 1 that it is not possible to derive syntactic combinatorics from purely semantic considerations, which means that, to at least some extent, syntactic possibilities require specific licensing conditions which make no reference to the meaning of the words combined to form the sentence. But we still have no idea of what the form of those conditions actually looks like. To explore this question, we need to examine a range of data and work out, in a practical fashion, the simplest set of restrictions that does what we need it to do.

We start with the sentence in (2):

(2)   The supposed messengers from Ghent finally arrived in Aix.

The supposed messengers from Ghent can easily be shown, through pronoun replacement, to be an NP: *They finally arrived in Aix.* Systematic examination of what can be done with this NP reveals the following spectrum of data:

(3)
$\Bigg\{$
a. the supposed messengers from Ghent
b. *the supposed messengers from
c. *the supposed messengers Ghent
d. the messengers from Ghent
e. messengers from Ghent
f. supposed messengers from Ghent
g. the supposed messengers
h. the messengers
i. *supposed from Ghent
j. *the supposed from Ghent
k. supposed messengers
l. messengers
$\Bigg\}$
finally arrived in Aix.

The forms in (3) following (3)a reflect the possibilities corresponding to the omission of various nonhead elements. As discussed in the first chapter, the only essential element in a phrase such as *the supposed messengers from Ghent*, so far as its distributional possibilities are concerned, is the noun *messengers*; it was for this reason that we settled on the description of such constituents as *noun* phrases in the first place, identifying the noun (here *messengers*) as the head of the syntactic unit which here takes the form *the supposed messengers from Ghent*. To ensure that (3)a is available as an NP, we have little choice but to simply state that an NP may consist of a determiner, an adjective, a noun, and a PP, in that order (as dictated by the badness of e.g. *The from Ghent messengers supposed arrived in Aix*, *Supposed the messengers from Ghent arrived in Aix*, *From Ghent messengers supposed the arrived in Aix*, etc.). Similarly, we can account for the goodness of (3)k by specifying that an NP may also consist of an adjective and a noun, in that order. We can make these statements a bit less long-winded by introducing a rightward arrow to mean 'may consist of' and using the conventional abbreviations introduced in the first chapter. The statements of possible NP forms corresponding to (3) will then take the form shown in (4):

(4) a.   NP → Det A N PP
    b.   NP → A N PP
    c.   NP → Det N PP
    d.   NP → N PP
    e.   NP → A N
    f.   NP → Det A N
    g.   NP → Det N
    h.   NP → N

(4)a, according to the notation we've introduced, can be stated as 'An NP may consist of a determiner followed by an adjective followed by a noun followed by a prepositional phrase'; the second as 'An NP may consist of an adjective followed by a noun followed by a prepositional phrase', and so on. By adding a sufficient number of such statements together, we guarantee the existence of all of the well-formed examples in (3). Each statement of this kind tells us that a certain sequence of words satisfying the category description on the right-hand side of the arrow forms a unit, and that this unit has the distributional properties corresponding to the left-hand side category. For example, the statement NP → Det A N means that a sequence $[_{DET} \ldots][_A \ldots][_N \ldots]$ is one of the forms possible for a constituent in which the N is the head. Since our lexicon for English will make explicit the facts that *the* is a determiner, *supposed* an adjective and *messengers* a noun, we know that $[_{DET}the][_A \ supposed][_N \ messengers]$ is a sequence with the properties that make it describable as an NP.

Readers who find this array of stipulations to still be a bit drawn out are justified in their skepticism. It certainly seems unnecessarily expensive to use eight separate statements to capture the possibilities latent in a constituent which is four elements long at the longest. But the situation is actually a good deal worse than the preceding paragraph indicates. When we look not just at the number of licensing statements, but also at what those statements are actually *doing*, it appears that the total effect of the statement in (4) consists of nothing more than a list of unrelated possibilities.

This is a point that deserves to be amplified. In principle, the conditions in (4) could be *anything* at all. Since, separately stated as they are, no logical linkage exists among any of them, the fact that they cumulatively express exactly all of the logically possible combination of categories belonging to the maximum string Det A N PP, with only N always represented – and *only* that combination – seems a remarkable coincidence. Eight formally independent licensing statements, unlinked to each other in any way, which nonetheless divide the labor so precisely in expressing a single, well-defined notion, amount to a rather implausible fluke. The statement in (4) is not incorrect because it gets the bare facts wrong, but rather because, by presenting the possibilities for NP as a series of seemingly random, disconnected facts, it in an important sense misses the point completely. As syntacticians like to put it, (4) fails to capture a major generalization.

In order to eliminate the role of coincidence in specifying the possible form of NPs, we need an alternative way of encoding explicitly what the separate statements in (4) express as an accident – the identification of N as obligatory within the NP, and all other elements as optional, with no further linkage between them, occurring in the fixed constant order amongst the parts of the NP that (3) exhibits. Such a statement could take the following form:

(5)   NP → (Det) (A) N (PP)

The parentheses in (5) mark an element whose (non)occurrence is acceptable and unconnected to the (non)occurrence of any of the other, similarly marked optional elements.

Comparison of (5) with (4) is an illuminating exercise. A licensing statement to the effect that, in the absence of special restrictions, an NP may consist of an N followed by a PP, for example, will admit an unboundedly large set of strings consisting of a word of category N followed by a string which meets the description PP, that is, an open-ended set of word sequences which all meet the description [$_{NP}$ [$_N$ ...] [$_{PP}$ ...]], or, in tree notation,

Both (4) and (5) admit the trees shown in (6).

(6)

In terms of the actual set of possibilities they license, (4) and (5) are therefore equivalent. But, as already suggested in connection with the highly coincidental nature of the rule system in (4), this fact in itself in no way entails equal value for them as accounts of the English NP.

We can sharpen this critique by introducing a second system, similar to (3), as given in (7):

(7) a.   NP → Det A N PP
    b.   NP → A PP N
    c.   NP → Det N PP
    d.   NP → N PP
    e.   NP → A N
    f.   NP → Det A N
    g.   NP → Det N
    h.   NP → N

This set of statements is almost identical to the one given in (4); the only difference is that in (4)b the noun is described as preceding the PP – as is the case in all of the other three statements where N and PP appear, and which can be summarized very simply (in a way that (4) does not) by saying that in NPs, N precedes PP. In (7), however, N follows PP just in case there is an A but not a Det in the statement. This situation is clearly extremely idiosyncratic and constitutes a major deviation from the simplicity of the pattern in (5) – but (7) is no more complex *as a system* than (4) is! There are exactly the same number of rules, the same number of symbols, and the symbols are identical in both cases. What this means is that (4) completely fails to encode the systematicity of the various forms of the English NP. Compare this situation with the alternative expression of the same set of possibilities in (5): the constant order of N with respect to PP is literally built into the structure of the statement. Regardless of which options one takes or declines, any sequence involving N and PP will necessarily display the first to the left of the second. More generally, for any pair of terms, there is a constant ordering among the different categories throughout all of the possible forms of the NP, and this constancy is inherent in the form of (5) itself.

The reader might suppose that all that would be necessary to achieve the effect of (7), given (5), would be to add the rule (7)d to (5) – a move which would itself double the number of statements. But in fact all that would be accomplished under this scenario would be to allow N to either precede PP when A but not Det was present (by virtue of (5)a) *or* follow PP under those conditions (by virtue of (7)). The ordering N PP would not, on this scenario, actually be subtracted from the set of possibilities. It is a major virtue of (5) that there is in fact no way to alter the set of possibilities that it expresses so as to give rise to (7).

The general point of this example is that compact notations such as the use of option parentheses in stating patterns are highly valued, not simply because they take up less space on the page, but also because – all other things being equal – the more compact statement incorporates a more regular and fundamentally simpler pattern, and makes a stronger claim. Thus, the use of such devices, which appears at first to be only an abbreviatory convenience, turns out to be a measure of how well a given set of licensing statements expresses the maximum degree of generality in the formulation of the grammar.

The licensing statements we have introduced and compared, such as (4), (5), and (7), belong to the class of formal devices called *context-free phrase structure rules* (CF-PS rules), all of which have the general form

(8) $X \rightarrow Y$

where X is a single symbol and Y is a sequence of one or more symbols. Such statements are rules, in that they impose conditions on the possible form of phrases in the language; they are phrase-structure rules by virtue of the fact that they specify the structure of phrasal objects, in terms of domination relations; and they are context-free rules in the specific sense that any category which meets the description indicated by the label X, no matter what larger structure it appears in, can always take the form specified by the sequence of daughters notated in (8) by the cover symbol Y. Simple rules of this type can, so far as we are aware, express *most* of the dependencies found in human languages, and are particularly easy to use in implementations of grammars, such as computational applications and models of language learning (but see the remarks on Shieber (1985) in the Suggestions for Further Reading at the end of this book).

2.2.1   Phrase Structure Rules, Continued

We have obtained an economical rule that licenses several different kinds of strings, all of which have the distributional properties that we attribute to NPs. We need to provide similarly wide coverage for all of the other phrasal types we've identified. Just as in the case of NPs, we proceed by looking at sentences which exhibit a variety of forms taken by one or another kind of phrase, and then write the most compact rule set that licenses all the observed cases.

Consider, for example, the following data:

(9)   Robin {
            slept
            ate breakfast
            broke with a radical sect
            gave a book to Terry
            gave Terry a book
            drove from Berlin to Paris
        }.

You can show that in each case, the string of words following *Robin* is a VP.

Practice Exercise

For all of the examples in (9), use whatever test you can to demonstrate that the sequence of words after *Robin* merits the description VP.

Problem

Having shown that all of the possibilities in (9) consist of the NP *Robin* followed by a VP, you now need to determine the structure *within* each of these VPs. In particular, before any rules for VP can be written, it is necessary to identify the structural relationship between the verb and the other elements that appear within the VP headed by that verb. For example, in *Robin gave Terry a book*, there are three possibilities – *gave* is a sister of both *Terry* and *a book*; *gave* is a sister of *Terry* but not *a book*; *gave* is a sister of neither. If, for example, *a book* is not a sister to *gave*, then the only other possibility is that *gave* and *Terry* themselves form a phrase *within* the VP, so that the structure would correspond to the tree

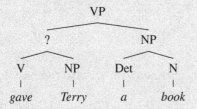

To solve this problem, you need to answer two questions:

i.   Given that the larger structure is a VP and that *gave* is the only verb within this larger VP, what category must '?' stand for?

ii.   Having answered (i), what tools are available to you to determine whether the preceding tree is correct or not?

Once you've answered ii, carry out the test that you've identified and provide an answer to the question of what the internal structure of *gave Terry a book* is. Then apply the same test to the other VPs in (9).

If you've worked out the correct answers to these questions, you'll have found that all of the cases in (9) correspond to sequences with a verb followed by zero, one or two sisters. This result dictates the form of the rules we need to write for English VPs. The following possibilities must be licensed:

(10) a.   V
      b.   V NP
      c.   V PP
      d.   V NP PP
      e.   V NP NP
      f.   V PP PP

The situation can be described as follows: in general, a verb, like all other lexical heads, can in principle appear on its own. In addition, it can be followed by either an NP or a PP, each of which can be followed by nothing, or else by another instance of either NP or PP – except that the order PP NP does not seem to be particularly well-formed:

(11)   *I gave to my cousin presents.

But such data is somewhat misleading. Cases such as (12) are actually quite good, and one would hardly want to write a set of phrase structure rules which excluded them:

(12)   I gave to my cousin a large and lavishly illustrated book about the great wine-producing chateaux of Bordeaux and Burgundy.

When the NP which follows the PP *to my cousin* is long and/or complex – a situation which syntacticians often refer to as an instance of a 'heavy' NP – there seems no problem with having a $[_{vp}$ V PP NP] sequence. We will, for the time being, assume that such structures are to be licensed by the same rule system as the cases in (10), and under this assumption, we can write all of the possibilities in the form shown in (13):

$$(13) \qquad V \left(\left\{ \begin{array}{c} NP \\ PP \end{array} \right\} \right) \left(\left\{ \begin{array}{c} NP \\ PP \end{array} \right\} \right)$$

VPs are in fact a bit more complex than this, however. We are also responsible for sentences such as the following:

$$(14) \qquad John \left\{ \begin{array}{c} knows \\ told\ Mary \\ mentioned\ to\ Sue \\ bet\ Steve\ forty\ dollars \end{array} \right\} (that)\ Mike\ is\ a\ spy.$$

Practice Exercise

Construct arguments supporting the treatment of the verb + following material in (14) (including the clausal constituent outside the curly braces) in all instances as a VP.

Again, we can summarize these possibilities for VP schematically as in (15):

(15) $\quad V \left(\left\{ \begin{array}{c} \text{NP} \\ \text{PP} \\ \text{NP PP} \end{array} \right\} \right) \text{S}$

These possibilities combine with those in (13) in the system given in (22) below.

Next we turn to prepositions and the phrases built up from them. Here too there are a number of possibilities that must be taken into account.

(16) a.   Robin walked out.

  b.   The twins walked out the door.

  c.   We hauled some beer out from under the bed.

  d.   I'm annoyed at Dana constantly complaining about everything.

The preposition *out* can appear on its own, as in (16)a, as well as with a following NP, as in (16)b. Example (16)c shows that prepositions can appear with other PPs.

Practice Exercise

Use whatever tests work to show that in (16)c, *under the bed* is a constituent and that *from under the bed* is also a constituent. Then show that the same methods support the interpretation of *from under the bed* and *out from under the bed* as constituents in (16)c.

The final example (16)d is a bit different from the others. We can show that *Dana constantly complaining about everything* in this example is a constituent, using two variants of the displacement test:

(17) a.   It's Dana constantly complaining about everything that I'm (so) annoyed about __. (cleft test)

  b.   What I'm so annoyed about is Dana constantly complaining about every-thing. (Pseudocleft test)

The so-called pseudocleft construction illustrated in (17)b is somewhat different from the other displacement tests; what is important for our current purposes is that the position following *is* in the construction is reserved for constituents exclusively. So we have reason to believe that *Dana constantly complaining about everything* is a constituent, but what kind? A major clue is the fact that the adverb *constantly* appears following *Dana*. Such adverbs are used freely in VPs, and we can in fact replace *complaining about everything* with *doing so*, indicating its VP status. *Dana*, as in the case of other proper names, is an NP. We therefore have a constituent comprising an NP and, as the *do so* replacement test shows, a following VP – exactly the kind of phrases which, as we saw in the first chapter, are the immediate constituents of sentences. There is then justification for concluding that in (16)d, *about* is associated with a following clause (a term which applies both to free-standing sentences and to material dominated by an S node contained within larger sentences) displaying a particular kind of morphology, the so-called gerundive *ing* suffix. We see similar examples in cases such as

(18) a.   With Dana constantly complaining about everything, no one will be able to have any fun.

   b.   Dana constantly complaining about everything is the last thing I want to listen to all weekend.

We therefore have a set of structures for PPs that we can write as

(19) $$P \left(\left\{ \begin{array}{c} NP \\ PP \\ S \end{array} \right\} \right)$$

Example (19) needs to be refined; as it stands, it would allow **I'm annoyed at* [$_s$ *Dana is constantly complaining*]. The correction required turns out to require only a little extra machinery to identify clauses whose VPs are headed by Vs with gerundive morphology, all of it independently well-motivated. The necessary innovations will emerge in the discussion in Chapter 3.

   Finally, we turn to adjective phrases, as in (20):

(20) a.   Robin is angry.

   b.   Robin is angry $\left\{ \begin{array}{c} \text{with} \\ \text{at} \end{array} \right\}$ Terry.

   c.   Robin is angry that Terry didn't call back.

Practice Exercise

Show that *angry that Terry didn't call back* is an AP, based on the displacement and replacement tests you applied to argue for the reality of APs in Chapter 1.

On the basis of these data, we can state the AP possibilities in English as

(21) $$A \left(\left\{ \begin{array}{c} PP \\ S \end{array} \right\} \right)$$

The results of this brief (and very incomplete) survey of English phrasal types and their possible forms are summarized in (22), beginning with a rule S → NP VP that states the immediate constituency of sentences, as illustrated in Chapter 1. Note that we have a slightly modified version of the later rule, based on the form that internal sentences – sentences occurring within larger sentences – can often take. In later chapters, we refine this treatment of the structure of sentences considerably.

(22)   S → (*that*) NP VP

   NP → (Det)(A) N (PP)(S)

   $$VP \rightarrow V \left(\left\{ \begin{array}{c} NP \\ PP \end{array} \right\} \right) \left(\left\{ \begin{array}{c} NP \\ PP \end{array} \right\} \right) (S)$$

$$PP \rightarrow P \left(\left\{ \begin{array}{c} NP \\ PP \\ S \end{array} \right\} \right)$$

$$AP \rightarrow A \left(\left\{ \begin{array}{c} PP \\ S \end{array} \right\} \right)$$

The rules in (22) jointly constitute a definition of the set of possible tree structures in English. Note that the reappearance of the 'start' symbol S and the occurrence of each of NP and PP in the rules expanding each other allows us to license trees in which an NP indirectly introduces a possible internal NP, and a PP introduces a possible internal PP, as per (23):

(23)

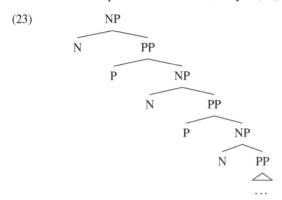

Since each tree structure in turn corresponds to a sentence of English (which itself may be ambiguous), the rule system given indirectly allows for an unboundedly large number of English sentences, assuming that there are no further conditions imposed on the grammar, in much the same way that a restaurant menu 'licenses' a certain set of meals, or a musical score 'licenses' a certain set of actual performances. The rules contain information not present in the trees; as one should expect, choice braces and option parentheses are confined to rules, since trees represent the structural properties of actual linguistic objects, as opposed to abstract specifications of possible forms a given phrasal type may take.

As noted earlier, these rules cannot be regarded as complete; in each case, there are structural possibilities which do not appear on the right-hand side of the arrow. But the set in (22) will serve the purpose of the discussion below, whose main point is that context-free phrase structure rules such as those given above are themselves not the most insightful mechanism to express the phrasal possibilities of human languages. The following section sets the stage for a fundamental rethinking of how structural representations are to be licensed.

Practice Exercise

Provide an account of the phrase structure of the NP *My comment to Dana that Leslie was rude*. Use the set of rules given in (22) to license a tree structure where replacement of all the lexical categories at the bottom of the tree with actual vocabulary items will result in this string of words.

2.3   The Valence Problem

In spite of our success to this point in characterizing English sentence structure, a little reflection should convince the reader that at the moment, we have no way to exclude the starred examples in (24):

(24) a.   *The lawyers put.
  b.   *Some crafty lawyers put the issue.
  c.   Various lawyers talked.
  d.   *Various lawyers talked the obscure issues.
  e.   Various lawyers talked about the obscure issues.
  f.   *Some lawyers discussed.
  g.   Some lawyers discussed the issues.
  h.   *Some lawyers discussed about the issues.

As example (24)c makes clear, our rules must be able to define a VP consisting of a single V – yet once we've done so, we have no way to ensure that such a VP can be headed by *talked* but not *put* or *discussed*. The existence of (24)e and f make clear that verbs must be able to appear with NP and PP sisters, but again we lack formal means to exclude *talked* in the first context and *discussed* in the second. Without such means, we can do no more than itemize the possible forms that VPs – and phrases in English generally – may take, without being able to exclude any ill-formed string of words which happened to comply with the PS rules of English. Since English speakers recognize which of the examples in data such as (24) are well-formed and which are not, we need some way to make the necessary information available, along the lines of (25) and (26):

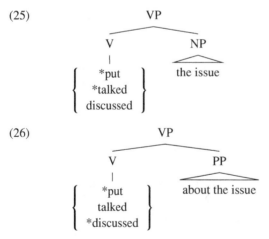

(25)

(26)

Matters are actually still more difficult than this, because getting the facts right is not simply a matter of ensuring that one verbal head can only appear with an NP sister while another appears with a PP sister. We saw in the first chapter that what were called verbs of judicial sanction – *accuse, indict, charge* – all require PP sisters, but in each case only a particular member of the lexical class P will do as the head of this PP. Somehow information about *which* P is head of a given PP must be made explicit, and the same mechanism that requires *put* to have both an NP and a PP sister but, for example, *hesitate* to have *no* sister will impose, in addition to an NP, a *with*-headed PP on *charge* but an *of*-headed PP on *accuse*.

Such examples reinforce the point, stressed in Chapter 1, that meaning differences provide little motivation for the distribution of lexical heads. Again, consider the data in (27)–(28):

(27) a.   Robin had eaten a steak.

   b.   Robin had eaten.

(28) a.   Robin had devoured a steak.

   b.   *Robin had devoured.

Eaten and *devoured* overlap considerably in meaning: to devour something means to eat something in a particular fashion. We might identify this fashion via the adverbs *ravenously* or *rapaciously*, so that the possibilities in (29)a are essentially indistinguishable in meaning. Yet the facts in (27)–(28) are strictly parallel to those in (29)b–c:

(29) a.   Robin $\left\{ \begin{array}{l} \text{ate a steak ravenously} \\ \text{devoured a steak} \end{array} \right\}$.

   b.   Robin ate ravenously.

   c.   *Robin devoured.

Even though *devour* and *eat ravenously* mean the same things, they still correspond to markedly different possible VPs. Or consider *answered* and *replied* (where (*...) means the option must not be taken and *(...) means the option *must* be taken):

(30) a.   Robin answered (*to) the question.

   b.   Robin answered (*to) Leslie [on the reading where *answer* indicates a response to a question.]

(31) a.   Robin replied *(to) the question.

   b.   Robin replied *(to) Leslie.

On the interpretation in which *answer* and *reply* are essentially identical in meaning, the former requires an NP sister and is incompatible with a PP sister, while the distribution of the latter is exactly the opposite. Or again, you can be angry *with* someone but you must be mad *at* them; you can be offended *at* someone's rudeness but you can only be insulted *by* it. Such examples, which are legion in the syntax of English, make it clear that each lexical head must be regarded as picking out a particular (sub)set of compatible sister categories as a kind of inherent property, not reducible to any other characteristic that we might reasonably attribute to it.

Our 'everyday' view of the properties of lexical items is reflected in the information we find in dictionaries. The pronunciation, denotation, irregular morphological forms of words and syntactic category, among other attributes, are typically unpredictable, and hence must be listed in the dictionary for the benefit of speakers who don't already know one or another of these properties; yet for any vocabulary item, many native speakers know what these four properties are – a fact which entails the existence of some component of the speaker's knowledge of their language where such facts 'live'. In this sense, the particular set of categories that a lexical head is able to combine with requires us to specify properties of its possible sisters in just the same way that we must explicitly identify its pronunciation, meaning, syntactic category, and so on.

Practice Exercise

For each of the following sets of words, identify, for every item listed, the kinds of category or categories it can combine with:

i.   {*dispute, wrangle, debate*}
ii.   {*pretend, feign, act*} (where *act* has the sense of behaving deceptively, e.g., *Robin acted as if she didn't speak any French at all.*)

But the 'reach' of this kind of selection, where a lexical head in effect picks and chooses the number and kind of categories it can appear with in the phrase it heads, extends even further than what we have seen so far. In the examples in (32), it is clear that not only are the sisters of a verb determined by that verb, but *subjects*, structurally some distance away from the verb, are also sensitive to which verb is the head of the VP that the subject combines with. We have, in English, data such as the following:

(32) a. $\left\{ \begin{array}{c} \text{There} \\ \text{*It} \\ \text{*Robin} \end{array} \right\}$ is nothing easy about solving that kind of problem.

b. $\left\{ \begin{array}{c} \text{It} \\ \text{*There} \\ \text{*Robin} \end{array} \right\}$ would bother me for Leslie to go spying for the Ostrogoths.

c. $\left\{ \begin{array}{c} \text{Robin} \\ \text{*It (dummy intepretation)} \\ \text{*There} \end{array} \right\}$ felt ambivalent about being chosen Person of the Year.

In later chapters, we will consider the kinds of phenomena in (32)a and b in much more detail. But the importance of this kind of data is that it imposes on us a dual burden of analysis: not only must we formulate a mechanism guaranteeing the kind of selectivity illustrated above, but this mechanism must be able to carry information outside the VP, ultimately determining what kind of subject can be the sister of that VP.

A certain caution is necessary here. Many verbs, and lexical items generally, are quite particular about the semantic properties of the constituents they combine with, so that the kinds of expressions that they can appear with are predictable on the basis of meaning alone. Note for example (33):

(33) a. $\left\{\begin{array}{c}\text{A year}\\ \text{Several weeks}\\ \text{Robin's term of office}\\ ^{\#}\text{Robin}\end{array}\right\}$ elapsed.

   b. $\left\{\begin{array}{c}\text{The crowd}\\ \text{Soldiers}\\ ^{\#}\text{Robin}\end{array}\right\}$ dispersed.

   c. A plangent $\left\{\begin{array}{c}\text{note}\\ ^{\#}\text{rumor}\end{array}\right\}$ reached my ears.

Here the notation $^{\#}$ denotes semantic strangeness, rather than the kind of ill-formedness we reserve the asterisk notation for. By virtue of its very meaning, *elapse* requires a subject which either overtly or implicitly denotes a time interval, while *disperse* demands a subject referring to some kind of aggregate being, such as a crowd or a cloud of vapor, since the meaning of *disperse* is the breaking up of that mass object into its component units, and *plangent* requires something denoting an acoustic event, since it characterizes a particular deep reverberant quality of a sound and makes no sense except in connection with sounds. It would be both mistaken and unnecessary to try to build the pattern shown in (33) into the syntax of these three words. But not all restrictions on subjects or the modification targets of adjectives fall out in this relatively simple way from the meaning of the verb or adjective.

Consider, for example, (34):

(34) a. It $\left\{\begin{array}{c}\text{turned out}\\ \text{proved to be the case}\end{array}\right\}$ that Robin was a spy.

   b. That Robin was a spy $\left\{\begin{array}{c}\text{*turned out}\\ \text{proved to be the case}\end{array}\right\}$.

The data in (34)a make it plain that the meanings of *turn out* and *prove to be the case* are very close to being indistinguishable. But whereas the VP *prove to be the case* allows a clausal subject in (34)b, *turned out* does not; the only subject this VP can have – on the interpretation of *turn out* denoting the same thing as *prove to be the case* – is a particular version of the pronoun *it*, whose properties and distribution are considered in detail in Chapter 6. Somehow, this kind of fact needs to be formally encoded in the lexical description of *turn out*, since it does not seem to be possible to derive it from the meaning of the expression. That is, it is a sheer, irreducible property of this lexical item that, just as it is pronounced [təˈndæ^{w}t] and means something paraphrasable as 'prove to be the case', it does not allow a *that* clause as its subject when it has no sister.

In thinking about how to express this information, it's well to bear in mind that sometimes brute force is the most elegant solution. If we simply *state* just which categories must correspond to the sisters of the lexical head, and then inspect the tree representation for any word string to check whether or not each lexical head in the tree actually has the sisters that its lexical entry says it must have, then we automatically guarantee that only those structures will survive scrutiny which have the property that every lexical head in the structure selects the appropriate set of sisters. This approach to the problem yields a significant and quite unexpected benefit: we now no longer need the phrase structure rules introduced earlier, as will be made clear below. What is required to make this line of analysis work is a completely explicit way of itemizing, in each lexical entry for any given head, exactly what properties are possessed by the categories selected by that head. Typically, those properties crucially involve the part of speech associated with each selected item (shared with it's own head), but there are often many others as well.

We also need to clarify just which elements within a phrasal constituent are actually selected by the lexical head of that phrase. Consider the word string *at noon*, which can easily be shown to be a prepositional phrase in the sentence *Robin will put the book on the table at noon*. In the previous chapter, we saw that *put* can only appear as head of VP if it has an NP sister and a PP sister. But we also can say *Robin will put the book on the table at noon*.

Practice Exercise

On the basis of the displacement and replacement tests, show that in *Robin had put the book on the table at noon*, *put the book on the table at noon* is a VP.

Since *the book* and *on the table* are constituents within the VP *put the book on the table at noon*, it looks as though *put* can here appear with *three* sisters. Appearances are quite deceiving in this case, however, because we can show, using our replacement test discussed earlier, that *at noon* is not a sister of *put*, as per data such as (35):

(35)   Leslie was supposed to have put the book on the table before breakfast, but
instead she $\left\{ \begin{array}{c} \text{put the book on the table} \\ \text{did so} \end{array} \right\}$ at noon.

This data should recall one of the exercises that you were asked to complete in Chapter 1. What (35) tells us is that, within the string *put the book on the table at noon*, *put the book on the table* behaves exactly the way an ordinary VP with the right semantic properties behaves: it is replaceable by *do so*, and hence is entitled to be identified as a VP constituent on its own. Taken together, the exercise just carried out and the structural relationships reflected in (35) constitute evidence for bracketing *put the book on the table at noon* as [$_{VP}$ [$_{VP}$ put the book on the table] [$_{PP}$ at noon]] or – in the more transparent tree notation we use – as

(36)

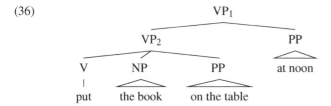

The geometric relationships among the subconstituents of the root VP reflect the fact that the PP *at noon* cannot be a sister to the verb *put*, but rather a sister to the whole VP that most closely dominates *put*. Not coincidentally, this PP is also completely optional. As we have seen in the first chapter, *put* is particularly strict about what kinds of phrases it appears with to form a VP, but *at noon* and similar PPs seem to deviate from this pattern: they come and go freely, so to speak. We have similar results for the phrase *(rather) reluctantly*, which is headed by the adverb *reluctantly*, per the following data:

(37)   Robin

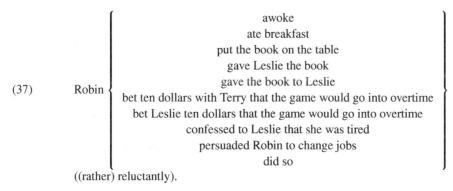

((rather) reluctantly).

The material in the braces can in every case be replaced by *did so*, identifying it as a VP. Regardless of what the head verb is, or what sister categories appear with the head verb, the resulting VP can always – but *need not* – be accompanied by either *reluctantly* or *rather reluctantly*. If the adverbial phrase does appear, the sequence VP + *rather reluctantly* can always be replaced by *did so*, showing, just as with the data in (35), that we have a two-level structure of the form:

(38)

VP
VP   XP
| |
... ...

Given the existence of this alternative kind of structural relationship, and the fact that it seems to be invariably associated with (i) the optionality of the VP's sister and (ii) a general indifference to the identity of the particular verb which is the head of the VP on the left, we are justified in concluding that the head V does not select XP in (38). It follows that the role of the head in picking out what constituents can accompany it is restricted to those which appear with it under the *lowest* VP, with the higher VP assembled in a way which does not depend on the choice of verb (this last point being vividly illustrated by (37)). This conclusion in turn means that, however the higher VP is put together, the identity of the lexical head verb plays no role. A VP simply combines with some other category to produce a 'bigger' VP along the lines displayed in (38).

The scenario just outlined does not ensure that all such combinations are well-formed. Consider the following data:

(39) a.   The square root of 9 equals 3 $\left\{ \begin{array}{l} \text{exactly} \\ ^{\#}\text{reluctantly} \end{array} \right\}$.

b.   Robin put the book on the table $\left\{ \begin{array}{l} ^{\#}\text{exactly} \\ \text{reluctantly} \end{array} \right\}$.

It is not difficult to see how this strangeness arises: the meaning of *reluctantly* incorporates an assumption that, roughly speaking, the VP it modifies specifies a situation in which some element of deliberate intent is involved. We can metaphorically extend this notion, in examples such as *After our repeated efforts, the bolt reluctantly slid into the slot*, which seems to be on the same order as statements such as *It wanted to rain all day, but couldn't quite manage to* and other kinds of implicit comparisons of nonsentient entities to human inclinations. But there is no doubt that such usage is delicate and constrained, and that the equality relationship between mathematical objects is well outside the limits of this kind of meaning extension, at least among nonmathematicians.

In short, the anomalousness of the *reluctantly* example in (39)a can be attributed purely to the fact that given what *reluctantly* means, the sentence doesn't make sense, even figuratively. A similar analysis holds for (39)b, given the meaning of *exactly*. Both cases lie on the far, unacceptable end of a spectrum of possibilities which become less and less semantically intelligible – a very different case from what happens when a necessary sister of a lexical head is omitted, or a phrase which is forbidden as a sister to the head appears nonetheless. We have already seen that there is no reason why *Robin devoured* should not mean the same thing as *Robin ate ravenously*; the difference is purely syntactic – *devour* requires an NP sister, while for *eat* an NP sister is strictly optional. In cases such as (39), therefore, we have no reason to suppose anything other than a free attachment of phrases of various kinds to VP, with the meaning of the attached phrase taken to modify or specify the meaning of the VP in some specific respect, with any difficulties arising as a result of semantic incompatibility.

At this point, some terminology will help us keep track of the key distinctions introduced in the discussion so far. In general, when we have a structure such as those in (40), the circled constituent is referred to as an *adjunct*:

(40)   a.   XP   b.   XP

          XP (YP)   (YP)   XP

On the other hand, in a structure such as (41), the circled constituent is referred to as a *complement*:

(41)

We can and will accommodate the combination of phrases with adjuncts in a very general way, but for the time being, the reader will get the idea of the more general approach by considering the VP rules in (42):

(42) a.   VP → VP XP
     b.   VP → XP VP

These rules will supply a VP with a phrasal sister, either preceding or following. There are different restrictions on what kind of phrasal categories can precede and follow the daughter VP respectively, but it seems clear that we can deal with adjuncts very simply, just by adding rules of this sort to the grammar. This conclusion still leaves us with the problem of accounting for how the idiosyncratic properties of lexical heads ensure the appearance of just the right set of complements for each such head.

2.4   The Valence Solution

The most straightforward way to correlate particular lexical items with their corresponding complements is, as hinted earlier, simply to specify just what the complements for each head can be, as part of the information tied to each lexical item. The list of complements, and the associated length-one list characterizing the possible subjects, for any given head are jointly referred to as that head's *valence* (though, as we will see shortly, valence encompasses a bit more than a verb's subject and complement affinities). The trick is to guarantee that this specification is respected in building up the phrase which any given lexical item is the head of. The key to solving the puzzle that valence seems to pose for us is to start by reconsidering what syntactic categories are and how we represent them. As we've already noted, a given word's valence is typically idiosyncratic and semantically unpredictable, just as its pronunciation, and the pairing of that pronunciation with the word's meaning, is unpredictable. The same holds for syntactic properties such as part of speech, which neither pronunciation nor meaning allow us to predict. We can express exactly the same idea either by saying *Robin was desperately hungry* or in the form *Robin starved*, so that the core idea – the physical sensation of needing food – can be encoded either as an adjective or a noun. By the same token, *Robin is a sadist* and *Robin is sadistic* are semantically equivalent, so that nouns and adjectives must also be regarded as candidates for the expression of the same concept. For basic forms of the language, then, pronunciation, meaning and part of speech are all unpredictable, and must be *listed* somewhere in the grammar. Given what's already been said, it seems reasonable to specify the word's valence properties – the subject and sisters it may or must combine with – in the same 'place' in the grammar as these other idiosyncratic properties.

Suppose we associate, with the word *put*, the following partial description:

(43)
$$
\begin{bmatrix}
\text{PHON(OLOGY)} & [\text{pʊt}] \\
\text{P(ART) of S(PEECH)} & \text{V} \\
\text{SEM(ANTICS)} & \ldots
\end{bmatrix}
$$

Such boxes or matrices provide a set of what are called *feature/value* pairs: each feature name identifies a particular property of a word, and the associated value given represents the particular 'setting' for that property, in much the same way that the label WEIGHT identifies a particular physical property of some object, and the number supplied for that property indicates where on the scale of possible values for that property the object falls. In the case of *put*, we give a phonetic representation to indicate a value for this verb in terms of its pronunciation, identify its 'part of speech,' and provide a representation of its meaning, on the understanding that the whole issue of meaning in natural language and how it should be represented is a vast and controversial set of questions. For this reason, we will for the time being simply assume that there is some empirically ideal way to encode the formal aspects of a word's meaning in a manner revealing how such meanings for all the words in a sentence combine to yield the meaning of the whole sentence. To the three features mentioned in (43) we now add two more: one identifying the inventory of possible sisters for each lexical item, as depicted in (44) under the label *complements*, and the other identifying what kind of subject can appear with a phrase headed by the particular word in question. We use the name COMP(lement)s for the first and SUBJ(ect) for the second, so that a more complete entry for *put* will look something like (44):

(44)
$$
\begin{bmatrix}
\text{PHON} & [\text{pʊt}] \\
\text{POS} & \text{V} \\
\text{SEM} & \ldots \\
\text{SUBJ} & \langle \text{NP} \rangle \\
\text{COMPS} & \langle \text{NP,PP} \rangle
\end{bmatrix}
$$

The notation classifies *put* as a member of the lexical class V(erb), and identifies the subject of the verb as of category NP (though for the moment we make no distinction between ordinary NPs and dummy pronouns such as *it*). The complements of this verb are specified as a single instance of an NP and a single instance of a PP, in that order. The use of angled brackets ⟨⟩, rather than set braces {} is, at this point, best understood as a way to notate the left-to-right sequence of the constituents within the brackets, though later on this characterization of the elements within these brackets will be somewhat modified. Set notation implies that there is no ordering among the members of the set, whereas angled brackets are generally understood in descriptions of formal systems – where they are often referred to as *lists* – to imply such ordering, so that $\langle 1, 2 \rangle \neq \langle 2, 1 \rangle$. Use of this notation will enable us to identify the particular requirements that each verb, and more generally each lexically distinct head, imposes on the syntactic structures in which it appears.

Our next step is to decide how to *use* the information about valence that will, on this general approach, be included in the lexical description of every potential head word in the lexicon. The notion of a list here is suggestive. Imagine going to a supermarket with a list of things you need to purchase (naturally taking for granted the fact that the names on the list stand for, but are quite distinct from, the actual items whose names appear on the list), and crossing each item off that list as soon as you've put it into your cart. The remaining list gets smaller as the number of items in your cart gets larger, until eventually all the items on the list are gone. The critical aspect of this analogy is that the list ensures that everything named on the list actually winds up in your cart, and we can make the analogy still more appropriate by assuming that you are determined to buy only those things which are on your list. As you add each item to your cart, the corresponding name is canceled from the list, and nothing else can be added.

We can make a first pass at building up a phrase from a word and its valence list by thinking about how this cancellation procedure would yield the right kind of phrase in the case of *put*, whose lexical description is given in (44). To keep things as simple as possible, we omit everything in that description except the information needed to build up a VP in which *put* shows up with sisters of the kind specified on its COMPS list:

(45)

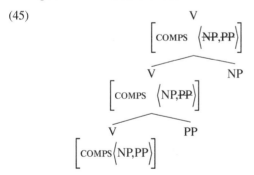

This tree graphically illustrates the idea that by supplying an actual phrasal structure matching each category label appearing on the COMPS specification, we wind up eliminating the list of required complements as a consequence of satisfying the head's valence requirements. But there is a critical problem with (45): it implies that at each step where a new sister is 'supplied', we have a phrasal constituent. That would entail the constituency of *put on the table*, however – the very first step in the construction of the tree in (45) – a result which, as we saw in the first chapter, cannot be maintained in the face of evidence from both displacement and replacement that *put the book* is *not* a phrasal unit. At this point, it seems, there is a mismatch between the grocery cart analogy and the actual structure of the VP.

And once we've noticed this mismatch, the solution becomes relatively simple. The problem with the grocery cart analogy is its suggestion that, in the syntactic sphere, we do the same thing that we normally do shopping: put items into the cart one at a time. This is certainly a possibility, and there is no reason why a language might not work this way, but English does not, nor do many other languages. In effect, what happens in the grammar of English is more like the case of someone who takes a list of groceries into a store and loads everything that's on the list into the cart *simultaneously*, canceling out the whole list in one go. We therefore want something more along the lines of (46):

(46)

$$
\begin{array}{c}
\text{V} \\
\left[\text{COMPS} \quad \langle \text{NP,PP} \rangle \right]
\end{array}
$$

$$
\begin{array}{ccc}
\text{V} & \text{NP} & \text{PP} \\
\left[\text{COMPS} \quad \langle \text{NP,PP} \rangle \right] & &
\end{array}
$$

Notice that the principle is the same – you cross off the list exactly what you put into the cart – but the 'loading procedure' is different.

This line of reasoning mandates three new components for our grammatical machinery:

- features that express valence information about the particular combinations of complements that lexical heads can combine with to form phrases;
- something like a cancellation procedure which eliminates from the COMPS requirements of a phrase all of the complements which the head of that phrase combines with in order to form the phrase;
- some kind of principle forcing all the items mentioned in a head's COMPS list to be 'supplied' at the same time.

In addition, we must ensure that anything not mentioned on the original list is barred from appearing as a complement to the head, and that if something is on the list but fails to match an actual complement to the head, the resulting structure is blocked.

The reader might feel a bit frustrated at the direction this discussion has taken. There appears to be quite a bit that the grammar now has to deal with which wasn't apparent early in this chapter, when it seemed possible simply to state a few rules covering a very broad swathe of the grammatical possibilities. But a bit of reflection should convince the reader that actually, things can be seen as a good deal *simpler* than they were before. What we have now determined is that, given a verb, we are guaranteed of getting a verb phrase by doing nothing more than consulting the verb's valence requirements and then, so to speak, supplying it with what we find there. As long as there is a guarantee that a VP is formed just in case the verb appears with its COMPS elements – no more and no fewer – a long, complex rule summarizing all the different forms the VP can take is completely unnecessary. In other words, instead of something along the lines of the VP rule in (22), we can simply write something like

(47)   VP → V XP*

with XP* an arbitrary sequence of phrasal sisters, on the assumption that the necessary principles already alluded to are in place: that unless the sequence of sisters abbreviated XP* matches the list specified in the COMPS feature exactly, the result will be ruled out. In fact, we can generalize this schema along the following lines:

(48)   YP → Y XP*

with X, Y ranging over all of the major categories N,V,A,P – as long as we can ensure that the restrictions built into our grammar will assign defective status to all combinations of lexical heads and sisters which do not respect the head's valence. Example (48) represents the payoff of the approach we've followed: it actually *replaces* all of the CF-PSGs in (22) except the rule for S, as long as a few very general constraints, alluded to earlier and discussed in detail below, are satisfied.

It is formally convenient to assume that list cancellation takes the form, not of a strikeout, as in (114)–(115), but rather of something like erasure – the canceled COMPS element simply disappears from the COMPS list of the phrase which results from supplying the complement phrase itself to the lexical head. Under this interpretation of cancellation, we can restate (46) as

(46′)

$$
\begin{array}{c}
\text{V} \\
\left[\text{COMPS} \ \langle \ \rangle \right]
\end{array}
$$

$$
\begin{array}{ccc}
\text{V} & \text{NP} & \text{PP} \\
\left[\text{COMPS} \ \langle \text{NP,PP} \rangle \right] & & \\
| & & \\
\text{put} & &
\end{array}
$$

To ensure that we obtain only the correct structures, we posit a few very general rules. Any phrasal tree which is not allowed through the operation one of these rules is ruled out as a possible structure of the grammar. To ensure that only (46′) is an allowed licensing for the combination of *put* with its complements to form a VP, we state a preliminary form of a phrase structure rule that ensures what we might think of as the 'saturation' of the head verb's requirements: it supplies a sequence of sisters each of which satisfies exactly one and only one of those listed requirements:

(49)   **Verb-complement Rule:**

$$
\begin{bmatrix} phrase \\ \text{SS} \begin{bmatrix} \text{POS} & \text{V} \\ \text{COMPS} & \langle\,\rangle \end{bmatrix} \end{bmatrix} \rightarrow \begin{bmatrix} word \\ \text{SS} \begin{bmatrix} \text{POS} & \text{V} \\ \text{COMPS} & \langle X_1,\ldots,X_n\rangle \end{bmatrix} \end{bmatrix}, \qquad X_1,\ldots,X_n
$$

$$\qquad\qquad\qquad\qquad\qquad\qquad\qquad HEAD \qquad\qquad\qquad\qquad\qquad COMPS$$

In (49), the ellipses are interpreted as denoting everything on the right side of
the rule apart from the head daughter, which is notated on the right-hand side
of the rule as *HEAD* below the schematic description of the head daughter.
In general, we will follow this format throughout: the left-hand side of each
rule specifies the description of constituents which are legal in case they have
as daughters a set of constituents satisfying the description on the right, in
conjunction with the general feature-matching principles whose application is
determined by the relationship of each constituent to the mother category (e.g.,
the constituent corresponding to the description identified on the right as the
head must not only comply with the specific description given in the rule, but
also with the general requirement, which we formalize below, that certain of
its feature values are identical to those of the constituent satisfying the specific
description of the mother in this rule). This rule – very general, with minimal
detail since the latter will be supplied by the lexical entries in conjunction with
other principles – introduces a major distinction between what are called *types*,
or *sorts*, in the theory of syntax. Each type represents a different species of object,
a fundamentally different kind of entity from those belonging to a different
type. We make a fundamental distinction between *word*-type things and *phrase*-
type things here; words do not have syntactically visible internal parts, while
phrases do. The above rule identifies a phrase in English as having a lexical
daughter – a word, which is the head – along with a set of unspecified sisters
(notated by $X_1, \ldots, X_n$). The mother's COMPS list is empty just in case each of
the items on its head daughter's COMPS list matches exactly one corresponding
sister. In the case of *put*, with its [COMPS $\langle$NP,PP$\rangle$] value, the lexical head must
therefore be accompanied by an NP and a PP sister.

At the same time, the rule schema in (49) incorporates a significant break
with the interpretation of tree-licensing implicit in context-free rules. The comma
following the portion of the right-hand side which specifies the head indicates
that the rule imposes no linear ordering restrictions on the elements itemized
following the arrow. Linear ordering statements can be abstracted from specific
categories, and shown to hold amongst daughter constituents *regardless of the
mother's phrasal category*. In particular, we find that, across the board, there is a
restriction in English statable as (50):

(50) i.   signs of type *word* precede signs of type *phrase*;
      ii.   NPs precede sisters of all other phrasal types;
      iii.   nonadjunct phrasal projections of V follow nonadjunct phrasal projections
            of all other lexical categories.

The rule-template in (49) thus no longer represents a generalization of PS rules, but rather constitutes an *immediate dominance* schema, indicating only that a phrase may dominate a lexical head and just those constituents meeting in one-to-one fashion the descriptions provided on the mother's COMPS list. All linear ordering relations in tree representations fall out directly from the interaction of schemata such as (49) with the precedence restrictions just given.

We can illustrate this general architecture with a specific case. Based on its COMPS specifications, the verb *put* will necessarily take two sisters, an NP and a PP, yielding a phrase of category V, all of whose complement requirements have been eliminated by the appearance of its NP and PP daughters. Thus, the VP *put a book on the table* will necessarily have the following form, as per (46′):

(51)

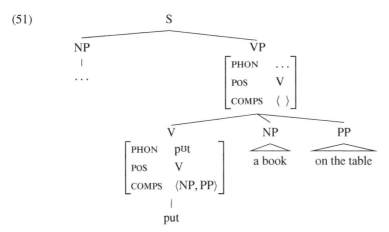

Henceforth, we shall simply remove the deleted items from the COMPS list rather than showing them crossed through. The left-to-right linear order is imposed by the COMPS list order ⟨NP, PP⟩.

Under this conception of the grammar, we will have a lexicon filled with entries that can be partially described along lines such as (52):

(52)   **Lexical items:**

$$\textit{hesitate:} \begin{bmatrix} \text{PHON} & \text{hέzətεʸt} \\ \text{POS} & \text{V} \\ \text{COMPS} & \langle \ \rangle \end{bmatrix}$$

$$\textit{discussed:} \begin{bmatrix} \text{PHON} & \text{dIskʌst} \\ \text{POS} & \text{V} \\ \text{COMPS} & \langle \text{NP,PP} \rangle \end{bmatrix}$$

$$\textit{talked:} \begin{bmatrix} \text{PHON} & \text{tɔkt} \\ \text{POS} & \text{V} \\ \text{COMPS} & \langle \text{PP} \rangle \end{bmatrix}$$

We can pair each such item with any combination of complements we like, but only the combination which matches the head's valence specifications will be admitted. In practice, testing out the correct possibility for, say, *talk* might work something along the following lines: we start with the Verb-complement Rule in (49), which allows us a structure along the lines of Step 1 in (53).

(53)   Step 1:

Since the verb is the head, the resulting phrase will be a VP – that is, as explained above, a V which has had all its valence requirements satisfied and hence has an empty COMPS list. This situation is depicted in Step 2.

Step 2 (by free lexical insertion):

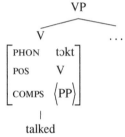

In order to be sanctioned by the Verb-complement Rule, the verb must have exactly as many complements of the right kind as are necessary to cancel every element on its COMPS list. This means that *talked* can be provided with exactly one sister, a PP, which will cancel out the PP on *talk*'s COMPS list, yielding a phrase of category V with an empty COMPS list as mandated by the Verb-complement Rule, as indicated in Step 3.

Step 3 (by the Verb-complement Rule):

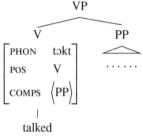

Suppose, however, we insist on supplying the verb with an NP, rather than a PP. In that case, we will not be able to perform the cancellation required to yield a mother with an empty COMPS list, because NP and PP are irreconcilably distinct categories, and hence the NP sister cannot be identified as corresponding to the PP complement demanded by the verb. The result will be a category which is not a VP, as per Misstep 3.

Misstep 3 (*not* by the Verb-complement Rule):

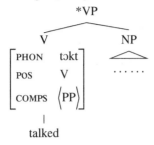

Since the one rule for forming clauses introduced in the first chapter, S → NP VP, is quite explicit that only a VP will do as a sister to the NP daughter, it is evident that the non-VP *talk* + NP cannot combine with a subject to form a sentence, and therefore that (54) is not a legal string, since there is no legitimate structure corresponding to it.

(54) a.   *Robin talked the attorneys.

   b.

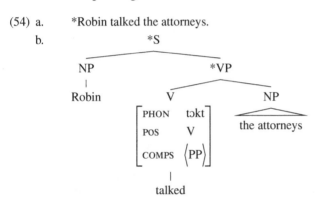

Practice Exercise

Use the approach just outlined to provide an account of the facts about *eat* vs *devour* and *answer* vs *reply* that were discussed earlier in this chapter. For each of these pairs of words, construct a partial lexical entry, along the lines illustrated in (44) for *put*, and then, using the kind of reasoning just illustrated, show how this entry forces a combination of that lexical item with a complement which is different from the combination permitted for the other member of the pair.

2.5   Refinements

The approach introduced in the preceding discussion is sometimes referred to as 'shake-and-bake' syntax – the idea being that, in effect, you put a lexical item into a bag with any number of possible phrasal sisters, twirl it about (metaphorically), and what will come out of the bag will be a structure with exactly the right number and kind of complements for that particular lexical item to project to a phrase. But the alert reader will probably have some pointed questions to ask about the details provided so far.

For example, we have introduced the valence mechanism to provide an explicit account of selectional differences among lexical items – which frequently require finer discriminations than mere categorial identity of the NP vs PP sort. Our discussion of verbs of judicial sanction, for example, revealed that such verbs not only require PP complements, but PP complements headed by particular prepositions, with the relevant data repeated as (55):

(55) a.   The DA charged the defendants $\left\{ \begin{array}{c} \text{with} \\ \text{*of} \\ \text{*for} \end{array} \right\}$ racketeering.

    b.   The DA accused the defendants $\left\{ \begin{array}{c} \text{of} \\ \text{*with} \\ \text{*for} \end{array} \right\}$ racketeering.

    c.   The DA indicted the defendants $\left\{ \begin{array}{c} \text{for} \\ \text{*of} \\ \text{*with} \end{array} \right\}$ racketeering.

Similar facts hold for certain verbs of presentation, as in (56):

(56) a.   I $\left\{ \begin{array}{c} \text{conferred} \\ \text{bestowed} \end{array} \right\}$ the award $\left\{ \begin{array}{c} \text{on} \\ \text{*to} \end{array} \right\}$ Robin.

    b.   I $\left\{ \begin{array}{c} \text{gave} \\ \text{presented} \end{array} \right\}$ the award $\left\{ \begin{array}{c} \text{to} \\ \text{*on} \end{array} \right\}$ Robin.

How can such information possibly be made visible to a selecting head in a way which will allow the latter's COMPS specification to single out exactly the right subclass of PPs necessary for a resulting well-formed VP? More generally, how are we to account for certain facts when it does not seem that the information relevant to any account of those facts is available on the proposal considered? Every meaningful hypothesis must be able to meet challenges of this sort, with details laid out as fully as necessary to ensure that no problems remain. The difficulty here is substantive: at present, our treatment of prepositional phrases does not enable us to identify just which preposition is the head of a PP. Something more must be added to our technical toolkit in order to overcome the problem that PP selection poses.

Again, it will help to rethink just what it is that cases such as verbs of judicial sanction tell us about the nature of information flow within a phrase structure representation. The fact that a verb such as *put* is sensitive to the category type of its sisters means, in effect, that those sisters receive a kind of abstract 'coloration' by virtue of the fact that their heads belong to certain categories. In some cases, knowing categorial type is all that is needed; thus, a verb such as *devour* seems to only require an NP, not an NP of a particular kind. Of course, a randomly chosen NP may not be semantically compatible with the meaning of *devour*, but even in such cases, speakers of English have a considerable capacity to work out a figurative interpretation, as in *Robin devoured the scenery* or *The twins devoured War and Peace*, where *devour* no longer has its literal meaning referring to an act of nutritive ingestion, but something related to the notion 'intake' more generally, with the clear implication of intensity. Oversimplifying somewhat, we can say that *devour* only requires that its sister be an NP, and any difficulties with the result can be attributed to semantic incompatibility. But there are many cases in the grammar of English, and natural languages generally, in which the syntactic information available to the head must be finer grained; semantic considerations are not enough to distinguish the well-formed cases from those which are ill-formed when the head combines with its sister, and there is no way to get certain combinations to work by the kind of generous interpretation that gives rise to the figurative uses of *devour*. In other words, it is often not enough just to get the category type of the complement correct; there are other attributes of the head's sister(s) which must reflect particular values, or the combination of head and sister will fail.

The case of the prepositional distinctions reflected in verbs of judicial sanction shows that we need to treat the identity of the actual preposition heading a PP as such an attribute – a property of that PP which, like the simple fact that the head is indeed a preposition, 'colors' the phrase projected from it. The key idea, then, is that there is certain information which is shared between heads and their mothers, with category type being the most obvious example (the head of an NP is always an N, the head of a VP is always a V, etc.); in addition, as we see, prepositional identity – the *name*, so to speak, of the preposition – needs to be shared as well in the case of Ps and the PPs built from them. But how should this information be encoded?

We start with the general strategy adopted earlier in which syntactic categories are taken to be complex objects, whose properties are made explicit in terms of feature/value pairs. Any information we wish to categorize as an attribute of some category must be expressed as the value of some feature. Since the information we wish to encode in this case is the identity, or form, of the preposition itself, the name of the feature we designate to carry the necessary information is P(reposition)FORM, with the value of PFORM being the ordinary spelling of the preposition itself. Thus, the PFORM value of *of* is *of*, and so on.

In order to make this information available as part of the description of the PP built from a given P, we need to ensure that PFORM is identified in the grammar as a feature which is necessarily shared between a head and its mother. This requirement might appear at first somewhat stipulative – an ad hoc add-on that we've pulled out of thin air because we need a particular piece of information. But, as just observed, we already *know* that there are other properties that are shared between phrases and their head daughters. The sharing of category identity, for example, was the whole basis of our choice of names for different kinds of phrases based on what category their heads belong to. Similarly, the noun *cat* is singular, with a plural counterpart *cats*, and when we investigate the agreement properties of NPs – the fact that we say *The cat is meowing* but *The cats are meowing* – we see that the singularity or plurality of the noun head has become an attribute of the NP that requires a specific alignment with the morphological form of the verb: singular/*is*, plural/*are*. So it appears that the number value of a given noun is projected, along with nounhood itself, to the NP mother of the noun. And, as we will see in the next chapter, VPs with auxiliary verbs as heads differ in their distribution from those whose heads are not auxiliaries in ways which demand that the property of (not) having an auxiliary head daughter must register on the VP mother. These and many other examples make it clear that, rather than being an isolated phenomenon, this sharing of information between a phrase and its head daughter is widespread in English, and in human languages generally. All we need do to implement the solution for verbs such as *accuse*, therefore, is assume that PFORM is one of the features which must have the same value on heads and their mothers.

To generalize over all such features, we posit the existence of a feature HEAD, which takes as its value a set of other features – varying, perhaps, from category to category. That is, we assume that the feature NUMBER is somewhere specified in the set of HEAD features of noun-type categories, but not preposition-type categories; conversely, we take PFORM to be a preposition-type feature, not a noun-type feature. With these assumptions in place, we write the lexical entries for the Ps *to*, *with*, and *on* as the following data structures, where the feature name POS is the formal expression of the notion 'part of speech':

(57) a.
$$
\begin{bmatrix}
\text{PHON} & \text{tʊ}^{\text{w}} \\
\text{HEAD} & \begin{bmatrix} \text{POS} & \text{P} \\ \text{PFORM} & \textit{to} \end{bmatrix} \\
\text{COMPS} & \langle \text{NP} \rangle
\end{bmatrix}
$$

b.
$$
\begin{bmatrix}
\text{PHON} & \text{wɪð} \\
\text{HEAD} & \begin{bmatrix} \text{POS} & \text{P} \\ \text{PFORM} & \textit{with} \end{bmatrix} \\
\text{COMPS} & \langle \text{NP} \rangle
\end{bmatrix}
$$

c.
$$
\begin{bmatrix}
\text{PHON} & \text{an} \\
\text{HEAD} & \begin{bmatrix} \text{POS} & \text{P} \\ \text{PFORM} & \textit{on} \end{bmatrix} \\
\text{COMPS} & \langle \text{NP} \rangle
\end{bmatrix}
$$

POS is now a HEAD feature specified for all categories, and PFORM is a HEAD feature of prepositions generally. To ensure that HEAD features are indeed shared among mothers and head daughters, we impose a second principle regulating the composition of adjacent generations in tree structures:

(58)   **Head Feature Principle:** The value of the HEAD feature on a phrasal category *C* is identical to the value of HEAD on *C*'s head daughter.

In considering this principle, the reader is urged to take particular note of the fact that the attribution of 'sharing' in (58) makes no mention of a source, or 'point of origin', or anything at all along lines suggesting that the information held in common starts at one point in the structure and percolates or diffuses to another point. (Readers with some background in general linguistics might compare this view of feature sharing with the notion of spreading in autosegmental phonology, where phonological rules are stated in a form which takes for granted that a feature specification associated with one point on some autosegmental tier is transferred from that point to another one – one which, at some stage in derivational history, did not bear it.)

But at this point we need to consider exactly what the contents of the HEAD feature are for any given category. In the case of prepositions, there must be a PFORM value, while, as we'll see in the next chapter, verbs must have a VFORM value and a specification of whether or not they belong to the class of auxiliaries. Suppose we say that the value of every HEAD specification is a certain type of object, call it *head*, which identifies a particular set of attributes or properties specified for each category, and which must be shared between any constituent belonging to that category and any phrase that that constituent is the head of. In all the cases just alluded to, we can show that the relevant information supplied by these features – PFORM value, (non)auxiliary status and so on – must be shared between phrasal constituents and their head daughters. But at the same time, the different kinds of information that must be supplied for each different lexical class suggests that the information shared between mothers and head daughters is in some sense *defined* by what part of speech the head daughter belongs to. Thus, what POS tells us about a linguistic expression – what its part of speech is – is not simply another kind of feature value; it is, rather, what *determines* the kind of HEAD information that must be shared between that expression and the phrases projected from it. We can capture this intimate connection between part of speech and the kind of information that is shared under the Head Feature Principle by rethinking the relationship between the feature HEAD and the syntactic category of specific words and phrases along the following lines: rather than use a separate feature specification POS to identify this category information, we take *head* to be a kind of cover term for a set of subtypes *verb*, *noun*, *preposition*, each of which imposes a certain set of attributes that must be specified respectively. In each case, these attributes and their values jointly constitute the value of the HEAD feature itself. Thus, as we'll see in Chapter 4, nouns and verbs must be specified for certain kinds of agreement information via a feature AGR, whereas in English, where neither prepositions nor adjectives display morphological agreement, neither the *adj* nor the *prep* subtypes of head will mandate specification of AGR. We can display these sorts of type-imposed requirements as follows:

(59)

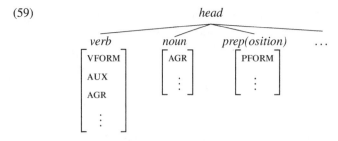

Each head type imposes a constraint on the particular set of attributes which must be specified as the value of HEAD, automatically ensuring that only that information is shared between a phrase and its head which is appropriate to the specific part of speech to which the head belongs.

At the same time, it will prove extremely convenient to group together the HEAD and valence information, along with the relevant information about the representation of the semantic contribution that the constituent makes to the meaning of the larger constituents within which it appears, under a single attribute which separates out the morphosyntactic and semantic specifications of the sign from phonological information. There are several reasons for doing so, but the most obvious is that we do not want to have the option of specifying some particular phonological condition on the complements that a verb in English (or any language, for that matter) can select. For example, there is no verb in English which selects complements whose initial phonological value must be a fricative. Such phonologically determined valence requirements have in fact never been observed in any human language, and there is excellent reason to think that no language would adopt such requirements. So in specifying that a head is seeking a complement with certain properties, our options in identifying those properties should be constrained in advance so that we do not allow for possibilities that, 'purely coincidentally,' are never realized. Assuming in advance that the only kinds of objects which can appear on COMPS lists are descriptions of morphosyntactic and semantic properties ensures that the possibility of phonological selection simply never arises. Furthermore, as we'll see later on in this chapter, it is also very useful to separate syntactic and semantic properties from each other.

From this point on, therefore, instead of writing, for example, (60)a, we assume the feature architecture in (60)b:

(60)   a. $\begin{bmatrix} \text{HEAD} & \begin{bmatrix} \dots \\ \text{POS} & verb \\ \dots \end{bmatrix} \\ \text{SUBJ} & \dots \\ \text{COMPS} & \dots \end{bmatrix}$ b. $\text{S(YN)S(EM)}\begin{bmatrix} \text{SYN} & \begin{bmatrix} \text{HEAD} & \begin{bmatrix} verb \\ \dots \\ \dots \end{bmatrix} \\ \text{SUBJ} & \dots \\ \text{COMPS} & \dots \end{bmatrix} \\ \text{SEM} & \dots \end{bmatrix}$

An adequate treatment of the semantics for natural languages requires an appeal to certain mathematically demanding logical formalisms that we cannot survey within the scope of this textbook. I will therefore describe, in informal terms, various semantic properties of signs and their combinatorics, where these properties are relevant, but our attention will be restricted throughout this book to the strictly syntactic aspects of such combinatorics. We will therefore make no further reference to the SEM attribute in sign descriptions, and adopt the convention that unless we need to make specific reference to SYN, morphosyntactic attributes will be listed directly under SYNSEM, which, as indicated in (60)b, we abbreviate ss.

In order to use the lexical entries in (57) to compose a PP, we need an explicit rule which works exactly the same way for prepositions as for verbs – it combines the preposition with a sequence of sisters which match in one-to-one fashion the items on the preposition's COMPS list. We could state this rule as a near-copy of the Verb-complement Rule stated in (49), with appropriate changes of V (or head type *verb*, in our current setup) to P/*prep*. But since we have adopted the Head Feature Principle, we no longer need to state either the Verb-complement Rule, or the corresponding Preposition-complement Rule given below by making specific reference to the HEAD feature on the right side of the arrow. Whatever the HEAD value (as notated by HEAD) of the lexical item which is taken to be the head, corresponding to the right-hand side of a rule such as (49), the mother in the structure which is licensed by the rule must have the same HEAD value. Hence, we can omit all reference to part of speech on the right of the arrow, and state the two rules as follows:

(61)   a. **Verb-complement Rule**

$$
\begin{bmatrix} phrase \\ \text{SS} \begin{bmatrix} \text{HEAD} & verb \\ \text{COMPS} & \langle\,\rangle \end{bmatrix} \end{bmatrix} \rightarrow \underset{HEAD}{\begin{bmatrix} word \\ \text{COMPS} & \langle X_1, \ldots, X_n \rangle \end{bmatrix}} \quad \underset{COMPS}{X_1, \ldots, X_n}
$$

b. **Preposition-complement Rule**

$$
\begin{bmatrix} phrase \\ \text{SS} \begin{bmatrix} \text{HEAD} & prep \\ \text{COMPS} & \langle\,\rangle \end{bmatrix} \end{bmatrix} \rightarrow \underset{HEAD}{\begin{bmatrix} word \\ \text{COMPS} & \langle X_1, \ldots, X_n \rangle \end{bmatrix}} \quad \underset{COMPS}{X_1, \ldots, X_n}
$$

For the time being, let us leave aside the question of how the subject of a sentence is connected to that sentence's VP. Then these rules are virtually identical, except for the difference in the mother category's HEAD type. If *verb* and *preposition* had been the only two lexical category types in English, then we could be assured that collapsing these rules along the lines (62) would always give the correct results:

(62)   **Head-complement Rule**

$$
\begin{bmatrix} phrase \\ \text{SS}|\text{COMPS} & \langle\,\rangle \end{bmatrix} \rightarrow \underset{HEAD}{\begin{bmatrix} word \\ \text{COMPS} & \langle X_1, \ldots, X_n \rangle \end{bmatrix}} \quad \underset{COMPS}{X_1, \ldots, X_n}
$$

where SS|COMPS α is a convenient abbreviation for

$$
\begin{bmatrix}
\cdots \\
\text{SS} \quad \begin{bmatrix} \cdots \\ \text{COMPS} \quad \alpha \\ \cdots \end{bmatrix} \\
\cdots
\end{bmatrix}
$$

Whatever the COMPS value of the lexical item which appears in the structure licensed by (62), the only way to obtain an empty COMPS list on the mother is to provide a set of sisters for the head word which match the latter's COMPS value in one-to-one fashion, and the Head Feature Principle ensures that the HEAD specifications on the mother and on the lexical head in the structure are identical. The interaction of these few, very general principles guarantees that all and only legal structures with lexical heads are licensed.

Let's look at a concrete application of these general principles. Given the Head-complement Rule, and the lexical item in (57)a, we know that structures of the form in (63) must be admitted:

(63)

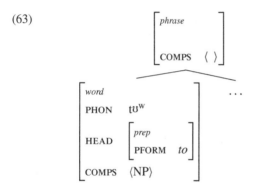

where $\langle\ \rangle$ is the type of an empty list. But since this representation must also respect the Head Feature Principle, we also know that the mother must display the same value for HEAD as its head daughter:

(64)

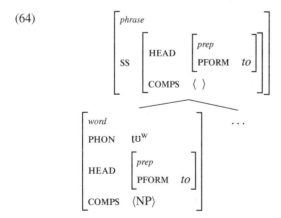

At the same time, the Head-complement Rule entails that the COMPS list of the head be identical to the list of the head's sisters. It follows that there is an NP sister to the head, which, when combined with the mother's empty COMPS list, yields a COMPS list containing only NP, identical to the head's [COMPS ⟨NP⟩] specification. Thus, we know that the structure in (65) is licensed:

(65)

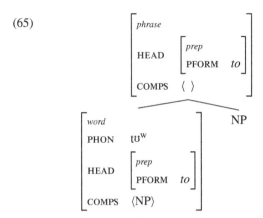

Since the category label PP identifies an expression with the *head* type *prep* whose combinatorial requirements have been fulfilled (as reflected in an empty COMPS list), we can relabel the mother category in (65) simply as PP. With appropriate simplification of the descriptive notation, we wind up with the following as a legal phrase structure:

(66)

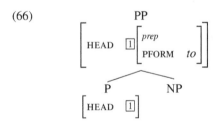

where the notation ①️ labels a particular *head*-type object, and the appearance of ①️ as both the mother and the head daughter's HEAD value means that the same *head*-type object is the HEAD value for both of them. The information that *to* is the head of the PP is thus available to any head which requires a PP complement headed by a specific preposition. For example, we state the lexical entries for *conferred* and *presented* along the lines displayed in (67):

(67) a.

$$conferred: \begin{bmatrix} word \\ \text{PHON} \quad \text{knfŗd} \\ \text{HEAD} \quad verb \\ \text{COMPS} \quad \left\langle \text{NP, PP}\begin{bmatrix} \text{PFORM } on \end{bmatrix} \right\rangle \end{bmatrix}$$

b.

$$\text{presented: } \begin{bmatrix} word \\ \text{PHON} \quad \text{p.iəzɛntəd} \\ \text{HEAD} \quad verb \\ \text{COMPS} \quad \left\langle \text{NP, PP}\begin{bmatrix}\text{PFORM } to\end{bmatrix}\right\rangle \end{bmatrix}$$

The appearance of a PFORM specification on the PP mother in such a structure provides the necessary information for an account of the possibilities in (56), and similarly with (55) (see Problem 1 on page 76).

2.6   Subject Selection

Nothing said so far explicitly refers to the combination of subjects with VPs to form *clauses* – a term which embraces both sentences, which correspond to stand-alone utterances (*Robin has been a spy all along*), and phrases, which are identical in syntactic structure to sentences but which occur *within* sentences (e.g., the bolded parts of *Leslie is convinced that because* [$_s$ ***Robin has been a spy all along***], [$_s$ ***the war is already lost***]. The NP+gerundive VPs we noted earlier in §2.2.1 are examples of the latter. We will in later chapters explore a variety of subject selection phenomena, but for the time being it is important to see how the technology developed so far for complements can be applied with very little elaboration to the combination of VPs with various kinds of categories to yield the possibilities that we observe.

We have seen that some predicates can take clausal subjects and some cannot. This difference can be enforced by using a feature SUBJ, alluded to earlier, to identify what possibilities exist for any given verb. For example, consider the following contrast:

(68) a.   That Robin might have been a spy $\left\{ \begin{array}{l} \text{??*interrupted} \\ \text{wreaked havoc with} \end{array} \right\}$ our planning.

    b.   That Robin is a spy $\left\{ \begin{array}{l} \text{bothers} \\ \text{*harasses} \end{array} \right\}$ me.

These judgments may not be universal, but they reflect the grammar of a certain subset of speakers whose grammars constitute a valid topic of investigation. And such an investigation must come to terms with the fact that while *interrupt* and *wreak havoc with* differ in their semantics much more in terms of degree than of kind, they exhibit, for the speakers in question, a marked difference in compatibility with clausal subjects such as *that Robin might have been a spy*. One might argue that in addition to being more general, *interrupt* also requires a concrete subject (*Robin interrupted my work*). But this alternative account is factually untenable; we can say *Various distractions interrupted our planning*. The empirically correct generalization rather seems to be that *interrupt* does not accept a clausal subject. In the same way, *bother* allows a clausal subject but *harass* does not. And again, while we might seek a solution here based on incompatible meaning, it would be hard to argue that *harass* does not allow abstract subjects; thus, we find on the internet examples such as

> The nagging feeling of self-doubt, as Derrick describes it, harassed him not only as an artist but also at the thought of becoming a teacher.

(at www.inmagtexas.com/2013/01/self-doubt-squashes-creativity-artist-feature-derrick-white/). How can we build this kind of apparently syntactic restriction into our grammar? At present, the rule we have provided in (22) combining an NP and a VP to yield an S is inadequate, because we know that many sentences do have clausal subjects (*That Robin is a spy annoys the hell out of me*). But so far we have no way to sort between VPs which take a clausal sister to form a clause and those which cannot.

Clearly, the key difference in the examples given is the difference in the verbs: *interrupt* vs *wreak havoc with, harass* vs *bother* respectively. It follows, on the simplest account, that it is this difference which somehow 'permeates' the VPs formed by the two respective verbs in each case, making it possible for one VP to accept, while the other must reject, a clausal subject. The verbs themselves cannot literally carry out the selection, because, unlike complements, subjects do not occur as sisters to verbs, and hence it is not possible to define conditions on the verb which make reference to a sister subject:

(69)

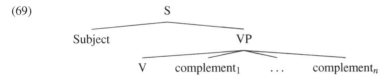

It is only possible to talk about what kind of subject a given verb *phrase* will accept or reject as a sister. And at present we have no explicit account of that.

But it may have occurred to you that we can use essentially the same mechanism to account for subject/VP combination that we have used for a head/complement combination. Schematically, the relationship between the two can be depicted as in (70):

(70)   a.   VP   b.   S

         V $\overset{\text{COMPS}}{\longrightarrow}$ XP   XP $\overset{\text{SUBJ}}{\longleftarrow}$ VP

Clearly, another general rule along the same lines could do the same work in the case of subjects as with complements. We can in fact ensure the correct combination of subjects with the VP by imposing the condition stated in (71):

(71)   **Head-subject Rule (preliminary version)**

$$\begin{bmatrix} phrase \\ \text{SUBJ} \quad \langle \, \rangle \end{bmatrix} \rightarrow \underset{HEAD}{\begin{bmatrix} phrase \\ \text{SUBJ} \quad \langle Y \rangle \end{bmatrix}} , \qquad \underset{SUBJ}{Y}$$

along with the condition in (72):

(72)   All categories of type *phrase* must have empty COMPS lists.

Since in order to be of type *phrase* a sign must have an empty COMPS list specification, we know that the COMPS list on the right side of (71) must be ⟨ ⟩; hence we need make no mention of COMPS on either side of the arrow in (71). Now the Head Feature Principle (58) and the two rules (49) and (71) replace all of the phrase structure rules posited so far, except the one which combines adjuncts with phrasal heads to form another phrase of the same kind, to which we turn in the following section.

To see how all these pieces of our system work in tandem, we reconsider the verb *put* and the VP projected from it, amending our description of it to take into account the [SUBJ ⟨NP⟩] specification we posited for it in (44):

(73)

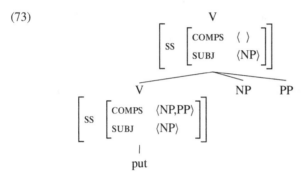

In order to ensure that this structure is licensed, the Head-complement Rule must be written so that a lexical head will, loosely speaking, have a SUBJ list equal to the SUBJ list of its mother (since, in the first stage of combination, that head may only combine with elements corresponding to the complement daughters of the mother category, and there are therefore no signs which can saturate the SUBJ valence specification). So far as the COMPS list of this lexical head is concerned, the story is quite different: the COMPS list of *put* and the COMPS list of its mother will necessarily differ, given the lexical entry for the former and the description mandated by the Head-complement Rule for the latter. We therefore revise this rule to read:

(74)   **Head-complement Rule**

$$
\begin{bmatrix} phrase \\ \text{SS|COMPS} \quad \langle \ \rangle \\ \text{SUBJ} \quad \boxed{1} \end{bmatrix}
\rightarrow
\begin{bmatrix} word \\ \text{COMPS} \quad \big\langle X_1, \ldots, X_n \big\rangle \\ \text{SUBJ} \quad \boxed{1} \end{bmatrix}
\quad X_1, \ldots, X_n
$$

                    HEAD   *COMPS*

The Head-complement Rule formulation in (74) now entails not only sister signs for *put* which exactly match its own COMPS list, but also a subject requirement for the VP projected from *put* which is exactly the same as the subject requirement specified in the lexicon for *put* itself. Thus, *put* will appear with exactly one NP and one PP sister, and will seek an NP subject as sister to this V NP PP constituent. The phrasal constituent licensed by the combination of *put* with its sisters may now, as the head/subject rule (71) tells us, combine with another element to form a structure such as the one in (75):

(75)

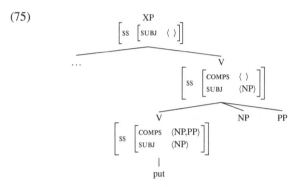

What can we say about XP, sitting at the very top of the structure? We know that its head is the V[ss|COMPS ⟨ ⟩] in (75), since this is mandated by the Head-subject Rule; hence, by the Head Feature Principle, XP must be a verb-type phrase of some kind. We also know that its SUBJ list is empty, and that, by virtue of (71), its COMPS list is empty as well. XP therefore may combine with nothing further, and, in compliance with the Head Feature Principle, we must 'fill in' (75) as in (75'):

(75')

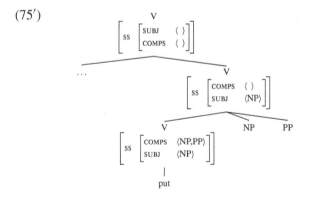

Again, the Head-subject Rule entails that the difference between the SUBJ list on the VP (i.e., ⟨NP⟩)) and that on the mother (i.e.,⟨ ⟩) corresponds to the VP's sister. Thus we can 'solve' the ellipses in (75') to yield NP. The two rules we have introduced and the lexical entry for *put* interact to allow us to identify (75″) as a legal structure of English.

(75″)

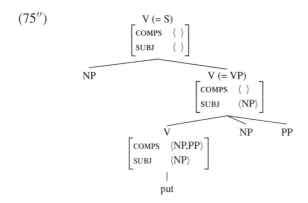

Omission of a subject, or attempting to supply two or more subjects, would lead to a violation of the Head-subject Rule, just as supplying too few or too many complements for a given verb is prohibited by the Head-complement Rule.

Problems

1. State lexical entries for *gave*, *bestowed*, and *presented* and show how these lexical entries, along with those in (67) – in conjunction with the principles and constraints stated in the grammar so far – automatically give rise to the data in (56).

2. Consider the following data:

The committee $\left\{\begin{array}{l}\text{dissented from}\\ \text{disagreed with}\\ \text{disputed}\\ \text{argued against}\end{array}\right\}$ the position that spies are untrust-

worthy.

Provide lexical entries for two of the verbs shown listed in braces in this example, along with lexical entries for any associated prepositions. Using one of the verbs you've chosen which takes a PP complement, build up a tree for the whole sentence step by step, showing how the interplay of the principles that have been introduced in this chapter allows us to license these trees completely without any reference to phrase structure rules.

2.7   NPs

We now turn to the phrasal system projected from nominal heads. In our previous discussion on NPs, we provided a rather 'flat' structure in which determiners, adjectives and PPs appearing under NP were all sisters of the head N. But in English, flat structures are somewhat unusual, and the internal architecture of the NP is no exception to this tendency.

2.7.1   *One* Replacement

We start with the data in (76).

(76) a.   Robin and Terry were arguing with each other in a restaurant.

   b.   Terry and Robin were arguing with each other in a restaurant.

Constructions in which *and, or* and a few other words which correspond to English 'logical' vocabulary are said to exhibit the coordination phenomenon. The question of what is actually being coordinated isn't necessarily always obvious, however. One excellent test is to look at the string containing the coordination and then switch the positions of the strings you think are being coordinated, as in (76). For example, it's conceivable that the coordinated strings in (76) are *Robin* and *Terry were*; but if that were so, we'd expect **Terry were and Robin arguing with each other in a restaurant* to be good – which it definitely isn't. We can therefore be confident that in (77)a, *the King of France* and *Queen of Spain* are not the strings being coordinated:

(77) a.   The King of France and Queen of Spain were arguing with each other in a restaurant.

   b.   *Queen of France and the King of Spain were arguing with each other in a restaurant.

   c.   The Queen of Spain and King of France were arguing with each other in a restaurant.

What *does* work is switching the positions of *King of France* on the one hand and *Queen of Spain* on the other. Since, in general, strings that can be coordinated correspond to constituents, we have some plausible evidence that *Queen of Spain* and *King of France* are constituents.

But the evidence goes from fairly good to excellent when we consider the replacement pattern in (78):

(78) a.   I like THIS King of England better than THAT one. (*one* = 'King of England')

   b.   Some students of chemistry are smarter than other ones. (*ones* = 'students of chemistry')

   c.   Leslie found a new book of poetry after Terry bought a used one. (*one* = 'book of poetry')

One here seems to have no meaning of its own; but it does pick up a meaning from the syntactic context it appears in. It also has a plural form:

(79)   Robin likes these books of poetry better than those other ones.

On this basis, it seems fair to conclude that *one(s)* is a proform for a subportion of an NP, which in turn means that that subportion is itself a constituent, a conclusion which dovetails nicely with the coordination facts.

But a skeptic might well argue that we're jumping to conclusions here: what about cases such as (80)?

(80)   Leslie bought me a book and Terry bought me $\left\{ \begin{matrix} \text{a book} \\ \text{one} \end{matrix} \right\}$ as well.

In (80), *one* appears to have replaced *a book* in its entirety. This challenges our description of it as a proform for what would have to be analyzed as a structural component of NP constituents consisting of everything except the determiner, for in (80), the entire NP *a book* has to be taken to be what was replaced; clearly *book* cannot be replacing only *book* here, given the badness of **Leslie bought me a book and Terry bought me book as well.* On the other hand, it is difficult to see how the *one* which appears in (40) could be an NP along the lines of *him, her, it* and so on, since in (78) it forms a constituent with a determiner, and hence cannot be a complete NP itself. We therefore need to consider the possibility that the different instances of *one* in (78) on the one hand and (80) on the other are actually different linguistic expressions, one of which is indeed a sub-NP proform and the other of which can indeed serve anaphorically for a complete NP.

This suggestion may strike the reader as rather suspect: is it not a bit of a coincidence that two forms which appear to be doing quite similar work are distinct objects which just happen to have the same form? But the evidence of the data in (81) bears out this suggestion:

(81)   Leslie bought me some books and Terry bought me $\left\{ \begin{matrix} \text{some books} \\ \text{*ones} \end{matrix} \right\}$ as well.

The plural form of the *one* which appears in (80) in place of a singular NP cannot replace a plural NP. What *can* appear in such contexts, rather, are cardinal numbers:

(82) a.   Leslie bought me $\left\{ \begin{matrix} \text{a book} \\ \text{two books} \\ \text{three books} \\ \vdots \end{matrix} \right\}$ and Terry bought me $\left\{ \begin{matrix} \text{one} \\ \text{two} \\ \text{three} \\ \vdots \end{matrix} \right\}$

        (of them) as well.

On the other hand, in exactly the same contrastive environments that sub-NP *one* can appear in with a singular antecedent, *ones* can appear with a plural antecedent:

(83) a.   *Robin bought me some books and Terry bought me ones (of them) as well.
     b.   Robin bought me some new books and Terry bought me some used ones.

The *one* in (80) thus appears to represent nothing more than an anaphoric use of the numeral, overlapping in pronunciation, but not denotation, with the sub-NP replacement *one*, which we can now consider ourselves justified in taking to be a proform belonging to a category which, taken together with a determiner, constitutes an NP, and we need to adopt a notation for it in phrase structure trees such as (84):

(84)

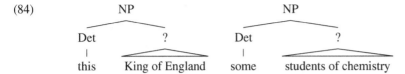

There is in fact a standard notation for the mystery label '?' in these examples. From the early 1970s on, the sub-NP nominal sister to the determiner has been written N̄. The question then arises as to how to analyze the NP *a used one/some used ones* along the lines of (83)b. Here, *one* itself replaces *book of poetry*, but we need to arrive at analysis of the subphrase *used one*. The data in (85) speak to this question:

(85) a.   Robin bought me THIS new book of poetry and Terry bought me THAT one.
      (*one* = 'new book of poetry')

 b.   Robin bought me a new book of poetry and Terry bought me a used one.
      (*one* = 'book of poetry')

The distribution of *one* in these examples, which we can take as a reflection of positions in the configuration where N̄ appears, indicates that *both* of the strings *book of poetry* and *used book of poetry* are instances of N̄:

(86)   [$_{NP}$ this new book of poetry]

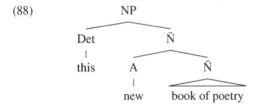

The evidence from *one* replacement thus supports the analysis of *this new book of poetry* in terms of the structure displayed in (87)–(88), giving both the bracketed and the tree form of the configuration:

(87)   [$_{NP}$ this [$_{N̄}$ new [$_{N̄}$ book of poetry]]]

(88)   NP
         ┌──────┴────┐
        Det   N̄
         │   ┌─────┴─────┐
        this   A   N̄
                │   ┌─────┴─────┐
               new   book of poetry

We also have evidence for adjuncts on the right side of the nominal head. Consider the data in (89):

(89) a.   I like the student of Scottish origin better than the one from Ostrogothia.
      (*one* = 'student')

 b.   I like THIS student of Scottish origin better than THAT one. (*one* = 'student of Scottish origin')

Again, the *one* replacement possibilities strongly suggest that both *student of Scottish origin* and *student* itself should be analyzed as instances of N̄ here. Compare these data with the results in (90):

(90) a.   I like THIS student of chemistry better than THAT one. (*one* = 'student of chemistry')

b.   *I like the student of chemistry better than the one of physics.

The fact that *one* replacement is blocked in (90)b makes credible the distinction in structural representations displayed in (91):

(91)

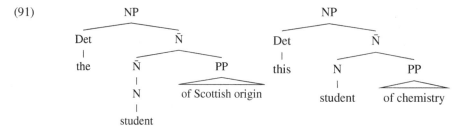

Apparently, some PPs are adjuncts to N̄ and some are complements to the lexical head of the NP. The NP system thus appears to be formulable in terms of the compact set of rules given in (92):

(92)   NP → (Det) N̄
         N̄ → A N̄
         N̄ → N̄ PP
         N̄ → N (PP)

It follows from the form of these rules that in a string [$_{NP}$ older student of Scottish origin], we have two possible structural analyses:

(93)   a.

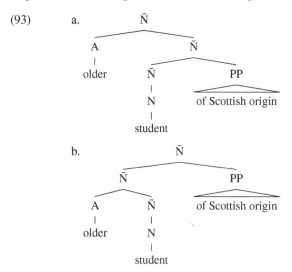

This is indeed a correct prediction, as we see from data such as (94):

(94) a.   I like the younger student of Scottish origin less than the older one.

b.   I like the older student of Ostrogoth origin more than the one of Scottish origin.

Since we have readings in which the contrast in (94)a is between two students both of Scottish origin, one older and one younger, and (94)b between two older students, one of Ostrogoth origin and one of Scottish origin, it appears that the structural ambiguity depicted in (94) does correspond to a motivated difference in representations along the lines shown.

The rule system in (92) has an interesting consequence for the way we interpret NPs containing adjuncts. Notice that for a string such as *the former high roller with a dubious reputation*, there are two logically somewhat independent interpretations: the individual so described may be someone with a dubious reputation who was but is no longer a high roller, or someone who used to be a disreputable high-roller but is no longer, as in *The former high roller with a dubious reputation had reinvented himself as a charismatic community activist and advocate for the disenfranchised*. In one case the sense carried by *former* – that the following description held at an earlier time but does no longer – applies only to the information carried by the description *high roller*; in the other, it applies both to the description *high roller* and to *with a dubious reputation*. The two descriptions correspond to the two different structures corresponding to this string licensed under (92):

(95)   a.

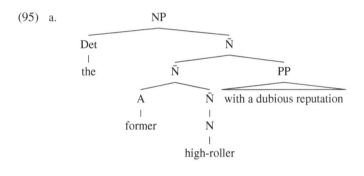

b.

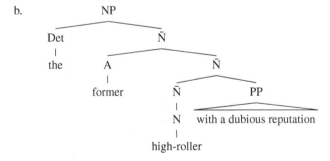

If (95)b identifies a former high roller of current poor reputation, we predict that replacing [$_{\bar{N}}$ *former high roller*] with *one* will preserve that meaning while suppressing the other sense, and it does:

(96)   The former high roller with all those community service awards wasn't nearly as interesting as the one with the dubious reputation.

Here the only interpretation is that *the one with the dubious reputation* refers to a former high roller who is currently viewed with a certain suspicion. What this example makes clear is that the restriction of *former*'s meaning to the sense of *high roller*, exempting *with a dubious reputation* (and hence allowing it to be interpreted as a current property) correlates with the structural position of the PP outside the innermost N̄ dominating *former*.

2.7.2   Generalizing the NP System

The rules just given correctly characterize a large range of NP structures, but, compared with the rule we've stated for VP and PP, the system looks rather arbitrary. Having worked out a plausible configurational description of the NP, our next task should be to eliminate any redundant information that the rules contain, and given the Head-complement/-subject Rules and Head Feature Principle we arrived at earlier, it should be clear that many aspects of (92) are redundant, and can be suppressed, if we 'farm out' as many of the specifics which show up in these rules as possible.

We've already seen how to do this, extrapolating from the VP rules to a system which includes PPs as well. We can eliminate reference to nounhood on both sides of the arrow in each of these rules, since the Head Feature Principle guarantees that if the mother is [HEAD *noun*], the head daughter will be and vice versa. Nor do we need to say anything about complements: the Head-complement Rule will force exactly the complement sequence associated with each lexical head that is mandated by the latter's COMPS list. What we're left with in (92) that can't be accounted for completely under the present system is the presence of adjuncts, to which we turn shortly, and the rule expanding NP as an optional determiner+N̄.

There are two possibilities: either determiners are adjuncts or they have some other sort of structural relation to the nominal head. If they were adjuncts, they would have to combine with N̄ to yield an N̄, just as adjectives, PPs and other sorts of constituents do. What happens instead is that they in effect close off the nominal phrase to which they belong from further structural elaboration. We start with a noun, combine it with a complement to get an N̄, then possibly add any number of adjuncts one at a time, licensing a new N̄ with each addition, until we combine an N̄ with a determiner, at which point we have a complete NP, which can then serve as a complement or possibly an adjunct (e.g., *I'm going to Paris* [$_{NP}$ *the week after next*]), or part of a coordination. So determiners definitely do not constitute modificatory material which leaves the category they compose with the head unchanged. Another possibility is that they are markers, like the *that* and *for* which appear with finite and infinitive clauses respectively in *I know that Robin is a spy, I'm waiting for Robin to be revealed as a spy*, discussed at length below. But whereas markers have a marginal semantic role in the interpretation of the constituents they appear in, determiners are crucial: *Every arrow hit the target* is dramatically different in meaning from *No arrow hit the target*, where *every* and *no*, syntactic determiners, have the status in logic of *generalized quantifiers*, whose specific identity is crucial to the denotation of sentences. More to the point, some determiners enter into number agreement patterns with respect to their N̄ sisters that no English markers do – but which is a prominent part of the grammar of the subject/verb relationship. On the whole, then, the most plausible structural status to assign to determiners is that they, like the subjects of clauses, are valents of the phrasal head.

The parallels between determiners and subjects is appealing. Compare the structure of *Robin supposedly criticized Leslie in a fit of jealousy* on the one hand and *the supposed usurper of the throne from Corsica* on the other:

(97) a.

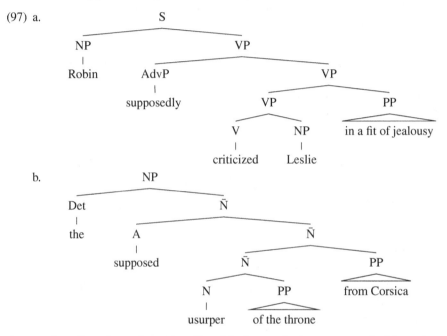

As noted earlier, determiners in effect block any further structural elaboration of nominal phrases, just as subjects terminate the development of the VP. Like subjects in clauses, there is only one determiner allowed at the 'top' of the NP. And, like subjects, the class of forms which can occur in the structural position occupied by determiners is actually somewhat categorially diverse:

(98) a.   [_{NP} [_{DET} that] picture of Leslie]
 b.   [_{NP} [_{POSS}[_{NP} Robin] 's] picture of Leslie]
 c.   [_{NP} [_{POSS}[_{VP} being smart] 's] sake]
     (at http://campusprogress.org/articles/five_lessons_mlk_we_can_use_today/:
     'When King talked of intelligence plus character, he meant that there was
     more to life than being smart for being smart's sake.')

Nonnominals in the possessive position in NPs are quite unusual – even more so than nonnominal subjects, perhaps – but, per (98), are apparently not ruled out. Possessives – which in some cases have certain semantic properties in common with determiners, but in others seem quite different (e.g., (98)c) – make particularly clear the parallelism between what we may call the specifier position of NPs and the subject of clauses. A particularly telling kind of construction, in this regard, is exhibited in (99):

(99)   What really annoyed me was Robin('s) constantly saying nasty things about Leslie.

Without the possessive *'s*, (99) illustrates a kind of clause called *gerundive* in which the verb is marked with an *ing* suffix, but which otherwise has completely parallel structure to clauses with a finite verb. But when *'s* is present, we have an apparent NP, since, apart from the gerundive construction, VPs simply cannot appear with possessors. The proof that in *Robin's constantly saying nasty things about Leslie*, *constantly saying nasty things about Leslie* really is a VP is the adverb *constantly*: the string cannot be a nominal phrase, because nominals can only take adjectival modifiers preceding the head, never adverbial. Thus, the constituent *Robin's constantly saying nasty things about Leslie* seems to be a strange kind of mixed category, which tests positive, so to speak, for two parts of speech *at one time*: nominal, because of the possessor preceding the head, but also verbal, because of the VP that seems to be the head. A detailed analysis of this perplexing construction would take us much too far afield, but for our purposes, the central point is that the parallelism between the subject NP *Robin* and the possessive specifier *Robin's* is close enough that in this particular syntactic context, the two appear to be conflated, with the specifier appearing in a context which we would expect to be clausal, as an apparent alternative to a subject specification.

It follows from this discussion that, all other things being equal, we should treat subjects and determiners as being different expressions of the same valence requirement. That is, determiners satisfy the 'last slot' requirement in the phrasal system projected from nouns in precisely the same way that subjects satisfy a 'final slot' requirement in the phrasal hierarchy based on the verb. To implement this unification of the verb and noun phrasal systems, we identify a valence attribute SP(ECIFIE)R:

(100)   **Head-specifier Rule**

where, by removing the [HEAD *noun*] restriction, we no longer confine the Head-specifier Rule to specification of nominal phrases; whatever syntactic type is identified as the value of HEAD in any phrasal sign licensed by this rule will be shared between that sign and its head daughter, and if that value is *verb*, the sign will be interpreted as S and its specifier daughter will saturate the head daughter's SPR requirement, corresponding to what we will continue to refer to as the subject, now understood to be the specifier daughter of a clause. This rule, together with the Head-complement Rule, restated here, and the two rules in (102), constitute the whole of our grammar to this point.

(101)   **Head-complement Rule**

$$\begin{bmatrix} phrase \\ \text{SS|COMPS} \quad \langle \; \rangle \end{bmatrix} \rightarrow \underbrace{\begin{bmatrix} word \\ \text{COMPS} \quad \langle X_1, \dots, X_n \rangle \end{bmatrix}}_{HEAD}, \quad \underbrace{X_1, \dots, X_n}_{COMPS}$$

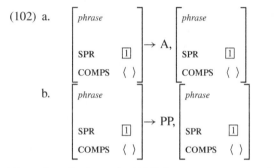

(102) a.

$$\begin{bmatrix} phrase \\ \text{SPR} \quad \boxed{1} \\ \text{COMPS} \quad \langle \; \rangle \end{bmatrix} \rightarrow A, \begin{bmatrix} phrase \\ \text{SPR} \quad \boxed{1} \\ \text{COMPS} \quad \langle \; \rangle \end{bmatrix}$$

b.

$$\begin{bmatrix} phrase \\ \text{SPR} \quad \boxed{1} \\ \text{COMPS} \quad \langle \; \rangle \end{bmatrix} \rightarrow PP, \begin{bmatrix} phrase \\ \text{SPR} \quad \boxed{1} \\ \text{COMPS} \quad \langle \; \rangle \end{bmatrix}$$

The rule subsystem in (102) is a counterpart to the specific rules for VPs in (42), an instance of the schematic adjunction rule in (40). These rules break rank fairly dramatically with the Head-specifier and Head-complement Rules we've focused our attention on so far, in that they make no reference at all to valence properties of the head. This is as it should be – in essence, the definition of adjuncts is that they are sisters of phrasal heads which are unselected by those heads – but clearly a more general treatment which expresses the idea of adjuncthood cross-categorially is needed. In particular, it would be desirable to unify the adjunct rules as a single schema to the greatest extent possible, and we turn to the question of how to achieve this unity in the following discussion.

2.8   Adjuncts

The syntax of adjuncts is, as just suggested, rather different from that of subjects and complements. The latter are selected by heads; adjuncts, in contrast, occur outside the phrasal constituent immediately dominating the selecting head, and are therefore 'invisible' to the latter. The fact that the valence preferences of some XP's lexical heads play no role in determining the adjunct sisters of those XPs does not mean, however, that no properties of XP are relevant to its adjunct possibilities. Meaning compatibility unquestionably plays a role in accounting for the goodness (or not) of examples such as those in (103):

(103)   Robin spoke to me in a $\left\{\begin{array}{c} \text{haughty} \\ \text{\#parametric} \end{array}\right\}$ tone of voice.

(104)   Robin's solution to the resonance problem involved introducing a $\left\{\begin{array}{c} \text{parametric} \\ \text{\#haughty} \end{array}\right\}$ scaling factor into the damping term.

The anomalous examples in (103) and (104) are difficult or impossible to interpret in terms of normal circumstances, but not for reasons that we would want to attribute to some formal property of the NPs in either case. Tones of voice are the kind of things which can be haughty, but there is no obvious sense in which the meaning of *parametric* can characterize a tone of voice. By the same token, a scaling factor in some mathematical model can be parametric – determined, for example, by several independent variables – but an abstract object by its very nature cannot be characterized in terms of attitude, which is what *haughty* denotes. It would be very difficult to identify plausibly the source of these meaning difficulties with some mismatch of formal features, if for no other reason than that there seem to be an arbitrary number of properties with respect to which an adjunct might be an inappropriate modifier for a given noun or verb. Thus, we would be better advised to assign the determination of judgments such as those in (103) and (104) to whatever mechanism of the grammar is responsible for assessing whether or not the meanings of the parts of some sentence make sense when put together.

But there *is* a formal difference which is responsible for the mirror-image contrasts in (105) and (106):

(105)   Robin drove $\left\{\begin{array}{c} \text{recklessly} \\ \text{*reckless} \end{array}\right\}$.

(106)   Robin's $\left\{\begin{array}{c} \text{reckless} \\ \text{*recklessly} \end{array}\right\}$ behavior could get him into trouble.

The meaning of *reckless* and *recklessly* are essentially identical; where the two adjuncts differ is in the kind of category to which they may be adjoined respectively: *reckless*, like other adjectives, must modify phrasal projections of nouns, while adverbs of manner, such as *recklessly*, modify nonnominals, including not only VPs, as in (105), but APs and PPs:

(107)   Recklessly $\left\{\begin{array}{c} \text{out of control} \\ \text{aggressive} \end{array}\right\}$ Robin may be __, but she is also very lucky.

The fact that the strings containing *recklessly* are fronted shows that they form a constituent dominating both the adverb and the prepositional and adjectival heads. It follows that there must be some kind of interaction between the adjunct and the constituent to which it attaches, even though this interaction can't involve selection of the latter by the former. In other languages, there is still stronger indication of this connection. The case of French adjectival modification is representative of a large class of languages in which certain properties of heads register morphologically on at least a subclass of modifiers:

(108) a.   la grande maison 'the big house'
      b.   les grandes maisons 'the big houses'

(109) a.   le grand livre 'the big book'
      b.   les grands livres 'the big books'

(110) a.   Les maisons sont grandes. 'The houses are big.'
      b.   Les livres sont grands. 'The books are big.'

In French, nouns are assigned to masculine and feminine gender classes, and are morphologically either singular or plural. Appropriate values for both of these two-way distinctions must appear on adjectives modifying, or, as in (85), predicated as a value of a nominal category, as part of the French agreement pattern. In the case of (110), the French analogue of English *be*, *être*, takes the adjective as a complement and the number/gender-marked NPs as subject, making it possible to state the agreement pattern directly. In the case of (108)–(109), however, there is no linkage between the adjunct and the nominal head of the phrase other than the structural fact of sisterhood. This entails that the necessary cross-checking of gender and number information between the nominal and its adjectival modifier must somehow be written into whatever rule we state that licenses adjunct structures – an issue that we take up in more detail in Chapter 4.

One strategy for accomplishing this goal would be to require any category appearing in a head/adjunct configuration to be compatible with morphosyntactic properties of the head by in effect specifying what kind of SYNSEM values that head could be assigned. We would want the feminine form of the adjective in (108)–(110), *grande(s)*, to appear as an adjunct always and only when the noun head of the phrase that the adjective was a sister to was assigned feminine gender in the French lexicon. Since there is no valence relationship involved, the match in gender values must be a consequence of the rule itself whereby heads of some category X appear with a sister A under a mother of category X. This line of solution presupposes that there is some property of the adjunct – call it MOD(IFIED) – which specifies the conditions that a head must satify to form a constituent with that adjunct. On this approach, MOD is correlated in the head-adjunct rule with the SYNSEM value of the head, so that, for an adjunct of a certain class, the value of MOD must match the SYNSEM value of the phrase to which the adjunct is structurally attached. Informally, we want the rule for adjuncts to indicate that an adjunct can only be sister to a head whose SYNSEM value is the same as the MOD value of the adjunct, which provides the necessary cross-checking of features, and we want the adjunct's MOD value to only have specifications that allow the adjunct to be a sister to some constituent if the adjunct itself has the right specifications for other features. We can illustrate how this works most simply in the case of the adverb/adjective distinction in English: by correlating adjectives with heads which have [HEAD *noun*] specifications, and adverbs with HEAD values which are not *noun*, we rule out the possibility of getting the wrong modifier/head pairings. An adjective such as *honest*, for example, will have the partial description

(111)
$$
\begin{bmatrix}
\text{PHON} & \text{honest} \\
\\
\text{SS} & \begin{bmatrix} \text{HEAD} & \begin{bmatrix} \textit{adjective} \\ \text{MOD} & \begin{bmatrix} \text{HEAD} & \textit{noun} \\ \text{COMPS} & \langle\,\rangle \end{bmatrix} \end{bmatrix} \end{bmatrix}
\end{bmatrix}
$$

while an adverb such as *brutally* would meet the description

(112)
$$
\begin{bmatrix}
\text{PHON} & \text{brutally} \\
\\
\text{SS} & \begin{bmatrix} \text{HEAD} & \begin{bmatrix} \textit{adverb} \\ \text{MOD} & \begin{bmatrix} \text{HEAD} & \neg\textit{noun} \\ \text{SPR} & \langle\ldots\rangle \\ \text{COMPS} & \langle\,\rangle \end{bmatrix} \end{bmatrix} \end{bmatrix}
\end{bmatrix}
$$

To license the combination of such adjuncts with their heads, we first make a small adjustment in our feature geometry, taking COMPS and SPR to be specified as the values associated with an inclusive attribute VAL(ENCE):

(113)
$$
\begin{bmatrix}
\text{VAL} & \begin{bmatrix} \text{SPR} & \textit{list} \\ \text{COMPS} & \textit{list} \end{bmatrix}
\end{bmatrix}
$$

We can now state the Head-adjunct Rule in preliminary form as follows:

(114)   **Head-adjunct Rule (Preliminary version)**

$$
\begin{bmatrix}
\textit{phrase} \\
\text{SS} \; \boxed{0} \begin{bmatrix} \text{HEAD} & \boxed{1} \\ \text{VAL} & \boxed{2} \end{bmatrix}
\end{bmatrix}
\rightarrow
\begin{bmatrix}
\textit{phrase} \\
\text{SS} \; \boxed{3} \begin{bmatrix} \text{HEAD} & \boxed{1} \\ \text{VAL} & \boxed{2} \end{bmatrix}
\end{bmatrix},
\begin{bmatrix} \text{MOD} & \boxed{3} \end{bmatrix}
$$

$$\qquad\qquad\qquad\qquad\qquad\quad \textit{HEAD} \qquad\qquad\qquad \textit{ADJUNCT}$$

We cannot identify the SYNSEM values of the mother and the head, because the SEM value of the two differ; the mother's SEM value will reflect the meaning added by the modification contributed by the adjunct. But clearly a generalization is still being missed here. The Head-adjunct Rule essentially tells us that you can put a modifier together with a sign to form a larger constituent which is morphosyntactically no different from its head daughter, and although the *meaning* of the resulting constituent will differ from that of its head precisely in incorporating this modification, the combinatoric properties of the mother phrase will be no different from those of its phrasal head. In a nutshell, valence is unaffected by modification. The right way to capture this pattern is to use the feature architecture introduced earlier in this chapter, in which SYNSEM, taken to identify the strictly morphosyntactic and semantic properties of signs, is decomposed as a specification of two properties SYN and SEM, where SEM specifies the meaning of the sign in terms of one of the higher-order logics that formal semanticists have found necessary for the complete encoding of the truth conditions on natural language sentences. As noted earlier, the technical demands of such logics preclude inclusion of any discussion of them in this book, but we can exploit the distinction between SYN and SEM to simplify considerably the Head-adjunct Rule in (114). The identities in (115) can be captured by the rule in (115), where ss|SYN identifies the SYN value of ss

(115)   **Head-adjunct Rule:**

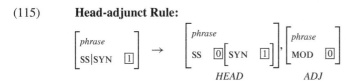

This rule applies indifferently to VPs and NP, and indeed to any kind of phrasal projection of a lexical head (although the combinatorial requirements for semantic composition will rule out the possibility of an adjunct predicate such as *clever* applying to a structure in which a nominal specifier has already combined with an N̄ to yield an NP. Here we gloss over the thorny problem of ordering adjuncts with respect to their sisters). But the fundamental simplicity of the Adjunct-head rule gives us an adequate preliminary foundation for further investigation, and on its own concisely expresses a range of facts which hold cross-categorially.

2.9   Markers

Finally, we need to address the large-scale organization of clauses – in particular, the status of what are usually referred to as *complementizers*: the *that* in *I know that Robin never arrives on time*, *for* in *I'm hoping for Terry to get the job*, *if* in *I wonder if Leslie knows we're here*, and several more. Early work on syntax often assumed that the first of these examples had the structure in (116), reflecting the rule we gave above in (22):

(116)

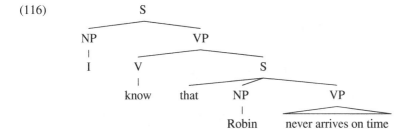

The category status of *that* was, in the earliest days of modern grammatical theorizing, not entirely clear, and the trinary-branching structure in (116) seemed a reasonable assumption, embodied in a PS rule S → (*that*) NP VP, where the correlation between *that* and finite clauses on the one hand and *for* and infinitives on the other was taken to arise from the same structure-changing rules thought to take finite clauses into infinitive counterparts. Regardless of the framework in which the original proposals were embedded, we need to assess whether or not (116) and analogous structures or other complementizers are the right way to analyze such sentences, and here we can use coordination and displacement facts to good advantage.

To begin with, let's examine some of the consequences of (22). The data in, e.g., (117) are quite difficult to account for in a straightforward way on the analysis of clausal structure imposed by this rule:

(117)   I know that $\left\{ \begin{array}{l} \text{a. it rains a lot in Seattle} \\ \text{b. there is a lion in the garage} \end{array} \right\}$.

In our earlier overview of subject selection, we observed that such data provide support for the treatment of subjects as instances of valence satisfaction. But the analysis corresponding to the Head-subject Rule is unavailable if we assume the flat structure in (116). The difficulty is that ordinary subject selection, as discussed above, is part of the formation of clauses from subject and VP daughters. Clearly, complementizers are not subjects, or even co-subjects; as argued later in this section, the places where clauses with complementizers can appear depend in part on the identity of the complementizer, and information about valents is not accessible above the point where the selected phrase appears. This fact, combined with the distributional requirement just noted, means that complementizers cannot be selected by the verb serving as the lexical head of the selecting VP (or the necessary information about their identity would be lost). But in that case, it is very difficult to account for a structure such as *that* [$_{NP}$ it] VP: how does VP get to combine with both the *it* subject and the complementizer simultaneously, as must be the case in a flat structure such as (116), if the former is selected but the latter is not? And if the VP cannot select the subject as part of combining with it to form a clause, then it is difficult to see how sentences such as those in (117) are licensed at all. Note that substituting *there* for *it* in (117)a, and conversely in (117)b, yield results which are ill-formed in a way strictly parallel to the illformedness of the corresponding root counterparts *There rains a lot in Seattle/It is a lion in the closet. But again, this parallelism is inexplicable on the structure in (116).

Another serious difficulty emerges when we consider examples such as (118):

(118)   That Robin was a spy and no one even suspected are both very improbable.

The first thing to observe about this example is that the verb displays plural form, which strongly suggests that that subject has the form of a coordination of categories. We see the distinction, for example, in the case of the ambiguous NP subject in (119):

(119)   That friend of Robin and Leslie $\left\{ \begin{array}{c} \text{is} \\ \text{are} \end{array} \right\}$ here.

The plural marking alone is possible when we shift the positions of the substrings *that friend of Robin* and *Leslie*:

(120)   Leslie and that friend of Robin $\left\{ \begin{array}{c} \text{are} \\ \text{*is} \end{array} \right\}$ here.

There are two different analyses of (119) which correspond exactly to these data: we have two NPs, *that friend of Leslie* on the one hand and *Robin* on the other, which, when coordinated yield the structure in (121)a, while the coordination of *Robin* with *Leslie* will yield the structure in (121)b:

(121)   a.

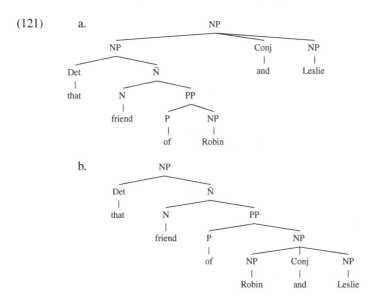

In (121)a, we have a coordination of two NPs at the highest level under the 'root' NP, which naturally corresponds to a plural number value for the whole NP itself, whereas in (121)b, the singular marking is exactly what we predict, given the analysis of the NP in terms of a singular head *friend* which takes a PP in which the object of the preposition *of* is coordinated: only a single friend is involved, regardless of the number of people who that individual is the friend of. The strings corresponding to these two analyses are the same, but the string corresponding to the subject in (120) is only possible when the form of the coordination is as in (121)a. Such examples support a view of plural marking on the verb as associated with a coordination of the form XP *and* XP, so that the appearance of the plural in (118) strongly implies the coordination of two clauses. The question now is what the form of each of the S categories in the coordination takes.

One possibility is the structure in (122):

(122)

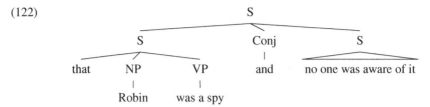

This would give rise in a straightforward way to a structure representing a coordination of clauses, but there is a major difficulty which arises as a consequence of having *that* 'buried' inside the first conjunct: in sentences such as (123), a displaced NP is located immediately following the complementizer, offering no way to connect this NP with the gap in the second conjunct S:

(123)   Everyone loves Chris, but I can tell you that TERRY, the twins don't like __at ALL and Robin actively DETESTS __.

Schematically, we have

(124)

In Chapter 6, we develop the formal technology to handle displacement as a phenomenon in its own right, and it is evident, in light of the mechanisms necessary to establish linkage between the filler *Terry* and the gap site in the right-hand conjoined S, that a structure such as (124) cannot be correct. At the very least, the filler must have a parallel structural relationship to the two conjoined clauses, so that we cannot account in a satisfactory way for such sentences with any less structure than what is shown in (125):

(125)

This in fact is still unsatisfactory, since, again, it requires what turn out to be two completely separate mechanisms to license (123) on the one hand and (126) on the other:

(126)   Terry, the twins don't like __at all.

The sole basis for the difference in how the filler is linked to the gap in (125) and (126) is the a priori assumption of the flat structure in (125). But notice that even the latter takes the NP+VP components of the clause to form a constituent as vs the complementizer. In a sense, then, we have already been forced to abandon the structure posited in (122).

Suppose then we *begin* with the premise that, contrary to the above rules, S simply takes the form *that*+S as one of its possible forms. Then, assuming that an ordinary S can take the form of a coordination of Ss along the lines of any other category, we predict a structure

(127)

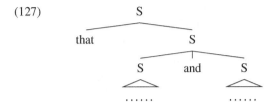

In a single move, we have now eliminated all of the problems that we encountered on the 'flat' analysis. If, along the lines independently developed in detail in Chapter 6, we assume an analysis for (126) of the form in (128)a, then, in conjunction with our conclusions about the coordination of Ss as simply another specific instance of the coordinability of like-category constituents, we obtain the structure in (128)b.

(128)   a.

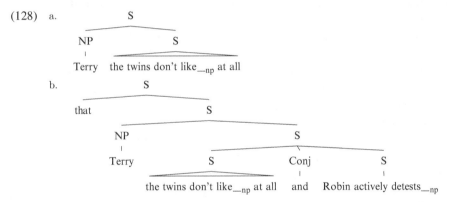

It is worth stressing that none of the components of our reasoning here have required anything special about complementizer+S sentences to be taken on faith, as it were: the difficulties associated with the flat structures we have examined are based on empirical patterns – the conditions which must hold in order for fillers and gaps in the displacement phenomenon to connect, the way in which coordination works for like categories across all major categories, even the way in which coordination interacts with the subject agreement system in English – that are logically quite separate from the status of *that*+S structures. Furthermore, under the assumption that NP and VP combine first, according to the phrase structure schemata introduced earlier in this chapter, and that only then does *that* combine with the resulting clause, we no longer have a descriptive anomaly to account for in the face of (117): subject selection works exactly as it does when no complementizer is present. In effect, there is no longer anything to explain.

There are several frameworks in which complementizers such as *that* are treated as heads and the clauses they appear with as their complements, though there is little evidence presented to support this analysis. One typical argument is that there are contexts in which, for example, *that* is obligatory – those we characterized earlier as left-peripheral positions – but it has also been observed (Huddleston and Pullum 2002: 952) that these are precisely the contexts in which omitting *that* would lead to serious 'garden path'/false-start effects, in which a clausal subject or filler, appearing without some marker indicating that it was only part of the larger structure, would be initially interpreted as the main structure itself, creating nontrivial parsing problems for the hearer. It's not unusual for grammatical options minimizing real-time psychological processing difficulties to achieve the status of very strong preferences, ultimately incorporated into the grammar as formal rules, but this historical pattern is hardly the same thing as awarding phrasal headship to morphemes which arguably might assist in simplifying the processing task. In other discussions, the choice of complementizers as heads is made apparently on the basis of purely theory-internal a priori decisions about the status of clausal and NP categories, or given no explicit justification at all. The key fact, so far as our treatment of clausal categories in the rest of this book is concerned, is that in almost all contexts where the position of clauses within sentences precludes their misinterpretation under a false-start assumption about their structural status, *that* is freely omissible. This behavior is dramatically different enough from what we find with uncontroversial phrasal heads that taking *that* to be a clausal marker of some sort, rather than the head of the clause, seems the clear null hypothesis.

What about other complementizers, such as *for*? Here the situation is very different. If a head selects an infinitival clause with a *for* complementizer, there is supposedly no version of that head which selects strictly parallel infinitival clauses consisting of just an NP and an infinitival VP (e.g., *I was waiting/hoping/intending *(for) her to get a promotion*), in clear contrast to the behavior of verbs selecting *that* clauses.[1] Some investigators appear to have conflated this observation with a much stronger claim, that the *only* infinitival clauses we ever observe are accompanied by the complementizer *for*. This is an

---

[1] The generalization itself may not be tenable; we have attestations of both *He would prefer him to get the job* (www.independent.co.uk/news/blair-may-support-morgan-for-wales-1082868.html) and *we would prefer for him to get registration first* (www.tripadvisor.com/ShowTopic-g293916-i3687-k7523468-Teaching_in_International_Schools_General-Bangkok.html). There are good reasons for thinking that in the first of these, *him* is the subject of an infinitive VP, rather than being a complement of *prefer*, along the lines discussed in Chapters 4 and 5. If so, *prefer* would constitute a serious counterexample to this generalization. For some speakers, *want* has a parallel distribution (*I want for her to have more money than me* along with *I don't want her to be a person who gives up when things get tough* (https://books.google.com/books?id=PfZ8AAAAQBAJ&pg=PA156&lpg=PA156&dq=\%22want+for+her+to\%22&source=bl&ots=hbsTWE_xAL&sig=oC3U0ZLwm0QN5gAzyfAfcK5WZuo&hl=en&sa=X&ved=0ahUKEwjr5_-x_6fKAhUJNxQKHWucDY4Q6AEILzAD#v=onepage&q=\%22want\%20her\%20to\%22&f=false).

incorrect generalization, however. Note, for example, the following natural data from the internet:

(129) a.   What I intended was her to use more of a medieval sword (http://herxg-sticky-rice.deviantart.com/art/Lucinda-Sketch-18420669).

b.   And what I'm looking for is him to just say, maybe people are making mistakes. But it's always this conspiracy thing. (http://en.wikiquote.org/wiki/Michael\gapMoore).

c.   What I'm hoping for is him to start spilling the beans about the massacre . . . (www.mangashare.com/forums/threads/15058-Naruto-480-Discussion-481-Predictions/page24).

d.   What I really want is him to at least come and visit me and spend time with me, rather than me always spending time with him.

As noted above, the construction illustrated in these examples, the pseudocleft, is a robust test for constituency: in the frame

(130)   wh [$_s$ . . . __] be α

the string α is always a constituent. The above examples – a very small sample out of many – illustrate the constituent status of NP VP[*inf*] structures, and motivate a parallel treatment of *that* and *for*, with the two in complementary distribution: *that* appears only with finite clauses, *for* only with infinitive clauses. This strict parallelism and complementarity mandates a uniform treatment of both complementizers, so that, given the evidence for the nonheadship of *that*, our default assumption must be that *for* is not a head either.

We now have two related questions to answer: how are we to license complementizer + S constituents, and how are we to align the identity of the complementizer in each case with the relevant properties of the clause? Our analysis must preserve the clausal identity of complementized and complementizerless clauses, explain the impossibility of iterated complementizers, and account for the fact that the particular identity of the complementizer is sometimes relevant to the distribution of the complementizer + S constituent, in (131):

(131)   Our decision depends on $\left\{ \begin{array}{c} \text{whether} \\ \text{*if} \end{array} \right\}$ Robin provides us with the necessary information.

While it might seem tempting to treat complementizers in a fashion parallel to determiners in the nominal system, as instantiating a specifier valent requirement for type *verb*, note that such treatment, which requires us to take *that*, *if*, and so on to saturate the verb's SPR list value, would make it difficult to recover the identity of the particular complementizer associated with the maximum projection of the verb head without some dedicated piece of ad hoc machinery. It would in consequence be much more difficult to motivate naturally the kind of distributional facts represented in (131). So although, as discussed in the next section, treating complementizers as specifiers for the *verb* type would add an attractive symmetry to the overall architecture of category properties, the facts dictate a different solution, one in which complementizer identity is visible on the phrasal head S.

To this end, we identify a feature MARKING, whose value is a category specification of type *marker*, one of whose subtypes is *complementizer*, itself represented by the subtypes *that, if, for*, and so on. *Marking* works within our system in a loosely parallel fashion to PFORM: a clausal category specified for a MARKING value dominates a complementizer daughter which uniquely shares the MARKING value of the clause, and a clausal head daughter, which is specified for a *nil* MARKING value. Then the rule we need can be stated as follows (where we assume a VALENCE attribute whose value is an object specifying COMPS, SUBJ, and SPR):

(132)   **Head-marker Rule**

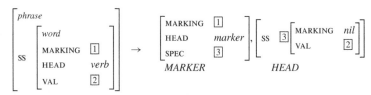

The rule as given ensures that the valence values on the mother and head daughter are identical. Each complementizer will identify, via its SPEC value, the properties of the *verb* projection that it can combine with. Thus, we have the following partial description:

(133)   a.
$$\begin{bmatrix} \text{PHON} & \text{that} \\ \text{SS} & \begin{bmatrix} \text{MARKING} & \textit{that} \\ \text{SPEC} & \begin{bmatrix} \text{VFORM} & \textit{fin} \\ \text{SPR} & \langle\,\rangle \\ \text{COMPS} & \langle\,\rangle \end{bmatrix} \end{bmatrix} \end{bmatrix}$$

b.
$$\begin{bmatrix} \text{PHON} & \text{for} \\ \text{SS} & \begin{bmatrix} \text{MARKING} & \textit{for} \\ \text{SPEC} & \begin{bmatrix} \text{VFORM} & \textit{inf} \\ \text{SPR} & \langle\,\rangle \\ \text{COMPS} & \langle\,\rangle \end{bmatrix} \end{bmatrix} \end{bmatrix}$$

c.
$$\begin{bmatrix} \text{PHON} & \text{whether} \\ \text{SS} & \begin{bmatrix} \text{MARKING} & \textit{whether} \\ \text{SPEC} & \begin{bmatrix} \text{VFORM} & \textit{fin} \\ \text{SPR} & \langle\,\rangle \\ \text{COMPS} & \langle\,\rangle \end{bmatrix} \end{bmatrix} \end{bmatrix}$$

d.
$$\begin{bmatrix} \text{PHON} & \text{whether} \\ \text{SS} & \begin{bmatrix} \text{MARKING} & \textit{whether} \\ \text{SPEC} & \begin{bmatrix} \text{VFORM} & \textit{inf} \\ \text{SPR} & \langle\ldots\rangle \\ \text{COMPS} & \langle\,\rangle \end{bmatrix} \end{bmatrix} \end{bmatrix}$$

We see that *that* can, under the terms of its own SPEC value, appear as a complementizer just in case the head of the clausal constituent is finite, whereas *for* can appear with a clausal sister only if the latter is infinitive. The case of *whether* is particularly interesting: it can appear as a complementizer under two conditions – with a finite clausal sister and with an infinitive VP sister, as in

(134)   I wonder whether $\left\{ \begin{array}{l} \text{I should call Robin} \\ \text{to call Robin} \end{array} \right\}$.

No other complementizer can appear with a VP, and there appears to be some question in the literature as to whether *whether* is actually a complementizer at all; an alternative analysis takes it to be an adverb. But there is very clear evidence that *whether* is indeed a complementizer. There is a restriction on displacement in English which prohibits a subject from being displaced following a complementizer:

(135) a.   I think (that) Robin should get the job.
      b.   Who do you think (*that) __should get the job?

(136) a.   I am anxious for Robin to get the job.
      b.   *Who are you anxious for __to get the job?

(137) a.   I wonder if Robin will get the job.
      b.   *Robin is the person who I don't know if __will get the job.

When an adjunct intervenes between the complementizers and the gap site, however, a dramatic improvement can be observed in the cases apart from *for*:

(138) a.   Who do you think that under current hiring restrictions __should get the job?
      b.   Robin is someone who I don't know if in the current circumstances __is the best person for the job.

Thus, there is a clear difference between complementizers and adjuncts so far as licensing subject gaps is concerned: the former drastically reduce the possibilities and the latter make them available again.

Against this background, consider the following instance of *whether* interacting with subject displacement:

(139) a.   *Robin is someone who I wonder whether __is the right choice for the job.
      b.   Robin is someone who I wonder whether in the current economic climate might not be the best person to hire.

The pattern here – displacement after a complementizer blocked, but then allowed if an adverb intervenes between the complementizer and the gap site – is the unique characteristic signature of complementizers; no other grammatical category of signs displays that particular behavior, and on that basis we can confidently assign *whether* to the same category as *that*, *if*, and *for*.

We therefore add (132) to our compact rule set for English syntax, and turn now to the broader question of further generalization and simplification in the system induced by those rules.

2.10   A Unitary Architecture for Syntactic Categories?

At this point, it's worth pausing in the development of the framework to take stock of the view of category architecture that we seem to have arrived at. We've seen, in the NP system, evidence for an intermediate category N̄ which contains everything except the specifier. There is a parallel organization in clauses: we have verbs, VPs which contain everything in the clause except the subject, and Ss, which add a subject to the VP. In both of these domains there are three levels: the unsaturated lexical item which serves as the ultimate head of the whole constituent, a nearly saturated phrasal level, in which all complements have combined with that head, and a saturated category which in effect has nowhere to go in terms of further elaboration. Again, in both the nominal and the verbal projection systems, the possibility exists of adjuncts combining with the nearly saturated projection of the head, iteratively without any limit, at least so far as the grammar itself is concerned. We can illustrate this 'blueprint' for categories in the following schema:

(140)

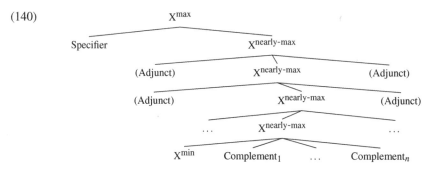

In terms of this schema, VP is $V^{nearly-max}$ and $\bar{N}$ is $N^{nearly-max}$; S is V^{max} and NP is N^{max}. Moreover, it seems possible to plausibly extend this model of category architecture further, to projections of *preposition*. We have assumed that a string such as *on the edge of the table* is a PP, based on the arguments given in the first chapter, in particular proform replaceability: *The sliding coin stopped [$_{PP}$ at the edge of the table/there]*. But consider the data in (141):

(141) a.   The sliding coin stopped (right/just) $\left\{ \begin{array}{c} \text{at the edge of the table} \\ \text{there} \end{array} \right\}$.

b.   It was (right/just) at the edge of the table that the sliding coin stopped __.

In (141)b it is clear, via one of the forms of the displacement test, that *right/just at the edge of the table* is a constituent. *There* replaces all of this constituent in (141) except the lexical items *right* or *just*. Evidently, these morphemes are not the heads of the phrase – they are optional, but if they're present without a following preposition (and possibly following material), the example is bad: **The sliding coin stopped just*. Again, it seems as if *just* and *right* are either adjuncts or something else, and, maintaining the same meanings, it does not seem possible to 'stack' these words: **It's right just there/*It's just right there*. This behavior is consonant with an analysis of these forms as, in effect, specifiers in the prepositional system. If so, then *at the edge of the table* is not a PP but rather $\bar{P}$.

We can extend this approach to APs as well. We have data such as

(142) a.   He's obviously upset and you seem so as well

(www.loveshack.org/forums/general/archive/13089-why-he-avoiding-me).

    b.   Your blog is so lovely, and you seem so as well
        (http://flashesofstyle.blogspot.com/2012/12/the-big-holiday-
        giveaway.html).

    c.   Don't hold the beer in front of your gut it actually subconsciously makes
        you more nervous and closed off and will make you appear so as well
        (http://archive.foolz.us/sp/thread/24778654/).

These examples suggest, as briefly mentioned in Chapter 1, that there is a *so* in English which plays the role (inter alia) of a pro-AP. And we find degree markers showing with them:

(143) a.   Voting is Critical, Diversity even more so
          (www.kc-makers.org/voting-is-critical-diversity-even-more-so/).

      b.   The birth is important, but she is much more so
          (http://prolificmother.blogspot.com/2007/02/work-in-progress.html).

      c.   Robin is very worried about Terry, and Leslie is even more
$\left\{ \begin{array}{c} \text{worried about Terry} \\ \text{so} \end{array} \right\}$.

One might suppose then that such degree markers play the role of specifiers to $\bar{\text{A}}$ categories. It seems that the specifiers here would not constitute a closed class – we have *Terry is very/extremely/(in)sufficiently/comparatively/...* ; moreover, it's not clear that only degree adverbs can play this role, for example, *Terry was inappropriately worried about Leslie*. The real issue here is whether or not these adverbs are specifiers in the AP system or are adjuncts. It is conceivable that the degree adverbs are indeed specifiers, but manner adverbs such as *inappropriately* are adjuncts. Examples such as *Terry was very (in)appropriately worried about Robin's performance* have a bearing here, but the issues would take us too far afield to explore adequately. As we'll see shortly, this kind of issue is rather less critical than it appeared to be in an earlier period in syntactic theory.

    The schema in (140) goes back quite far in the literature, although it was much more commonly notated as in (144):

(144)

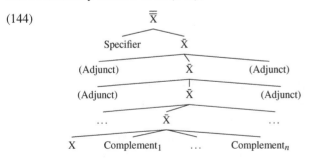

where $\bar{\bar{\text{X}}}$ is used in place of X^{max} and $\bar{\text{X}}$, as we've already seen, is the long-established convention for writing what we have discussed as nearly saturated categories. This way of representing what has been given in (140) wasn't merely an abbreviation – it was thought that such bar systems were a primitive of the grammar, a fundamental part of category structure that had to be regarded as an ingredient of innate linguistic knowledge. There was considerable discussion and argumentation about how many bar levels were required for an adequate representation of grammatical structure, and the role of bar levels was accepted cross-theoretically, with one version of one approach ancestral to the framework in this textbook even taking BAR to be a syntactic feature, like COMPS and PFORM.

It is therefore very important to appreciate the fact that in our current framework, the structure of (140)/(144) is completely derivative from the valence specifications for lexical categories and the way in which those specifications can be satisfied, in terms of the rule schemata stated earlier. Words must be saturated for COMPS before either their specifier or subject valence requirement is met, and before they can combine with adjuncts. This priority, imposed by the form of the combinatory rule schemata, entails a characteristic branching structure for all phrases in English syntax, where the role of linear ordering constraints, as discussed earlier, plays a significant role. The combination of these ordering constraints winds up imposing on typical clauses a relentlessly right-branching structure, as illustrated in (145) and reflected in the trees displayed throughout this and the preceding chapter.

(145)

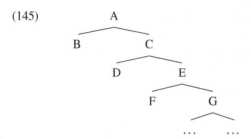

The source of this right-branching is the interaction of independent linear precedence conditions on categories and, again, the way in which valence requirements are saturated under the conditions imposed by the interactions of the principles introduced in this chapter.

2.11   What Comes Next?

We began this chapter by introducing context-free phrase structure rules as a way to license the tree structures revealed by the constituency tests in Chapter 1. While these rules do the necessary work of enumerating what kinds of phrase structures correspond to the hierarchical organization of words within sentences of some human language, they provide no way to control which words can actually appear in which of these structures. In the course of developing a solution to this problem, we ended up replacing these rules with a small number of far more general principles which yield the same structures as the CF-PSGs we wrote, building hierarchical arrangement of word strings directly, based on information in the lexicon specifying each word's combinatory requirements, which we call valence. The general strategy behind the constraint system that has been proposed in this chapter can be illustrated and summarized for the specific case of verbs fairly simply: combine them with the kinds of categories that they need to have as sisters (stated explicitly by their COMPS specifications). Take the result of that combination and combine it with the kind of subject that the verb demands. At this point, no further combinations are mandated by the head verb, and, since all necessary principles have been followed, the result will be a sentence of the language.

The foregoing, and the material in this chapter generally, represents a fairly simple illustration of the general approach to syntax that will be pursued in this book. There are two directions in which the discussion will proceed from here. On the one hand, we will apply the valence-based approach outlined in this chapter to patterns of dependency in English, showing that the methods already developed to capture the co-occurrence of lexical heads with appropriate sisters and subject winds up giving simple accounts of a large number of such patterns, with essentially no extra machinery. On the other hand, what we have covered in this chapter barely begins to lay out the relevant details of English phrase structure, and a number of issues (such as the actual constituent breakdown constituency of a sentence such as *It bothers me that Robin is a spy*, or the question of whether determiners and adjectives within noun phrases really are sisters of the head, as per the rules in (22)) need to be carefully studied and resolved. These two lines of development are in fact intertwined, and both will be pursued in the remainder of this book. We begin this double-edged approach in Chapter 3 with an analysis of English auxiliaries, one of the earliest topics of study in modern theoretical syntax.

3   The Auxiliary Dependency

A little history, to begin with: the phenomena that come under the heading 'English auxiliaries' were instrumental in bringing about the contemporary era in syntax, and, beyond syntax, in linguistics as a field. In Chomsky's watershed 1957 monograph *Syntactic Structures*, these phenomena were perhaps the key setpiece for the pivotal argument in the book that context-free phrase structure rules, of the sort that we first formulated to capture basic phrasal constituency in English, get crucial facts about the language wrong. Chomsky's point was not that such rules cannot summarize our observations about what we find in English, but rather that, implicitly, they deny the existence of a certain kind of pattern that can in fact be shown to exist, and therefore are wrong, not about the data, but about recurrent patterns in the data. The new kind of rule that Chomsky proposed to deal with this difficulty (a more user-friendly version of a kind of mechanism that certain logicians and linguists of the preceding generation (in particular Emil Post and Zelig Harris) had devised and experimented with) had the apparent virtue of being able to express these patterns easily. A good deal of the development syntax has experienced in the last quarter of a century reflects a somewhat belated counting of the costs incurred by Chomsky's innovation, and a gradual realization that there were far simpler, more economical solutions to the problem he pointed out with empirical coverage considerably better than what he had proposed in 1957.

The particular virtue of Chomsky's approach, then, is not the particular solution he advanced, which has become progressively less attractive as time has passed (even independently of framework-internal changes in the specific theory he inaugurated), but rather the enhanced scope of the linguist's intellectual responsibilities that it assumed. Recording the facts correctly no longer had the status of a sufficient activity, even with a convenient classification and organization of those facts; what was now essential was motivating those facts, by showing how they were manifestations of underlying patterns and their interaction. One could characterize most previous work in linguistics as at best proto-scientific, in the sense that recording and classification are crucial to the actual business of science, but are not themselves that business, which is to identify a domain of phenomena and discover the general principles governing the behavior of the phenomena in that domain. This is probably the one enduring contribution that Chomsky's work will ultimately be judged to have made to linguistics: the kind of question that his writings (particularly the early ones) pose, rather than the answers they provide.

It will be instructive to see how all this played out in connection with auxiliary phenomena. The first thing we have to do is justify talking about 'auxiliaries' at all. Why do we think there actually is such a class? The term itself comes from traditional grammars of English, and receives definitions such as

> ***auxiliary*** noun Abbr. aux. or aux. v.: A verb, such as *have*, *can*, or *will*, that accompanies the main verb in a clause and helps to make distinctions in mood, voice, aspect, and tense. (*The American Heritage Dictionary* 2000)

Such definitions, of course, beg a number of questions. Is *go(ing)* an auxiliary? After all, in the sentences

(1)   I $\left\{ \begin{array}{l} \text{will} \\ \text{shall} \\ \text{am going to} \end{array} \right\}$ read this book.

the notion of 'futurity' is clearly involved, and in much the same way. Does this make *go(ing)* an auxiliary? It is not regarded as such by any grammarians in the earlier tradition which is the source of the terms 'auxiliary.' What about *used*, as in

(2)   I $\left\{ \begin{array}{l} \text{was skiing} \\ \text{used to ski} \end{array} \right\}$ a long time ago.

Again, *used* appears to have both tense (*past*) and aspectual (habitual) meaning; does that make it an auxiliary? Here again, the verdict, for many if not most speakers, appears to be 'no'. So just what makes something an auxiliary?

3.1   Auxiliary Phenomena: *What Are Auxiliaries?*

Fortunately, we don't need to rely on the kind of vague, impressionistic definition of 'auxiliary' just cited. It turns out that the notion of auxiliaryhood is useful precisely because it labels a class of items which have specific unique distributional features in English. Most members of this class have all four, but there are several which display only one or two. Nonetheless, these distributions are specialized enough that showing up in even one of them is prima facie evidence that the description 'auxiliary' is motivated. Furthermore, they manifest certain fixed patterns of linear order which reinforce their membership in a special class of lexical items. And as we shall see, they reflect a special kind of syntactic dependency which the technology of valence that we have been developing is well suited to capture.

3.1.1   The NICE Properties

Auxiliaries behave in a fashion different from any other verbs in English, and they do so, for the most part, in an across-the-board fashion.

3.1.1.1   Negation

(3) a.   Robin is not eating.

 b.   Robin has not eaten.

 c.   Robin will not eat.

The negative marker *not* can appear in all of these sentences, immediately following *be/have/should*, with the meaning 'it is not the case that Robin is eating/has eaten/will eat.' Compare the distribution possibilities of *not* in (3) with those in (4):

$$\text{(4)} \qquad \text{*Robin} \left\{ \begin{array}{l} \text{eats} \\ \text{sleeps} \\ \text{walks} \\ \text{fell} \\ \text{hesitates} \end{array} \right\} \text{not.}$$

To express the negation that the data in (4) appear to correspond to, we need the forms

$$\text{(5)} \qquad \text{Robin doesn't} \left\{ \begin{array}{l} \text{eat} \\ \text{sleep} \\ \text{walk} \\ \vdots \end{array} \right\}.$$

The generalization here seems to be that *not* can only show up following a specific class of items that includes *have, be, will, would, shall, could, can, should*, and a few others.

At first glance, this claim appears to be flat-out wrong, in the face of examples such as (6):

(6)   Robin tried not eating.

The giveaway here is that unlike the pattern in (3), the meaning corresponding to (6) is not the negation of the meaning of the sentence left when *not* is removed (which is what would be instead expressed as *Robin didn't try eating*), but rather the negation of only the part corresponding to *eating*. Furthermore, compare the pattern in (7)–(8):

(7) a.   You should try not eating.

 b.   It is NOT eating that you should try.

(8) a.   You might not get the job.

 b.   *It is NOT get the job that you might.

This suggests a significant structural difference between the position of *not* in (7) and (8) respectively: the displaceability of *not eating* in the former, in contrast to the inability of *not get the job* in the latter, suggests that *not* forms a constituent with the VP *eating* (*It is NOT doing so that you should try* seems unexceptionable), whereas *not* in (8) does not form a constituent with the VP *get the job*, and hence cannot be displaced with it.

To follow up on this possible source of the difference between the two cases, we might consider a further implication of the structures under consideration, depicted in (9):

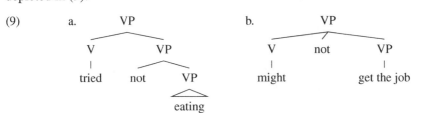

(9)   a.   VP   b.   VP

         V   VP   V   not   VP

          | ⌒ | |
        tried   not   VP   might   get the job

                        ⌒
                      eating

These trees are premature, because the necessary structural arguments have not been put forward to support them in all relevant details. But in one respect we do have the necessary evidence, in the form of the data in (10), that in the case of (9)a, the lowest VP is the head of its own VP, whereas in (9)b it need not be and, as will be argued below, in fact is not. There is a general pattern in English that heads do not displace. If the analysis in (9) is correct, we should expect to find that *eating* in (7)a, the head of the larger VP, does not displace. And this is exactly what we find:

(10)   a.   *Eating, you should try NOT __.
         b.   Get the job, you might NOT __

(What is possibly surprising is the fact that in (10)b, the displaceability of *get the job* strongly suggests that it is not the head of the VP. Much of this chapter is devoted to arguing that this is indeed the case.) The data in (10) offer robust support for the difference in structure posited in (9) and on this basis, we have excellent reason to believe that negation, in the sense of *not* appearing as a sister to a lexical head, is restricted to auxiliaries.

3.1.1.2   Inversion

The same class of forms which supports negations, in the sense specified in the preceding section, also supports inversion with respect to the subject. We think of interrogatives, typically, in connection with inversion.

(11)   a.   Is Robin eating?
         b.   Has Robin eaten?
         c.   Should Robin eat?

(12)   a.   *Ate Robin?
         b.   *Tried Robin eating?

c.   Did Robin $\left\{ \begin{array}{c} \text{eat} \\ \text{try eating} \end{array} \right\}$?

But we also have inversion triggered by negative/*so* expressions, as in (13)a, and counterfactual inversion, shown in (13)b:

(13) a.   . . . and $\left\{ \begin{array}{c} \text{neither} \\ \text{so} \end{array} \right\}$ will I.

b.   Had I known you were worried, I'd have reassured you.

And as with negation, other verbs are blocked in these contexts:

(14) a.   *. . . and neither thought I.

b.   *Figured I you were worried, I'd have said something.

A caveat is called for here: not all forms which are reliably identified as auxiliaries are able to appear in inversion contexts.

3.1.1.3   Contraction

Contraction is actually a special form of negation, but it's usually considered to be a separate diagnostic for auxiliary hood:

(15) a.   Robin isn't eating.

b.   Robin hasn't eaten.

c.   Robin shouldn't eat.

(16) a.   *Robin aten't.

b.   *Robin triedn't eating.

There is some evidence that the contracted forms should be considered distinct words, with their own lexical entries, synchronically independent from the uncontracted forms. For example, in many British and American dialects, *ain't* is the default expression of finite nonpast forms of *be* under negation. But there is no *ai form such that *ai+not* → *ai+n't* = *ain't*. Similarly, there is an inverted form of finite, nonpast *be* under negation – *aren't* – which corresponds to the first person subject:

(17) $\left\{ \begin{array}{c} \text{*Amn't I} \\ \text{Ain't I} \\ \text{Aren't I} \\ \text{Am I not} \end{array} \right\}$ $\left\{ \begin{array}{c} \text{talking to the right person?} \\ \text{clever!} \end{array} \right\}$

Unlike the case of *ain't*, there *is* an uncontracted form of the verb root which can be separated from the contracted negation, namely *are*, but – crucially – this form of *be* cannot appear with first person subject uncontracted, whether inversion is involved or not:

(18) a.   *I are $\left\{ \begin{array}{c} \text{-n't} \\ \text{(not)} \end{array} \right\}$ $\left\{ \begin{array}{c} \text{talking to the right person} \\ \text{clever} \end{array} \right\}$.

b.   *Are I not $\left\{\begin{array}{c}\text{talking to the right person?}\\ \text{clever!}\end{array}\right\}$

The *aren't* form thus displays two properties which appear to separate it decisively from any analysis as a mere phonological by-product of contracting *are* with *not*: it alone can show up associated with a first person subject (which *are* cannot), and then only in inverted position. This last fact eliminates a possible counteranalysis to the effect that the *are* which shows up with *not* has the option of selecting a first person subject, for if that were the case, why would *Aren't I talking to the right person* be good but **I aren't talking to the right person* be bad? And if we then tried to save the counteranalysis by claiming that the *are* which takes *not* and a first person subject must also invert, however this is stipulated, then why is (18)b bad? On the other hand, if *aren't* is a separate lexical entry which selects a first person subject just in case *aren't* is of the inverted variety, then all of these problems disappear.

For all these and still other reasons, then, it might be wise to consider the negative contracted forms of auxiliaries to be distinct lexical items with significantly different distributional properties, at least in some cases. This view of things supports the inclusion of contraction as an independent NICE property, and is at least equally compatible with the fact that certain items which pass the test of auxiliaryhood in other respects, such as *better* (*I better not do that*), lack contracted forms. Auxiliary *better* manifests not only negation but also ellipsis, the final diagnostic discussed immediately below; but it lacks the other two signature properties of auxiliaryhood.

3.1.1.4   Ellipsis

Ellipsis, in the context of auxiliaries, refers specifically to VP ellipsis – the permitted omission of a VP, with the missing element interpreted in, so to speak. We have

(19) a.   Robin isn't leaving, but I am (leaving).
  b.   Robin hasn't left, but I have (left).
  c.   Robin shouldn't leave, but I should (leave).

A very few other verbs can omit their VP complements, but there are good reasons to believe that the cases are not the same. Compare

(20) a.   Robin tried to get a job, and Leslie tried as well.
  b.   If you never try, you never succeed.

with

(21) a.   ??Robin attempted to get a job, and Terry attempted as well.
  b.   ??*If you never attempt, you never succeed.

A case could therefore be made that *try* and a few other nonauxiliaries have, in effect, intransitive forms, and that that's what (20) reflects. But the great majority of verbs fail this test, for example, *hope (to succeed)*, *propose (speaking to the*

Committee about the matter), and so on. The only lexical forms which reliably allow the ellipsis of the VP which would otherwise follow them are those which support negation (and, usually, inversion).

The NICE properties thus pick out a small closed class of English lexica which display four characteristic (morpho)syntactic properties, three of which are logically independent. There are, however, other distinctive patterns that the auxiliaries display which constitute nontrivial descriptive problems, giving us a clue to their essential syntactic nature. We outline these problems, and their solutions, in the following sections.

3.1.2   The Auxiliary System Dependency

The auxiliaries were recognized as a distinct subclass of lexical items at the time Chomsky's *Syntactic Structures* appeared. The pivot of his argument in that work was a particular pattern of behavior manifested by these items, reflected in the following representative data:

(22) a.   Robin is { eating / *eats / *ate / *eaten / *eat } breakfast.

  b.   Robin has { eaten / *eats / *ate / *eating / *eat } breakfast.

  c.   Robin should { eat / *eats / *ate / *eaten / *eating } breakfast.

  d.   Robin { eats / ate / *eating / *eaten / *eat } breakfast.

The examples in (22) display a striking correlation between the lexical identity of the auxiliary and the morphology of the following verb. The descriptive generalizations evident in these data can be summarized quite simply as in (23):

(23) i.   Modal X-∅

  ii.   *have* X-*en*

  iii.   *be* X-*ing*

The term 'modal' refers to a subclass of the auxiliaries – items such as a *can*, *should*, *will*, *ought*, and the like – which, in contrast to *have* and *be*, do not manifest normal inflectional behavior parallel in all respects to that displayed by ordinary nonauxiliary verbs. Modals, unlike normal verbs, instead exhibit invariant morphological form regardless of the subject's person and number properties. Example (24) illustrates their failure to participate in typical morphological subject/verb agreement:

$$(24) \quad \left\{ \begin{array}{c} \text{I} \\ \text{You} \\ \text{(S/he)/It} \\ \text{We} \\ \text{They} \end{array} \right\} \left\{ \begin{array}{c} \text{can} \\ \text{will} \\ \text{shall} \\ \text{must} \\ \vdots \end{array} \right\} \text{think about that.}$$

A second point the modals have in common, as vs *have* and *be*, is the particular morphological form that the following verb must take. All of the modals require a completely uninflected form of their sister verb – a pattern which is particularly clear in the case of the copula, whose 'bare' form, *be*, is – uniquely among English verbs – morphologically totally unrelated to any of its tensed forms:

$$(25) \quad \text{You} \left\{ \begin{array}{c} \text{must} \\ \text{should} \\ \text{could} \\ \text{might} \\ \text{ought not} \\ \text{better} \\ \text{would} \end{array} \right\} \text{be more cooperative than you feel like being.}$$

A final property that the modals have in common is that in all cases, they must appear first in a series of auxiliaries. The behavior of *should* is completely representative:

(26) a.   Robin should have been eating breakfast.
    b.   *Robin have should been eating breakfast.
    c.   *Robin have eating should been breakfast.
    d.   *Robin been have should eating breakfast.

$$\vdots$$

Modals thus correlate morphological invariance with two seemingly separate restrictions: (i) correlation of following verb form with the lexical identity of the preceding auxiliary, and (ii) fixed order of auxiliaries. More generally, the auxiliaries all impose characteristic morphological shapes on the verbs which follow them, and occur in a particular place in a fixed sequence of precedence relationships:

(27)   Modal $\prec$ *have* $\prec$ *be* $\prec$ nonauxiliary V

where $A \prec B$ means that A linearly precedes B.

3.1.3   How Modals Reveal Themselves to Be Verbs

For syntacticians, the parallel behavior of auxiliaries in all the respects so far identified puts a premium on an analysis of them as a unitary class – which, at the most basic level, demands that they be treated as reflecting the same lexical category. In the following section we present some of the data that makes such a unitary analysis very plausible.

3.1.3.1   The Sequence of Tenses Argument

There is a somewhat subtle but quite effective test for tense – and consequently verbhood – that we can apply to the modals. Consider the following data and try to formulate a generalization which covers the facts displayed.

(28) a. $[_{S_{t_0}}$ I think $[_{S_{t_0}}$ Robin knows about that]]

 b. $*[_{S_{t_1}}$ I thought $[_{S_{t_1}}$ Robin knows about that]]

 c. $[_{S_{t_1}}$ I thought $[_{S_{t_1}}$ Robin knew about that]]

 d. $*[_{S_{t_1}}$ I thought $[_{S_{t_2}}$ Robin knew about that]]

where t_0 is the time of utterance, $t_2 \prec t_1 \prec t_0$, and a clause subscripted with t_n means that the activity denoted by the root verb – the structurally highest verb under that S – took place at time t_n. We see in (28)a that when the intended time of thinking is the same as the time of the utterance, and the intended time of knowing is the same as the intended time of thinking, the morphological form of *know* matches that of *think*, both of them being nonpast. In (28)c we see that when the time of the thinking precedes the time of utterance, and the time of knowing and the time of thinking are to be interpreted as coextensive – in other words, as though the sentence *I think Robin knows about that* is to be evaluated for truth with respect to some past time, not the time of utterance – again, both *think* and *know* have the same morphological form, the past tense. What (28) tells us is that this identity of morphological form permits only one interpretation: that the thinking and knowing were going on at the same time. When the time of knowing precedes the time of thinking, where the latter is set in the past, then the two verbs may not share the same morphological form; to express this temporal relationship, we must say *I thought Robin had known about that*. The generalization then is that, whether at or preceding the time of utterance, when the time setting of the event described by the root verb is the same as the time setting of the event described by the verb of the internal sentence, both verbs have the same morphology – a phenomenon often referred to as the Sequence of Tenses phenomenon.

This pattern gives us a powerful diagnostic weapon. Consider examples such as those in (29):

(29) a.   I think that Robin **can** do that.

 b.   ??*I thought that Robin can do that. (on the intended reading, where t_0 is the time of utterance, $t_1 \prec t_0$, and both the time of the reported belief ('thought that...') and the time of the action defining the content of the believe ('do that') are t_1)

c.   I thought that Robin **could** do that. (on this same reading)

Comparing (28) and (29), we see that the following relationship holds: *think* is to *thought* as *know* is to *knew* as *can* is to *could*. In a word, *could* behaves exactly as we would expect it to do if it were the past tense of *can*. An exactly parallel pattern holds for *will/would*: *I wonder if Robin will do that/I wondered if Robin would do that*, *I suspect that Robin may do that/I suspected that Robin might do that*, and so on. While not all modals behave in precisely parallel fashion in terms of the sequence of tenses (in some cases because there seems to be no 'tense partner' for some of the modals, such as *ought* and *must*), enough of them do to make it clear that the auxiliary subclass of modals comprises verbs with, in many cases, morphologically 'frozen' past tense forms no longer recognizable as such.

3.1.3.2   Orthography

There is another bit of support for the analysis of modals as verbs, at least from a diachronic perspective. English spelling is often denounced because of its phonetic opaqueness – it's often hard to determine the pronunciation of a word from its spelling, although English is far more transparent in this respect than, for example, Irish – but the price one pays in the difficulty of converting letters to sounds is more than made up for by the evidence contained in the writing system attesting to the language's earlier phases. Past tense forms are typical in this respect: we find a very wide spectrum of transparency in the relationship between the pronunciations of verbs in the past tense and in the nonpast, but it is often the case that allegedly obscure or eccentric spellings preserve links to the history of tense morphology which have long been lost in the phonetic form of the words. Consider, as one not particularly unusual instance, the relationships revealed in the following comparison of the verbs *bake*, *sleep*, and *seek*:

(30)   *bake*   [beʲk]   *sleep*   [slIʲp]   *seek*   [sIʲk]
         baked [beʲkt]   *slept*   [slɛpt]   *sought* [sɔt]

The phonetic relationship between *bake* and its past tense form is transparent, and the orthographic relationship mirrors this transparency. The case of *seek* is quite different: the velar has disappeared entirely, in clear contrast to what we find for *bake*. But the *gh* in the spelling of *sought* represents a graphic clue to the lost velar which is typically the segment responsible for the *gh* spelling convention in the spelling of a particular word: compare, for example, *bring* and *brought*, and *right*, related to *reckon*. There is a good deal of history, much of it quite old, attested in English spelling.

With this in mind, compare the forms in the following table, where *would* and *should* are the forms that consistently appear in the 'succession of tenses' test contexts when the matrix verb tense is in the past tense.

(31)   *will*   [wɪl]   *shall*   [šæl]
      would   [wʊd]   *should*   [šʊd]

We have in each case two forms, one with an *l* as the terminal phonetic segment and one with *d*, which in the succession-of-tenses argument correspond to each other, at least in the case of *will/would*. The phonetic form of present-day English gives no hint that a lateral was ever present in both forms – but the spelling contains a crucial hint that once upon a time, *would* was (in effect) *woul+d*, with the lateral disappearing before the obstruant. And this is exactly what we would expect, if *would* is the past tense form of *will*, *should* the past tense of *shall*, and so on.

3.1.3.3   Conclusion: Modals Are Verbs

Based on the facts we have surveyed so far, a very simple picture of the auxiliaries begins to emerge: auxiliaries, including modals, are nothing other than a particular subclass of verbs, which have certain syntactic properties that allow us to isolate them as a distinct species, and semantic properties which distinguish them from most (though not all!) nonauxiliary verbs. At this point, we need to take stock of the evidence bearing on this point and drive it to its logical conclusion.

Looking at the auxiliaries from this point of view, the relationship between *may* and *might*, or something rather unexpected (but perhaps it shouldn't be!) – *owe* and *ought* (*You ought not do that/Ought we do this, really?*) where *aught* survived as the past tense of *owe* with the semantics of *owed* in East Anglian dialects into the early nineteenth century – shows us that when it comes to the modals, we are dealing with items which, at least historically, were true verbs. In every case, we find that the final *t* or *d* in the subset of auxiliaries which display these final alveolar stops were tense morphemes attached to ordinary verbs. *Would*, for example, was the past tense of a verb *will* which still exists in English ('to will something'); *shall* comes from the Anglo-Saxon **sceal* 'to owe', with **sceolde* the past tense form. *May* is from Anglo-Saxon **mag(en)* 'to be able', with past tense *mihte*, but notice that the *gh* of *might* echoes the original velar terminal of the root. The take-away message from these facts is that the modals originated as verbs in virtually every case (though there were later 'recruits' to the class, such as *better*, which has a more complex history).

So we know, first of all, that the modals had their origins in ordinary verbs. More than this, however, the succession of tenses argument shows that at some level we are aware of the grammatical tense of these modals and use them in a way which parallels the alternation of nonpast and past tense forms of obvious verbs. While the first of these might not be significant on its own, when combined with this second consideration we have excellent reason to regard the modals as tense-bearing words (although without normal past tense semantics) and therefore as legitimate claimants to the category 'verb'. And if modals are verbs, then it is obvious that any phrase they count as the heads of must be VPs. And *this* is the important point of our investigation into the status of modals; the whole question of the basic structure of the sentence in English revolves around whether we can treat sequences of auxiliaries simply as (hierarchically deep) VPs.

The fact that, on the basis of our analysis in the preceding section, we can legitimately identify auxiliaries as a whole as just another class of Vs suggests that indeed, we should *expect* these Vs to head their own VPs. After all, that's what verbs do! But the issue is made complicated by the question of just what VPs headed by auxiliaries would look like. What would the complement(s) of an auxiliary be?

3.2   What Is the Phrase Structure of Clauses with Auxiliaries?

3.2.1   Auxiliaries as VP Heads?

3.2.1.1   Auxiliaries Are VP Heads: The Fronted *So* Inversion Construction

Consider (32)–(33):

(32) a.   Robin has figured out the solution, and Terry has $\left\{\begin{array}{l}\text{figured out the solution}\\\text{done so}\end{array}\right\}$ as well.

b.   Robin has figured out the solution, and $\left\{\begin{array}{l}\text{so has Terry}\\\text{*Terry has so}\end{array}\right\}$ as well.

(33) a.   Robin has been telling the truth all along, and Terry has $\left\{\begin{array}{l}\text{been telling the truth all along}\\{}^{\#}\text{done so}\end{array}\right\}$ as well.

b.   Robin has been telling the truth all along, and so has Terry.

There are some very important diagnostic facts exhibited here. First of all, we see that the standard *do so* test works as expected when the auxiliary is followed by a verb such as *figure out*, as illustrated in (32)a; but things don't go nearly so well when we try to replace *been telling the truth* with *did so*. The result of the replacement isn't ill-formed, but it doesn't correspond to the meaning of *been telling the truth*, and hence, so far as the interpretation in question is concerned, is semantically anomalous. Specifically, *Terry has done so* conveys the sense that on some specific occasion, Terry told the truth; but there is no sense that *Terry has done so* refers to a series of repeated episodes, or a continuous episode, of truth-telling. Rather, *Terry has done so* corresponds to the meaning that at least once in the past, Terry has told the truth – what would in fact be conveyed by, *Terry has told the truth*. For some reason, *do so* replacement does not capture the semantics of the progressive corresponding to *been telling the truth*, or any other progressive construction with *be* V-*ing* form.

But *so has Terry* is not subject to the same restrictions. One can say, *Robin told the truth, and so did Terry*, with a strictly one-time, punctual interpretation, but (33) conveys the progressive of *been telling the truth* without the slightest interference; in fact, it is quite difficult to get any other interpretation from (33) than the progressive aspectual one. Note that the *so* here is quite different from the *so* in the *do so* proform. We do not have, for example, any of the examples in (34)b matching those of (34)a:

(34) a.   Terry $\left\{ \begin{array}{l} \text{is } [_1 \text{ telling the truth}] \\ \text{has } [_2 \text{ told the truth}] \\ \text{will } [_3 \text{ tell the truth}] \end{array} \right\}$, and $\left\{ \begin{array}{l} \text{so}_1 \text{ is} \\ \text{so}_2 \text{ will} \\ \text{so}_3 \text{ will} \end{array} \right\}$ Robin.

b.   Terry $\left\{ \begin{array}{l} \text{is } [_1 \text{ telling}] \\ \text{has } [_2 \text{ told}] \\ \text{will } [_3 \text{ tell}] \end{array} \right\}$ the truth * $\left(\text{, and Robin} \left\{ \begin{array}{l} \text{is so}_1 \\ \text{has so}_2 \\ \text{will so}_3 \end{array} \right\} \right)$ (as well).

Fronted *so* constructions are thus typically *not* associated with 'in situ' analogues (where *so* appears in what would be its normal position in an uninverted context). The fronted *so* construction is separate, and, as (34)a shows, the *so* which shows up in it reliably 'stands in' for what, by any of our previous tests, corresponds to a VP. But unlike the *do so* test as discussed above, inverted *so* includes not just unquestionable VPs with ordinary nonauxiliary heads, but also strings of words which would, if they were constituents, be VPs containing various forms of *be* in the position normally reserved for the head of the phrase.

To make sure we're not jumping to conclusions without justifying those conclusions fully, we need to proceed step by step.

- We begin with the use of the *so* inversion test as a diagnostic for normal VPs. We have excellent reason to regard fronted *so* as a corroborating test for VP-hood, based on data such as the following:

    (35) a.   Robin will [$_1$ put the book on table], and so[$_1$] will Terry __$_1$.
    b.   *Robin will [$_2$ put] the book on the table, and so[$_2$] will Terry __$_2$ the book on the table.
    c.   *Robin will [$_3$ put the] book on the table, and so[$_3$] will Terry __$_3$ book on the table.
    d.   *Robin will [$_4$ put the book] on the table, and so[$_4$] will Terry __$_4$ on the table.
    e.   *Robin will [$_5$ put the book on] the table, and so[$_5$] will Terry __$_5$ the table.
    f.   *Robin will [$_6$ put the book on the] table, and so[$_6$] will Terry __$_6$ table.

    It's clear that the only substring which *so* can replace is the same substring *put the book on the table* which both *do so* replacement and displacement can apply to, making an overwhelmingly strong case that *so* inversion is yet another diagnostic for VPhood.

- But in addition to the facts in (35), where the *so* inversion phenomenon overlaps pretty much completely with the results of displacement/replacement, we find that *so* also applies to sequences such as *been telling the truth all along*, as in (33)b. Since we've already seen that *so*-inversion is a reliable test for VPhood, data such as (33)b constitute very strong evidence that subsequences of the form *be* V*ing*... are also VPs.

• At the same time, we know that in a sentence such as *Robin has been telling the truth all along*, *telling the truth all along* is itself a VP:

(36) a.   ...and telling the truth all along, Robin HAS been.

       b.   ...and Robin has been doing so as well.

So, for *Robin has been telling the truth all along*, we have evidence supporting the bracketing in (37):

(37)   Robin has [$_{VP}$ been [$_{VP}$ telling the truth all along]]

• But now we cannot avoid facing the question, which constituent determines the VP status of the outer/upper VP in (37)?

What we have in (37) can perhaps be more easily visualized as a tree:

(38)

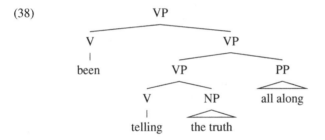

There are two possibilities:

i.   the VP *been telling the truth all along* is headed by the VP *telling the truth all along*; or,

ii.   the VP *been telling the truth all along* is headed by the verb *been*.

How to decide between these alternatives? It's actually quite easy. There is a basic test for headship, which we discussed very early on, and you will apply it in the following problem to determine an unequivocal answer to the question of whether (i) or (ii) is correct.

Practice Exercise

Use the criterion for headship alluded to in the preceding paragraph to decide whether, in (37), the VP *telling the truth all along* is the head or *been* is. Correct application of the test will yield an absolute result which immediately identifies which of the two possibilities for the headship of the larger VP is correct. Explain your reasoning in just enough detail to establish that your answer is the right one.

3.2.1.2   Auxiliaries Are VP Heads: Absolute Adjuncts and Perfective *Have*

The next question we need to answer is what the status of *have eaten lunch* is in a sentence such as *Robin should have eaten lunch*. The initial reports are not encouraging:

(39) a.   *. . . and have eaten lunch, Robin definitely should __.
      b.   *Leslie should have eaten lunch, and Robin should do so as well.
      c.   *Robin should have eaten lunch, and so should you.

Example (39)a is just bad outright. Examples (39)b and c are not ill-formed in themselves, but *are* unacceptable on the intended interpretation – that the sense of (39)b, for example, is that Robin should have eaten lunch already, just as Leslie should have. What *Robin should do so* conveys here is rather that Robin should eat lunch, *now*. Parallel observations hold for (39)c. There is no way that the 'perfective' aspect, contributed by *have. . . -en*, survives replacement of the latter by *do so* or *so*.[1]

The burden of proof therefore definitely rests on anyone who wants to argue that some form of *having + eaten lunch* is a constituent. As it happens, there is evidence strong enough to bear this burden comfortably. The fact is that we can actually display *have* + VP sequences in contexts where only VPs are able to appear. The class of positions are often referred to as *absolutive adjuncts*, and are illustrated in boldface in the following examples.

(40) a.   **Speaking quickly to keep the crowd distracted**, John managed to unobtrusively attach a small spy-mike to the bottom of the council chamber desk.
      b.   **Striding into the room briskly**, the Detective Superintendent immediately took control of the briefing.
      c.   **Grabbing an orange from the bowl and shoving it into her pocket**, Mary rushed out the door, down the stairs and into the street in hot pursuit of her university-bound bus.
      d.   Mary rushed out the door, down the stairs and into the street in hot pursuit of her university-bound bus, **grabbing an orange from the bowl and shoving it into her pocket**.

Absolute adjuncts attach to whole clauses, with the morphology displayed typical: a verb with some kind of *ing* affix, lacking a subject (although this is not essential), and positioned at the front (as in (40)a–c) or the end (as in (40)d) of the sentence. The form of the verb which appears in the examples in (40) is not the ordinary *ing* progressive that we see in sentences such as *Robin is eating a sandwich*. We can show this by considering the data in (41)–(42):

---

[1] But there may be some speaker variation involved here. Huddleston (1974) notes with approval the example *They say that Tom will have been singing, and so he will*, with *so* standing in for *have been singing* (p. 216). This example does seem somewhat better than (39)c, and it may be that *will* supports the interpretation of *so* more robustly than *should*, which doesn't strike me as nearly as good when substituted into Huddleston's example.

(41) a.   Bill $\left\{ \begin{array}{c} \text{knows} \\ \text{*is knowing} \end{array} \right\}$ the answer.

   b.   Sue $\left\{ \begin{array}{c} \text{seems} \\ \text{??*is seeming} \end{array} \right\}$ to pay attention.

(42) a.   Knowing the answers in advance, Rocco found his attention wandering in amusement to the agonies of his fellow exam-takers.

   b.   Although seeming to pay attention to the lecture, Mary actually spent two hours paying most of a month's bills during her computational æsthetics class.

Verbs such as *know* and *seem* do not have a present progressive form in English. But they appear in completely well-formed absolute constructions. Another place where we see verb forms such as *knowing* is in data such as

(43)   Scott knowing the head of the company and his completely inexperienced cousin getting a high-paying job there to do nothing are completely unrelated facts.

The verb form in question, appearing as part of the subject in (43) is identified as the *gerundive* form, and we will assume, based on the evidence, that the gerundive is one of the forms of the verb mandated by the absolute.

The crucial point of introducing these constructions is the evidence that they provide for auxiliary-headed VPs involving *have*.

To begin with, notice that nonconstituents cannot appear as absolute adjuncts:

(44) a.   Hastily putting the books under the table, Luanne searched desperately for a place to hide.

   b.   *$\left\{ \begin{array}{l} \text{Hastily putting} \\ \text{Hastily putting the books} \\ \text{Hastily putting the books under} \\ \text{Hastily putting the books under the} \end{array} \right\}$ Luanne searched desperately for a place to hide.

Using this pattern as a diagnostic for constituency, we can show that *have* + VP does indeed form a constituent. The facts in (45) are decisive:

(45) a.   Having hurriedly put the books under the table, Luanne was able to pretend that she hadn't stopped off at the library on the way home.

   b.   They told me to send a job application to the company, and, having done so willingly, I am now waiting for a reply from them.

   c.   Having been sitting on the stairs for three hours waiting for them to come home, Constance was enraged when her kids finally showed up at two in the morning.

Since only constituents can show up in absolute adjunct position, we have immediate prima facie evidence that *having hurriedly put the books under the table, having done so willingly* and, particularly importantly, *having been sitting on the stairs for three hours waiting for them to come home* are all constituents. And we know that *having* is a verb bearing the *-ing* marker of the gerundive form. We therefore have the following general structure for these adjuncts:

(46)

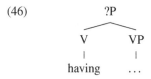

There are two daughters of ?P here, both of them corresponding to the part of speech *verb*. It would therefore be very strange if ?P, which gets its part of speech identity from its head, were not a VP, because both of the rivals for the status of 'head' in this structure are, indeed, verb-type structures. Even more to the point, virtually any absolute adjunct with a nonauxiliary head can be replaced by *doing so*:

(47)   Luanne remembered that she needed to set the alarm; hastily doing so, she then slipped out of the house and down the lane to the bus stop.

Hastily doing so in (47) definitively identifies the adjunct as a VP, the proform standing in for *setting the alarm* and the adverb uninterpretable as anything but a VP adjunct, with the combination itself a VP. So we now have evidence that absolutive phrases are VP constituents, that, for example, *having been sitting on the stairs for three hours waiting for them to come home* is a VP. From *so* inversion, we know that *been sitting on the stairs for three hours waiting for them to come home* is a VP as well. The facts then support the following bracketing:

(48)   [$_{VP}$ having [$_{VP}$ been [$_{VP}$ sitting on the stairs for three hours waiting for them to come home]]]

Again, we have to ask, what is the head of this whole VP? Just looking at the structure, it seems very likely that *having* must be taken to be the head. For one thing, *having* certainly isn't an adjunct, which it would be if *been sitting on the stairs for three hours waiting for them to come home* were the head. As an adjunct, it would be omissible – but you can't say, **Been sitting on the stairs for three hours waiting for them to come home, Dana was enraged when her kids finally showed up at two in the morning*. The absolute allows gerundive *ing* morphology, and that shows up on the head of the VP appearing in absolute position. So the fact that *having* is the bearer of this morphology makes the case extremely strong that the head of this VP is indeed *have*. We see then that the tree structure corresponding to such VPs should be analyzed as

(49)

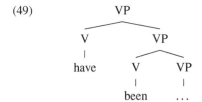

So far, then, a consistently right-branching structure for the *have* and *be* auxiliaries has emerged. But what about the modals? Do they work the same way?

3.2.1.3   Auxiliaries Are VP Heads: Modals and VP Coordination

Modals present a special difficulty for the line of inquiry we've been pursuing to this point. It is a fact about the English modals that they only appear in finite form. That means that they are beyond the reach of any VP constituency test (such as the absolute adjunct context) which requires a nonfinite head verb form. Furthermore, since they're finite, and there is no verb in English which shows up with finite VP complements, there's no way they can be displaced (because, given what's just been said, they can't be the heads of complements to any verb). So it seems that we have no way to test the hypothesis that modals parallel *have* and *be* in heading VP and appearing with VP sisters.

Nonetheless, there are certain considerations which allow us to make a plausible case for a parallel treatment of modals and *have/be*. We have two possibilities: on the one hand, just this kind of uniform treatment, and on the other, a 'flat' structure, depicted in (50)a and b respectively:

(50)   a.

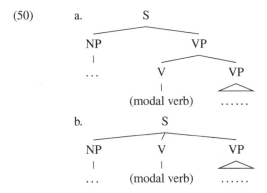

If (50)b were the correct analysis of clausal phrase structure when modals were involved, the modal would have to be the head of the whole sentence, but there would be no structural connection between the modal and the VP. This would mean that the particular correlation between the modal verbs and the completely uninflected form of the following verb would have to be built into the sentence rule itself. In terms of the rules previously introduced in Chapter 2, we would have the following corresponding to the single rule for complete saturation offered there:

(51)
$$\begin{bmatrix} phrase \\ \text{SPR} \quad \langle\,\rangle \\ \text{COMPS} \quad \langle\,\rangle \end{bmatrix} \rightarrow \boxed{1}\text{XP}, \underbrace{\begin{bmatrix} word \\ \text{HEAD} \quad modal \\ \text{COMPS} \quad ? \\ \text{SPR} \quad \langle\boxed{1}\rangle \end{bmatrix}}_{HEAD}, \text{VP}\,[\text{VFORM } bare]$$

where we have had to separate the modals out as a named subtype of *verb*. The ellipsis facts illustrated in (19) make it clear that by the omissibility criterion, the modal in (50) is the head. But if it selects all its sisters, as in (51), then the VP is a complement, the NP is a subject, and (51) constitutes a completely new rule which specifically allows a verb to saturate both its SUBJ and its COMPS specifications simultaneously. This is far from out of the question – it is, in fact, the basis for our analysis of subject/auxiliary 'inversion' in the last section of this chapter – but apart from doing no work that the independently motivated structure in (50)a already does not (as per our analysis of *have* and *be* above), it comports badly with the fact that the modal verb, an ordinary major class word, does not precede the subject phrasal constituent, regardless of category, in spite of the fact that, as we observed in Chapter 2, it is a general fact of English that words precede phrases, regardless of category. Again, we could work out a way to exclude the version of modals which appears following subject phrases from this generalization. But the critical point is that once again, we would be supplying an after-the-fact correction motivated not by any gain in empirical coverage, but in order to repair a major misprediction that, if we assume (50)b instead, never arises in the first place.

Straightforward methodological considerations such as these shift the burden of proof onto the flat structure hypothesis embodied in (50). Certainly, prior to adopting this alternative we would want some very good reason to reject the branching alternative in (50)a in favor of (50)b.

One argument to this effect, of course, is that *do so* replacement fails in the case of structures where the 'top' auxiliary is a modal. But as we've seen, *do so* replacement doesn't work for *any* auxiliary construction, so this argument doesn't really have much force. And, as already observed, the restriction of modals to tensed forms means that various other tests, which appear to implicate nonfinite form for the candidate VPs being tested, will be inapplicable.

There is, however, a simple empirically driven reason to take the sequence modal+VP to be a constituent – the evidence of coordination.

3.2.2   Coordination

3.2.2.1   What Can be Coordinated, and What Is the Result?

The coordination test is probably the trickiest of the major diagnostics for constituency. What makes it so difficult to apply confidently is the fact that many apparent nonconstituents appear to be coordinable. Nonetheless, there are limits to this flexibility that make coordination a useful tool for investigating constituency, if applied with suitable caution.

It should be noted that even frameworks which speak of the coordination of nonconstituents don't exactly mean that one can coordinate nonconstituents; rather, apparent nonconstituent coordination is handled by showing that the coordinated elements really are constituents, but just don't look like constituents, for whatever reason. The idea is that genuine nonconstituents really do *not* coordinate. To see how this works, consider the following data:

(52) a.   Robin was looking up the $\left\{ \begin{array}{c} \text{staircase} \\ \text{phone number} \end{array} \right\}$ when the call came through.

   b.   Up which $\left\{ \begin{array}{c} \text{staircase} \\ \text{*phone number} \end{array} \right\}$ was Robin looking when the call came through?

These data suggest that the sequence *up the staircase* is a PP constituent in (52)a, but not (52)b, correlating with displaceability vs nondisplaceability. To check whether this is a correct analysis, we can formulate another prediction and then test it against the facts: we know that in PPs, the preposition can never follow the noun – *talked to Robin/*I talked Robin to; I put the book on the shelf/*I put the book the shelf on*, etc. If the *up* in *look up the phone number* deviates from this pattern, it's excellent evidence that it's not part of a PP, but something else. And this is just what we find.

(53)   Robin was looking the $\left\{ \begin{array}{c} \text{phone number} \\ \text{*staircase} \end{array} \right\}$ up when the call came through.

We therefore have ample empirical justification for positing the following bracketing:

(54) a.   Robin was looking [$_{PP}$ up the stairs].

   b.   Robin was [$_V$ looking up] [$_{NP}$ the phone number].

The payoff of this analysis is that we can confidently identify *up the phone number* as a nonconstituent in *Robin was looking up the phone number*. In light of this discovery, consider now the facts reported in (55):

(55) a.   *Robin was looking up the $\left\{ \begin{array}{c} \text{stairs} \\ \text{address} \end{array} \right\}$ and up the phone number.

   ⱳ.ᵇ   Robin had looked up the attic staircase and down the basement staircase and still hadn't identified the source of the strange creaking noises she was hearing.

   b.ᶜ   Robin had [looked up the phone number] and then [looked up the stairs].

We cannot coordinate *up* NP with either *up* NP or PP ((55)a); we can, however, coordinate PP with PP ((55)b) and VPs headed by both ordinary *look* and by the apparent compound verb *look up* ((55)c). All of these facts fall out immediately if we assume the following principle:

(56)   Only constituents can be coordinated.

But what is still left unresolved by (56) is the question, what do we actually
get when we coordinate constituents? And what kinds of constituents can be
coordinated in the first place?

First consider the following data:

(57) a.   I want to talk to you.
     b.   I want a book.
     c.   *I want to talk to you and a book.
     d.   ??*I want a book and to talk to you.
     e.   I want to talk to you and I want a book.

The simplest account of such data is that only members of the same category
can be coordinated. Furthermore, other data strongly suggest that the result of
coordinating two constituents of the same category is a larger constituent of the
same category:

(58) a.   I put [$_{NP}$ the books and the CDs] on the table.
     b.   I put the books [$_{PP}$ under the table or on the shelves].

We know that the coordinate categories in these examples must be NP in (58)a
and PP in (58)b because that's what the verb *put* demands. On this basis, we
reformulate (56) as (59):

(59)   Coordination applies to constituents of the same category and yields a larger
           constituent of that category.

We now apply these results to the problem of modal auxiliary syntax.

3.2.2.2   What coordination tells us about the modal auxiliaries

We start by noting what looks like the strongest possible evidence
that the sequence modal+VP should be treated as a constituent.

(60) a.   Robin feels proud of herself and *should* feel proud of herself.
     b.   The twins could have been successful and still can be successful.
     c.   I tried getting her on the phone all day but probably won't reach her till the
           weekend's over.

We can be sure that the two strings being coordinated by *and* in (60)a are *feels
proud of herself* and *should feel proud of herself*. Of course there are other
possibilities: so, for example, *Robin feels proud of herself* might have been
coordinated with *should feel proud of herself*. But if that were the case, we
would expect that (making allowance for predictable semantic differences) we
could have reversed the order of these two strings to get *Should feel proud of
herself and Robin feels proud of herself*. In fact, there is no interpretation of what
is being coordinated here which passes this reversibility test except for *feels
proud of herself* and *should feel proud of herself*. But given what we've said in
(59) about coordination as a test for constituency, it follows that we must have,
for (60)a, the analysis

(61)   Robin [$_{VP}$ [$_{VP}$ feels proud of Leslie] and [$_{VP}$ *should* feel proud of Leslie]]

This conclusion represents a confirmation of our preliminary decision to treat modal+VP as a constituent – a decision, it should be recalled, strongly suggested on a priori grounds by the constituency tests showing that the modals' fellow auxiliaries, *have* and *be*, form larger VPs in combination with the VPs which follow them, and are the heads of the VPs so formed. The second conjunct in (61), in particular, will be analyzed as

(62)

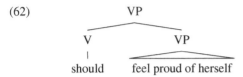

We now only need to decide on which of the daughters of VP in (62) is the head, and the decision here is easy: *Robin should* is good, while **Robin feel proud of Leslie* is ill-formed. If the VP sister to *should* contains the copula, the effect is even more striking: *Robin should be very proud of Leslie, and you should, too* vs **Robin should be very proud of herself, and you be very proud of Leslie.* Clearly, *should* is the head of its own VP, and we now have an extended argument that modals, along with *have* and *be*, are the heads of their own VPs. Based on the evidence adduced to this point, we can therefore confidently analyze, for example, *Robin should have been eating breakfast*, as in (26), as

(63)

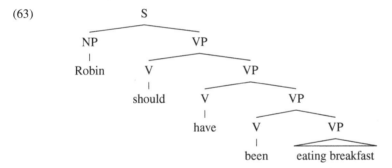

On the assumptions made so far, the auxiliary system proves to have a consistently right-branching hierarchical phrase structure in which each auxiliary is the head of a VP, and has a VP sister. In terms of the system outlined in the previous chapter, this sister is a complement of the auxiliary head, and appears by virtue of the phrase structure rule schemata already described.

3.2.3   Null Subjects: An Alternative That Doesn't Work

But one might not accept the assumptions on which the analysis in (63) is based. Suppose, instead, that we analyzed (61) as:

(64)   [$_S$ [$_{NP}$ Robin] feels proud of herself] and [$_S$ [$_{NP}$ ∅] *should* feel proud of herself]

The innovation in (64) is the null subject ∅. The claim here is that English sentences can have such subjects, and that in cases of apparent coordination of components which don't otherwise pass tests for constituency, coordination of clauses with null subjects may be involved. But this analysis doesn't come for free. It would entail certain commitments from advocates – predictions about what is and is not possible that, as we will see, don't square at all well with the available evidence.

Consider the data in (65):

(65) a.   Robin only rarely will talk about it or will make any comments.
     b.   Robin only rarely will talk about it or he will make (noncommittal) comments.
     c.   *Robin only rarely would talk about it or he will make any comments.

The data show that *only rarely* can apply to the string *will talk about it or will make any comments* (as per (65)). But when *only rarely* occurs within the first of two full *clauses*, it does not modify the second. And when an item such as *any* appears in the second clause, the example is bad. *Any* belongs to a class of elements called *negative polarity items* (NPI)s, for which the general principle holds that such items can only appear in a local context of a certain level of logical negation (e.g., *reluctantly* implies negativity but not enough to make **Robin reluctantly bought any apples* good), and cannot scope into another clause which is structurally too far separated from that negation. If we use the symbol $\neg^{\alpha}$ to indicate the necessary level of negation to license an NPI α, we can illustrate the situation as in (66):

(66)

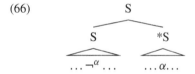

The item corresponding to α in (66) is structurally inaccessible to $\neg^{\alpha}$, so that the second S makes the whole sentence ungrammatical. This principle would explain the data contrast in (65) perfectly – on the assumption that *would talk about it or would make any comments* is a VP, and therefore both parts of the coordination are subject to modification by a negative adverb sister to their common mother:

(67)

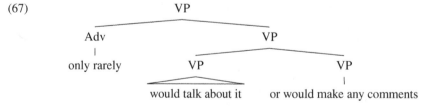

Given this structural argument, the 'covert subject' analysis faces the difficulty that it must somehow account for the goodness of ∅-subject analogues of both (65)b, where *only rarely* is not allowed to scope, and (65)c, where the point is driven home by the inability of *any* to appear in the second clause. Since the badness in these cases appears to be caused by structural properties that in no way depend on the phonology of the subject NP, it is very difficult to see why *only rarely* has no access to the second clause when the subject is overt, but gains such access when the subject is unpronounced.

A second point which supports the VP coordination analysis over its null-subject analysis competitor is afforded by the behavior of doubly marked coordination constructions such as that displayed in (68):

(68) a.   Robin both likes her job and is good at it.
     b.   ??*Robin both likes her job and she is good at it.

(68)a appears to be telling us that *both/and* coordination is ruled out when *both* is in a separate sentence from *and*. We see this effect with the coordination both of *has*-headed VPs and with modal-headed VPs:

(69) a.   Robin both likes her job and has taken the trouble to become good at it.
     b.   ??* Robin both likes her job and she has taken the trouble to become good at it.

(70) a.   Robin both wants to do a good job and should be EXPECTED to do a good job.
     b.   ??Robin both wants to do a good job and she should be EXPECTED to do a good job.

The parallel is exactly what we would expect if *has* and *should* also paralleled each other in projecting VPs which entered into coordination in (69) and (70).

3.3   Capturing Auxiliaries

3.3.1   Some Stocktaking

It will be worthwhile at this point to survey our progress to this point. We now know what makes something an auxiliary – what the signature properties of this class are – and, in addition, that auxiliaries are, at the end of the day, just verbs – verbs with idiosyncratic properties, but verbs, not some exotic grammatical beast that needs its own unique category. We would expect, on the basis of this knowledge, that auxiliaries, like other kinds of verb and, more generally, as members of one of the major syntactic categories, would be able to head their own VPs, and all of the evidence considered above suggests that the auxiliaries as a class do indeed head their own VPs. Furthermore, we can actually derive some useful information from the fact that the VPs projected from auxiliary Vs do not allow displacement or *do so* replacement: these facts mean that the VP mothers of auxiliary heads register the fact that their head is an auxiliary. Most critically, we have been able to use a variety of supplementary tests – *so* inversion, absolutive adjunct distribution, and coordination – to make a strong case for the constituency of all auxiliary+VP sequences, and employed two logically independent tests (NPI distribution and binary coordination facts) to refute an alternative approach to coordination which denies the existence of VPs headed by modals. Taken together, these analyses lead us to posit a right-branching structure for multiple auxiliary constructions of the sort depicted in (63).

If the arguments to this point are on the right track, then the next phase of the account must work out exactly why the auxiliary dependency exists in the form we observe, and why auxiliaries occur in the order we find them in. It turns out that these two questions are intimately connected – a somewhat surprising and very welcome aspect of the analysis we propose directly.

3.3.2   Solving the Auxiliary Puzzle Via Valence

We begin with the morphosyntactic dependency issue. How does the right-branching structure of the auxiliary system allow us to explain the correlation between the particular identity of the auxiliary and the morphological form of the following verb? We can begin by rethinking the view of things implicit in the preceding sentence: the 'following verb' is, as the structure in (63) shows, the head verb of the auxiliary's VP sister. By the Head-complement Rule, each such sister VP must be on the auxiliary's COMPS list – which means that the auxiliary has control over what kinds of properties its eventual sister VP possesses. Being 'visible', via the COMPS list, to each selecting auxiliary head, the VP sister of that auxiliary must display whatever formal attributes the auxiliary imposes on its complements. And this particular aspect of the system we've developed – the linkage between what the selecting head requires from its sister and the form that sister can take – gives us the key to the auxiliary dependency. If any particular auxiliary can determine some property of its sister VP, and if that property is in turn shared between the sister VP and its head daughter, then, indirectly, the auxiliary is able to force that property to be part of that head daughter's description. Is it possible to make this two-step linkage between the auxiliary and the 'following verb' work?

The V+PP dependency problem we looked at in the previous chapter – the correlation of the lexical identity of the selecting V with the particular form of its selected PP sister, as in *accuse of/charge with/indict for* – shows us the route to a solution. To account for that dependency, we added information about the identity of prepositions to their lexical entries via the PFORM feature, and – crucially – ensured the sharing of that information between the PP mother and its head P daughter by making PFORM be a HEAD feature. By the Head Feature Principle, we then have a structure with the general form

(71)

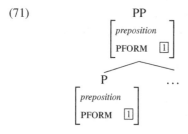

as discussed in Chapter 2. But a moment's thought should convince the reader that what we face in establishing a controlling relationship between auxiliaries and the heads of the VPs they select is exactly parallel to the problem we faced, and solved, in establishing a controlling relation between verbs and the heads of the PPs they select. We can solve the V+VP dependency problem in the same way as we solved the PP dependency problem – by adding information about the form of its head to the feature specifications of the VP by means of a HEAD feature which specifically encodes that information, just as PFORM did.

What we need, therefore, is a feature which does for verbs what PFORM does for prepositions. There is a slight difference in what such a feature would have to do in the case of verbs: whereas PFORM picks out an entire preposition uniquely – *in*, or *for*, etc. – the corresponding feature for verbs should identify only the morphological form of the verb. Suppose, following our choice for prepositions, we call this feature VFORM. VFORM will identify the inflectional properties of the verb: the progressive *ing*, the gerundive *ing*, the 'perfective' *en*, and so on – including a specification for a completely uninflected, bare form. We don't need to get individual verbs – the auxiliary *have* doesn't require a specific verb to head its VP complement; it just requires that whatever verb does head that VP be in the *en* form (or the *ed* form, depending on which verb is involved: we have *had broken*, but *had baked*).

This proposal is hardly very radical or unintuitive; morphological form is a property of particular words, and inflectional differences in morphological form must therefore be encoded as part of the inventory of a word's attributes. We know, when we see *am*, that we're looking at a particular form of *be*, one that corresponds to the nonpast tense (as well as a first person subject, but that's a different story, one we'll deal with in the next chapter). The lexical entry for any word is a summary of its attributes – a cluster of values for specific features appropriately specified for a word of whatever type it is. So our knowledge of the nonpast tense (i.e., finite) grammatical status of *am* corresponds formally to a lexical entry for *am* which records this information. And since feature/value pairs are the means this framework uses to express properties, we need a feature which carries the necessary information – hence, VFORM is required.

We use the verb *eat* to illustrate how all this works. Each morphological form of *eat* will correspond to a different value for the feature VFORM. We therefore have the array of (partial) lexical entries in (72):

(72) a.   *eats*: $\begin{bmatrix} \text{HEAD} \begin{bmatrix} verb \\ \text{VFORM} & fin \\ \text{TNS} & nonpast \end{bmatrix} \\ \text{COMPS} \langle \text{NP} \rangle \end{bmatrix}$

b. *ate:* $\begin{bmatrix} \text{HEAD} \begin{bmatrix} verb \\ \text{VFORM} \quad fin \\ \text{TNS} \quad past \end{bmatrix} \\ \text{COMPS}\langle\text{NP}\rangle \end{bmatrix}$

c. *eating:* $\begin{bmatrix} \text{HEAD} \begin{bmatrix} verb \\ \text{VFORM} \quad prog \end{bmatrix} \\ \text{COMPS}\langle\text{NP}\rangle \end{bmatrix}$

d. *eaten:* $\begin{bmatrix} \text{HEAD} \begin{bmatrix} verb \\ \text{VFORM} \quad perf \end{bmatrix} \\ \text{COMPS}\langle\text{NP}\rangle \end{bmatrix}$

e. *eat:* $\begin{bmatrix} \text{HEAD} \begin{bmatrix} verb \\ \text{VFORM} \quad bare \end{bmatrix} \\ \text{COMPS}\langle\text{NP}\rangle \end{bmatrix}$

These descriptions imprint the correct VFORM value on each of the different forms of *eat*. So, parallel to the structure in (71) we have

(73)

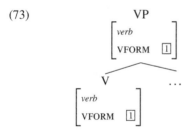

Each lexical entry for *eat* – and for all verbs, in general – will contain a specification of some VFORM value, which, as (73) depicts, will appear simultaneously in the mother node of any phrase formed by combining that version of *eat* with its complement phrase.

Our Head-complement Rule from the previous chapter gives us general structures of the form in (74)a. When a lexical item such as *was* appears as the V head, the details sharpen quite a bit. Based on what we need to say about *was* – a finite verb in the past tense whose COMPS list comprises a VP[VFORM *prog*] specification – we will wind up with something along the lines of (74)b:

(74) a.   VP
          /‾‾‾‾\
        V   ...

b.

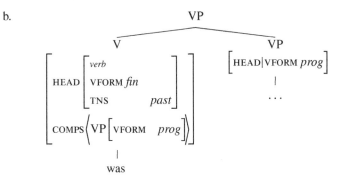

The example in (74) introduces a general convention that will be followed in subsequent chapters: in a situation such as that described in (75)a, all of the statements in (75)b hold:

(75) a.

$$
\begin{bmatrix}
\text{FEATURE-1} & \begin{bmatrix} \text{FEATURE-10} & \alpha \\ \text{FEATURE-11} & \beta \\ \text{FEATURE-12} & \gamma \end{bmatrix} \\
\text{FEATURE-2} & \begin{bmatrix} \text{FEATURE-20} & \delta \\ \text{FEATURE-21} & \epsilon \end{bmatrix} \\
\text{FEATURE-3} & \begin{bmatrix} \text{FEATURE-30} & \sigma \\ \text{FEATURE-31} & \tau \end{bmatrix}
\end{bmatrix}
$$

b. $\begin{bmatrix} \text{FEATURE-1}|\text{FEATURE-10} & \alpha \end{bmatrix}$

c. $\begin{bmatrix} \text{FEATURE-1}|\text{FEATURE-11} & \beta \end{bmatrix}$

d. $\begin{bmatrix} \text{FEATURE-1}|\text{FEATURE-12} & \gamma \end{bmatrix}$

e. $\begin{bmatrix} \text{FEATURE-2}|\text{FEATURE-20} & \delta \end{bmatrix}$

f. $\begin{bmatrix} \text{FEATURE-2}|\text{FEATURE-21} & \epsilon \end{bmatrix}$

g. $\begin{bmatrix} \text{FEATURE-3}|\text{FEATURE-30} & \sigma \end{bmatrix}$

h. $\begin{bmatrix} \text{FEATURE-3}|\text{FEATURE-31} & \tau \end{bmatrix}$

In other words, in a structure such as (76)a, we can trace a kind of pathway of information specification from F_1 to F_2 to F_n and write that pathway as in (76)b:

(76) a.

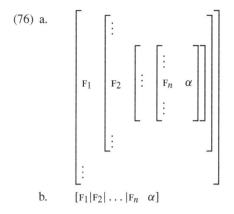

b. $[F_1|F_2|\dots|F_n \;\; \alpha]$

In the case of (74), we read the pathway [HEAD|VFORM *prog*] as 'the HEAD feature's VFORM value'.

We now have to complete the representation in (74) by fleshing out the form of *was*'s VP[HEAD|VFORM *prog*] complement. We know that by virtue of the HFP, the head daughter of this VP is also a *verb*-type object specified as [HEAD|VFORM *prog*]. Essentially *any* VP which meets these specifications can therefore appear as the complement here, which means that the following is a legal structure:

(77)

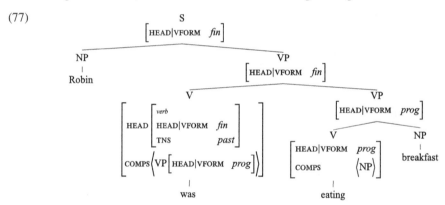

This treatment can be extended to all the other auxiliaries, and yields the correlation between particular auxiliaries and the morphological form of the following verb.

It's worth mentioning that every form of *eat*, regardless of its VFORM value, will have the same valence: [SPR ⟨NP$_{normal}$⟩, COMPS ⟨NP$_{normal}$⟩]. In order to ensure that this is the case, we will need a specific kind of rule that states generalizations about lexical items. By the same token, given the pattern displayed in (78), all variants of the progressive *be* will be specified as selecting a VP with the specification [VFORM *prog*] as in (79):

(78) $\left\{ \begin{array}{c} \text{is} \\ \text{was} \\ \text{been} \\ \text{be} \end{array} \right\}$ eat**ing**

(79)   all forms of *be*:
$$\begin{bmatrix} \text{HEAD} & \text{VERB} \\ \\ \text{COMPS} & \left\langle \text{VP} \begin{bmatrix} \text{HEAD|VFORM} & prog \end{bmatrix} \right\rangle \end{bmatrix}$$

This pattern seems quite natural – why would the progressive form of a given verb select a different list of complements from the bare form? But it's far from universal; there is, for example, an often-noted pattern in a certain paradigm class in Russian whereby certain nonpast verbs lack first person singular subjects. On the line of analysis pursued to this point, we would say that in the case of these verbs, the inflectional classes specified as past and nonpast tense display different valence possibilities (the former admits specifications of the form in (80), the latter does not):

(80)
$$\begin{bmatrix} \text{SPR} & \left\langle \begin{bmatrix} \text{SS} & \begin{bmatrix} \text{HEAD} & \begin{bmatrix} noun \\ \text{PER} & 1 \\ \text{NUM} & sing \end{bmatrix} \end{bmatrix} \end{bmatrix} \right\rangle \end{bmatrix}$$

Here then is a clear case where valence partially depends on inflectional form, in two respects: on the one hand, the restriction just noted in connection with (80), and on the other, the fact that this restriction itself only holds in one specific class of Russian conjugations.

Practice Exercise

i.   Provide lexical entries for *had* and *must* which account for the VP structure in the sentences

   Robin had remembered the password.

   Robin must remember the password.

ii.   Show how these lexical entries interact to give rise to the correct verb structure in

   Robin must have remembered the password.

   Present a full annotated tree – a tree with detailed feature specifications, along the lines illustrated in (77) – for the preceding sentence, using the lexical entries you provided in part (i) of this exercise for *had* and *must*.

Having completed this exercise, you should now have a good sense of the way the feature COMPS, in conjunction with the Head Feature Principle, the Head-subject Rule and the Head-complement Rule allow us to correlate particular classes of auxiliary with the suffixal morphology of the head of the auxiliary's complement VP. But very little if any extra machinery beyond what was introduced in Chapter 2 has proven necessary. This result constitutes a dramatic illustration of the way in which locally satisfied feature-matching principles can model the flow of information within a structural configuration to yield observable effects. One more piece of the puzzle is still needed, however – an account of the linear order possibilities among the auxiliaries.

3.3.3   Capturing Auxiliary Ordering

So far, we've said very little about linear ordering possibilities. The order of elements on the COMPS list reflects the relative 'ranking' of major components of the clause, with direct objects ranked highest, indirect or 'second' objects (such as *a book* in *Robin gave Leslie a book*) next, and so on. But such a scheme is not really very exact, and as stated, it doesn't take into account the appearance of subjects, of adjectives and other adjuncts, and so on. We can introduce various fixes for these particular cases, but what is really needed is a general theory of linear order. Such a theory is available within the overall framework already presented, but it requires a higher degree of technical detail than would be useful to go into at this point. This is unfortunate in terms of the present discussion, because what we need is a way to account for the ordering of the auxiliary elements. Does this mean we need to regard this issue as unsolvable, given the tools we've developed to this point?

Before giving up on the question, it might be worthwhile thinking about just what the question *is*, and whether it might be reframed in a way that leads to a solution along different lines. What we see, looking at (63) again, is that the order of auxiliaries actually corresponds to their structural height within the tree, and so asking why the modals always precede any other verb in clauses which contain them is, in effect, to ask why the modals must always be the highest verb in any sentence in which they occur. Let's take another look at (63), but this time annotate it with information about VFORM values, which are the key to which VPs are allowed to appear as sisters to which auxiliaries:

(63′)

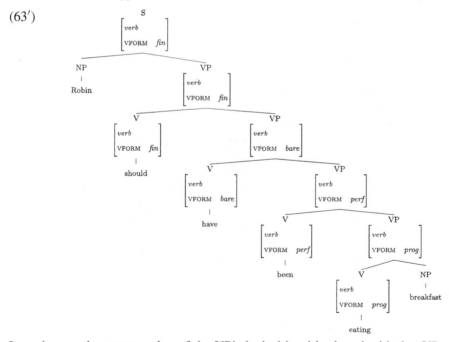

In each case, the VFORM value of the VP's lexical head is shared with that VP, which then becomes eligible for selection by the next higher auxiliary in the structure. At the top, we find the auxiliary *should*, which as we know represents the past tense form of the verb whose nonpast tense is *shall*. What would happen if *should* occurred to the right of its position in (63′), following some other auxiliary? Obviously, it would have to project its VFORM value to its mother VP to make the latter selectable by the preceding auxiliary. But that would mean that its mother, which would be VP[VFORM *fin*], would satisfy the valence requirements of either *have* or *be* – and neither of those verbs selects a finite VP. So the only way *should*, and the VP it heads, could appear to the right of either auxiliary would be to replace *should* with the perfective or progressive form of the modal *shall* – and no such form exists in English!

What this conclusion means, in turn, is that *should*, and the modals in general, appear in the leftmost position in all auxiliary sequences because, in effect, they do not have the morphological resources to appear anywhere else. They have only finite forms; the lexicon does not contain any nonfinite modals, and so the only place the VPs they head can appear is where these are not selected by any other verb – namely, at the very highest position in the clause, where they are an immediate constituent of S itself. What appears to be a precedence condition (leftmost position) turns out to be a dominance condition (structurally nearest the root S) based on the selectional requirements of the various auxiliaries, interacting with the morphological properties of the lexicon. There simply are not *enough* words related to *shall*, or the other modals, in the lexicon to permit the modals to appear anywhere else but the very top of the clausal VP – and therefore at the left edge of that VP.

Once we appreciate this point, we can provide a parallel account for the remaining auxiliary ordering puzzle: the fact that *have* invariably precedes *be*. And now it's *your* turn to provide the explanation.

Practise Exercise

i.   Using the solution provided in the preceding discussion for the ordering of the modals prior to *have/be* as a model, explain the invariant ordering of *have* and *be* with respect to each other.

ii.   If you've solved (i) correctly, the unwary might be skeptical of your solution on the grounds that there's nothing wrong with *having* in absolute constructions such as *Having lost the race, Terry courteously congratulated the winner*. Why might they think this a problem for your solution? Why is it *not* a problem for your solution?

3.4   Auxiliaries and Subject Selection

We aren't quite done with the technical issues that auxiliaries confront us with. So far, everything that's been said bears either on the complement possibilities of the auxiliaries or on their own morphosyntactic form, as reflected in various HEAD feature specifications. But there is something else about auxiliaries that we need to pay attention to, a pattern exhibited in the following data:

(81) a.   It rained.
    b.   *There rained.
    c.   *The day rained.

(82) a.   It is raining.
    b.   *There is raining.
    c.   *The day is raining.

(83) a.   It has been raining.
    b.   *There has been raining.
    c.   *The day has been raining.

(84) a.   It might have been raining.
    b.   *There might have been raining.
    c.   *The day might have been raining.

(85) a.   There is nothing wrong with you.
    b.   *It is nothing wrong with you.
    c.   *Robin is nothing wrong with you.

(86) a.   There has been nothing wrong with you.
    b.   *It has been nothing wrong with you.
    c.   *Robin has been nothing wrong with you.

(87) a.   There may have been nothing wrong with you.
    b.   *It may have been nothing wrong with you.
    c.   *Robin may have been nothing wrong with you.

(88) a.   Robin bought ice cream.
    b.   *There bought ice cream.
    c.   *It bought ice cream.

(89) a.   Robin is buying ice cream.
    b.   *There is buying ice cream.
    c.   *It is buying ice cream.

(90) a.   Robin had been buying ice cream.
    b.   *There had been buying ice cream.
    c.   *It had been buying ice cream.

(91) a.   Robin may have been buying ice cream.
    b.   *There may have been buying ice cream.
    c.   *It may have been buying ice cream.

We can think of this pattern as reflecting a kind of *transparency* effect: the subject of the auxiliary is exactly the right one given the particular VP which lies at the bottom, so to speak, of the VP 'staircase' created by the complement valence requirements of the auxiliaries as a class. Notice that what is at stake is not simply a matter of a single intermediate VP: in (84)a, information about what the required subject is must reach through three separate levels of the VP hierarchy in order to link *it* at the top with *raining* at the bottom. We can depict the problem schematically as follows:

(92)

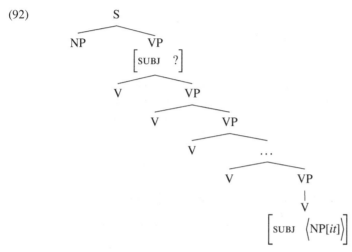

The evident difficulty here is that subjects are determined by a combination of the Head-specifier Rule and the SPR specification of the highest verb, the head of the highest VP in the sentence. How does this topmost verb 'know' what the verb of the lowest VP requires for its subject?

Given the restrictions of the framework that we've taken on, there isn't a great deal of latitude available to us in approaching this question. We must ensure that in the case of (82)a, *is* selects an *it* subject, but only if its VP complement is headed by a verb such as *raining* which itself also requires an *it* subject. And the same must be true for *have*, as per (83), as well as any modal auxiliary (*It will rain/*There will rain/*The sky will rain*, etc.). In short, any auxiliary that combines with a VP requiring *it* must itself select *it*. But an exactly parallel requirement holds for auxiliaries that combine with a VP selecting *there* – and, for that matter, for auxiliaries combining with VPs that demand a 'normal' subject. The list doesn't stop there: certain verbs, such as *bother*, can take a clausal subject (*That Robin spies for the Ostrogoths bothers me*), and auxiliaries combining with VPs headed by these verbs – and these alone – also can take clausal subjects:

(93)   That Robin spies for the Ostrogoths
$\left\{\begin{array}{l}\text{bothers}\\\text{is bothering}\\\text{had bothered}\\\text{had been bothering}\\\text{must have bothered me}\\\text{must have been bothering}\end{array}\right\}$
me.

Substitution of the appropriate form of, say, *harass*, which does not accept clausal subjects, yields a clearly ill-formed result in all the contexts in (93). Once again, it appears that all auxiliaries are sensitive to all the subject selection possibilities and restrictions of the VPs they combine with.

The simplest way to capture the fact that auxiliaries match the subject specifications of their complement VPs is to state the fact as an obligatory property of the English lexicon. Suppose auxiliaries bear a HEAD feature [AUX +]. We impose the following restriction on all lexical entries bearing that specification:

(94)
$$[\text{AUX} +] \quad \supset \quad \begin{bmatrix} \text{COMPS} & \langle \text{VP}[\text{SUBJ} \; \boxed{1}] \rangle \\ \text{SUBJ} & \boxed{1} \end{bmatrix}$$

This constraint forces every auxiliary in English to share its subject specification with its VP complement. Completing the following two exercises should make it clear to you how this restriction enables us to capture the subject transparency effect noted above.

Practice Exercise

Present a full lexical entry for the auxiliaries *must* and *have*, based on the preceding discussion, and in particular the requirement (94).

Practice Exercise

Using the lexical entries you've worked out for the preceding exercise, present a completely annotated phrase structure tree for the sentence *It must have rained*, with each step justified via the operation of the various combinatorial principles introduced in Chapter 2. Explain how the components of your account also rule out *There must have rained*.

3.5   Where Does Inversion Come From?

We've used the NICE properties as a diagnostic probe for auxiliary status, but each of them is a grammatical phenomenon in its own right with, typically, a very deep literature and much ongoing debate about its proper analysis even now. Nonetheless, it will be useful to see how this phenomenon can be accommodated in a framework such as the one we've been developing. As noted at the very beginning of this chapter, the auxiliary system as a whole was one of the centerpieces of the transformational paradigm, and the putative ease with which one could derive inverted structures on the basis of the independently required uninverted structures transformationally was contrasted with the awkward and redundant behavior of early versions of the present framework which, it was claimed, inevitably failed to express the simple generalizations which related inverted word order to uninverted. The very name of the phenomenon, adopted across all frameworks and in current use as the default term for the order of elements in questions, counterfactuals, and the other uses of inversion cited at the beginning of this chapter, takes the essence of the construction to be a *change in order*, presupposing that there was some other order originally in effect in the structures which give rise to 'subject-auxiliary inversion' and that inversion itself arises as a rule applying to this original order to yield subject-second sentences.

The claimed advantage for this analysis was the fact that in the inverted structure, the order of auxiliaries and the morphological marking on any given verb following some auxiliary were the same as in the uninverted structure. If the uninverted structure fixed the auxiliary order and the morphological marking to begin with, then subsequent reordering of the leftmost auxiliary with respect to the subject would leave both aspects of the clause unchanged. A number of highly parochial and idiosyncratic transformational rules were required to gain this advantage, but the costs appeared to be justified by the generalizations gained.

In terms of the phrase structure-based approach we've taken in this book, the main issue that needs to be addressed is the fact that in a structure in which the auxiliary is separated by an NP from the VP it would normally select, it does not seem possible to maintain the $[_{vp}$ V VP] constituency which corresponds to the selection mechanism guaranteeing the correct VFORM on the VP complement and the proper sharing of SUBJ information between the 'inverted' auxiliary and the VP corresponding to its COMPS specification. But further reflection will show that this problem is completely illusory. As long as the VP to the right of the subject saturates the 'inverted' auxiliary's COMPS specification, that VP's SUBJ specification will match the auxiliary's, and the NP to its right must therefore match the latter's SUBJ value, and hence that of the complement VP, just as in the uninverted case. And at the same time, since the VP matches the auxiliary's COMPS value, it must bear the morphology imposed by the auxiliary's COMPS value, again just as in the uninverted case. The obvious problem is that given the structure we are assuming here, $[_s$ V NP VP], we must combine V *simultaneously* with its subject and complement. And none of the schematic rules given above for combining heads with valents allows us to do that.

That deficiency in our grammar is easily remedied, however. We can state a new rule which specifies that a sentence can have an auxiliary as a head daughter. The rule will look very much like the following:

(95)   **Head-specifier-complement Rule (preliminary version)**

$$
\begin{bmatrix} phrase \\ \text{SS} \begin{bmatrix} \text{COMPS} \langle \ \rangle \\ \text{SPR} \quad \langle \ \rangle \end{bmatrix} \end{bmatrix} \rightarrow \underbrace{\begin{bmatrix} word \\ \text{AUX} \quad + \\ \text{COMPS} \ \langle X_1,\dots,X_n \rangle \\ \text{SPR} \quad \langle Y \rangle \end{bmatrix}}_{HEAD}, \underbrace{\begin{bmatrix} phrase \\ \text{SS} \quad Y \end{bmatrix}}_{SPR}, \underbrace{\begin{bmatrix} phrase \\ \text{SS} \quad X_1 \end{bmatrix}, \dots, \begin{bmatrix} phrase \\ \text{SS} \quad X_n \end{bmatrix}}_{COMPS}
$$

This remarkably simple schema turns out to be almost all that is needed to get exactly the inversion possibilities in English. Consider how (95) works: we have structures of the form in (96) licensed by this schema:

(96)

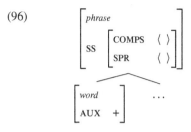

Since only verbs are ever specified as [AUX +], this structure can only be further specified as

(97)

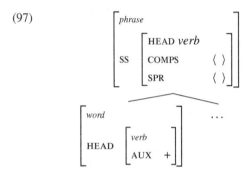

The auxiliary can be any of the lexical items whose entries specify [AUX +]. Suppose we allow *should* to appear in this structure:

(98)

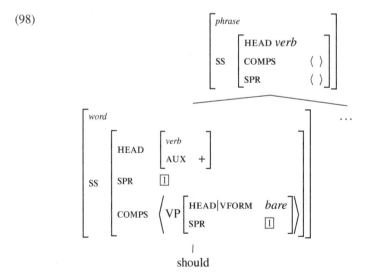

The Head-specifier-complement Rule ensures that there is exactly one sister to the verb corresponding to each COMPS list item, and likewise for the SPR list. Let's assume that its SPR specification is ⟨NP⟩. Then *should* must have a sister which

satisfies this specification, a phrasal sign with a HEAD value of type *noun*, and, on the same grounds, a VP[*bare*] sister whose SPR specification is identical to that of the auxiliary's NP subject, exactly as per the conditions imposed by *should*'s valence requirements, and completely unaffected by the fact that *should* and that VP don't actually form a constituent.

But exactly where do these sisters mandated jointly by the Head-complement/Head-sister Rules and the COMPS/SPR lists of various phrasal heads appear in the tree? It turns out that their order is completely determined by the linear precedence restrictions stated in the previous chapter, where it was noted that words precede phrasal sisters and NPs precede all other phrasal categories. The auxiliary head of the sentence, a word, therefore precedes the NP and VP sisters which satisfy its valence requirements, and the NP subject precedes the VP complement. Supplying the relevant values on these syntactic arguments as dictated by *should*'s SPR and COMPS values, we therefore can replace the ellipses in (98) with

(99)

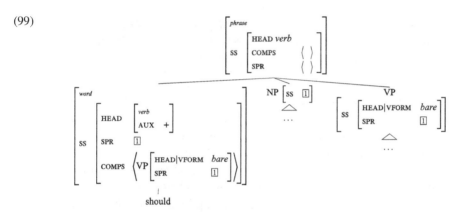

The VP complement of the auxiliary head will have exactly the same form as in any uninverted sentence in which it combines with *should* to form a constituent. Hence, if this VP has the form *have been paying more attention*, we will license both *Robin should have been paying more attention* and *Should Robin have been paying more attention?* with nothing more elaborate than the single additional rule schema in (95). No generalization about the parallels in constituent ordering or morphological marking are lost, and no rule which is qualitatively different from any of the other phrase structure schemata we have already introduced is required.

While space considerations preclude any kind of detailed discussion, it can easily be shown that (95) interacts with negation in a very simple way to yield the full range of data in which both inversion and negation are in evidence. The negation marker *not* must be exempted from the general word-before-phrase ordering requirement; with this one wrinkle, and the independently supported assumption that the *not* associated with sentential negation is an additional complement selected by auxiliaries, we can obtain the facts in (100) directly:

(100) a.   Shouldn't Robin have been paying more attention?

   b.   Should Robin not have been paying more attention?

   c.   *Should not Robin have been paying more attention?

We take neg-contracted forms such as *shouldn't* to be full lexical items, as discussed earlier. These will pattern in a fashion completely parallel to nonnegated forms of the auxiliaries, yielding (100)a. The example in (100)c will be ruled out by the ordering restriction that nonadjunct *not* always follows NP[ss ⬜] when it is a sister of V[SPR ⬜]. The case of (100)b is addressed in the following exercise.

Practice Exercise

Assume that one of every auxiliary's lexical entries specifies the negation marker *not* as a complement, in addition to the usual VP element on its COMPS list, with *not* an adverb bearing a MOD *nil* value.

i.   Write out the specific entry for *should* which would license *Robin should not have been paying more attention*.

ii.   Show, in step-by-step fashion along the lines shown for *Should Robin have been paying more attention* above how the inversion licensing based on (95) already given allows us to license (100)b.

There is one more refinement we need to make, however. As stated, (95) predicts that all auxiliaries undergo inversion. But this is not the case. Ellipsis and negation show that *better* is an auxiliary, but we do not have **Better you (not) do that?* parallel to *You better (not) do that*. A slightly more complex issue is raised by *ought*, which seems to come in two versions: an inverted kind, which for at least some speakers requires a bare complement (*Ought you (??*to) be so direct about this matter?*) and an uninverted kind requiring an infinitive (*You ought *(to) be more direct about this matter*). In both cases we find the need to control the invertibility of the auxiliary, but there is no mechanism available for us to do so at present.

   Two other considerations suggest that we need a way of separating out the auxiliaries which appear in inverted contexts from those which do not. We know of at least one instance in which an inverted form of an auxiliary has different morphosyntactic properties from its uninverted form. The contrast alluded to earlier in this chapter between **I aren't clever* and *Aren't I clever!* shows clearly that inversion is associated with an agreement possibility which is not available to the uninverted version of *aren't*, which means that we again need to keep track of lexical entries for inverted forms of auxiliaries as versus those which are not inverted. Finally, it has been noted in the semantics literature that inverted auxiliaries in some cases have a subtly different meaning from their uninverted counterparts: *We shall dance* is completely synonymous with (though stylistically marked as a bit 'tonier' than) *We will dance*, but *Shall we dance?* has what logicians call a *deontic* interpretation – conveying a sense of some kind of

moral requirement or, at least, desirability in terms of a shared set of criteria –
that *Will we dance?*, which simply invites a prediction, does not carry at all.
Here again, we need to distinguish the inverted from the uninverted version of
the auxiliary in order to accommodate the facts.

These various considerations jointly amount to a strong basis for positing a
feature, INV, which is specified as + only for a subset of auxiliaries, and as −
for all other verbs. Both *better* and the infinitive-seeking *ought* in the particular
group of English speakers mentioned earlier are specified as [INV −]; the version
aren't which is specified as [INV +] has agreement specifications (which we look
at in more detail in the following chapter) compatible with first person singular
subjects, and so on. The statement in (95) is therefore too strong; what we want
is the version in (101):

(101)   **Head-subject-complement Rule (final version)**

$$
\begin{bmatrix} phrase \\ SS \begin{bmatrix} COMPS & \langle \ \rangle \\ SPR & \langle \ \rangle \end{bmatrix} \end{bmatrix} \rightarrow \underbrace{\begin{bmatrix} word \\ AUX & + \\ INV & + \\ COMPS & \langle X_1,\ldots,X_n \rangle \\ SPR & \langle Y \rangle \end{bmatrix}}_{HEAD}, \underbrace{\begin{bmatrix} phrase \\ SS & Y \end{bmatrix}}_{SUBJ}, \underbrace{\begin{bmatrix} phrase \\ SS & X_1 \end{bmatrix},\ldots,\begin{bmatrix} phrase \\ SS & X_n \end{bmatrix}}_{COMPS}
$$

This formulation will correctly restrict the structures licensed by the rule to those
in which an auxiliary marked [INV −] in its SYNSEM attributes appears as the head
of the inverted clause.

3.6   What Comes Next?

The point of departure for this chapter was a set of facts about the
auxiliaries reflecting a particular pattern of dependency that was mysterious and
intractable in terms of pre-transformational approaches to syntax, but which
could be stated succinctly in terms of the far more powerful rule system
introduced by Chomsky in his work in the mid-1950s. Having shown that the
auxiliaries have distinctive distributional properties that warrant their traditional
identification as a unique subclass of lexical items, and having shown that the
auxiliaries are in every case verbs, we then considered a variety of evidence
which points to their appearance as heads of their own VPs. This review of the
data and arguments made it clear that the auxiliary system allows a consistently
right-branching structure, reflective of the selectional preferences of the different
subclasses of auxiliaries. Moreover, the headship of auxiliaries within their VP
allowed us to state their COMPS specifications in such a way that in each case
their VP complement reflects the correct morphology, which we implemented
via a new feature VFORM. The correspondence of verbal morphology with the

identity of a preceding auxiliary then emerges as a simple matter of valence specifications, in conjunction with the head/mother sharing information enforced by the Head Feature Principle motivated in Chapter 2 and stated in (58) in that chapter. As a bonus, we have shown that the linear order facts for auxiliaries fall out directly from the fact that in certain cases their morphological realization is incomplete, barring them from certain positions which demand selection on the basis of VFORM values which do not exist for them.

The auxiliaries thus demonstrate the remarkable effectiveness of the valence mechanism in enforcing the correlations between different parts of syntactic structure that come under the heading of 'dependencies.' It turns out that we can see many of these dependencies as nothing other than the satisfaction of lexically imposed valence requirements – just as in the case of the auxiliaries. In the next chapter, we'll extend our coverage to a number of other canonical dependencies in English, and show how in each case the data can be motivated completely on the basis of selectional requirements associated with specific classes of lexical items.

4   Local Dependencies and Lexical Rules

The auxiliary dependency analyzed in the preceding chapter takes the form of a complex network of distributional facts emerging as the consequence of a simple set of purely lexical properties. Both (i) the relative order of auxiliaries and so-called 'main verbs' (a notable misnomer, in our terms, since 'main verbs' in sentences with auxiliaries are actually deeply buried), and (ii) the morphology of clauses containing auxiliaries are due to the selectional properties of individual words, and the characteristic existence of gaps in the lexicon, along with a requirement that the top hierarchical level of English sentences be finite. Given these properties of individual words, the independently motivated feature-matching requirements of the grammar, as laid out in the preceding chapters, automatically yield the correct morphosyntactic dependencies with no more effort than is required to specify that *talk* requires a PP complement and *discuss* an NP. This demonstration offers strong support for the general approach taken so far, but it would be reassuring to find that there are other, unrelated phenomena which can be satisfactorily described using the same machinery. In this chapter, we briefly survey several grammatical patterns in English and a range of other languages which can be captured rather simply using the same technology already implemented in the auxiliary analysis presented in the preceding chapter.

4.1   Case and Agreement

4.1.1   Case

The first of these patterns, referred to as case, identifies a generally systematic marking of the dependents of a head which often correlates with what would be called grammatical relations (subject/object/indirect object/adjunct), but which typically have additional semantic content; thus we talk about 'dative' case, associated with a beneficiary role, corresponding to *Robin* in *I gave Robin a book* (although this case is not realized in the form of English words) in which the transfer of some benefit to the individual marked with dative morphology is conveyed (though dative case may show up in nonbenefactive contexts as well, as we'll see below), or the possessive, as in *Where is my book?*, where possession is conveyed by *my*. In some languages, such as English, case is vestigial; although its distant ancestor Anglo-Saxon had a rich case system,

reflecting the grammar of its own pan-Germanic ancestor and, ultimately, the
ancestral Indo-European proto-language, English has lost almost all vestiges of
this system. The only elements of English which bear morphological marking
for case are pronouns, for example, *I* vs *me*, and even here, the system is
evaporating; the relative and interrogative pronoun *whom*, corresponding to the
accusative *me/him, her/us/them*, is often replaced by *who*, which is also used for
the nominative form (corresponding to *I/(s)he/we/they*). In addition to these, we
find a third morphological form of pronoun which appears in expressions such
as *a friend of mine, that attitude of yours*, and so on, and which I will refer to
as the *genitive* case. This subclass of proforms has some interesting properties,
including its rather specific meaning, which invariably indicates possession.
Mine, yours, hers, ours, and *theirs* can in effect appear in the same set of contexts
as full possessive NPs such as *Robin's house, the King of England's crown*, and
so on, and overlaps in distribution with accusative pronouns:

$$(1) \qquad \text{I remember} \left\{ \begin{array}{c} \text{her} \\ \text{hers} \\ \text{*she} \end{array} \right\} \text{from the cat show last year.}$$

$$(2) \qquad \text{The judge argued with} \left\{ \begin{array}{c} \text{me} \\ \text{mine} \\ \text{*I} \end{array} \right\} \text{during the trial.}$$

$$(3) \qquad \text{What I can't imagine is} \left\{ \begin{array}{c} \text{them} \\ \text{theirs} \\ \text{*they} \end{array} \right\} \text{being on the best seller list for that long.}$$

In each instance, the genitive pronoun is interpreted with respect to some object
owned by or in some other way connected to an individual picked out by the
person/number/gender of the pronoun – perhaps a cat in (1), a lawyer in (2), a
novel in (3) – as part of the relevant context. What *cannot* appear in any of the
contexts in (1)–(3) is a nominative proform, as these examples make clear. There
is exactly one syntactic context in English in which we find *she, I,* and *they* – in
the subject position of a finite clause; in that context, accusative pronouns cannot
appear – but genitive pronouns can:

$$(4) \qquad \left\{ \begin{array}{c} \text{I} \\ \text{mine} \\ \text{*me} \end{array} \right\} \text{expects to do well on the exam.}$$

On the basis of these facts, we can sum up the evident distributional patterns
as follows: nominative pronouns appear always and only as finite subjects,
accusative pronouns always and only elsewhere, and genitive pronouns appear
freely everywhere. Formally, we can implement these patterns in various ways;
as it happens, there are certain advantages to the following formulation:

(5) i.   All signs of type *noun* are specified for a feature CASE, whose value in pronouns must be one of the following: *nom, acc, gen*.

ii.   An NP daughter satisfying the SPR specification of a finite verb must not be [CASE *acc*].

iii.   All other NP daughters must not be [CASE *nom*].

iv.   Nonpronouns are specified as [CASE *neut(ral)*].

The distribution specified in (5) is an extreme example of case which is structurally assigned. What matters in English is the configurational position occupied by a particular NP; the individual identity of the selecting head plays no role whatever. This total correlation of case value with structural position is far from universal; in many languages, case displayed on an NP is determined at least in part by the specific lexical item that selects that NP, a property of the grammar that, in parallel with English's structural case pattern, we may call lexical case.

An example of lexical case as extreme in its own way as the English structural case property is afforded by its fellow Germanic language Icelandic, where we encounter the following kinds of data:

(6)   Drengurinn   kyssti stuúlkana   í bílnum.
        the-boy(nom) kissed the-girl(acc) in the-car(dat)
        'The boy kissed the girl in the car.'

(7)   **Accusative subjects**

a.   Mig   langar að fara til Íslands.
     me(acc) long   to go to Iceland
     'I long to go to Iceland.'

b.   Bátinn   rak   á land.
     the-boat(acc) drifted to land
     'The boat drifted to land.'

c.   Hana   dreymdi um   hafið.
     her(acc) dreamed about the-sea
     'She dreamed about the sea.'

d.   Drengina   vantar mat
     the-boys(acc) lack   food(acc)
     'The boys lack food.'

(8)   **Dative subjects**

a.   Honum   mæltist vel í kirkjunni.
     him(dat) spoke   well in the-church
     'He spoke well in the church.'

b.   Mer   sýndist   álfur.
     me(dat) thought-saw elf(nom)
     'I thought I saw an elf.'

c.   Barninu   batnaði   veikin.
      the-child(dat) recovered-from the-disease(nom)
      'The child recovered from the disease.'

(9)   **Genitive subjects**

a.   Verkjanna   gætir   ekki.
      the-pains(gen) is-noticeable not
      'The pains are not noticeable.'

b.   Konungs   var þangað von.
      the-king(gen) was thither expectation(nom)
      'The king was expected there.'

These data, due to Avery Andrews (Andrews (1982)), make clear the irrelevance
of structural concerns to the determination of CASE values. As Andrews himself
notes, 'while there is a good deal of systematicity to case selection, there is
no invariant meaning that one can assign each case which will then provide
an explanation of its distribution. Rather, case selection is basically lexical and
idiosyncratic, but subject to regularities keyed to the semantics of its matrix verb'
(p. 464). The upshot of Andrews' detailed investigation of the case data is that
there is no way to avoid specifying, for any given verb, which respective values
of CASE appear on its various valents. We must therefore include case information
in the valence specification of each verb in the lexicon individually.

4.1.2   Agreement

A second local morphological kind of dependency abundantly exhibited in the world's languages is usually referred to as *agreement*, which refers
to systematic covariation between some aspect of some class of linguistic signs'
morphosyntactic properties and morphological marking elsewhere in the structure. English displays agreement phenomena, in two domains: the morphology
of finite verbs with respect to the person and number of their subjects, and of
determiners with respect to certain aspects of the nominal heads which select
them, often identified as number, though things seem to be a bit more complex
than this. The agreement pattern is in most respects far from regular: many verbs
display only a very restricted kind of morphological covariation with subjects,
and, as we've seen in the preceding chapter, the great majority of auxiliaries
exhibit no agreement morphology at all. The several auxiliary verbs which are
identified as *be* show a uniquely well-developed agreement pattern – *be* is the
one verb in English in which the first person singular is differentiated from the
second person singular and the plural forms (*am* vs *are*), and where number and
person are both taken into account in the past vs nonpast forms (*I/he/she/it was*
vs *you/we/they were*), although again the pattern is still somewhat idiosyncratic.
For all other verbs, apart from the invariant modals, the only difference in the
form of verbs which reflects person/number properties of the subject is that

which appears in the form of the nonpast third person singular, vs all other person/number combinations.

In the case of determiner/nominal agreement, the pattern is still more idiosyncratic. Some determiners show invariant form: *the/some/which*. These determiners are themselves neutral with respect to number; others only co-occur with morphologically singular (*a/each/every book(*s)* or plural (*all/most/few book*(s))* forms. Others show variation that is not entirely straightforward. Even as supposedly straightforward a case as the contrast between *this/that* vs *these/those* turns out to lead to nontrivial complexity when examined closely. The simple pattern in the table in (10) would naturally lead us to post the labeling given in the columns:

	Singular	**Plural**
Proximate	*this book*	*these books*
Distant	*that book*	*those books*

(10)

But a slightly wider range of data makes the singular/plural gloss at least appear somewhat problematic. Consider for example (11):

(11)   **That** [ₙ man and woman] **were** arguing at the top of their lungs.

If the *was/were* contrast signals singular vs plural number in the subject, then why do we see a singular determiner used in combination with a coordinate subject whose number, as reflected by the appearance of *were*, is plural? One possible approach would be to say that determiners are sensitive to purely grammatical registrations of plurality; that is, their plural forms only show up when some kind of morphological marking of plurality appears on the nominal expression that selects them, which is not the case in (11), since *man* and *woman* are both grammatically singular. Presumably, on this approach, the plural form *were* reflects the plural *meaning* of the phrase *man and woman*. But this initially plausible proposal is undercut by the fact that we must use *were*, and other plural forms of verbs, in contexts where there is semantic singularity but morphological plurality. Take, for example, the use of so-called 'singular *they*,' often seen in contexts where the speaker wishes to avoid assuming the gender of the person being spoken about. In (12), we see a simple example of this:

(12)   So if someone you've never seen before comes up to you and they start talking to you like they've known you all your life, you should be very suspicious!

Clearly only a single person is intended here. Interestingly, however, the plural form of verb agreement appears on verbs taking such singular-intended plurals as subject:

(13)   I was talking with someone at my office yesterday and they were all worried about the takeover rumors we've been hearing.

Similarly, when the Queen of England's appointments secretary tells her, 'Your Majesty is due to meet with a delegation from a veteran's charitable trust tomorrow afternoon,' rather than 'Your majesty are due to meet...' – in spite of the fact that 'Your Majesty,' the required formula for the monarch, in this case refers to the hearer (second person singular, which requires the *are* form) – the agreement pattern again reflects the grammatical (i.e., third person singular) rather than semantic properties of the subject. So the idea that determiners are sensitive to morphological form but verbs reflect meaning seems difficult to sustain, at least in that relatively coarse-grained formulation.

Another, quite different approach is to assume that the phrase *that man and women* as we pronounce it is a kind of disguised version of a coordination of two NPs *that man* and *that woman*, so that (11) corresponds to a grammatical (as opposed to phonological) expression *That man and ~~that~~ woman were arguing at the top of their lungs*, where the pronunciation of the second *that* is suppressed. This suggestion has been made in the literature, and a general mechanism relating syntactic to prosodic form has been invoked to implement it, but this proposal is, again, untenable, because of examples such as (14):

(14)   That mutually incompatible man and woman were arguing at the top of their lungs.

To license this example on the deletion account just sketched, the grammatical representation of the sentence would have to be, very roughly,

(15)   That mutually incompatible man and ~~that mutually incompatible~~ woman were arguing at the top of their lungs.

But this makes no sense at all: the meaning of *mutually incompatible* is such that there is no interpretation for NPs such as *that mutually incompatible man*. This solution, then, achieves consistency in the treatment of *that* in terms of singular agreement at the cost of forfeiting any kind of plausible semantic interpretation for cases such as (14).

English then is perhaps not a particularly good example of how agreement works as a core part of grammar. But many other languages exhibit much richer, more far-reaching and grammatically more regular agreement systems. We find several subsystems of agreement in French which the grammatical machinery already introduced allows us to capture fairly straightforwardly.

The sentence in (16) is a good illustration of the multiple instances of agreement we frequently observe in French data:

(16)   Ces   petites   chiennes   grises   sont   bruyantes.
        Det-pl small(fem)-pl dogs(fem)-pl grey(fem)-pl be(3rd/pl) noisy(fem)-pl
        'These small grey she-dogs are noisy.'

Every word in this sentence shows agreement for at least number, and most of them mark gender agreement as well. The forms that show agreement are the determiner, the noun head, the verb, and the adjectives, which are of two kinds: adjuncts to the head (*petites* and *grises*) and the complement (*bruyantes*) of the verb (*sont*). While the relationships among the determiner, adjuncts, and noun head and between the NP *ces petites chiennes grise* and the verb (*sont*) are completely local, the relationship between the predicate adjective *bruyantes* and the head of the NP *chiennes* appears structurally far more indirect.

To capture this pattern, we need to take into account possibly its most striking feature: the formal parallel of number and gender throughout (16). This is certainly reflected in the orthography, at least, but in at least certain aspects of the pronunciation as well. Thus, *chien* identifying a dog whose gender is not specified (and which is morphologically treated as male) is pronounced [šʲɛ̃], but *chiennes*, 'female dog', is [šʲɛn]. And the presence of the 'covert' plural marker *-s* in French will likely be revealed by so-called liaison phenomena in the speech of at least some native speakers of French when texts are read aloud; thus, *les chiennes ont aboyé* 'The female dogs barked' may be pronounced with an overt [s]. The specific signature for number (final *-s*, at least potentially realizable phonetically in particular contexts), appears in every word in (16), and feminine gender (preservation of a final obstruant which is lost in the masculine forms) on the noun head, adjunct modifiers, and the predicate adjective. Agreement in this component of French grammar takes the form of multiple copies of the same morphological marking (and hence parallel realizations in pronunciation) on nominal heads, their adjuncts and specifier valents, and on at least adjectival predicates which select the phrases projected from these heads. This generalization holds for both gender and number: while the plural determiner *ces* displays only number agreement, the corresponding singular displays a regular gender contrast: *ce chat* 'this cat' but *cette souris* 'this mouse,' where *souris* is one of the animal names in French whose default gender is female.

We must therefore ensure that the items in agreement share a value for some morphosyntactic attribute that will be 'read' by whatever part of the grammar maps such values into phonological form. Suppose we call the attribute in question AGR, evidently a HEAD feature since the relevant properties of the lexical head are visible to predicates for which the NP projected from that head is a valent. Then our framework must guarantee that all of the words in (16) share the value for AGR given in (17):

(17)

$$
\left[
\text{AGR} \quad
\begin{bmatrix}
\text{PER(SON)} & 3 \\
\text{NUM(BER)} & plu \\
\text{GEN(DER)} & fem
\end{bmatrix}
\right]
$$

In order to distribute this specification to the constituents implicated in the agreement pattern, we need to impose the following restrictions on nominal heads and their adjuncts:

(18)

$$
\left[\text{SS} \left[\begin{array}{ll} \text{HEAD} & \left[\begin{array}{ll} \textit{noun} \\ \text{AGR} & \boxed{1} \end{array} \right] \\ \text{SPR} & \left\langle \boxed{2} \right\rangle \end{array} \right] \right] \supset \boxed{2} \left[\text{AGR} \quad \boxed{1} \right]
$$

$$
\left[\text{SS} \; \boxed{2} \left[\text{MOD|HEAD} \left[\begin{array}{ll} \textit{noun} \\ \text{AGR} & \boxed{1} \end{array} \right] \right] \right] \supset \boxed{2} \left[\text{AGR} \quad \boxed{1} \right]
$$

$$
\left[\text{SS} \; \boxed{2} \left[\text{SUBJ} \left\langle \left[\text{HEAD} \left[\begin{array}{ll} \textit{noun} \\ \text{AGR} & \boxed{1} \end{array} \right] \right] \right\rangle \right] \right] \supset \boxed{2} \left[\text{AGR} \quad \boxed{1} \right]
$$

The first of these constraints imposes on the selecting head the restriction that its specifier valent must be required to mirror the head's own AGR value. The second demands of adjuncts that they share the AGR specification of their modification target. The third is the most interesting, for it shows how the sharing of AGR specifications can propagate, in a strictly local way, over nonlocal syntactic domains. To keep the presentation as simple as possible, the following somewhat schematic tree is offered to display the way AGR information is connected in cases such as (16).

(19)

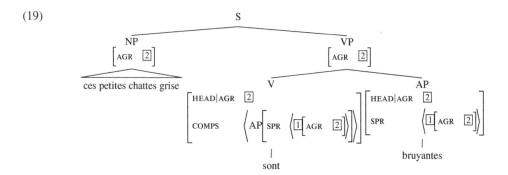

The third of the constraints stated in (18), in conjunction with independent properties of the copula auxiliary, forces all the feature identities marked by the appearance of the tag $\boxed{1}$. Starting at the bottom of the tree, this constraint requires that the predicate adjective, which specifies an NP subject with a particular AGR value, must carry that same AGR value. The third person plural form of the copula *être*, like other auxiliaries in French, identifies its own SUBJ with that of its complement; therefore it too must, by the third condition in (18), display the same AGR value as does *bruyantes*. The SPR value of *sont* is shared with its mother VP along the same lines as in English, as per the operation of the French analogue of the rule schemata system given in Chapter 2; and as a consquence, a subject NP must be present in the structure which displays the AGR value required, ultimately, by *bruyantes*. We could, of course, have proceeded in the other direction, noting the AGR value of the subject and tracing its sharing downward until the licensing bottomed out in the identification of the SPR value of *bruyantes* with that of *sont* and the consequent requirement that the predicate adjective display the same agreement properties as *sont*'s subject. As always, the directionality has no significance of its own; the essential point is that the constraint setup in (18) ensures the crucial identifications in (19), as well as those within the subject NP itself.

Case and agreement are both tremendously various, often extremely complex domains which in fact interact with each other (one familiar form of agreement is case agreement, widespread in the grammar of Latin and many other case languages). The foregoing is just a brief introduction to these topics and how one might approach them using the analytic tools already developed.

4.2   Passive

4.2.1   The Basic Cases

The passive is one of the three 'classic' phenomena on which Noam Chomsky (Chomsky (1957)) built his arguments for a particular view of linguistics in his watershed volume, *Syntactic Structures*. The burden of his argument was that in each of the cases he discussed – English auxiliaries, the passive construction, and coordination – there were significant generalizations to be captured which were beyond the reach of syntactic mechanisms available at that time, and that far more powerful devices were needed in linguistics in order to account in an economical fashion for the patterns in the data that he had called attention to. Much has changed since then, and while the first of Chomsky's claims may have been true, it has been recognized for roughly the past thirty years that the second is *not*. As we shall see directly, the formal setup we've used to this point is more than up to the task of handling the passive data in a way which captures all the generalizations that Chomsky adduced – *and more* – with no actual extension of the power of the grammar, and none of the eccentric properties of the syntax in *Syntactic Structures* in order to get the specific proposal for passives to go through.

We begin with a review of the basic data. As (20) shows, we find systematic relationships between sentences in which there is a normal transitive verb with a direct object and sentences whose subject corresponds to the direct object of the first type of sentence.

(20) a.   Rocco noticed the error.
    b.   The error was noticed (by Robin).

(21) a.   Rocco gave a book to Melinda.
    b.   A book was given to Melinda (by Rocco).

(22) a.   Rocco gave Melinda a book.

   b.   The announcer told us that the sky was falling.

   c.   The audience expected Luanne to avoid certain subjects.

   d.   The police suspected Rocco of forgery.

   e.   The police suspected Rocco knew about the forgery.

(23) a.   Melinda was given a book (by Rocco).

   b.   We were told that the sky was falling (by the announcer).

   c.   Luanne was expected to avoid certain subjects (by the audience).

   d.   Rocco was suspected of forgery (by the police).

   e.   *Rocco was suspected knew about the forgery (by the police).

We see here a very general pattern: if we have a nonpassive form of the sentence where a verb takes a set of sisters (corresponding, of course, to its COMPS specifications) and a subject, it will be matched in every case by a form of the verb with characteristic passive morphology which projects a VP taking, as its subject, the element which was the highest-ranked element on the nonpassive verb's COMPS list, and with its passive head combining with all of the other elements on the nonpassive head's COMPS list. In effect, to get the passive form of the verb, we find the highest-ranked COMPS element on some nonpassive form of the verb, shift it to the SPR valence list (where it replaces the nonpassive subject description on the list), and leave all the other COMPS elements as they were.

Formulating things in this way immediately accounts for the seeming anomaly presented by (22)e/(23)e. In all of the (22) examples, the verb is immediately followed by an NP, and in every case, there is a passive analogue in which this NP appears as the subject. What's wrong with (22)e, where this pattern breaks down? The answer, in terms of what's just been said, is straightforward: in all of the cases where there is a passive analogue to the 'active' form, the NP which appears as subject represents a valence element for the nonpassive form of the verb. But in (22)e, that's not the case: the NP directly following *suspected* is not a valence element of the verb, but rather part of a separate clause – an internal sentence. We can see this by a variety of tests, including the so-called Heavy NP shift test, which allows phonologically complex NPs (notated in what follows as $NP^{\perp}$) to appear after phrases that they normally precede, for example, *I gave to Rocco *presents* vs I gave to Rocco [a collection of rare and intricate wooden puzzles from Indonesia]$^{\perp}$. Note that this test also gives positive results in the case of *I expected to be arrested [every one of those so-called Tolstoy scholars who were clearly foreign operatives in disguise]$^{\perp}$, but cannot apply to finite subjects (*I know (that) likes cats [the hereditary heir to the Ostrogoth throne]$^{\perp}$) – and it cannot apply in the case of (22)e (*The police suspected [knew about the forgery the hereditary King of Ostrogothia]$^{\perp}$). If the passive pattern applies only to valents of a nonpassive verb, then it is to be expected that (22)e should have no passive correspondent, and as (23)e shows, that expectation is correct.

Notice that this perspective implies a relationship between the active and passive sentences determined not by a deformation of the structure assigned to the first into that assigned to the second, but rather by a systematic relationship between nonpassive and passive verbal heads from which, respectively, active and passive sentences are projected by application of the licensing principles of the grammar. We must now state the nature of the nonpassive/passive verb relationship in a way which yields the data we've already seen as consequences. In particular, we need to ensure that a passive version of the verb is available *just in case* the verb in question has a NP as its highest ranking COMPS specification. Interestingly, even a PP which seems to be nothing more than an NP with a preposition serving as a kind of case marker, such as *at Robin*, does not manifest a passive form:

(24) a.   Everyone looked coldly at Robin.

  b.   *At Robin was looked (coldly) (by everyone).

Compare this example with *Everyone regarded Robin coldly/Robin was regarded coldly (by everyone)*.

It was this dependency of the passive on the existence of a nominal object for the corresponding nonpassive that was the heart of Chomsky's case in 1957 that a very powerful new kind of rule was needed to literally alter the structure of active sentences into one that supported the form of passive sentences. But was such a move really necessary?

Given the primitive theoretical resources available at the time, where the only formal models of grammars available were virtual automata – mathematical objects which generated strings of symbols one at a time, with a change of state in the object each time a symbol was generated – it's probably the case that there was no good alternative to the rule-system analogues of such models. That limitation is now at least two generations out of date: the introduction of a lexicon in syntactic theory in Chomsky's 1965 monograph *Aspects of the Theory of Syntax* made the earlier, automaton-based models obsolete in a foundational way. But it would be another decade and a half before the resources of the lexicon were effectively exploited to produce an empirically competitive and fully explicit alternative which did not require the excessive power built into that model. One culmination of that alternative approach might be seen to be the following rule, which captures exactly the relationship between nonpassive and passive verbs that we have been considering:

(25)

$$
\begin{bmatrix} \text{HEAD} & \begin{bmatrix} verb \\ \text{VFORM} & \neg passive \end{bmatrix} \\ \text{SUBJ} & \langle \text{NP} \rangle \\ \text{COMPS} & \langle \boxed{1}\,\text{NP} \rangle \oplus \boxed{2} \end{bmatrix} \supset \begin{bmatrix} \text{HEAD}|\text{VFORM} & passive \\ \text{SUBJ} & \langle \boxed{1}\,\text{NP} \rangle \\ \text{COMPS} & \langle \boxed{2} \rangle \oplus \langle (\text{PP}[\text{PFORM } by]) \rangle \end{bmatrix}
$$

This statement is given in the form of a logical implication, and that's exactly what is intended. Implications – logical statements of the form $\varphi \supset \psi$ – are false if and only if φ is true but ψ does not hold. The licensing mechanisms introduced in previous chapters are, in effect, the inference rules of a kind of logic whose notion of validity is interpreted not in terms of truth values, as in classical logic (and its variants), but rather in terms of structural well-formedness. The example in (25) introduces a new VFORM value *passive* – a feature specification justified by the fact that the passive has its own characteristic morphology, although one that it happens to share with the perfective (so we have, for example, *John had baked a cake/The cake was baked by John; Mary had broken the window/The window was broken by Mary; The twins had sung that song/That song was sung by the twins*, and so on). What (25) says is that, for any object that meets the partial description on the left-hand side of the implication operator, there is an object that meets the right-hand side description. Given that we have a verb meeting the description in (26)a, then, we are guaranteed to find a verb meeting the description in (26)b (where $\oplus$ denotes an operator which combines two lists so that the members of the second list follow the members of the first in the combined list, which preserves the original list ordering; for example, $\langle a, b, c \rangle \oplus \langle e, f, g \rangle = \langle a, b, c, d, e, f, g \rangle$):

In the case of verbs with a nonempty COMPS list $\boxed{2}$, the COMPS list of the passive will take the form of the list obtained by combining $\boxed{2}$ with the optional *by*-PP.

Problems

1.   The pattern in (27) is quite widespread in English:

(27) a.   This bed was slept in by George Washington.
     b.   Rocco has been spoken to by the management.

- What are the implications of such data, in view of the proposed solution in (25)?
- Can you think of a solution? Describe your idea informally but carefully.

2.   Use the machinery developed to this point to account for the pattern in (28)–(29) (where % in (28)d identifies the example as being well-formed in the grammars of a certain speech variety of English).

(28) a.   Rocco **was** arrested (by the police).
     b.   Rocco **got** caught (by the police).
     c.   Chris saw Rocco arrested (by the police).
     d.   %This statement **needs** investigated (by the police).

(29) a.   *Rocco didn't intend arrested (by the police).
b.   *Chris feared arrested (by the police).
c.   *Pat avoided arrested (by the police).

4.2.2   Passive Imposters

The data in (30) appear at first glance to be nothing more than another instance of the passive relationship discussed in the preceding section:

(30) a.   The reports horrified Rocco.
b.   Rocco was horrified by the reports.

Given the lexical specification required for (30)a, we predict, on the basis of (25), that (30)b will be well-formed.

Practice Exercise

Write out a lexical entry for *horrified* on the basis of (30)a and show that (1) does indeed allow us to license (30)b.) But the failure of (31)b is a big hint that something else may be going on here.

(31) a.   I was very horrified by his way of talking.
b.   *His way of talking very horrified me.

The contrast between (30) and (31) is not an isolated, idiosyncratic phenomenon, as we see from (32)–(33):

(32) a.   I wasn't too horrified by what I heard.
b.   *What I heard didn't too horrify me.

(33) a.   I was most alarmed (by his views).
b.   *His views most alarmed me.

In the case of (33)a, there is no need for the context in which the sentence is uttered to contain anything *else* that alarmed the speaker, as would be the case if *most* were being used in an actual comparison; in this case, however, a reasonable alternative phrasing which preserves the particular sense of *most* as used here would be *I learned his views, and was most alarmed*, with stress falling most heavily on the second syllable of *alarmed*. *Very*, *too*, and *most* are often referred to as degree adverbs, but interestingly, as the data just given illustrates, they do not seem to be able to modify VPs. What these degree adjuncts modify are *adjectives*:

(34)   Rocco was $\left\{ \begin{array}{c} \text{very} \\ \text{too} \\ \text{most} \end{array} \right\} \left\{ \begin{array}{c} \text{agreeable} \\ \text{enthusiastic} \\ \text{attentive} \end{array} \right\}$.

And since adjectives cannot combine directly with subjects, and are not selected as complements of auxiliaries other than various forms of *be*, it makes sense that if the words *horrified* and *alarmed* which appear in (32)–(33) are adjectives (as they must be, in order to combine with these degree modifiers), the resulting forms, which do involve such forbidden combinations, will be ruled out, just as *His views (most) agreeable me* and *She (very) enthusiastic Rocco* are ruled out. The only difference between these last examples and those involving *horrified/alarmed* and the like is that the former don't look even a little bit like actual verbs, so we don't find it at all surprising that obvious adjectives, appearing in exclusively verbal environments, yield bad judgments. The problem thus becomes one of identifying how it is that items which look like passive participles wind up leading a double life as adjectives in addition. Strictly speaking, this question is one that doesn't belong to syntax proper, and it's one that most syntacticians would probably prefer to leave to morphologists, the linguists who study the restrictions that determine the form of words. But roughly speaking, we can identify the relationship between passive verbs and corresponding adjectives as belonging to a general class of correspondences labeled *zero derivation*, in which a word which originates as one part of speech winds up being 'recruited' to a different lexical category in addition, with no evident change in form. The word *telegraph* originated as a noun at the end of the eighteenth century; in the following decade, it began to be used, unchanged, as a verb. Similarly, the word *referee* began as a noun in the early 1600s, but acquired its verbal identity late in the nineteenth century. The process works in the other direction as well; thus the verb *disconnect* seems to have become a noun in certain varieties of late twentieth-century English; *comic*, an old adjective, became a noun referring to a story presented in cartoon form at the end of the nineteenth century. This last case is interesting, in that the *ic* ending on *comic* seems to establish its identity as an adjective quite clearly – compare *nomad/nomadic*, *Iceland/Icelandic*, *myth/mythic* – yet there is no difficulty at all in reassigning this overtly adjectival form to the nominal category. Something similar appears to have happened with the passive, but on a wholesale basis: any passive form appears to be at least eligible to serve as an adjective (though not all possibilities are realized: *Rocco kicked the wall* but *??*The kicked wall looked unstable*).

Once a form has passed through the zero-derivation process, it will very likely undergo further morphological operations which clearly separate it from its category of origin. Consider the pair *Rocco's skill impressed the audience/The audience was very impressed by Rocco's skill*. As we've already seen, the appearance of *very* clearly announces that we're dealing with an adjective, not a verb, and therefore it's not surprising to find data such as *His energetic tunes had the impressed audience smiling.* (www.okgazette.com/oklahoma/tag-0-1-The%20Rural%20Alberta%20Adva.html). But since *impress* is an adjective, it can enter into morphological relationships that are available only to the latter.

There is a prefix *un* in English, for example, which contributes negation to the meaning of any adjective it combines with; for example, if *happy* is taken to denote a certain set of people who satisfy a particular set of semantic criteria, then, roughly speaking, the meaning of *unhappy* is everyone who *isn't* in that set. Thus if *Rocco is happy* is true, then *Rocco is unhappy* cannot be. This is a different suffix from the *un* in *untied* as in *Rocco untied the knot*, which means in effect that Rocco reversed the effect of the action of tying, not that Rocco didn't tie the knot. When we add the adjectival *un* to *impressed*, we get something which means, 'not [, impressed].' As it happens, the meaning of the verb *impress* is not one which can combine with the verbal *un* prefix just mentioned, so when we see the word *unimpressed*, it *has* to be the adjective. And that, of course, means that it cannot take a direct object NP. Therefore, we predict that **Rocco unimpressed me* will be ill-formed, and it is for exactly the same reasons that **Rocco unhappy me* is bad.

But this result in turn leads us to look at the *by* PP following *unimpressed* in a rather different light than we might have if we had restricted our view of such PPs to their association with the passives. It may be true that a *by* phrase associated with a passive is the only way that the 'agent' involved in the meaning of the passive clause can be expressed within the passive VP, but that doesn't mean that the passive is the only context where *by* + NP expresses agency. So consider, for example,

(35) a.   This concerto is by Vivaldi.

    b.   We convinced her by reverse psychology.

By in both cases seems to associate the existence of some object or the accomplishment of some event with the key involvement of whatever it is that the NP following *by* refers to. No passive is involved in either of these somewhat different instances. In the case of (35)a, the *by* PP is a complement of the copula, while in (35)b it can easily be shown to be an adjunct, but the core meaning it contributes, either as a logical argument or as a modifier, is at an abstract level essentially the same. The illusion in cases such as (30) that all we have is a simple passive is thus jointly created by (i) the zero-derivation process, which takes passive verb forms and in effect relabels them as adjectives, and (ii) the very general use of *by* PPs to express notions related to both agency and instrumentality – which is clearly related to agency, since doing something always presupposes some *means* of doing whatever it is that gets done.

There is an interesting and important consequence of this independence of the *by* PP from the passive: in the case of adjectives, it is quite possible that some other kind of PP can appear instead of the *by* PP to convey a similar meaning. This possibility is in effect a prediction of the analysis just given, and it certainly appears to be borne out:

(36) a.   Rocco appeared (very) impressed by all the pageantry.

    b.   Luanne appeared (too) impressed with all the pageantry.

c.   Duo was most unimpressed at the lack of attention he was getting. (www.google.com/#hl=en&output=search&sclient=psy-ab&q=%22most+ unimpressed+at+the%22&oq=%22most+unimpressed+at+the%22&gs_ l=hp.3..0i8i13i30.905.9901.0.10246.25.25.0.0.0.0.166.1758.23j2.25.0... 0.0...1c.9QIJCO-QRl0&pbx=1&bav=on.2,or.r_gc.r_pw.r_qf.,cf.osb&fp= b972a8d259da1dbf&biw=1309&bih=768)

Compare these data with:

(37) a.   Rocco was happy with all the pageantry.

b.   I feel so happy $\left\{ \begin{array}{c} \text{at} \\ \text{*by} \end{array} \right\}$ the effect it has on them as a person. (www .paddymcgurganartist.com/xml/biography.xml)

c.   *Melinda was happy by the pageantry/effect/thought/....

Other examples of adjectives appearing with *at* but not *by* include *sad, aghast, apoplectic, despondent, sick, angry, furious.*

Observant readers will have noticed an interesting morphological property of this last group of adjectives: none of them looks like a passive participle. As a rule, *by* is only available as a complement to adjectives when these are associated with passives by zero derivation. This distributional pattern suggests that in general, adjectives do not take *by* PP complements, but that the particular rule of the morphology which maps passive verb forms to adjectives preserves the complement structure of the 'source' passives, which will include the possible *by* phrase. The details are complex, and in any case not of immediate concern to us; the takeaway message from the preceding discussion is rather that one must be very careful in testing structures whose analysis is at first glance quite well-established, in order to avoid getting misled by the fact that some other, quite different structure is masquerading as the familiar, 'obvious' one – a point we've already encountered repeatedly in earlier chapters.

Problems

What can we conclude about the syntactic category of complements to *become*, *grow*, and *seem*, based on the following data? State your reasoning explicitly.

(38) a.   Rocco became alarmed by subsequent developments.
b.   Luanne became alarmed at subsequent developments.
c.   Sue became less alarmed $\left\{ \begin{array}{c} \text{by} \\ \text{at} \end{array} \right\}$ subsequent developments.
d.   *Terrence became struck by lightning.
e.   *Anne seemed more struck by lightning than Terrence.

(39) a.   Rocco preached to an (un)impressed congregation.
b.   Bill tried to comfort several alarmed shareholders.

4.3   Infinitival Complements

Another point which the discussion of passives raises forcefully is that the simplest, most straightforward account of some linguistic pattern – the one that we would on general methodological grounds take to be in some sense optimal, covering the maximum range of data with minimum special-purpose machinery – may have far-reaching consequences that we must be prepared to live with and accept as part of our framework. Suppose we look a bit more closely at (22)c–(23)c in the context of our passivization lexical rule. On the face of it, (22)c could have two different analyses, one in which *Luanne to avoid certain subjects* is a sequence of NP and an infinitive VP which does not form a constituent, and one in which this string is indeed a clause, consisting of a subject NP and an infinitive VP. We have reason in advance to suppose that the second analysis is at least possible; consider, for example, the following data:

(40) a.   What I don't expect is you to roll over at the first challenge and alter your world view. www.jonarcher.com/2010_02_01_archive.html

    b.   What I don't want is you to tell me that there should be a law preventing me from drinking on my boat when I'm anchored in a cove for the weekend. www.thehulltruth.com/boating-forum/356794-bui-while-anchored-its-happening-5.html#b

    c.   Even though we've struggled of late and winning is important, what I expect is us to play the game right. www.utsports.com/sports/m-basebl/recaps/051413aaa.html

The construction exemplified in these two examples, the so called *pseudocleft* construction, has already been mentioned as a robust constituency test: the material appearing after the copula in pseudoclefts – the so-called *focal* position – is necessarily a phrasal constituent, and it follows that the NP + infinitival VP sequences which occur in these examples are therefore constituents, to which it's difficult to justify assigning any category but S. So the idea of an infinitival clausal constituent can hardly be controversial at this point. But one might suppose that unlike the case of *that Rocco talks like that* – where we have excellent reason to believe that the complementizer is associated with a clausal constituent *Rocco talks like that* – the structure of the infinitival clause here is something like $[_s \ [_C \textit{for}] \ [_{NP} \textit{Rocco}] \ [_{VP} \textit{to talk like that}]]$, where the clause branches into three daughters with no 'internal' clause *Rocco to talk like that*. This position has in fact been maintained by certain analysts, on the grounds that while the sentences in (41), where the adjunct modifier directly follows an uncontroversial complementizer, are clearly good, the examples in (42), in which these modifiers follow *for*, are ill-formed:

(41) a.   Mary asked me if, in St. Louis, John could rent a house cheap.

    b.   He doesn't intend that, in these circumstances, we be rehired.

(42) a.   *Mary arranged for, in St. Louis, John to rent a house cheap.

   b.   *He doesn't intend for, in these circumstances, us to be rehired.

   (Ginzburg and Sag 2000: 47)

These examples are intended to demonstrate a divergence in behavior between
NP and finite VP strings (which as a sentential constituent can be modified by a
clausal adjunct) and NP and nonfinite VP strings, which cannot be; the idea is
that if NP VP[*inf*] do not form a clause, then the facts in (42) are automatically
explained, which wouldn't be the case if NP VP[*inf*] had clausal status. But the
examples in (42) are irrelevant in this context, because we already have excellent
evidence from (40) not only that NP VP[*inf*] strings are indeed constituents,
but also that such clausal constituents, even in contexts where their status as
infinitival sentences is indisputable, are incompatible with the kinds of adjuncts
displayed in (41)–(42):

(43) a.   *What I expect is in these circumstances us to play the game right.

   b.   *What I want is down the line us to be rehired.

Whatever the explanation for these effects, the problem is clearly independent of
the clausal status of NP VP[*inf*] sequences in English.

   We therefore have no reason to avoid positing a structure [, *Luanne* [, *to avoid
certain subjects*]], as in (44)a:

(44) a.

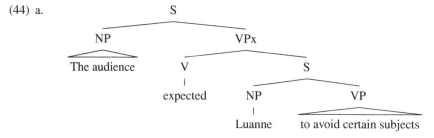

But the structure in (44)a is also certainly a candidate – after all, we know that
there are VPs of the form V NP NP, V NP PP, V NP AP (*Rocco drank the bottle
dry*), so there would be nothing surprising about a fourth sequence in which the
major phrasal category type VP followed NP, completing the pattern.

(44) b.

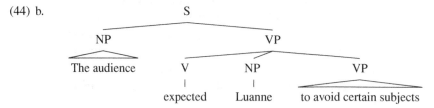

Is there any way to choose between these two candidate structures? One
possibility is afforded by the existence of sentences such as (45)a, which for
many speakers is a possible, and even preferred, variant of (45)b.

(45) a.   I believe to be still unresolved at least *some* of the major hurdles that have
           derailed negotiations at previous peace conferences.

     b.   I believe at least *some* of the major hurdles that have derailed negotiations
           at previous peace conferences to be still unresolved .

When one has a VP of the form V NP XP, and the NP is very long, and/or
complex – what is often referred to as 'heavy' in the syntactic literature – the
sequence V XP NP is often used instead of the more normal order, a move which
appears to yield an easier target for real-time sentence-processing requirements.
But such reorderings are not possible between a subject and its VP. So, for
example, note the contrasting pattern in (46):

(46) a.   I believe (that) at least *some* of the major hurdles that have derailed
           negotiations at previous peace conferences are still unresolved.

     b.   *I believe (that) are still unresolved at least *some* of the major hurdles that
           have derailed negotiations at previous peace conferences.

It appears, then, that this reordering of heavy NPs with respect to following
material, as in (45), is unavailable when the NP is a subject, which would of
course be a decisive argument in favor of (44)b. But the reader should not
concede the point just yet; after all, possibly the contrast here reflects nothing
more than a difference available to NP subjects of nonfinite clauses, but not to
finite subjects. Again, at the moment, we have no completely secure reason to
favor one or the other analysis.

What would lead us to feel at least reasonably confident in choosing between
these two possibilities? The reader should try to formulate an answer to this
question before going further. Given the specificity of the 'escape hatch'
possibility raised in the previous paragraph, it should be easy to at least envision
a certain class of data which would strongly support one or the other of the
positions on heavy NP rearrangements in finite as vs infinitive clauses.

(47) a.   *What I don't expect is [$_s$ __to roll over at the first challenge [**any of the
           many people I know who are capable of doing this job.**]]

     b.   *What I don't want is [$_s$ __to criticize me a [**lot of killjoy busybodies with
           too much time on their hands.**]]

Here the underlines mark the place where the 'shifted' heavy NPs would
normally occur. All such examples are consistently bad, however – an outcome
strongly supporting the view that Heavy Shift possibilities favoring infinitive
over finite syntactic environments are not a credible solution for the contrast
between (45) and (46).

The conclusion just reached thus directly leads to an analysis favoring (44)b,
with a sequence V NP VP, straightforwardly permitting heavy NP shift to occur.
In short, the NP in these kinds of infinitival construction is not a syntactic subject,
but rather an object complement of the head *expect, believe* etc.

As it happens, this is exactly the result we would expect if our approach to
passives, summarized in (25), is correct. The key point here is that in order to

relate an active V to a passive V, we must be able to identify the subject of the latter with an element selected by the former – that is, a complement. But if (44)a were the right analysis, then the passive rule would not be able to apply to any form of *expect* whose highest-ranking COMPS element was NP, because *expect* would be selecting an S, not an NP and a VP. Given that our independent tests lead us to prefer (44)b, we are also committed to the availability of a passive version of *expect* whose subject corresponds to the NP following the active version, and that is just what we find.

Problem

If we assume that passive sentences arise from a structural alteration of a configuration corresponding to an active sentence, what is the difficulty that (48) presents?

(48)   Rocco was said to be a spy/*They said Rocco to be a spy.

Does (48) present the same difficulty for an approach in which a rule along the lines of (25) guarantees that if a nonpassive verb takes an NP complement and other material, then there is a passive version of the verb which takes that other material plus possibly a *by* phrase as complements? Explain carefully what is and is not entailed by the account summarized in (25) that differentiates it from the treatment in which passive structures must come from the rearrangement of nonpassive structures.

We conclude this discussion of the passive by noting that the rule in (25) is a bit too narrow in its predictions. Passive verbs display not only NP subjects but entire clauses as well:

(49) a.   Most people $\left\{ \begin{array}{l} \text{knew} \\ \text{suspected} \\ \text{doubted} \end{array} \right\}$ that Rocco was a spy.

   b.   That Rocco was a spy was $\left\{ \begin{array}{l} \text{known} \\ \text{suspected} \\ \text{doubted} \end{array} \right\}$ (by most people).

The distribution of clausal passive subjects is somewhat complex; the passive of the verb *believe*, for example, supports sentential subjects, while the passive of the verb of judgment *hold* does not:

(50) a.   I $\left\{ \begin{array}{l} \text{hold} \\ \text{believe} \end{array} \right\}$ that Rocco has suffered enough, and is to be released from custody.

   b.   That Rocco had suffered enough was widely $\left\{ \begin{array}{l} \text{believed} \\ \text{??*held} \end{array} \right\}$.

Similar facts hold for cases such as, *know* vs *consider* (as in *I consider that Rocco has suffered enough*), *decree* vs *judge* (as in *I judge that Rocco has suffered enough*), and *assert* vs *insist*. In all these cases, the first of the contrasting pair of verbs has an alternate valence seeking an NP complement, whereas the second does not. This kind of fact has led some analysts to suppose that something much more complex than a simple extension of the rule in (25) is involved in cases such as (49); such cases are widely taken to reflect, rather, an ordinary passive construction in which certain extra grammatical possibilities give rise to a kind of disguised version of the passive in which it incorrectly appears that the *that* clause is the subject. On this account, the alleged fact that clauses cannot appear as passive subjects unless the passive verb has a nonpassive counterpart which can take an NP direct object is exactly what we would expect: in cases like the *believe* example in (50), only verbs which take a nominal direct object have passive forms which select clausal complements, because under one or another scenario, what they actually have is a covert NP subject that a *that* clause is somehow linked to. The analysis is complex, but the upshot is the claim that what appear to be clausal subjects are actually clauses appearing in fronted position – essentially, where the displaced material in topicalization appears, typically referred to topic position – before a subject NP which is either prosodically empty or simply missing; e.g., for *That Rocco showed up pleased us* we would have the representation in (51).

(51)

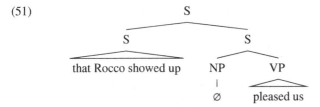

In cases such as (49)b, ∅ is in subject position via passivization. As it happens, for many speakers we can actually construct good examples of subject/object inversion in which clausal constituents participate in a fashion parallel to NP and other subjects. It is true that the 'inversion' represented in (52) is ill-formed:

(52) a.   [ₛ That Rocco showed up] pleased us.

b.   *Did [ₛ that Rocco showed up] please you?

But it has been noted in the linguistics literature that this effect is dramatically ameliorated when the length of the clausal subject relative to the rest of the sentence is reduced:

(53) a.   (?) To what extent did [that Fred failed to show up] anger those of his devoted fans who had waited by the stage door since dawn of the previous day? (Delahunty 1983)

b.   Should [whether Leslie or Terry got the job dishonestly] become the main issue under discussion at this afternoon's meeting? (based on examples given in Borsley 1992)

These examples show that sentential constituents such as *that* and *whether* clauses do indeed fulfill the role of subject valents specified as such on SPR lists, as is required for them to appear in inversion constructions under our analysis

of this phenomenon in Chapter 3. We can extend this range of examples to the
clausal subjects of passive verbs:

(54) a.   Was [ₛ that Rocco had been innocent] finally accepted by the angry members
           of the community whose lives had been disrupted by the violent spree?

     b.   Will [ₛ whether (or not) Rocco goes to prison] be decided by the three-judge
           panel at tonight's sentencing hearing?

In these examples, we see passive VPs (*finally accepted...*, *be decided...*)
appearing following a clause which is itself preceded by an auxiliary, yielding a
straightforward yes/no question – the signature of root clause interrogatives.

There is still more evidence that clauses really must be able to appear in the
subject position of passive clauses. One of the most problematic phenomena in
grammatical theory is the possibility of sentences in which we find a coordination
of constituents belonging to different categories. For example:

(55)   People won't appreciate Rocco's petty arrogance and that he's so pleased
           with himself all the time.

The verb *appreciate* is well-behaved with respect to the passive rule in (25), and
we therefore anticipate that the somewhat mysterious constituent *Rocco's petty
arrogance and that he's so pleased with himself all the time* is very likely to be
able to appear as a passive subject, which is indeed the case:

(56)   Rocco's petty arrogance and that he's so pleased with himself all the time
           won't be appreciated to any great extent by his supervisors and colleagues
           in his office.

Our hypothesis that apparent sentential subjects of passives are indeed subject
valents of the VP leads us to predict that the coordinated subject in (57) can
appear in an inverted interrogative construction, and so it proves:

(57)   Will Rocco's petty arrogance and that he's so pleased with himself all the
           time be appreciated to any great extent by his supervisors and colleagues in
           his office?

The example in (57) is an instance of an NP coordinated with a finite S –
an instance of a puzzling phenomenon called unlike category coordination
which contradicts one of our assumptions about what restrictions apply to
coordinations, that all conjuncts must be of the same syntactic type. It's not at all
clear what the category of the conjunction here is, so one possible response to
such data might be that whatever that category is, it isn't the same as S and
therefore (57) can't count as evidence for clausal subjects. But consider the
further data in (58):

(58) a.   John working on behalf of the enemy would compromise our security.

     b.   Would John working on behalf of the enemy really compromise our
           security?

     c.   Could John working on behalf of the enemy and that Mary then found out
           about it be the story behind that bizarre accident he had last year?

The string *John working on behalf of the enemy* is clearly a constituent, as demonstrated by its occurrence as an invertible subject in the first two examples, and it is straightforward to show that *working on behalf of the enemy* is a (gerundive) VP. We thus have in (58)a–b an NP and a VP[*ger*] forming a constituent in subject position (one which moreover, in view of its invertibility, cannot be analyzed as a displaced clause in topic position). The coordination of the gerundive and finite *that* clauses in (58)c therefore must have clausal status, and its invertibility again shows that it cannot be analyzed as a topic, but rather must be regarded as a true subject. The analysis of *that* clauses in subject position as instances of topicalization is now in the position of having to suppose that *that Mary then found out about it* must be taken to be in topic position when it appears on its own, but a co-inhabitant of subject position when coordinated with another clause – a far less plausible conclusion, and one requiring a good deal more in the way of special mechanisms than the analysis of *that*+ S as a legitimate occupant of clausal subject position.

The great weight of evidence thus suggests that clausal complements behave with respect to the passive lexical rule in a way strictly parallel to what we observe in the case of NPs. We therefore have plausible grounds to amend (25) along the following lines:

(59)

$$\begin{bmatrix} \text{HEAD} & \begin{bmatrix} verb \\ \text{VFORM} & \neg passive \end{bmatrix} \\ \text{SPR} & \langle \text{NP} \rangle \\ \text{COMPS} & \langle \boxed{1}\,\text{NP}\vee\text{S} \rangle \oplus \boxed{2} \end{bmatrix} \supset \begin{bmatrix} \text{HEAD}|\text{VFORM} & passive \\ \text{SPR} & \langle \boxed{1} \rangle \\ \text{COMPS} & \langle \boxed{2} \rangle \oplus \langle (\text{PP}[\text{PFORM } by]) \rangle \end{bmatrix}$$

This formulation allows either an NP or an S highest-ranked COMPS specification to appear as the description of the subject sought by VP[*pass*]. The account of passive summarized in (59) is still not complete, as our preceding discussion of coordinated unlike category passive subjects makes clear, but it significantly extends our coverage of this phenomenon.

The question of course remains why, in the case of certain verbs at least, passive clauses cannot have a clausal subject. This issue goes well beyond the coverage possible in a textbook such as this one, but it might be noted that, in many cases where *that* clauses are available for subject selection by passive VPs, the result of substituting the NP *the truth of the proposition that* S is that an acceptable sentence with equivalent meaning results, whereas in the case of *consider, judge,* and so on, this replacement is not possible (compare 'I believe the truth of the proposition that S' with 'I judge the truth of the proposition that S'). Verbs such as *judge, hold,* and so on, when they take S[*that*] complements, reflect something a bit stronger than just an attitude toward the proposition expressed by their clausal complement; rather, they convey a kind of rendering of a *verdict* on the truth of that proposition, with a kind of background deliberation and critical assessment implied. Other verbs which also resist clausal passive subjects, such as *insist*, have a still stronger extra component of what we might think of the social context involved in the relationship between the proposition and the subject of the verb which takes the sentence expressing that proposition as its complement. This sort of consideration represents a reasonable starting place for an exploration of the nonsyntactic factors at play in the determination of passivizability for verbs which take clausal complements.

4.4   Extraposition

The discussion of passives in the previous section shows that a systematic structural resemblance beween whole classes of sentences can be achieved without saying anything at all about the actual syntactic structure of these sentences. All that is necessary is a relationship between the valence specifications of lexical heads (accompanied, possibly but not necessarily, with a systematic change in the phonology of the head, corresponding to morphological differences, as with the active/passive forms). Exactly the same rules of structural combination are utilized in licensing both the active and the passive classes of sentences; the structural correspondences between them are nothing more than a by-product of the correspondence between their selectional requirements. Relationships between classes of sentences (where such classes are sometimes referred to as *construction types*) are typically referred to in the literature as relational dependencies, and it's easy to see why: notions such as subject and object come under the general heading of *grammatical relations*, and what rules such as (25) enforce is a systematic connection between what the SPR and COMPS specifications of the passive form are on the basis of what the values for those features are in the specification of the active form. Since it is these valence features which determine how the subject and object(s) of the passive form are determined, it makes sense to talk about a dependency here; and that dependency corresponds to a regular matching between the subject of the passive and the object of the active.

How common are such dependencies in human languages? In the very earliest phase of modern theoretical linguistics, they received by far the lion's share of attention from researchers, and quite a few phenomena were treated as relational dependencies that we would now regard quite differently, as our discussion of *there* phenomena below will illustrate. It turns out that in English, at least, and probably in many, if not most, other languages, there is a relatively small set of syntactic relationships that suggest treatments employing lexical rules such as (25). One particularly clear instance of such a case in English is what is called the *extraposition* construction, exemplified in the following section.

4.4.1   Basic Data

Typical cases of extraposition are given in (60)–(62)

(60) a.   That Rocco is a spy bothers me.
    b.   It bothers me that Rocco is a spy.

(61) a.   That Rocco is a spy annoys me.
    b.   It annoys me that Rocco is a spy.

(62) a.   That Rocco is a spy worries me.
    b.   It worries me that Rocco is a spy.

Readers will have no trouble convincing themselves that for any verb which can appear with a *that* clause as a subject, there is a predictable related sentence in which *it* appears as the subject (as can easily be shown using basic tests for subjecthood, such as the inversion of auxiliaries and subjects in questions, as discussed in Chapter 3), and a clause appears following the verb. What is at issue is how to capture this extremely regular, general pattern. The productivity of this pattern is even greater than in the case of the passive, because, while there are certain verbs which appear to take direct objects but which do not undergo passivization (e.g., *Rocco strikes me as odd/*I was struck by Rocco as odd*), there appear to be no exceptions to the pattern in (60)–(62).

Before we can provide an account of this phenomenon, however, the constituency relations involved must be determined on an empirically secure basis, which means recourse to all the familiar tests – and possibly others that are not so familiar.

4.4.2   Phrase Structure of the Extraposition VP

To begin with, we note that the tests in (63) support the treatment of *bothers me* in these examples as a VP, just as one would expect in advance.

(63) a.   This question bothers me, and so does that one.
    b.   This question bothers Rocco now, and bother him I am sure it always will __.
    c.   This question [$_{VP}$ bothers me].

But as we know from the evidence given in Chapter 1, the fact that strings such as *bothers me* can constitute a VP in one syntactic context is no guarantee that they have the same status elsewhere. Our decision on this point, as always, must be based on distributional evidence: we have two possible structures that might plausibly be assigned to (60)b, and we need to apply whatever tests are available to choose between them: is the clause in the Extraposition VP a COMPLEMENT (a sister to the V) or an ADJUNCT (a sister to the VP)?

(64) a.   It [$_{VP}$ [$_V$ bothers][$_{NP}$ me] [$_S$ that Joe is a spy]]
    b.   It [$_{VP}$ [$_{VP}$ bothers me] [$_S$ that Joe is a spy]]

If (64)b is correct – that is, if *that Joe is a spy* is indeed an adjunct – then we would expect it to be replaceable in all such examples. But native speakers of English typically find such examples off-key, to a greater or lesser extent.

(65) a.   It amazes me that Rocco is a spy more than it amazes me that Leslie was a spy.

   b.   ??/*It amazes me that Rocco is a spy more than it does so that Leslie is a spy.

In considering the relevant evidence, it is important not to fall into the trap of taking (66)a, which superficially resembles (65)b, to support the adjuncthood of the *that* clause. As (66)b makes clear, the auxiliaries in these examples have a distribution which looks quite different from that of *do so*.

(66) a.   It bothers me that Joe is a spy more than it did that Luanne was a spy.

   b.   Joe found the phone numbers faster than Luanne did (*so) the addresses.

   c.   Anne told us the stories faster than Rocco will (*so) the race results.

There is another test we can apply to see if our preliminary conclusion – that the *that* clause in (64) is a sister to the verb, and to *me*, and hence must be selected by the former – is correct. Compare the following examples, where the subscript *i* indicates that the constituents so labeled are to be understood as referring to the same entities in the world:

(67) a.   You can't say anything to them$_i$ without [the twins]$_i$ getting offended.

   b.   *You can't tell them$_i$ that [the twins]$_i$ are behaving outrageously.

The difference is clear and quite dramatic. The crucial generalization here emerges when we compare (67) with (68).

(68) a.   Rocco wanted me to **say something to them**, but I can't **do so** without someone getting offended.

   b.   *Rocco thought that I had [**told the twins**] that we were worried, but instead I **did so** that we were very annoyed.

Clearly, the *without* clause is an adjunct, a sister of the VP *say something to them* which *do so* has replaced in (68)a. Conversely, in (68)b, *do so* cannot replace *told the twins*, indicating that the *that* clause is a complement of *told*. So the two different structures we are dealing with in (67) can be written explicitly as follows:

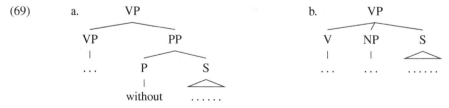

Given these general structures, it is clear that the contrast in (67) corresponds to the difference between the structures in (70):

(70)   a.

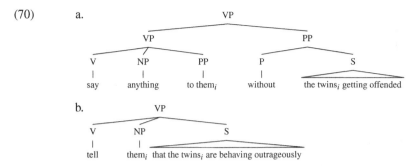

The key point of (67) can now be framed as follows: when the pronoun occurs within a VP whose adjunct contains the NP corresponding to that pronoun (as in (70)a), the shared reference is possible, but when the pronoun occurs as a sister to a constituent containing the corresponding NP, shared reference fails. These conditions on pronoun reference yield a straightforward prediction: if the object pronoun in the extraposition sentences can share reference with an NP within the *that* clause, then the latter must be an adjunct (corresponding to the structure in (70)a), whereas if it cannot, we have very strong evidence that the correct description is (70)b. And the data that we find point unequivocally to the latter conclusion as the correct one:

(71)   *It amazed him$_i$ that John$_i$ was so popular.

The sentence, *It amazed him that John was so popular*, is certainly possible in English; but it necessarily conveys the information that *him* and *John* identify two different people. Readers will be able to verify the representativeness of (71), supporting the conclusion that the *that* clause in extraposition sentences is indeed a valent of the head.

What makes this conclusion particularly important is that it points to the possibility of an account of the regular extraposition pattern which is parallel to the lexical rule treatment of the active/passive relation. We can now say, with empirical support, that in both cases there is a systematic correspondence between sentences in which a particular element appears as a subject and sentences in which it appears as a (possibly optional) object, with some other element appearing as the subject. In the case of extraposition, that other element is not a valent of the 'original' form of the verb, as it is in the case of the passive, but rather a dummy element, *it*. And the 'original' subject specification now corresponds (as we have just taken some pains to demonstrate) to a complement specification. The form of a verb such as *bother* which takes a clausal subject and an NP object will have a partial description of the form

(72)   *bother:* $\begin{bmatrix} \text{SPR} & \langle \text{S} \rangle \\ \text{COMPS} & \langle \text{NP} \rangle \end{bmatrix}$

while the version which takes a dummy *it* subject and a clausal complement (in addition to its 'original' direct object) will satisfy the description

(73)   *bother:* $\begin{bmatrix} \text{SPR} & \langle \text{NP[NFORM } it] \rangle \\ \text{COMPS} & \langle \text{NP, S} \rangle \end{bmatrix}$

These descriptions in fact correspond, as we noted above, to a very large class of verbs, including *trouble, distress, amuse, concern, intrigue, perplex, baffle, disturb, please,* and many others. All of them share, in one of their versions, the SPR and COMPS specifications given in (72), and in the other version, those provided in (73). In order to express the generalization that any verb which satisfies the first description (i.e., has a clausal subject and an NP object) will also satisfy the second (displaying a dummy *it* subject, we need do no more than state an implication relation between the first and the second descriptions:

(74) $\begin{bmatrix} \text{SPR} & \langle \text{S} \rangle \\ \text{COMPS} & \langle \text{NP} \rangle \end{bmatrix} \supset \begin{bmatrix} \text{SPR} & \langle \text{NP[}it] \rangle \\ \text{COMPS} & \langle \text{NP, S} \rangle \end{bmatrix}$

The rule in (74) expresses an implication: if a verb occurs in the lexicon with the description on the left of the implication sign, then it will also occur in the lexicon with the description on the right. Nothing else need be stated, and the rule as given makes a prediction: if a new verb appears in English which takes a clausal subject and an NP object, then it will also necessarily appear with an *it* subject and a clausal complement.

As stated, however, the rule is still insufficiently general. Consider the following data in terms of the rule in (74):

(75) a.   That Rocco is a spy is very odd.
     b.   It is very odd that Rocco is a spy.

(76) a.   That Rocco might be a spy has occurred to me from time to time.
     b.   It has occurred to me from time to time that Rocco might be a spy.

(77) a.   That Rocco will turn out to be a spy is $\left\{ \begin{array}{c} \text{very (un)likely} \\ \text{(im)probable} \\ \text{certain} \\ \text{conceivable} \end{array} \right\}$.

     b.   It is $\left\{ \begin{array}{c} \text{very (un)likely} \\ \text{(im)probable} \\ \text{certain} \\ \text{conceivable} \end{array} \right\}$ that Rocco will turn out to be a spy.

(78) a.   That Rocco was convicted on that perjury charge just feels wrong.
     b.   It just feels wrong that Rocco was convicted on that perjury charge.

(79) a.   That Rocco is a spy was (frequently) mentioned.
     b.   It was (frequently) mentioned that Rocco is a spy.

(80) a.   That Luanne is guilty is not in doubt.
     b.   It is not in doubt that Luanne is guilty.

None of these pairs of sentences reflect the generalization captured in (74), which is stated too narrowly to capture the fact that the same clausal subject/*it* subject + clausal complement matchup captured in that rule is evident also when the VP has the form [V AP], [V PP] and, as (79), shows, V VP, where VP has the VFORM value *passive*. We clearly need to generalize the rule in (74), but how?

A certain caution is called for here. As always, we need to ensure that we know just what the structural relationships involved are in some construction before we commit ourselves to a particular way of capturing those relationships. Consider (79): where does the clause *that Rocco is a spy* fit into the syntactic representation for the whole sentence? One very suggestive fact is that we have the following contrast:

(81) a.   It was frequently mentioned to Rocco$_i$ that he$_i$ worked too hard.

b.   ??*It was frequently mentioned to him$_i$ that Rocco$_i$ worked too hard.

A pronoun within a PP headed by *to* and various other prepositions is subject to the same conditions that it would if it appears in place of the PP itself: if its sister is a clause, then it cannot share reference with an NP within that clause, but if it belongs to a VP modified by an adjunct which contains an NP, then it *can* share reference with that NP. Given this restriction, we see immediately that of the two possible structures in (82), only the second is a plausible candidate as a depiction of the hierarchical relations among phrases in (79)b.

(82)

Adopting the empirically supported structure in (82)b, however, presents what appears to be a major difficulty for the formulation of the extraposition lexical rule. According to the latter, the verb whose subject is dummy *it* necessarily takes a *that* clause as its own complement. But since in (79) the verb in question is *was*, it appears at first blush as though *that Rocco is a spy* would have to be a sister of *was*, entailing a structure of the form

(83)

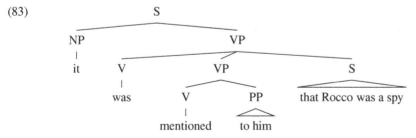

Obviously this structure would be all wrong. We've just shown that in *It was mentioned that Rocco works too hard*, *mentioned* has the complement *that* clause as a sister, yet in (83) we are forced to treat this clause as a sister, not of *mentioned*, but of *was*, creating a structure which completely mispredicts the possibilities of shared reference between the pronoun and some NP within the *that* clause, as already discussed. Hence (83) must be wrong. Rather, the correct structure must have the form:

(84)

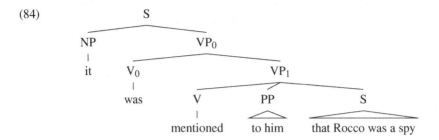

But now we seem to have backed ourselves into a very tight corner. No lexical rule can supply an *it* subject for some verb V_0, while at the same time inserting a *that* clause as a sister *within* some phrase – for example, VP_1 – which is a sister of V_0. Lexical rules cannot 'see inside' phrases of any kind; all they can do is specify alternative valence (or other) specifications for particular lexical items. If they apply to *was*, for example, they can associate this verb with an alternative set of feature values, but by their very nature they cannot 'see' anything but the properties of *was*, and are forever blind to the valence properties of any head that appears within some phrase that *was* selects; hence, they cannot 'reach inside' VP_1 to add a clausal complement valent to the latter. How then do we wind up with a structure of the form (84)?

As it happens, there is no contradiction or impasse here; we already have all the tools we need to license (84). The crux of the question is, how is it that *was* selects a dummy *it* subject while the *that* clause is a valent of *mentioned*? Recall that all forms of *be* are auxiliaries, which entails that any subject they select must reflect the SPR value of their VP complement – which is *mentioned that Rocco is a spy*. Hence, the latter must itself have a dummy pronoun subject, which *was* in (79) merely inherits its own subject specification from, along the lines considered in detail in Chapter 3. Now the problem is suddenly much simpler: we only need to determine how the passive form *mentioned* gets both its own [SUBJ *it*] specification and its clausal COMPS list value. More explicitly, we need to account for a lexical description of the form shown in (85):

(85)

$$
\begin{bmatrix}
\text{PHON} & \langle \texttt{mentioned} \rangle \\
\text{SS} &
\begin{bmatrix}
\text{HEAD} & \begin{bmatrix} \textit{verb} \\ \text{VFORM} \quad \textit{pass} \end{bmatrix} \\
\text{SPR} & \textit{it} \\
\text{COMPS} & \langle \text{PP}[\textit{to}], \text{S}[\textit{that}] \rangle
\end{bmatrix}
\end{bmatrix}
$$

And as it happens, we already have everything we need to license lexical entries which meet this description. It will prove worthwhile to review the reasoning which, on the basis of the analyses already presented, guarantees the availability of (85).

To begin with, as we saw earlier, the passive lexical rule must be formulated sufficiently generally that it applies not just to NPs but to *that* clauses whose sense has a certain semantic character in relation to the heads selecting those clauses. This relation holds between *mention* and its complement *that* clause, so that we predict the existence of a specification (86)b based on (86)a:

$$(86)\ a.\quad \begin{bmatrix} \text{PHON} & \langle\text{mention}\rangle \\ \text{SS} & \begin{bmatrix} \text{HEAD|VFORM} & \neg\,pass \\ \text{SPR} & \boxed{1}\langle\text{NP}\rangle \\ \text{COMPS} & \langle\boxed{2}\,\text{S}[that]\rangle \end{bmatrix} \end{bmatrix}$$

$$b.\quad \begin{bmatrix} \text{PHON} & \langle\text{mentioned}\rangle \\ \text{SS} & \begin{bmatrix} \text{HEAD|VFORM} & pass \\ \text{SPR} & \langle\boxed{2}\rangle \\ \text{COMPS} & \langle(\text{PP}[by])\rangle \end{bmatrix} \end{bmatrix}$$

The passive lexical rule thus guarantees the existence of a form of *mention* which has a *that* clause subject. But this form, necessarily belonging to the lexicon as per the passive rule, in turn guarantees the existence of a form of *mention* with an *it* subject and a *that* complement – if the extraposition rule is generalized to cover cases in which either nothing or a *by* PP follows the verb, rather than being restricted to just cases such as *bother* where an NP object is present. Such a generalization is equally motivated by cases such as *likely* (as in (77)), where we have reason to believe that *likely*, although an adjective, has a SPR value, one which may take the form of a clausal specification. While direct evidence for the status of the clause as a complement of *likely* is difficult to come by, we do not have any data contradicting this analysis, and similarly for *in doubt*, a PP, as in (80). The simplest approach, given these conclusions, is to extend the rule along the following lines (where $\boxed{1}$ ranges over lists of all lengths, including the empty list, corresponding to intransitive verbs such as *sucks/stinks/*):

$$(87)\quad \begin{bmatrix} \text{SPR} & \langle\text{S}\rangle \\ \text{COMPS} & \boxed{1} \end{bmatrix} \supset \begin{bmatrix} \text{SPR} & \langle\text{NP}[it]\rangle \\ \text{COMPS} & \boxed{1}\oplus\langle\text{S}\rangle \end{bmatrix}$$

Here we have in effect declared that if a lexical item selects a clausal subject, then it also takes an *it* subject and, in addition to whatever it selected as a complement along with the clausal subject, it adds a clausal complement to that list at the end. This extension, which represents a kind of simplification in the specifications of the original formulation of the rule, will give us all of the correspondences in (75)–(81), and many others as well.

Given the existence of the passive version of *mention* in (86)b, the licensing of (86) follows directly from the extraposition lexical rule, as generalized in (87). When a VP headed by this passive version of *mention* is selected by a finite copula, the latter, as an auxiliary, inherits the SPR specification of the VP, and the result is the structure in (84).

Problems

1.   Use the extended form of the extraposition lexical rule to show how (75)b is licensed, basing your explanation on the lexical form for *odd* that is required in order to license the unextraposed version in (75)a.

2.   Readers may have noticed that, if the association between verbs with clausal subjects and verbs with dummy *it* subjects is as complete as the previous discussion suggests, one might equally well state the relationship so that the implication was reversed: any word specified to take an *it* subject, and a clausal complement in addition to any others, will be matched with a version of that word specified for a clausal subject and a SISTERS list in which the COMPS list is the same except that the clausal complement is missing. Explain the implications of the following data for that proposed inverted formulation of the extraposition rule.

(88) a.   *That Rocco is a spy
$\left\{ \begin{array}{l} \text{seems} \\ \text{appears} \\ \text{happens} \\ \text{transpired} \end{array} \right\}$.

    b.   It
$\left\{ \begin{array}{l} \text{seems} \\ \text{appears} \\ \text{happens} \\ \text{transpired} \end{array} \right\}$
that Rocco is a spy.

3.   Assume that the verb *find* has, as one of its forms, a valence specification

$$\begin{bmatrix} \text{SPR} & \langle \text{NP} \rangle \\ \text{COMPS} & \langle \boxed{1}\,\text{NP}\;\text{AP}\begin{bmatrix} \text{SPR} & \boxed{1} \end{bmatrix} \rangle \end{bmatrix}$$

corresponding to, for example, *I found Terry excessively pleased with herself*. Write a lexical entry for the adjective *odd* such that (63) will be licensed, and explain the steps that are involved in licensing this sentence.

(89)   I find it odd that Leslie spies for the opposition.

4.5   *There*

The preceding discussion of the passive and extraposition relations brings to the foreground two critical points, one having to do with basic foundational issues and one having to do with what we might call 'good practices' on the part of working syntacticians trying to make sense of complex data.

The first point, noted in passing above, is that explaining structural parallels between classes of sentences does not necessarily require reference to structures themselves, in any direct way. If syntactic configurations are projected in large part by lexical specifications, as in the framework adopted here, then systematic relations in such specifications will *necessarily* correspond to predictable parallelisms in the structures projected from them – apart from the kinds of exceptions which always arise when we look at the lexicon of some language.

For example, the fact that the expected passive version of *That mountain resembles my brother's pig* is the unacceptable **My brother's pig is resembled by that mountain* has to be chalked up to some lexical property of *resemble*. The difficulty isn't semantic – compare *That mountain closely matches my brother's pig in appearance*, which means essentially the same thing, but where *My brother's pig is closely matched in appearance by that mountain* is perfectly good and means what we would have expected the ill-formed example with *resemble* to mean. There is nothing about the meaning of the passive (which, roughly speaking, preserves the meaning of the active) and the meaning of *resemble* (which is sufficiently close to that of *closely match in appearance*) which makes sense of the incompatibility between the two, and there is no phonological difficulty with the illegal passive form either. So there's nothing left except some kind of lexical property carried by *resemble* but not by *match*. We needn't be concerned about just how this property should be formulated, but it is important to note that we find exactly the same kind of exceptionality in morphology, where lexical rules have long been used to provide statements of basic regularities. Two examples will suffice: the fact that we must exclude, for example, *sing* from the operation of whatever rule is responsible for the overwhelmingly common appearance of *-ed* on verbs as the past tense form, and our example from Russian, discussed in Chapter 3, involving the somewhat strange lack of first person forms for a substantial number of verbs under certain inflectional conditions. There are countless other instances of this kind of exceptionality, and as we've seen in an earlier chapter in connection with the modals, the lexicon may simply contain gaps as the result of each word's idiosyncratic history. The fact that we encounter such gaps in the case of the passive in fact strongly suggests the correctness of the lexical treatment, because it is precisely in the lexicon that we expect to find such eccentricities.

The upshot of such cases is that a structural regularity does not *necessarily* demand that we formulate conditions or restrictions on structures directly. On the contrary, such a formulation may well constitute serious overkill. Appeals to structure typically allow a much wider syntactic reach than do lexical restrictions – a situation in which a strictly local phenomenon is treated by mechanisms which would only be called for in the case of syntactically much more far-ranging effects. And, as we shall see in the latter part of this book, even such effects may well turn out to be the result of an interlinked series of local interdependencies, and thus global in appearance only.

The methodological point that these proposals underscore is that one needs to be quite certain about the structures involved before concluding anything from particular examples. We saw instances of forms that looked like passives which turned out to be something quite different, along with data that seemed to suggest serious difficulties with the extraposition rule originally proposed, but which on closer examination turned out to be completely compatible with that rule once the identity of the forms which had actually been subject to the rule was clarified. In general, it is a serious error to conclude anything in particular from unanalyzed data; one needs as much as possible to consider what alternative structures could be assigned to the data in question, and try to assess the strength of the case for any of those alternatives before using the structure one thinks is correct as the basis for further analysis.

Both of these analytic caveats are relevant to the syntactic pattern to which we now turn, involving the distribution of one of the *there* morphemes in English, almost always identified as EXISTENTIAL *there*, and the syntactic contexts in which it appears as the existential construction. The source of the name is evident from the data presented in the following section: in the simplest form of the declarative existential construction, what is asserted is the existence of some entity in a particular location or context of action (although as we shall see in the examples in (93) below, this characterization is far too simple; the existential may equally well be used to DENY the existence of something in some particular context).

4.5.1   Basic Data

The existential examples we begin with appear in (90), and it is useful to compare them with the counterparts in (91), whose synonymy with the existentials was an important factor in the analyses this construction received in the early decades of modern theoretical syntax.

(90) a.   There is a lion in the garage.
     b.   There were some lions howling.
     c.   There is at least one lion tired of all these nosey photojournalists.

(91) a.   A lion is in the garage.
     b.   Some lions were howling.
     c.   At least one lion is tired of all these nosey photojournalists.

Although the details are not important at this point, readers may find it useful to understand some of the thinking that led the pioneer generation of syntactic theorists to regard the syntactic form of the examples in (91) as in a fundamental sense the *source* of their counterparts in (90), and why they did so. The data in (90) and the corresponding examples in (91) are truth conditionally equivalent – that is, in any conceivable situation in which a sentence in one of these data sets is true, its analogue in the other data set will be true, and where one is not true, the other will not be true either. Such a semantic relationship was, at an earlier time, assumed to hold when one structure was, in a special sense, derived by operations on another structure, and the plausibility of the latter was suggested by the fact that the subject in the first class of sentences appears to have been displaced to a position following the copula, with its original position occupied by *there* – a situation which many syntactic researchers regarded as similar to the relationship between active and passive sentences. Nonetheless, matters are a bit more complex than this. As long as one looks only at classes of data similar to (90)–(91), it seems evident that the existential is simply a variant of a construction with the schematic form NP *be* …; but consider the cases in (92)–(93):

(92) a. *Nothing is to it/*Nothing to it is.
      b. *Some problems are with your report/*Some problems with your report are.
      c. *No problems were at any point./*No problems at any point were.

(93) a. There is nothing to it.
      b. There are some problems with your report.
      c. There were no problems at any point.

There does not appear to be a source for (93) based on the structures in (92). Despite the possibility of various ad hoc expedients, the simplest approach seems to be to take the two classes of structures as separate, and allowing the various PPs that are forbidden in (92) to appear in the structures independently posited for (93). But we cannot implement this approach until we have a motivated account of the phrase structure of the existential construction. Such an account must supply answers to three questions:

- What is the grammatical relation between *there* and the rest of the sentence in which it appears?
- To which grammatical category does *there* belong?
- What is the structure of the VP in existential clauses?

And the corresponding answers to these questions are, as we shall see, the following:

- *There* is a subject.
- *There* is an NP.
- The VP of *there* clauses has the form

(94)

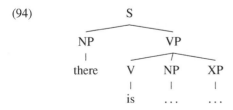

In addition, we will establish the following two points:

- *There* carries an (invisible) number distinction.
- The form of the VP that takes this *there* as a subject is unique.

All of these questions are amenable to either the various tests we've introduced, or to others which involve applying well-known, robust grammatical generalizations to the components of the existential construction and making the indicated inference. We start with the easiest question: what grammatical relation holds between *there* and the rest of an existential sentence?

4.5.2   *There* Is a Subject

We can establish the subjecthood of *there* in these sentences in the most direct way possible: all of the tests for subjecthood that work for ordinary subjects also work for existential *there*. Just considering two of these tests – the possibility of inverted position with respect to a following auxiliary, and appearance of a subject form in a tag question which shares reference with the clausal subject – leaves no doubt that the dummy *there* element is indeed a subject, and needs to appear as such in the SPR specification of whatever form of the copula is the head of the VP in existential clauses. As noted and discussed at length in Chapter 3, only subjects invert with respect to auxiliaries, and we find exactly this pattern in existential clauses:

(95) a.   There is a lion in the garage.
     b.   Is there a lion in the garage?

The structural probe employing tag questions is somewhat different. Tag questions are the sort of internal interrogative clauses one often finds playing a kind of support role for the main clause (e.g., *Terrence plays the violin, doesn't he/Terrence doesn't play the violin, does he?*, acting as a qualification of the latter which makes its content a bit more tentative than would otherwise be the case, and therefore less vulnerable to something like a challenge or outright contradiction; thus, *Rocco has a criminal record* sets up the possibility of a flat-out refutation (*No, Rocco does NOT have a criminal record!*), whereas *Rocco has a criminal record, doesn't he?* leaves the door open for a correction which will in all likelihood be much less direct (*No, actually, it turns out he doesn't*). Tag questions, at least on their most common use, thus serve to decrease the speaker's vulnerability to a combative response; but their chief syntactic properties are that (i) they invariably show auxiliary inversion with respect to a pronoun subject only (*Luanne doesn't like Italian food, does she/*Luanne*), and (ii) that pronoun targets the subject, not any other part of the sentence (*Rocco likes the twins, doesn't he/*don't they*, etc.). Compare now the two examples in (96):

(96) a.   Rocco saw the twins, didn't he/*they?
     b.   There are two lions hiding in the garage, aren't there/*they?

These distributional facts amply confirm the status of *there* as the subject: *there* can appear as the subject of the tag question in (96)b, and it is identical in morphological form to the *there* which appears preverbally in the declarative clause (compare (96) with *Two lions were hiding in the garage, weren't they/*?? *there?*).

4.5.3   *There* Is a (Pronominal) NP

The next stage of our demonstration is establishment of the claim that *there* is a nominal proform, that is, a pronoun. We've already seen, in the previous section, that *there* can occupy the subject position in tag questions, a position reserved for proforms; but it's conceivable that other kinds of pro-categories besides nominals could bear the subject function in tags. What are the possibilities? We know that *there* is a pro-PP, as discussed in Chapter 1. But we can show that existential *there* isn't the locational pro-PP *there*.

To begin with, we need to investigate what kinds of proform can appear in tag questions. We've seen that pronouns are fine as a tag-question subject. But of course there are other proforms, for example, *so* (pro-AP), and *there* (pro-PP). APs and PPs can indeed appear as subjects, so in principle, it's conceivable that the corresponding proforms would show up as subjects of corresponding tag questions. But do they? The facts strongly rule otherwise:

(97) a.   Luanne is proud of herself, and Terrence is so as well.

  b.   Proud of yourself isn't how you should be feeling right now, IS $\left\{ \begin{matrix} *so \\ it \end{matrix} \right\}$?

Now what's the pattern?

(98) a.   [Under the bed]$_i$'s a strange place to keep your beer, yet there$_i$'s where you keep your beer...

  b.   ...ISN'T $\left\{ \begin{matrix} it \\ *there \end{matrix} \right\}$?

In both cases, the evidence is clear that a nonnominal proform cannot appear as a tag question subject corresponding to a declarative clause in which a corresponding nonnominal phrase is a perfectly good subject. The bottom line appears to be that in (99), the tag question subject is not the locational PP, nor a PP (or any other kind of nonnominal proform) of any sort. The null hypothesis, therefore, seems to be that *there* here is a pronoun.

(99)   There's a lion in the garage, isn't there?

The defender of existential *there* as the pro-PP form has one last move available, however. Suppose the *there* which appears in tag questions is indeed a dummy, but the one which appears in a main clause subject position is the PP. Admittedly, this is somewhat far-fetched, if only because when a full locational PP appears as an indisputable main clause subject, it requires an *it*, not a dummy *there*, as its corresponding tag question:

(100)   In that gazebo seemed to be the right place to take the wedding photos, didn't
$\left\{ \begin{array}{c} \text{it} \\ \text{*there} \end{array} \right\}$?

This pattern in itself makes the last-ditch defense at issue seem too implausible to take seriously. But there is another fact about pro-PP *there* which undercuts the viability of this defense: the systemic difference in stress possibilities that are available for existential and locational *there* subjects respectively. In particular, note the following contrast:

(101) a.   There's where I WANT to live, and then there's where I LIVE. (*there* = [θəˈ])

      b.   (**pointing to ground under a bridge**) There is where I DON'T want to live! (*there* = [θeɹ])

Exchanging the reduced form of *there* for the unreduced form is legal in (101)a, but replacing the unreduced form in (101)b with the reduced form yields an ill-formed result.

These inquiries appear to answer our questions about the status of *there*. But what about the rest of the existential construction? Strictly speaking, it's in the existential VP that all the activity takes place: in *There is a lion in the garage*, the VP *is a lion in the garage* has all of the parts necessary to convey the content of the whole sentence; after all, *there* contributes nothing to the information obtainable by putting *a lion*, *is* and *in the garage* together. What is the structure of this VP?

4.5.4   *There* VPs Immediately Dominate the Predicate

We start with a demonstration that the existential VP is a trinary branching structure, that is, that both the postnominal NP (*a lion*) and the material following this NP (*in the garage*) are sisters of *is*. This structure is by no means the only one available. For example, we might take the data in (102) to suggest that all of the material which follows the existential copula constitutes a single NP, as in (103)b, as vs the structure just proposed, given in (103)c.

(102) a.   Yes, Virginia, there is a Santa Claus.

      b.   there is [$_{NP}$ a Santa Claus]

(103) a.   There is a lion in the garage.

      b.   There is [$_{NP}$ a lion in the garage]

      c.   There is [$_{NP}$ a lion] [$_{PP}$ in the garage]

Is there any actual evidence for an NP of the form *a lion in the garage*? There is, and it's quite strong:

(104) a.   A lion in the garage is bad for everyone's morale.

      b.   A lion in the garage, you just can't ignore __.

c.   Reflecting on the matter in my study, I realized that I considered

$$\left\{ \begin{array}{l} \text{a lion in the garage} \\ \qquad\text{Terrence} \\ \qquad\quad\text{him} \end{array} \right\} \text{ to be just another one of Rocco's grotesque}$$

fantasies.

In (104)a, *a lion in the garage* is demonstrably the subject, hence a single constituent, and in (104)b, the displacement test shows it to be a constituent as well. The object position of verbs such as *consider* is yet another position in which single constituents appear, and hence we have a series of robust and independent tests suggesting that *a lion in the garage* is indeed a constituent of English. The question is, is it a constituent in the existential sentence in (103)?

We've encountered this question already in this chapter – the problem of deciding between (44)a and b was another instance of exactly the same binary vs trinary problem, and we can use the same techniques to settle the issue in this case. So consider the following data:

(105) a.   There is an enormous and very hungry lion in that garage.
      b.   There is in that garage an enormous and very hungry lion.

We've already seen, in connection with the question of what structural representation is most motivated for (22)c, that this kind of heavy NP Shift is characteristic of structures of the form [$_{VP}$ V ⌄NP XP]. In contrast, when we examine the behavior of the same string in a context where it must be a constituent (as attested by the displacement test, as in (20)b, we find a very different range of possibilities:

(106) a.   I mentioned an enormous and very hungry lion under the bed.
      b.   It was [$_{NP}$ an enormous and very hungry lion under the bed] that I mentioned ___.
      c.   *I mentioned under the bed an enormous and very hungry lion.

We cannot understand *under the bed an enormous and very hungry lion* as a description of a lion who is under the bed. The phrase *an enormous and very hungry lion* cannot shift position with its sister constituent *under the bed* within the NP, and this is typical of such NPs; thus we have

(107) a.   I recognized a student with red hair.
      b.   It was a student with red hair that I recognized ___.
      c.   *I recognized with red hair a student.
      d.   *It was with red hair a student that I recognized.

Not only can (107)c not possibly be understood as an alternative ordering of (107)a, but also it doesn't seem possible to understand it in any way that makes it well-formed at all. The failure of displacement here makes it clear that *with red hair a student* does not have the status of a constituent.

A second diagnostic pattern emerges when we attempt to displace material from within an NP – a possibility in only a very limited class of NPs, and one which appears blocked in general for constituents which appear to be NP-internal adjuncts:

(108) a.   I bumped into an editor from New York.
       b.   It was [$_{NP}$ an editor from New York] that I bumped into __.
       c.   *From New York, I bumped into [an editor __].

We have

(109) a.   There is a lion in the garage.
       b.   *It is a lion in the garage that there is __.
       c.   In the garage, there is a lion.

This distribution of data runs exactly contrary to our expectations on the analysis in which *in the garage* is a constituent of an NP *a lion in the garage*, but coincides perfectly with what follows if this string comprises an NP and a PP which are sisters of each other and of the existential copula. The results of this displacement test thus mirror the distribution of data in the complex NP shift test, and justify our confidence in the claim that the VP in existential constructions does directly dominate the postnominal predicate (in this case *in the garage*, *howling* in (90)b, etc.).

Our findings to this point can be summarized in the phrase structure tree in (94) above. But this result only gives us a point of entry into the syntax of *there* and the existential construction, which displays several distributional peculiarities that must be addressed before we can construct a reasonably comprehensive proposal for its analysis.

4.5.5   Accounting for *There*

We begin with the fact that most verbs do not allow a semantically empty *there* subject:

(110) a.   There is a student in the library.
       b.   *There reads a student in the library.
       c.   *There mentioned someone to me that Rocco is a spy.
       d.   *There wagered a complete stranger fifty bucks with Christopher that Luanne was a spy.
       e.   *There ate the twins a steak.

It follows that the existential copula *be* must be specified as requiring an NP of the subtype *there*, just as *rain* and various other ambient weather predicates require similar specification for an *it*-type subject.[1]

---

[1] The copula is not unique in this respect; there is a class of verbs in English, which seems to consist largely (though not exclusively) of verbs of ordinary motion, which, under certain circumstances, permit the appearance of a *there* subject. *Emerge* is such a verb, and the following data pattern is representative:

(111) a.   A bear emerged from the cave.
       b.   ??*There emerged a bear from the cave.
       c.   There emerged from the cave a *(gigantic, foul-tempered grizzly) bear.

One of the most unexpected properties of the existential construction is the agreement pattern displayed in data such as (112), where we see the match in the verb's agreement morphology with not the subject but the NP following the copula:

(112) a.   A lion has been in the garage.
      b.   There has been a lion in the garage.

(113) a.   Two lions have been in the garage.
      b.   There have been two lions in the garage.

Since we've already established that *there*, not the post-copula NP, is the subject of existential clauses, we seem to be forced to conclude that the otherwise completely general agreement rule for English discussed earlier in this chapter is somehow suspended or overridden in the case of the existential. This seems a strikingly ad hoc move, a special additional condition imposed on the grammar for what appear to be unknown reasons. One could, of course, reject our original formulation of agreement in Section 4.1.2, replacing it by a semantically based one, in which the verb reflects the person and number values of the syntactic material in the clause corresponding to the logical argument that the meaning of the rest of the sentence applies to. In the case of the examples in (91), for example, we might say that the meaning of *in the garage* is a kind of operation which applies to whatever it is that the subject refers to and yields a claim that that entity is in the particular location designated by *in the garage*. Normally, this will be the subject, but in the case of the existential, the grammatical subject doesn't actually *have* a meaning, so the agreement is with the post-copula element, to which, by lexical stipulation, the meaning of the predicative phrase *in the garage* applies.

There is nothing in principle absurd about such a possibility. But the dependence of the form of agreement marking on the semantic properties of the relevant element entails a certain prediction: when we have a normal subject, one which unlike the dummy pronouns does refer to some element in the world in the ordinary way, we will get the agreement pattern that is consistent with the semantic properties of the object in question. Even if the number marking on the phrase referring to that object is itself plural, we would expect, on this approach, to see a singular marking on the verb, since the agreement pattern is, on this hypothesis, semantically based. What we find instead is quite different:

Emerge can indeed take a *there* subject, but there is a somewhat unusual restriction it imposes on its VP: the normal order V NP XP is blocked; rather, the NP must be heavy and follow the predicate XP. There are ways to achieve this objective in versions of our current framework in which word order is regarded as an essentially phonological effect, but the important point for our purposes is that the class of verbs to which *emerge* belongs, giving rise to what is usually called 'presentational' *there* sentences, seems to be a different sort of phenomenon from the existential *there* construction, in which no such Heavy Shift is necessary. This and other differences suggest the existence of two distinct subclasses of *there*-seeking verbs with, however, certain morphosyntactic similarities. In this chapter, we restrict our attention to the existential.

(114) a.   The scissors are/*is on the shelf.
b.   My trousers need/*needs to be dry-cleaned again.
c.   Your glasses are/is always so smudged-up!

When we say of someone that she was wearing glasses, we invariably mean that she was wearing a single optical-correction device, not two or more such devices; when we say that someone changed from pants into shorts, we are talking about getting out of one garment and putting on another. Yet the agreement is plural, as it would be if we were talking about multiple entities in all these cases. One might try to explain this phenomenon as an effect of scissors, trousers, and glasses being composed of two 'parts', but this is not particularly convincing, since, for example, each lens in the glasses someone is wearing can't be referred to as a 'glass', as we can see if we want to say that one of the two lenses in someone's glasses was damaged: #*Luanne had to go to the optician's shop today to get a broken glass replaced*, where the notation # identifies a sentence which is, in a particular context, semantically bizarre or uninterpretable in the way required by that context. In other words, the agreement pattern revealed in such examples seems to reflect the idiosyncratic plural morphology on the noun, not the kind of thing the noun identifies.

Comparison of *trousers* with *shirt* sharpens the point: it's true that trousers have two legs, but a shirt has two sleeves. Yet we do not say, *Your shirt are creased*. This example is just flat-out unacceptable, and so is, *That nutcracker are almost a century old*, even if the nutcracker is one of the old-fashioned metal types with two arms that are brought together to break the shell. We say *The catamaran was/*were speeding across the lake*, although a catamaran is typically a two-hulled boat or ship, joined by what is often quite minimal structure; what seems crucial, rather, is that *catamaran* lacks plural marking. There is, in short, no evident semantic basis for the agreement patterns that we see. What is relevant is just the morphological form of the noun which determines the agreement relation with the verb.

Similar considerations seem to be at work in cases such as the so-called 'royal we', famously exemplified in Queen Victoria's (probably apochryphal) utterance 'We are not amused,' and the *yours truly* locution, as in *Yours truly sticks his neck out for no one, sweetheart!*, in which *yours truly*, by an extension of its use as a parting salutation in traditional correspondence etiquette, has become specialized as a reference to the speaker; the third person singular form, not the first person form, is used here. Still another example of the same general sort is the singular use of plural forms as a way of ensuring gender neutrality, as per the discussion above in §4.1.2: *Suppose you meet someone$_i$ and they$_i$ insist(*s) they've met you before and you're sure that you never have; how should you deal with that situation?* In such cases, as noted earlier, the verbal agreement morphology (and various other markers of agreement) are identical to what we would expect in the case of the normal third person plural, in spite of the fact that the speaker intends, and is understood by everyone in the conversation to intend, reference to a single individual.

The defender of the semantic agreement theory might nonetheless retreat to a seemingly defensible position: yes, the morphology of agreement reflects the morphology of the element entering into the agreement relation with the verb, but *which* element that is is still decidable on a semantic basis. But this position itself fails on empirical grounds, for, as it happens, we can test it against another case in which a dummy pronoun appears in which the VP appears to be 'about' plural linguistic entities. Note the contrast in (115):

(115) a.   That Saturn has rings and the square root of nine is three amuse me to about the same degree.

b.   It amuse*(s) me that Saturn has rings and the square root of nine is three to about the same degree.

By exactly the line of reasoning favoring the semantic analysis of verb agreement in the existential, we would expect to find *It amuse me that Saturn has rings and the square root of nine is three to about the same degree* to be the favored form, whereas it is in fact unequivocally excluded. Since the *it* subject in (115)b has no reference, the semantically determined agreement position is committed to having the actual agreement morphology reflect the semantics of the content of the VP. But (115)a shows that in the completely synonymous clausal subject analogues of the *it*-subject cases, we find *plural* morphology – an unequivocal indication that the morphology of agreement in this sentence is associated with the coordination of clauses in the subject. The defender of semantic agreement now has a very unpleasant dilemma, for if the content of the VP in the second example is what determines number marking on the verb, then this content, identical as it is to the content of the first example's subject, should similarly mandate plural agreement, just as in the first example. But the result of such plural marking is flagrantly bad.

If, on the other hand, verbal agreement simply reflects the number marking on the subject, and if, as we have reason to believe from the contrast between *it* and *they*, *it* is always associated with a singular number value, then the facts in (115) are trivially predictable. But that conclusion leaves us again in the position of trying to make sense of the fact that the existential copula agrees with the nonsubject NP following it. Since the semantic solution does not go through, it seems as though we might have to allow for an arbitrary exception to the agreement rule based on the subject's number marking – a very undesirable conclusion.

But suppose that the normal agreement rule works here as well as in all other cases. That of course would be the best outcome, but it means that the *there* subject in (113)b is indeed specified as plural, as opposed to the *there* in (112)b. This proposal depends on two assumptions: first, that there are singular and plural descriptions of *there*, which are homophonous, and second, that the number specification on *there* in any sentence is correlated in one-to-one fashion with the number marking on the post-copula NP – that and the latter will be accessible to the former. Since both subjects and complements are valents of the head, this second requirement is straightforwardly satisfied. Suppose we identify a subtype of NP whose name is *there*. Then we can write

(116)

$$
\begin{bmatrix}
\text{SPR} & \left\langle \text{NP}\begin{bmatrix} \text{HEAD} & \textit{there} \\ \text{AGR} & \begin{bmatrix} \text{PERS} & 3 \\ \text{NUM} & \boxed{1} \end{bmatrix} \end{bmatrix} \right\rangle \\
\text{COMPS} & \left\langle \text{NP}\big[\text{HEAD}|\text{AGR}|\text{NUM} \quad \boxed{1}\big], \textit{phrase} \right\rangle
\end{bmatrix}
$$

where, critically, the number specification of the subject is required by the selecting head itself to be identical to the NP complement's number value. We can see how this solution yields the correct results for (96)b:

(117)

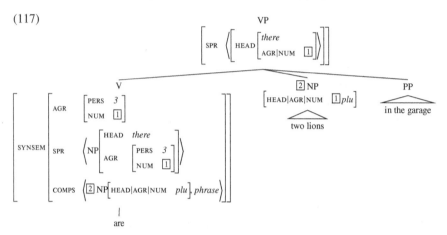

are

The critical point to note here is that by virtue of the agreement rule for English which corresponds to (18)a discussed above, the AGR value of the copula matches that of the subject, which in turn is shared with the copula's NP complement. Thus, the partial description in (116) is all that is necessary to ensure that the verb's morphology reflects the overt number marking on its NP complement. While this may seem a somewhat odd state of affairs, it is in fact no stranger than what we find in the auxiliaries, where in all cases the verb matches its own subject specification to that of its VP complement.

Moreover, the solution given here has a very welcome side benefit: it accounts for the fact that when the existential appears as part of an embedded VP under some finite verb, the correlation between the latter's subject and the now-distant NP complement of the copula still holds. We have examples such as

(118) a.   There have/*has been two lions in this garage.

b.   There appear(*s) to have been two lions in this garage.

Once the SPR specification corresponding to *there* is 'imprinted' with the number marking associated with the copula's NP complement, that number marking will be shared as far up the tree as the SPR specification is shared. The subject selection properties associated with auxiliaries (as well as verbs such as *appear*, *seem*, and *to*, as will be shown in the next chapter) therefore ensure that number information about the distant post-copula NP will be accessible for agreement.

Practice Exercise

Carry out a complete licensing for (118)a, noting specifically how the information relevant to the form of the top-level auxiliary is made available to ensure the correct agreement morphology.

The final point to make about the existential is that the structure *be* NP XP seems to be restricted to a form of *be* which selects *there* as its subject. There are examples such as (119), in which the word order is the same as in the existential. But in such cases, subsequent tests show that *a lion in the garage* is a constituent, and that, as already discussed, we predict the failure of PP extraction in this case (where in the following examples, *Roger* is the lion's name):

(119) a.   Roger is a lion in the garage.
      b.   What Roger is is a lion in the garage.
      c.   *In the garage, Roger is a lion__.

The same holds when *it* is the subject.

(120) a.   It's a lion in the garage.
      b.   *[In the garage, it's a lion__.]

The only way the strings with a fronted PP can be legal is if *in the garage* has the status of a VP adjunct, whose effect is to modify *is a lion* (or, arguably, the whole clause); the interpretation is something like, 'When Rocco is in the garage, s/he turns into a lion.' It appears at present, therefore, that the only form of *be* which demonstrably selects an NP and a second phrasal complement is the existential copula.

Problem

As always in syntax, things are a bit more complicated than one thinks they're going to be. We have data along the following lines, which are supported by a number of Google hits:

(121) a.   There was only $\left\{ \begin{array}{c} \text{me} \\ \text{us} \end{array} \right\}$ in the room.

      b.   There were only $\left\{ \begin{array}{c} \text{*us} \\ \text{*them} \end{array} \right\}$ in the room.

i.   Are the data in (121) consistent with the analysis summarized in (116)? Explain fully.

ii.   If you answered *yes* to i, show in detail how (116) allows us to license (120). If you answered *no*, identify one (or possibly more) lexical specifications for *be* that allow us to keep the broad coverage that (120) gives us while also allowing us to obtain (121).

4.6   Ergative and Antipassive

The preceding examples from English all reflect a particular association in the grammar among the subjects of transitive verbs and the subject of
intransitive verbs, as vs the object of transitive verbs. Morphologically, transitive
and intransitive pronoun subjects are treated identically, reflecting nominative
case when the verb is finite, whereas objects are invariably accusative, as per our
discussion of case in §4.1. Syntactically, the same association holds: the rule for
passives targets objects in the lexical entries for transitive verbs; the extraposition
rule applies to both transitive verbs such as *It bothers me that Rocco is a spy* and
intransitive verbs such as *stinks* which selects an AP complement (*It stinks that
Rocco wound up becoming a spy*), adjectives (*It's unlikely that Rocco is a spy* and
so on. This kind of patterning is usually referred to as *nominative/accusative*,
based on the way case values are assigned structurally in languages such as
English. There is, in fact, another far less common one, called *ergative* patterning,
sorting intransitive subjects with transitive objects. In English, such a sorting
would yield, not *She left (us)* vs *We left her*, as is in fact the case (with the
nominative *she* used for third person feminine pronouns in subject position in
both transitive and intransitive versions of *left*, and *her* reserved for transitive
object position), but rather *She left us* on the one hand and *Her left* on the
other (cf. *We left her*, with subject pronouns displaying accusative case in
both transitive object and intransitive subject position), with these grammatical
relations grouped together under the label *absolutive*. Syntactically, an ergative
version of English might locate the transitive subject in its standard position,
but leave the intransitive subject in the same position as the transitive object:
She left us but *Left her*. Ergative structure is relevant to the issue of relational
dependencies, such as those considered in the preceding section, because there
are analogues of such dependencies in ergative/absolutive languages which are,
in a way, mirror images of those in nominative/accusative languages, and the
same tools we use to capture these dependencies in English and other familiar
languages serve us equally well in the case of ergative dependencies.

The following data from the ergative language Chukchee illustrates one of the
most widespread of these relational dependencies.

(122) a. ətləg-e   keyng-ən penrərə-nen
          father-ERG bear-ABS attack-3SG/3SG/PAST
          'Father attacked the bear'

      b. ətləg-ən   penrərə-<u>tko</u>-nen   (keyng-etə)
          father-ABS charge-ANTIPASSIVE-3SG/PAST (bear-DAT)
          'Father ran at the bear'

In (122)a, we have the normal transitive pattern: the subject (or *ergator*, as the
transitive subject in such languages is called) bears the marking that distinguishes
transitive subjects from the absolutive arguments marked with *ən*, as in *keyng-ən*
'bear' in the same sentence. In (122)b, something quite different is presented: the

ergator in the preceding example is replaced with a form describing the speaker's father with the same morphology as the form identifying the bear, the target, displays in (122)a. The ergator in the first example has become the absolutive in the second, which now contains no ergator – which can only mean that the clause in (122)b is intransitive – the verb has only one valent, and the absolutive of the first example is now only an optional element, possibly an adjunct. The difference in meaning between the two is indicated in the translation – one might run at the bear with the intention of distracting it, rather than trying to harm it – but the key point is that, in a sense, the bear per se doesn't come into the situation described in (122)b at all: the speaker's father ran toward *something* with the intention of confronting it in some way, but there was only a weak relationship with respect to whatever that something was. The verb displays a special marker indicating the form of the verb reserved for the *antipassive*, underlined in the example given in (122)b.

The nature of the grammatical relationship between the two sentences should strike the reader as somewhat familiar: it echoes the relationship between the active and passive sentences, but in a kind of mirror-image way. Rather than a lexical rule whose effect is to promote an object to subject, the Chukchee rule demotes an ergator to an absolutive. Whereas the effect of the English rule is to license a valence specification in which the former top-ranked valent survives only as an optional *by*-phrase, the Chukchee process removes the transitive absolutive – the analogue of the English direct object – and makes *it* the marginal element, an optional analogue. Promotion from the bottom and dismissal at the top, in English; demotion at the top and dismissal at the bottom in Chukchee – and in both cases, the verb is marked with morphology that registers in effect the altered relationship between the highest-ranking valent and the verb. For this reason, the Chukchee construction, as well as others parallel in the relevant ways cross-linguistically, is referred to as the *antipassive*.

A particularly interesting aspect of the Chukchee antipassive is the way in which the marking of the optional 'demoted' element is determined. In English, the passive element agent corresponding to the nonpassive subject invariably takes the form of a *by* PP, with *by*, as discussed above, typically used to introduce reference to some means, method or technique or creative source (*We read a novel by Balzac*; *Terry flattened the can by hammering it*; *The police discovered the perpetrator dead by his own hand* etc). In Chukchee, however, the optional element corresponding to the absolutive in the normal transitive version of the construction takes one of three possible forms: the dative marking of (122)b, or one of the alternatives exhibited in (123):

(123) a.   Ɂaacek-ət   gənrit-ərkət   (qaa-k)
              boy-ABS/PL ANTIPASSIVE-guard-PRES/PL reindeer-LOC
              'The boys are guarding (the reindeer).'

        b.   muei   mət-<u>ine</u>-ret-ərkən   (kimitɁ-e)
              we-ABS 1°PL-ANTIPASSIVE-carry-PRES load-INSTR
              'We are carrying (the load).'

The particular case marking attached to the optional material corresponding to the absolutive in the transitive version of the sentence is not predictable on the basis of either the verb meaning or the NP meaning; it must be specified for each verb on an individual basis – which means that it must be recorded in the lexicon somewhere. We now face the problem of accounting for this pattern in a sufficiently general way, along the lines of the English relational dependencies discussed in preceding sections.

The first decision we need to make in approaching the transitive/antipassive relationship is how to incorporate the ergative/absolutive pattern into our framework. The nominative/accusative sorting we see in most of the world's languages treats an [SPR $\langle$NP$\rangle$] specification in verbs uniformly, regardless of the content of the COMPS list. If English were to adopt a thoroughly ergative architecture, where intransitive subjects pattern morphologically and syntactically in a way completely parallel to direct objects, matters would be quite different; in that scenario, an intransitive subject would presumably appear in the same valence-list slot as the transitive object, i.e., as the top-ranking member of the COMPS list, ensuring a morphosyntactically parallel treatment for the two. That is, we would have the partial description (124)a for the case in which NP$_1$ was the ergator and (124)b–c for cases in which it is the absolutive (the intransitive subject in b., the direct object in c.).

$$(124) \quad \text{a.} \begin{bmatrix} \text{SPR} & \langle \text{NP}_1 \rangle \\ \text{COMPS} & \langle \text{NP}_2 \ldots \rangle \end{bmatrix} \text{b.} \begin{bmatrix} \text{SPR} & \langle \ \rangle \\ \text{COMPS} & \langle \text{NP}_1, \ldots \rangle \end{bmatrix} \text{c.} \begin{bmatrix} \text{SPR} & \langle \text{NP}_3 \rangle \\ \text{COMPS} & \langle \text{NP}_1, \ldots \rangle \end{bmatrix}$$

Ergative patterning, on this account, reduces to the specification on intransitive verbs for an empty SPR specification – a requirement that we can formalize as the condition that a nonempty SPR specification entails the appearance of an NP as the highest-ranking COMPS list member. Since there is a regular relationship between the form of transitive constructions (124)a on the one hand and the antipassive (124)b on the other, we can appeal to a lexical rule of the same sort as for the relational dependencies we've already discussed to capture this regularity.

There is, however, the additional wrinkle noted above that the case marking associated with the optional 'counterpart' to the transitive construction's absolutive constituent is determined by the verb itself in a way that cannot be predicted. This information must be encoded somewhere in the transitive verb's specification, and referred to in the formulation of the antipassive rule, perhaps via a feature ABSCASE, which serves to record, for each transitive verb, the possible form of the antipassive counterpart to the transitive absolutive. Precisely how we treat this specification depends on the structural relationship between the 'counterpart' constituent and the antipassive form of the verb. (A second refinement we would need to make in a full treatment involves the fact, exhibited in the foregoing data, that there are actually two different ways of marking the antipassive in Chukchee, one involving the root suffix *ine*, the other based on the form *tku* which appears in either prefix or suffix position, depending on the root. There is a subtle meaning difference between the two, and in a full account of Chukchee, all such facts would have to be dealt with, but for current purposes we can ignore these questions.)

One possibility is that this counterpart constituent is actually a complement in the way *by* is with respect to the English passive. In that case, the nature of the rule would be straightforward: we want a lexical entry for a transitive verb to guarantee the existence of an antipassive version of that verb, so that for every description satisfying (124)a, there is a morphologically related form of the verb conforming to that description which satisfies (124)b. In addition, we need to ensure that there is an optional absolute counterpart constituent, marked according to the specification in the ABSCASE feature, and that the new verb form itself bears the relevant phonology signaling the antipassive form. All of these requirements are met in the following lexical rule:

$$(125) \quad \begin{bmatrix} \text{PHON} & \boxed{1} \\ \text{ABSCASE} & \boxed{2} \\ \text{SPR} & \langle \text{NP}_1 \rangle \\ \text{COMPS} & \langle \text{NP} \rangle \oplus \boxed{3} \end{bmatrix} \supset \begin{bmatrix} \text{PHON} & f_{antipassive}(\boxed{1}) \\ \text{SPR} & \langle \, \rangle \\ \text{COMPS} & \langle \text{NP}_1 \rangle \oplus \boxed{3} \left(\oplus \left\langle \text{NP} \begin{bmatrix} \text{CASE} & \boxed{2} \end{bmatrix} \right\rangle \right) \end{bmatrix}$$

Here the notation $f_{antipassive}$ denotes a function which, given the phonological form of any verb, returns the phonology of the antipassive form of that verb. Stated in the form given in (125), the rule will operate regardless of the number of other complements that intervene between the absolutive constituent NP_1 and the optional absolutive counterpart constituent. Alternative affixation patterns make the actual situation more complex than depicted in (125), so that we may have at least two different functors taking $\boxed{1}$ as an argument. But (125) reflects the essential form that any variant of the antipassive rule in Chukchee will have to take: it will yield an empty SPR list and an optional counterpart to the ergator.

On the other hand, suppose that the optional absolutive counterpart constituent is a syntactic adjunct. In accordance with the treatment of adjuncts in Chapter 2, we can ensure the correct correlation between the case of such adjuncts and the particular antipassive verb by appealing to the same ABSCASE feature already introduced in connection with (125). In the scenario just described, we would still have a rule along the lines of (125), but there would be no optional complement term NP[CASE $\boxed{2}$]; rather, the rule would take the form

$$(126) \quad \begin{bmatrix} \text{PHON} & \boxed{1} \\ & \\ \text{SS} & \begin{bmatrix} \text{HEAD}|\text{ABSCASE} & \boxed{2} \\ \text{SPR} \langle \text{NP}_1 \rangle \\ \text{COMPS} \langle \text{NP} \rangle \oplus \boxed{3} \rangle \end{bmatrix} \end{bmatrix} \supset \begin{bmatrix} \text{PHON} & f_{antipassive}(\boxed{1}) \\ & \\ \text{SS} & \begin{bmatrix} \text{HEAD} & \begin{bmatrix} \text{VFORM} & antipass \\ \text{ABSCASE} & \boxed{2} \end{bmatrix} \\ \text{SPR} & \langle \, \rangle \\ \text{COMPS} & \langle \text{NP}_1 \rangle \oplus \boxed{3} \end{bmatrix} \end{bmatrix}$$

where we assign the ABSCASE specification to HEAD so that it will be 'visible' in the VP projected from the antipassive verb. The output of this rule will have the same ABSCASE value as the input, and will interact (indirectly) with a class of adjunct entries all of which share the partial description

(127)

$$\left[\text{SS} \begin{bmatrix} \text{CASE} & \boxed{1} \\ \text{MOD|ABSCASE} & \boxed{1} \\ \text{VFORM} & \textit{antipass} \end{bmatrix} \right]$$

The following kind of structure will therefore be licensed:

(128)

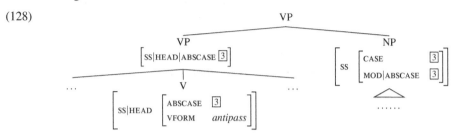

Our framework thus has the descriptive resources to capture economically both the relational dependency between transitive and antipassive constructions and the morphological dependency between the particular antipassive verb and the optional counterpart to the transitive absolute, whether the syntactic relationship between the two is head/complement or head/adjunct.

4.7   What Comes Next?

The brief survey of relational dependencies given in this chapter is of course no more than a point of departure – there is a considerable variety of such dependencies, with many differences in detail cross-linguistically; thus, the Coast Salishan language Halkomelen has an antipassive construction broadly parallel to that in Chukchee, with the possibility of an overt counterpart constituent, while the related Interior Salishan language Thompson has an antipassive in which the semantic role corresponding to the transitive absolutive is never overtly realized in any form – a situation which would be parallel to a language which had a passive construction similar to English but where there was no *by* phrase making overt the agent corresponding to the passive subject patient. Details of this sort are often extremely complex, particularly with respect to the morphology involved, but the fundamental dependency relationships themselves are straightforwardly embodied in the kinds of lexical generalizations about valence relationships exhibited in implicational rules of the kind displayed in this chapter.

As noted early in our review of these dependencies, earlier approaches to these kinds of relational dependencies assumed a kind of rule, labeled *transformation*, which mapped structures meeting particular descriptions into different structures, a mechanism far more powerful than necessary, reflecting the origins of this particular approach to syntax in formalisms in which the grammar did not contain an actual lexicon and categories were atomic, with no internal content. Although the picture is currently quite different, where the great majority of alternative approaches to syntax reject rules of this kind, there is an important point of resemblance between transformations and lexical rules: both kinds of statement are sensitive to the combinatorial details of the objects to which they apply. Transformations are applicable to structures only if certain structural conditions are met; lexical rules establish the existence in the lexicon of one class of forms given certain specific valence specifications of another, related class of forms. Thus, the existence of relational dependencies is predicated, within each approach, on certain assumptions about the structural properties of the classes of sentences that are related to each other by the appropriate rules in each of the two respective approaches.

There is, however, a significant asymmetry in this comparison. Transformational rules are inherently nonlocal, with much greater 'reach' than lexical rules, and hence the structures that can be related to each other by transformations can be much larger, with essentially arbitrary positions in trees connected via the application of such rules. Lexical rules, in contrast, cannot 'look' any further than the information made available on the valence lists of selecting heads. In effect, the trees which can be related to each other by the use of lexical rules – and then only indirectly – are restricted to the two-generation objects that are licensed by, for example, the Head-complement Rule, the Head-subject Rule and so on. Thus, while both transformations and lexical rules can be (and typically have been) used as probes and diagnostics for structure, the structures they point to are quite different classes of object. Where we see a grammatical dependency that can be captured by a lexical rule, the pattern of covariation revealed by that rule is completely local, which leads to radically different analyses of clause structure in the two approaches. In the following chapter, we will examine in detail one aspect of this divergence in perspectives, specifically, the configurational properties of infinitival complements, and various strands of evidence which can be brought to bear on the analytic issues posed by such complements.

5   Infinitival Complements

5.1   Consequences of the V NP VP Analysis

In the previous chapter, we saw evidence from a number of distributional patterns that strongly pointed in the direction of a nonclausal analysis as the right one for the sequence *Rocco to arrive early* in, for example, *I expect Rocco to arrive early*. As the discussion in Chapter 4 makes clear, the behavior of NPs with respect to the following infinitive VP when following the passive form of verbs such as *expect, believe, assume,* and many others strongly supports the analysis of both NP and VP as complements of those verbs (a conclusion, it should be stressed, perfectly compatible with the clausal analysis of NP VP[VFORM*inf*] mandated by cases such as *All I want is him to apologize* (see http://in.answers.yahoo.com/question/index? qid=20110601113931AAkfRdX, e.g., and the examples given in the preceding chapter). Once we adopt the NP VP[VFORM *inf*] analysis, of course, we have to live with the consequences – and those consequences are nontrivial. We know, for example, that verbs select subjects, sometimes in a very restrictive fashion, and that that selection is tied up with how the Head-specifier Rule interacts with the SPR specification of the selecting verbs. What we see in the case of verbs such as *expect* parallels the behavior of selected subjects even though no clausal structure is involved.

(1) a.   There is nothing wrong with you.

   b.   Most people expect $\left\{\begin{array}{c}\text{there}\\ \text{*it}\\ \text{*Rocco}\end{array}\right\}$ to be nothing wrong with you.

   c. $\left\{\begin{array}{c}\text{There}\\ \text{*It}\\ \text{*Rocco}\end{array}\right\}$ is expected to be nothing wrong with you.

(2) a. $\left\{\begin{array}{c}\text{It}\\ \text{*there}\\ \text{*Rocco}\end{array}\right\}$ will rain tomorrow.

   b.   Many people expect $\left\{\begin{array}{c}\text{it}\\ \text{*there}\\ \text{*Rocco}\end{array}\right\}$ to rain tomorrow.

194

c. $\left\{ \begin{array}{l} \text{*It} \\ \text{There} \\ \text{*Rocco} \end{array} \right\}$ is expected to be nothing wrong with you.

(3) a. $\left\{ \begin{array}{l} \text{Rocco} \\ \text{*There} \\ \text{*It} \end{array} \right\}$ buys ice cream.

b.   Many people expect $\left\{ \begin{array}{l} \text{Rocco} \\ \text{*there} \\ \text{*it} \end{array} \right\}$ to buy ice cream.

c. $\left\{ \begin{array}{l} \text{Rocco} \\ \text{*There} \\ \text{*It} \end{array} \right\}$ is expected to buy ice cream.

NP complement selection works in *expect* NP VP[*inf*] constructions in complete parallel to subject selection in finite clauses, in the sense that the NP and VP complement possibilities following *expect* are exactly what the NP VP possibilities are in finite structures of the form [$_s$ NP VP]. But, in the latter class of cases, it's the Head-specifier Rule which ensures the match between the SPR specification on the VP and the SYNSEM attributes of the subject daughter, whereas that clearly cannot be the scenario in [$_{vp}$ V NP VP] structures. Thus, despite the fact that – so far as passive structures are concerned, at least – the selected NP complement behaves, as per the discussion in the preceding chapter, exactly the way any transitive object should behave, we seem to be missing a generalization here, to the effect that NP VP sequences seem to behave the same regardless of whether they occur as clear Ss or as a series of constituents following verbs such as *believe*, *expect*, and so on. This generalization would, of course, be easily captured if we simply treated the NP VP[*inf*] sequences in these examples as instances of S[*inf*]. Indeed, this consideration was one of the principal reasons for the persistence of clausal analyses in the case of *expect*–type verbs. On the other hand, the negatives associated with such an analysis are obvious; for example, we no longer have a simple account of how the passive works, the susceptibility of infinitival subjects but not finite clause subjects to Heavy NP Shift becomes a matter of sheer stipulation, etc. Again, we seem to have reached an analytic impasse.

But the apparent impasse vanishes as soon as one adopts an analysis of lexical heads which allows them to specify their subject requirements as an inherent valence property via the SPR feature. The treatment of subject selection in the case of auxiliaries made it clear that the subject specifications of heads are *transferable*: as we saw in Chapter 3, when the head combines with complements to form a phrase which maintains the head's SPR value, that phrase may then be selected by a chameleonlike lexical item which adopts the same SUBJ value as its own. So far, we've attributed the subject-value sharing property only to auxiliaries. But there's no reason in principle to restrict this subject-sharing property to [AUX +]

heads exclusively. Suppose instead that there are nonauxiliary heads which, like auxiliaries, correlate certain of their own properties with attributes of their complements. *Expect* and *believe* select VP[*inf*]s freely, and have access to the SPR values of these VPs, but also, obviously, to the SYNSEM values of their other complements. It thus represents a natural possibility, under this architecture, that the two are connected – that certain verbs might identify their direct objects' SYNSEM values with the SPR values of their VP complements. The effect of this lexically based requirement would be exactly the same as the relationship between VP heads of clauses and their subjects: in both cases, a constituent must satisfy the description imposed by its sister VP's SPR specification. But in the case we're now discussing, this constraint is imposed by specific identities posited in the lexical entries for the verbs in question, rather than arising from a very general schematic rule of the grammar.

We can make this structural identity requirement precise along similar lines to our treatment of auxiliaries in Chapter 3. Equating the SPR specification of the VP to the selecting head's direct object valence requirement is as simple as writing

(4)
$$\begin{bmatrix} \text{PHON} & \langle \text{expect} \rangle \\ \text{SS|SYN|COMPS} & \left\langle \boxed{1}, \text{VP}\begin{bmatrix} \text{HEAD|VFORM} & \textit{inf} \\ \text{SPR} & \boxed{1} \end{bmatrix}\right\rangle \end{bmatrix}$$

The VP itself will, figuratively speaking, inherit its SPR specification from its head daughter, and this specification is aligned with the SYNSEM value of the NP complement in view of the conditions imposed by (4). Given a head *expect*, then, the tree in (5) is licensed:

(5)

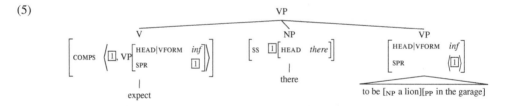

Assume for the moment that the critical properties of the VP *to be a lion in the garage* are the same as those of *is a lion in the garage* except for the infinitive VFORM specification. This assumption requires that the SPR specification on this infinitive VP be the same as that on the finite existential copula itself. The feature identities that *expect* imposes on its complement specifications in (4) are identical to those that any given auxiliary imposes on its own subject specification on the basis of its VP valent's subject requirements. Thus, the same valence mechanism accounts for both *There may be a lion in the garage* and *I expect there to be a lion in the garage*, except that in the second case, the identity between the SYNSEM value of *there* and the SPR of the VP headed by the copula is in effect imposed directly by *expect*, which, by fiat, enforces this requirement across the board between its NP complement and its VP[SPR] value. No structural relationship of the sort necessary to satisfy the Head-specifier Rule is required – putting it simply, the head of the VP itself does the work of ensuring that its direct object meets the requirements that its VP complement imposes on its subject.

This strictly lexical property of *expect, believe*, and similar verbs thus has the effect of creating a structural parallel between true clausal structure ($[_s$ XP[SYNSEM $\boxed{1}$] VP[SPR $\langle[\boxed{1}]\rangle$]]) and the complement structure of the verbs in question ($[_{vp}$ V XP[SYNSEM $\boxed{1}$]] VP[SPR $\langle[\boxed{1}]\rangle$]]). To the extent that the meaning of a linguistic expression is in part dependent on taking grammatical relations to translate into certain semantic roles – a point we return to directly – we have a compact account of the parallel semantics between *I expect Rocco to get the job* and *Rocco will get the job*, while at the same time making exactly the right predictions about the applicability of the passive lexical rule, the fact that *Rocco expects himself/*him to do better in competition than he has so far* (where the third person pronoun forms are intended to be understood as referring to Rocco), and so on.

Several interesting predictions follow from this analysis. Let's begin by comparing the meaning relationships in the following pairs:

(6) a.   I expect Rocco.

   b.   I expect Rocco to not show up yet again.

(7) a.   I believe Rocco.

   b.   I believe Rocco to be a liar.

(8) a.   I judge Rocco.

   b.   I judge Rocco to be outside my jurisdiction.

A striking feature of such examples is that they reflect a relationship of some kind between the speaker and Rocco in the (a) examples which does not hold in the (b) cases. In (7), for example, the speaker gives credence to Rocco himself, taking him as a truth-teller. Clearly that's not the case in the second sentence; even though we see *Rocco* as the direct object of *believe*, the speaker obviously does not give credence to Rocco, but rather to the assertion expressed by *Rocco to be a liar*. Thus (7)b can be paraphrased as *I believe that Rocco is a liar*, a phrasing which makes it clear that the belief relationship holds between the speaker and the claim that Rocco himself is *not* to be believed. Thus, there will need to be two *believe* verbs in the lexicon, one which specifies an NP object for *believe* and posits a particular kind of relationship between the subject of *believe* and its object, and a second *believe* which specifies an NP complement (or, more generally, an XP complement, as in *I wouldn't expect [*AP *proud of yourself] to be how you're feeling right now*) and a VP object for *believe* and posits a very similar relationship (though clearly not identical) between the subject and, in this case, the assertion itself.

Let us suppose now that the meaning of *believe* in (7) is the same as that of *believe* in *I believe that Rocco is a liar*, denoting a relationship between its own subject and some assertion of a logical truth – in the case of (7), the assertion that results from combining the meaning of its infinitive VP complement with the meaning of the NP complement satisfying that VP's SPR valence requirement. There are a variety of systems for the formal representation of meaning which will automatically make this combination of meanings exactly the same as that of the sentence *(that) Rocco is a liar*. On this account, the two sentences *I believe (that) Rocco is a liar* and *I believe Rocco to be a liar* are completely synonymous.

But the real payoff of this analysis emerges when we consider how to license examples such as *Rocco is believed to be a liar*, whose origins in the lexicon are guaranteed by the interaction between the entry for infinitive-seeking *believe* and the passive lexical rule. The passive rule will apply to (9)a and return a licensing of (9)b:

(9)
a.
$$
\begin{bmatrix}
\text{PHON} & \langle\text{believe}\rangle \\
\text{SS} & \begin{bmatrix}
\text{HEAD} & \begin{bmatrix} trans\text{-}verb \\ \text{VFORM} \quad bare \end{bmatrix} \\
\text{SPR} & \langle \text{NP}[norm] \rangle \\
\text{COMPS} & \left\langle \boxed{1}\,\text{NP}, \text{VP}\begin{bmatrix} \text{VFORM} & inf \\ \text{SPR} & \langle\boxed{1}\rangle \end{bmatrix} \right\rangle
\end{bmatrix}
\end{bmatrix}
$$

b.
$$
\begin{bmatrix}
\text{PHON} & \langle\text{believed}\rangle \\
\text{SS} & \begin{bmatrix}
\text{HEAD} & \begin{bmatrix} intrans\text{-}verb \\ \text{VFORM} \quad passive \end{bmatrix} \\
\text{SPR} & \langle \boxed{1} \rangle \\
\text{COMPS} & \left\langle \text{VP}\begin{bmatrix} \text{VFORM} & inf \\ \text{SPR} & \langle\boxed{1}\rangle \end{bmatrix} \right\rangle
\end{bmatrix}
\end{bmatrix}
$$

The passive version of *believe* which this rule posits in (9)b has an NP subject corresponding to the direct object of its corresponding nonpassive form. But the meaning of the active and passive forms are the same. In *Rocco is believed to be a liar*, the passive form *believed* still denotes a relation between some individual (who may not be identified, depending on whether the *by* phrase option is taken or not) and the assertion that takes Rocco to belong to a set of individuals meeting the description conveyed by *liar*: the passive subject SPR value, though (via the passive rule) no longer the direct object, is still identical to the subject specification of the VP that predicates being a liar of its own subject. The upshot is that *Rocco is believed to be a liar* is predicted by the lexical passive rule to assert some individual's belief that the property of being a liar holds of the NP which shows up as the passive subject and at the same time is the SPR value of *to be a liar*. We do not need *Rocco* to be, at any point, the *structural* subject of the infinitive VP – that is, a daughter of S, whose head daughter is the VP *to be a liar*. The critical aspect of the identical meaning conveyed by both *I believe Rocco to be a liar* and *Rocco is believed to be a liar* is the fact that *Rocco* is specified in the relevant head's lexical entry as the subject valent of *to be a liar*, and this effect is built into the very form of the passive lexical rule.

Similarly, in the case of examples such as (10), the relationship between the direct object of *expect* and the verb's infinitive VP complement also needs to be considered:

(10) a.   I expect several doctors to examine Rocco.

b.   I expect Rocco to be examined by several doctors.

The lexical entries for *expect* will parallel those for *believe* in most cases, and the VP in (10)a will take the form

(11)

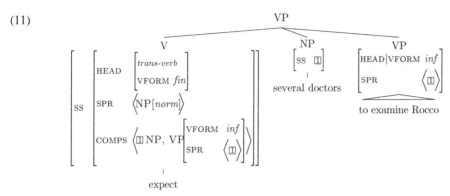

The lexical entry for *examine*, an ordinary transitive verb, interacts with the passive lexical rule to yield the (partial) description

(12)

$$\begin{bmatrix} \text{PHON} & \langle \text{examined} \rangle \\ \text{SS} & \begin{bmatrix} \text{HEAD}|\text{VFORM} & pass \\ \text{SUBJ}\langle \text{NP} \rangle \\ \text{COMPS}\langle \text{PP}[by] \rangle \end{bmatrix} \end{bmatrix}$$

and the Head-complement Rule headed by *expect* will be satisfied by a structure in which an infinitive VP is projected from this head if the former takes the form

(13)

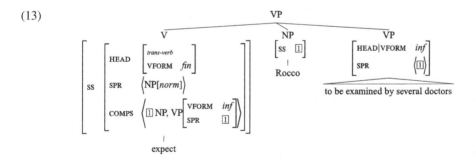

Again, *expect*, like *believe*, denotes a particular relationship between its own subject and an assertion or claim. The content of this claim arises from combining the semantic contributions of the complement NP (*Rocco*) with that of the complement VP (*to be examined by several doctors*), in exactly the same way that the meaning of the finite sentence *Rocco was examined by several doctors* arises from combining the meaning of *Rocco* with that of *was*

examined by several doctors. The passive rule, applied to *examine*, yields a form which preserves the relationship between Rocco and the doctors: in both cases, Rocco will be the target of the doctor's attention. So to expect Rocco to be examined by several doctors is to hold the expectation that Rocco will be the object of the doctors' examination, just as in the simple nonpassive version – because the passive rule leaves the semantic relationships of the passive subject unchanged from the semantic relationships holding of the nonpassive direct object. Thus, passive *expected* preserves the identification of the descriptions of active *examine*'s object on the one hand and the infinitive VP's subject on the other.

But things are quite different when we turn our attention to a different group of verbs, whose syntax is very similar to that of *believe/expect*. This second group of verbs is exemplified in the following data:

(14)   I $\left\{ \begin{array}{l} \text{a. forced} \\ \text{b. persuaded} \\ \text{c. begged} \end{array} \right\}$ several doctors to examine Rocco.

(15)   I $\left\{ \begin{array}{l} \text{a. forced} \\ \text{b. persuaded} \\ \text{c. begged} \end{array} \right\}$ Rocco to be examined by several doctors.

The a–c examples in (14) mean something quite different from their counterparts in (15), as attested by the fact that it is easy to imagine the situations communicated in one of these examples being true without the corresponding situations reported in the other being true as well – in marked contrast to, for example, the two examples in (10), where if one of these sentences is true, the other must be true as well, and likewise if one or the other is false. What's the difference here? The complement structure of both verb classes appears to be the same: heavy-NP shift examples such as *I've now persuaded to join us some of the most influential members of the Central Committee* show that the right analysis for such verbs is also [COMPS ⟨NP, VP [*inf*]⟩] – the same as that of verbs such as *expect* in the cases shown: both take a nominal direct object and an infinitive VP, and the object is mandated by the selecting head to match the subject specification of that VP. But there must be a difference somewhere that accounts for the behavior in (14)–(15).

A major clue to the contrast between these two classes of verbs becomes evident in contrasting pairs such as those in (16):

(16) a.   I $\left\{ \begin{array}{l} \text{believed} \\ \text{*convinced} \end{array} \right\}$ there to be a lion in the garage.

b.   I $\left\{ \begin{array}{l} \text{believed} \\ \text{convinced} \end{array} \right\}$ a lion to be in the closet.

Let's consider (5)→(16) in more detail.

In (16)a, the semantically meaningless NP *there* can appear as the direct object of verbs such as *believe*, which establish a meaning relationship between an individual (the subject) and the statement or claim whose truth that individual believes. As stressed above, these verbs in effect take no account of the meaning of the direct object. Instead, they link their object to the interpretation of *be a lion in the closet* by virtue of the identity condition they impose between their object value and the SPR value of their infinitive VP complement. And the semantically empty SPR value that *be a lion in the closet* thus acquires plays no more role in the semantic interpretation of this VP than it does in the stand-alone finite sentence *There is a lion in the closet*. The semantic translation mechanism which works in the latter case will work in exactly the same way in interpreting (16)a.

But (16)b is a different matter entirely. In the case of verbs such as *convince*, a relationship is understood to hold not only between an individual X denoted by the subject and a situation Σ denoted by the VP, but among Σ, X and a second individual Y who has a semantic relation to both of them: Y is the target of X's convincing, whose effect is that X's behavior causes Y to form an intention to carry out the action identified by the VP. Because the direct object NP has to have a semantic role in the relationship that the selecting verb denotes – identifying as it does the individual whose intention is so affected – a dummy element such as *there*, which denotes nothing that can form any intention (or indeed do anything else), makes the sentence impossible to interpret.

The telling point about (16) is that the two situations denoted by *A lion is in the garage* and *There is a lion in the garage* are identical, so the problem is not, per se, that a dummy element is in direct object position here; after all, (16)b shows that when a verb such as *believe* heads the VP, both the meaning-bearing NP and the dummy pronoun are perfectly fine, and mean the same thing. The robust contrast between the two sets of example in (16) falls out automatically on the assumption that *believe* and *convince*, in spite of their nearly identical syntax, differ in a critical fashion so far as the semantic status they assign to their valents: the direct object of the former will in general have no semantic relationship to the verb which selects it, whereas the direct object of the latter is assigned a semantic role by the verb and must therefore correspond to the sort of thing for which such a role makes sense.

A further consequence of this analysis is that a sentence such as (17)a will be perfectly good, and (17)b uncontroversially ill-formed:

(17)   There was $\left\{ \begin{array}{l} \text{a. expected} \\ \text{b. *persuaded} \end{array} \right\}$ to be a lion in the garage.

Practice Exercise

Explain precisely why the two examples in (17) have the respective degrees of acceptability that they display.

5.2   What Is Infinitival *to*?

In order to 'pin down' the syntactic aspect of the analyses just proposed, we need to characterize the infinitival marker *to*, which so far seems to be a bit of a mystery. We know that there is a *to* preposition in English, so the obvious place to start is with the hypothesis that infinitive *to* is that preposition, but the facts point overwhelming away from this possibility.

5.2.1   *To* as a Preposition?

It's worth recalling at this point the general methodological guideline that intuition is in general a poor guide to syntactic analysis. It's irrelevant whether or not, for any given speaker, *to* has the 'feel' or 'mental flavor' of a preposition; to take a by-now-familiar example, it's very likely that most speakers of English do not have the sense that *could*, for example, is a verb in the past tense, yet as we saw in Chapter 3, the evidence that modals are indeed verbs is very strong and yields an extremely simple, straightforward analysis of the English auxiliary system. Just as in the investigation of modals and their category status, the most direct way to assess the analysis of infinitival *to* as a preposition is to consider where it appears – that is, how much overlap there is in the respective distributions of infinitive and clearly prepositional *to*.

To begin with, consider the pattern of data in (18) vs that in (19):

(18) a.   For Rocco to do that would be strange.
    b.   It would be strange for Rocco to do that.

(19)   *For Leslie to Terry would be strange.

The extraposition pattern reflected in (18) shows that *For Rocco to do that* is a clausal subject, whose own subject is *Rocco*, making *to do that* a VP – a conclusion strongly reinforced by the fact that it can be modified by manner adverbials, which only attach to VPs, for example, *Why do you expect us cheerfully to do business with a business run with no ethics, that goes out of its way to annoy us, one more time?* (http://comments.gmane.org/gmane.comp .video.gimp.windows.user/11643) and many similar examples readily found on the internet. If *to* were a preposition, these infinitival VPs would have the structure in (20):

(20)   VP
       /\
   P   VP
   | |
   to ...

This is a highly anomalous configuration, however, in view of the fact that there is no evident example in English of a phrasal type whose leftmost daughter is a word belonging to a major lexical category (one for independent evidence exists that heads a class of phrases) and whose other daughter is a phrase, such that the category of the mother is that of the phrase, not the word. Given the absence of such [$_{VP}$ X YP] configurations in English, the analysis of infinitival *to* just sketched is already dubious. The framework developed in preceding chapters in fact guarantees this state of affairs as the default: if the VP in (20) were the correct structure, it would mean that the VP either had to take the lexical item *to* as a complement, which would be a contradiction since VPs by definition are saturated for their COMPS value, or as the SPR value, in which case *to do that* would be a complete clause on its own. But there would then be no way for *to do that* to combine yet again with, for example, *Rocco* in, say, *What I'm waiting for is Rocco to apologize to me* or *For Rocco to do that would be disastrous*.

The upshot is that an analysis of infinitives along the lines of (20) seems excluded at the outset by the framework itself. While this in itself might mean only that the framework needs to be revised, the conflict between the framework and the prepositional analysis of *to* concerns the violation represented by (20) of a very general pattern in English phrase structure that is, to a large extent, framework independent, as long as one is looking at phrase-structure-based approaches. Moreover, a further theory-neutral pattern is relevant here: in English, even neglecting the saturation issue just raised, heads invariably select complements which are to their *right*. Only subjects and determiners are selected by phrases to the left, and as we've seen, it doesn't seem possible for *to* to be a subject. The only alternative then is for *to* to be a specifier of some kind, but here again, as per the discussion in Chapter 2, we have no even moderately strong evidence that VPs in English *ever* have specifier arguments apart from their own subjects.

Suppose we were to ignore this last point and pressed on with the assumption *to* is some kind of preposition which serves as the specifier of a VP head. The result would be an empirical disaster. Consider what this analysis, representable as (21), would entail.

(21)

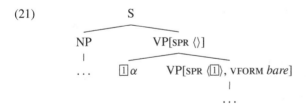

Imagine, that is, that α is [$_P$ *to*]. What would the VFORM value of the mother VP in (21) then have to be? Throughout the whole range of English verbal constructions, the VFORM value of the mother is shared with that of its *verb*-type head. This exceptionless pattern dictates that the VFORM value of *to apologize to me* is *bare*, which means that the infinitival VP is eligible to be selected as the complement of, say, *should* or any other modal, since VP[*bare*] complements are what these auxiliaries select exclusively. But the result of such a combination is completely ill-formed:

(22)   Rocco $\left\{\begin{array}{c} \text{should} \\ \text{will} \\ \text{can't} \end{array}\right\}$ (*to) apologize to me.

The proposal that *to* is a prepositional specifier therefore appears fundamentally inadequate to capture basic facts about the distribution of VPs in English. And since *to* cannot be a prepositional head, given the strong evidence that infinitivals are indeed VPs, the contraindications for the prepositional analysis of infinitival *to* are overwhelming.

5.2.2   *To* as a Complementizer?

There is yet another possibility we might consider, however. Recall from Chapter 2 that English finite clauses are often associated with a class of marker elements, illustrated in (23):

(23) a.   I believe (**that**) Rocco is a spy.

b.   I wonder $\left\{\begin{array}{c} \textbf{if} \\ \textbf{whether} \end{array}\right\}$ Rocco is a spy.

The *for* which shows up in infinitival clauses, discussed at length in the preceding chapter, appears to be an analogue of the finite complementizer *that* (though unlike the latter, it is obligatory in most occurrences of infinitive clauses):

(24)   *(**For**) Rocco to do that would be outrageous.

Complementizers have traditionally been grouped together with coordinating particles such as *and*, *or*, *but* and quantifying determiners (*the*, *some*, *all* etc.) as a 'minor' category, that is, one which does not head phrases. Nonetheless, there is a school of thought which takes the head of a *that* clause to be *that* itself, not the sentence which it is sister to. There are various arguments on behalf of this position, but none of them seems to have the *gravitas* of counterargument that no sentences can appear with these putative heads at the root level. *That Rocco is a spy* is irremediably bad, and so is every monoclausal sentence in English which begins with a complementizer. This seems strikingly bizarre behavior for material which is, as discussed in Chapter 2, the supposed core element of the clausal constituent, and the case is aggravated by the fact that, even internally, there are many contexts where the supposed 'head' is completely optional. The issue is not simple and deserves more extended discussion, but it seems prudent at this point to reject the hypothesis that the head of a clause with a complementizer is not the clause but rather the complementizer itself, until much more convincing arguments than have so far been offered on behalf of this proposal are put forward.

Recall from Chapter 2 that the Head-marker Rule can be stated as in (25):

(25)   **Head-marker Rule**

and that it licenses structures such as those in (26):

(26)

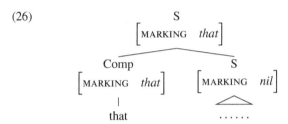

as well as the complement of *whether* in *I wonder whether to apply for this job*, while ruling out, for example, **I don't know if whether Rocco will apply for the job, *I know that that Leslie applied for this job once*, etc. The rule in (25) is stated so that the description of the head daughter on the right enforces a null MARKING value, ensuring, correctly, that we do not get strings of complementizers associated with a single S or VP.

The analysis embodied in (25) is predicated on the analysis of infinitival *to* as something other than a marker, an assumption which is arguably strongly supported by English data. If *to* were assigned to a category whose HEAD value was *marker*, we would have a structure along the following lines in the sentence *I wonder whether to apply for this job*:

(27)

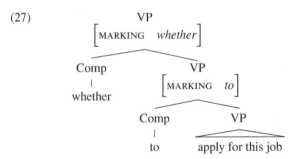

The configuration in (27) is immediately suspect: in English, sequences of markers for the same category are strongly prohibited (e.g., **I need to figure out whether if/if whether John is going into town*). The structure in (27) is therefore distinctly anomalous, requiring strong evidence to meet the burden of proof.

This conclusion is supported by a complex of phenomena involving displacement which unequivocally show that *to* cannot be a marker, or any other kind of nonhead. Much hangs on a robust generalization about displacement in English:

only dependents of heads can displace. As discussed in much more detail below, we find that complements, subjects, and adjuncts can all undergo displacement:

(28) a.   Those people, Rocco really likes__.
     b.   Those people I very much doubt__want to have anything to do with Rocco.
     c.   How prudently do the facts suggest Rocco acted__?

Heads, however, cannot themselves undergo displacement. Thus, while VPs can extract when they are themselves complements (all other things being equal), they cannot do so in their guise as, for example, adverbially modified heads:

(29) a.   Rocco could merely claim ignorance of the whole thing, and the case goes up in smoke.
     b.   And claim ignorance of the whole thing, Rocco could [vp (*merely) [__]] (assuming the same intonation pattern as in (29)a).

The difference between the possibilities in (29)b is that if *merely* does not appear, then *claim ignorance of the whole thing* corresponds to a displaced complement of *could*. But when *merely* appears, we have a configuration of the following sort:

(30)

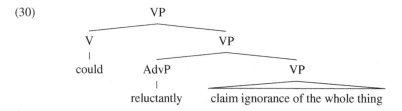

The VP *merely claim ignorance of the whole thing* is itself a complement of *could*, and as such can displace unproblematically:

(31)   Leslie suggests a conservative approach, that you merely claim ignorance of the whole thing – and merely claim ignorance of the whole thing you probably *could*__ – but I think there's a better strategy here.

But as (30) makes explicit, within the VP *merely claim ignorance of the whole thing*, the internal *claim ignorance of the whole thing* is the head, with *merely* only an adjunct. The contrast in behavior that (29)b–(31) exemplifies is completely representative of the contrast in extractability between dependents of heads and the heads themselves.

    Equipped with this test, we can now assess whether or not, in a sentence such as *I definitely intend to claim ignorance of the whole thing*, we can acceptably extract *claim ignorance of the whole thing*, in which case we would have powerful confirmation that *to* is optimally analyzed as a head. A negative result would not in itself rule out the headship of *to*, since there might be factors independent of headship that led to such an outcome, but the burden of proof on those taking *to* to be a head would be quite heavy. The data in (32) make it clear that the bare form VP following *to* can indeed displace:

(32)   ... and claim ignorance of the whole thing I definitely intend to__.

Note as well the following data, taken from sites on the internet:

(33) a.   I now have the evidence to enable me to challenge all those involved, and
           challenge them I intend to. (Peter, 1994, `http://menz.org.nz/cosa/`
           `horror-stories/`)

     b.   Whatever we saw and did was totally controlled, hopefully one day I can
           return at my own leisure and return I intend to. (www.solokat.com/`the`
           `-fortress-town-of-gyangze/`)

There is ample evidence that VP fronting from positions immediately following
to is no more problematic than from any other context. The clear inference from
these facts must be the head status of *to* within its VP.

This conclusion has a very counterintuitive consequence, however. We know
that sequences such as *to undergo such treatment* are VPs; for example, they
are modifiable by manner adverbs, as the following examples, all found on the
internet, make clear:

(34) a.   It well illustrates how low we must have sunk when they expect us quietly
           to undergo such treatment.

     b.   We cannot expect them quietly to fight on our behalf, if we do not look after
           their families who are left behind.

     c.   I want eventually to leave here.

But if infinitive *to* is a head, and its mother's category is VP, then this must mean
that *to* is a *verb*! This at first glance seems completely wrong. How could *to* be a
verb, when it exhibits virtually no morphological properties that link it to verbs
(or indeed, any morphological properties at all)?

Nonetheless, the analysis of *to* as a verb is not as aberrant as one might
think. For one thing, we already know of verbs which have extremely limited
morphological variation – the modals, for example, and among the modals, *ought*
is morphologically completely invariant, revealing its ancient connection with
verbal tense only in the morphologically vestigial final *-t* linking it to a past
tense form, as we found in Chapter 3. Another modal, the verb *need*, selects the
bare form VP valent typical for modals *She need not do this*, as vs the ordinary
nonauxiliary *need* which takes an infinitival VP *She needs to do this*; the first
can invert (*Need she do this?*) whereas the second cannot (**Needs she to do
this?*), and there are many other grammatically fundamental differences between
them, *including* the fact that the modal *need* is morphologically completely
fixed: **Needed she do that?, I don't think she need(*s) do that* and so on. So
morphological invariance is in itself not all that troublesome for *to*'s status as a
verb, particularly if it can be shown to be not just a verb, but an auxiliary – an
invariably *tenseless* auxiliary.

The hypothesis that *to* is an auxiliary makes sense: given that *to* is the head
daughter of its infinitival VP, it must be a verb, and auxiliaries are the class
of verbs with the greatest degree of morphological idiosyncrasy, and, like all

auxiliaries apart from the copula, infinitival *to* on this analysis only appears with VP complement sisters. Nonetheless, the identification in Chaper 3 of a class of one or more properties that qualify a word for membership in the auxiliary category mandates an application of these tests, the NICE characteristics, to determine if *to* qualifies. But before applying these tests, we need to reexamine them to determine the true conditions under which they apply, to ensure that we understand what we can expect to see if *to* is indeed an auxiliary.

5.2.3   NICE Revisited

The NICE properties examined in Chapter 3 which set the auxiliary verbs off as a class from others in terms of their distributional possibilities are actually more restricted than our earlier discussion indicated. There is a subtle but very important condition which applies to negation – in particular, the negative adverb *not* displays a distribution whose pattern is somewhat disguised, but which facts about contraction can help us tease out. The key examples involve the interaction between negation and the auxiliaries *can/could*. We have the following examples:

(35) a.   You could (just) not say anything.
    b.   You could not just say anything.
    c.   You could not have said anything.

Note that, when *just* is missing from the first example, the sentence is actually ambiguous: on the one hand, it can communicate the speaker's observation that it would not be possible for the addressee to say anything in some situation or other, and on the other it expresses a suggestion or recommendation – or at least itemization of a possibility – that the hearer remain silent in that situation. In the first case, we would say that negation has *wide scope*; that is, the possibility conveyed by, for example, *You could say something* is negated, so that we could paraphrase this reading of (35)a as *It would not be possible for you to say anything*. In the second case, the appropriate paraphrase would be something like *It would be possible for you to not say anything*. The difference is the size of the syntactic domain to whose meaning the adverb *not* applies negation: in the latter interpretation, *not* applies just to the meaning of *say anything*. *Could*, indicating possibility, is *not* negated. In this second sense, then, the negation of *say anything* is nothing more than an option available to the hearer. But in the first interpretation, *not* applies to the whole sense of the VP combination of *could* + the unnegated VP *say anything* – in effect, the negation cancels the possibility of any utterance on the hearer's part. The key structural correlate of this distinction is revealed, just as in the case of *Rocco tried not eating* in our discussion of negation in Chapter 3, when we displace first *say anything* and then *not say anything*:

(36) a.   . . . and say anything you could not__.
    b.   . . . and not say anything you (definitely) could__.

The displaceability of *say anything* in (36)a makes clear that here it is a complement of *could*, and hence there is no ambiguity: the displaced VP must be a sister to the head V *could*, or displacement could not take place. Corresponding to this elimination of the uncertainty in the identification of structure, we find only one meaning available: *not* scopes widely, since (36)a can only be understood as ruling out the possibility of you saying anything. On the other hand, (36)b can only have the reading which admits the possibility of you saying nothing. And here, we can see immediately that *not* must be part of an internal VP, rather than a sister to *could* as in (36)a. Thus, (32)a, suppressing a possibility, corresponds to (37)a, and (32)b, which communicates a possibility to the hearer, corresponds to (37)b:

(37)   a.   b.

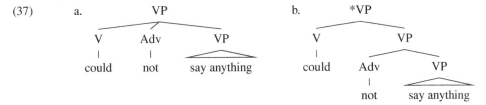

Consider now what happens if we realize the *just* option in (37)a. It is difficult or impossible to interpret *You could just not say anything* except as a case of narrow negation. This result follows automatically if *just* is assumed, as seems quite reasonable, to be a modifying adverb attached as an adjunct to a VP. If so, then necessarily the structure of this version of (37)a will contain a VP:

(38)

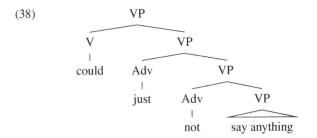

There are two points to take into account here. First, since *just* is a strictly left-attaching adjunct to a VP (so you cannot say *Leslie cannot stand Terry just*), the *not* which occurs to its right must be internal to that VP, as depicted in (38), and therefore cannot have been selected by the higher head verb *could*. Second, on the line of analysis taken here (based on the structural evidence provided by displaceability), the higher position of negation is associated with wider scope, and a lower position for *not* associated with *not* scoping lower, as in (37)b and (38). Given these two observations, the narrow-only interpretation we see for the examples in which *just* appears is an automatic consequence of the required phrase structure for such examples, based on the distribution of *just*. This prediction in turn adds further support for the plausibility of the two structural possibilities – complement and adjunct – we are considering for the placement of *not*, and for the association of wide and narrow negation as the respective meanings of these placements. We can summarize our diagnostic criteria to this point in the following chart:

(39)

	VP displaces	*not* + VP displaces	Negation scopes wide	Negation scopes narrow
Complement *not*	yes	no	yes	no
Internal adjunct *not*	no	yes	no	yes

These correlations between syntactic form and the semantics of negation have an important consequence bearing on the question of when negation via *not* is an applicable test for constituency. Notice that in (40)a, only narrow negation is available, as vs (40)b:

(40)   You could { a. have not / b. not have } said anything.

Based on what we've seen so far, this pattern is quite unexpected, given that *have* as an auxiliary should be able to select *not* as a complement. Moreover, this effect is quite general:

(41) a.   Rocco could be not sleeping.

 b.   Rocco could have been not sleeping.

In none of these cases where *not* follows a nonfinite auxiliary is it able to convey widest negation, applying to the highest VP. There are two possible explanations here:

•   selection of *not* complements is confined to finite auxiliaries; or

•   all auxiliaries can select *not*, but *not* complements are only able to apply negation to the VP projected from the head which selects them.

What this second possibility means is that in an example such as (41)a, with the structure (42), the highest scope that *not* can achieve – the largest 'chunk of meaning' that it can negate, so to speak – is the VP headed by *be*, which selected *not*.

(42)

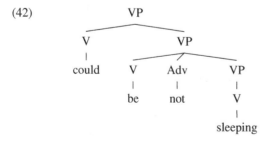

Since *could* did not select *not*, *not* fails to negate widely enough to include the part of the meaning that *could* contributes.

But if this second approach were correct, it should still be possible to displace the lowermost VP dominating *sleeping*, since this VP would after all be a complement of *be*, not a head on its own, just as we can do in, for example, ... *and sleeping, Rocco definitely is* __. What we instead find is the opposite:

(43) a. *... and say anything you could have not __.

b. *... and sleeping, Rocco could $\left\{ \begin{array}{c} be \\ have\ been \end{array} \right\}$ not__.

This failure of displaceability very strongly suggests that *not* is barred in complement position from such structures, and is simply unavailable as a selection possibility of nonfinite verbs. The verdict seems then to be that only finite auxiliaries have *not* complements. The examples in (42) are thus not legal, and in *Rocco could be not sleeping, not sleeping* must itself be a constituent with *not* in adjunct position, a sister to the VP *sleeping*.

There is, moreover, an additional fact which suggests that the restriction of wide scope negation to finite auxiliaries is the right analysis: the distribution of the contracted forms of negation consistently corresponds exclusively to finite contexts:

(44) a. Rocco couldn't have been sleeping at that time.

b. *Rocco could haven't been sleeping at that time.

c. *Rocco could have beenn't sleeping at that time.

Haven't exists as a morphological form, but only when the verb is finite. If contraction appears sensitive to finiteness, then this may well suggest that negation is not available to auxiliaries which are not finite.

This conclusion has immediate implications for the hypothesis that *to* is an invariable nonfinite auxiliary, in contrast to the invariably finite modals. In particular, we do not expect *to* to display contraction, and we do not expect any instance of *not* it appears with to have the status of a complement. In the latter case, we have positive structural evidence, parallel to the data in (43), that *to* does not tolerate a *not* complement:

(45) a. I hope to not have to talk to her about any of this.

b. *... and have to talk to her about any of this I hope to not__.

This pattern is completely general and is exactly what we expect in the scenario where *not* is adjoined under VP to the VP *have to talk to her about any of this*, as in (46):

(46)

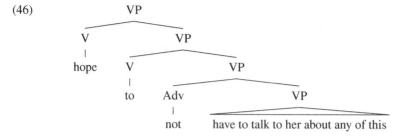

The upshot of all this is that contraction and *not* complement selection are reserved for finite auxiliaries, and that as an intrinsically nonfinite form, the N and C components of the NICE 'test suite' for auxiliary status are automatically inapplicable.

Similar restrictions also interfere with our use of I(nversion) to assess the status of *to*. Regardless of what work the inversion is doing – interrogation (*Had you known about Rocco's problems?*), Negative fronting (*Never till then had we met so many strange people in a single evening*) or counterfactuality (*Had I known then what I know now, I'd have acted much sooner*) – the only verbs we ever see in inverted structures are finite auxiliaries. This pattern needs to be formulated in the grammar in some appropriate fashion, but the descriptive generalization itself is exceptionless in English. If *to* is always and only nonfinite, then we expect that it will never undergo inversion, and that is just what we find. Thus, N, I, and C are all denied us as diagnostic tools simply on the basis of *to*'s inherent tenselessness.

But there is one test left, and it proves to be completely indifferent to VFORM value. Ellipsis is available across the whole range of auxiliary inflectional possibilities. Note the morphosyntactic range of the auxiliaries preceding the ellipsis site (notated with ∅):

(47) a.   Rocco isn't sleeping, but John is ∅. ([VFORM *fin*])

b.   John hasn't been sleeping, but Anne has been ∅. ([VFORM *psp*])

c.   Bill shouldn't have taken that exam, but Sue should have ∅. ([VFORM *bare*])

Regardless of the morphological form of the auxiliary, it supports ellipsis. And, usefully, nonauxiliaries, regardless of lexical class, which select VPs do *not* support ellipsis:

(48) a.   *Joe $\left\{ \begin{array}{l} \text{expects} \\ \text{appears} \\ \text{hopes} \end{array} \right\}$ to be in control of the situation, and Luanne

$\left\{ \begin{array}{l} \text{expects} \\ \text{appears} \\ \text{hopes} \end{array} \right\}$ ∅ as well.

b.   *Anne $\left\{ \begin{array}{l} \text{imagined} \\ \text{envisioned} \\ \text{contemplated} \end{array} \right\}$ (bravely) swimming the English Channel,

$$\text{and Bill} \left\{ \begin{array}{l} \text{imagined} \\ \text{envisioned} \\ \text{contemplated} \end{array} \right\} \varnothing \text{ as well.}$$

We thus have a very clear diagnostic that is still applicable. Verb phrase ellipsis is something that we see for every auxiliary and fail to see in the case of every nonauxiliary, with no morphological limits on its use as a probe. The hypothesis that *to* is an inflectionally defective tenseless auxiliary thus commits us to the prediction that of the NICE properties the first three will be inapplicable, but E will be relevant and will yield positive results. And this is just what we find:

(49) a.   Rocco wants to go to the movies, but Luanne doesn't want to ∅.
  b.   Rocco expects to succeed, and Sue expects to ∅ as well.

To thus fits the profile of a nonfinite auxiliary exactly, on the basis of the evidence so far, and given that basis, the burden of proof in the discussion falls on the shoulders of someone who objects to the classification of *to* as an auxiliary verb. There have in fact been various such objections over the years, but careful examination of them makes clear that their critical arguments fail to take into account the significant distributional differences between finite and nonfinite auxiliaries; when this error is corrected for, very little remains of the counterarguments offered in the challenges to auxiliary *to* that have been offered.

And there is additional evidence, if more were needed. Recent research in syntax has revealed a somewhat strange set of data in which what appears to be a nominal wh-form has been displaced from the complement position of an auxiliary head, a position known to host only VPs:

(50) a.   Luanne said we should visit the Cluny, [NP which] we will __VP next time we're in Paris.
  b.   If Bill asks me to wash the dishes, [NP which] I already have __VP at least twice today, I'm going to scream.

This phenomenon can be verified as a pattern of normal English speech by searching for internet hits, which yield many examples. What is particularly interesting is that, like ellipsis, the pattern is completely confined to auxiliaries, as we see by attempting to carry out displacement of *which* from the complement position of other verbs when it is interpreted as anaphoric to a VP:

(51) a.   Rocco seems [**to find fault with everything**].
  b.   *If you want [**to find fault with everything**], **which** Rocco seems __ , you won't have many friends left.

Another important class of such examples are verbs such as *let, make, had*, as in *I let/made/had Rocco do some work for us*. Before we can apply the *which* extraction test here, however, we need to establish that these verbs are indeed eligible to undergo displacement, bearing in mind that if the bare form VP here is not a complement of these permissive/coercive verbs, the test will be pointless, since heads cannot displace. The passive is at least a sufficient test of complement status for the VP when applied to a sequence V NP VP, since passivization of the NP will only be possible if V actually selects NP, in which case we know that the V is a sister of the NP, and therefore that the VP (apart from the possibility that it is an adjunct, which the failure of *do so* replacement rules out here) is as well. It appears that neither *make* nor *had* support passivization, but there are many examples available on the internet, including instances from current English, of *was let* VP. For example:

(52) a.   "Thank God", says he, as soon as he was let speak. (*Three Courses and a Desert*, William Clarke & George Cruikshank, p. 279 (1830))

   b.   I said no such thing and would appreciate if I was let speak for myself thank you very much. (http://forums.digitalspy.co.uk/showthread.php?t=612698)

   c.   After that, I was let do what I like. (from *Fanny's First Play*, by G.B. Shaw, 1914; available online at http://books.google.com/books?id=KzwWAAAAY AAJ\&pg=PA9\&lpg=PA9\&dq=\%22was+let+do+what\%22+-let's\& source=bl\&ots=Z73YXOeq6L\&sig=BH0U5KHMtz8bJlZG9X_ca1-4b Tg\&hl=en\&sa=X\&ei=wyUhUMrtKoeM6QH8kYBw\&ved=0CEcQ6 AEwBA#v=onepage\&q=\%22was\%20let\%20do\%20what\%22\%20- let's\&f=false)

   d.   I doubt he was let do what he liked without taking some hits. (http://forum .idwpublishing.com/viewtopic)

   e.   If he was never treated as a child, at least he was let do what he liked. (from *George Bernard Shaw, His Life and Works: A Critical Biography* by Archibald Henderson, 1911 available online at http://books.google.com/ books?id=L_ssAAAAMAAJ\&pg=PA17\&lpg=PA17\&dq=\%22was+let+ do+what\%22+-let's\&source=bl\&ots=EmUobMDjS1\&sig=FYiiVw2V p1QKa4ov0sq1iD5hyZc\&hl=en\&sa=X\&ei=yCchUIHLB8fF0AH94oB4 \&ved=0CE4Q6AEwAjgK#v=onepage\&q=\%22was\%20let\%20do\% 20what\%22\%20-let's\&f=false)

   f.   ...at the home i recently got him from he was let do what he wanted when he wanted. (http://ca.answers.yahoo.com/question/index? qid=20100612105831AA2VA9x)

   g.   He complained to the staff, and he was let speak instead of me. So I removed my stuff as most of the audience left. Someone wondered why he didnt do his session using Skype instead. (www.aidanfinn.com/?p=18167)

There is thus a certain amount of direct evidence that *let* should be analyzed as taking an NP and a VP complement. So far as *make/have* are concerned, things are less straightforward.

(53) a.   We $\left\{ \begin{array}{l} \text{made} \\ \text{let} \\ \text{had} \end{array} \right\}$ Terrence [**go to the movies alone**].

   b.   *If you saw Rocco [**go to the movies alone**], **which** we $\left\{ \begin{array}{l} \text{made} \\ \text{let} \\ \text{had} \end{array} \right\}$ Terrence __ , it would be worth mentioning the fact to Christina.

Note also the complement possibilities associated with verbs of perception/discovery:

(54) a. I $\left\{ \begin{array}{c} \text{saw} \\ \text{heard} \\ \text{found} \end{array} \right\}$ Rocco talking to some strangers.

b. Rocco was $\left\{ \begin{array}{c} \text{seen} \\ \text{heard} \\ \text{found} \end{array} \right\}$ talking to some strangers.

Again,the evidence is excellent that the finite head in all these VPs takes an NP and a gerundive VP as its complements. And in such cases as well, the *which* extraction pattern is blocked:

(55) *I saw Luanne [**talking to some strangers**], **which** I had previously $\left\{ \begin{array}{c} \text{seen} \\ \text{heard} \\ \text{found} \end{array} \right\}$ Rocco__.

It appears, in fact, that in every case where a verb selects a VP complement, save one, that complement cannot be displaced. That exception is the class of complements to auxiliaries. The recent research which uncovered this pattern supplies a possible explanation which requires more background to outline fully than is possible here, but the upshot can be stated fairly concisely: in this particular kind of displacement, *which* can indeed be shown to be an NP, and the possibility of a displaced NP linked to a VP gap site requires the head verb associated with the gap site to display a certain very specific selectional peculiarity which appears to be restricted to the class of [AUX +] verbs, among which it is universal. This specific displacement 'mismatch' is therefore a fully robust and highly specific test for auxiliary status, and given the fact that it is found exceptionlessly among verbs of this class, we have every right to demand that *to* supports this mismatched *which* displacement in an exactly parallel manner before we assign it to the class of auxiliaries.

In the event, *to* fulfills this requirement in every way:

(56) a. If I get this, which I hope to in the near future, that's what I'll be getting (attested at www.airsoftforum.com/board/Black-Tan-Scar-t154383.html &pid=18071732)

b. If I return to Salzburg, which I intend to in the near future, I will do it on my own or with a friend. (attested at http://www.igougo.com/journal-j16299-Salzburg-The_Birthplace_of_Mozart.html\# ReviewID:1230905

c. I think if I ever wrote a book (which I want to someday) it would be based off my experience of ending up pregnant at age 18 and giving birth to twin girls. (attested at http://yawriters.blogspot.com/2009/06/welcome-to-goddess-boot-camp.html)

    d.   Lately I've been feeling kind of melancholy that I've never been with another girl, and if I marry her (which I want to, eventually) I never will, and I feel I'm missing out. (attested at www.scarleteen.com/cgi-bin/forum/ultimatebb.cgi?ubb=get_topic;f=3;t=010083;p=1)

An abundance of such examples is available through internet search, and readers can verify for themselves that a sentence such as (56)a will be immediately accepted and interpreted by speakers in any context in which it makes sense and is a sensible thing to say at that point in the conversation.

The common behavior of *to* and the familiar uncontroversial auxiliaries puts so heavy a burden on the claim that *to* is anything other than an auxiliary that it is unlikely to ever be met. The evidence appears to be in, and overwhelming: immediate intuitions to the contrary, *to* is an invariably nonfinite auxiliary verb, and can be expected to display parallel behavior to the other members of the class of auxiliaries in all applicable respects.

There are, of course, questions that still remain about *to* which future research must address. One notable issue that requires clarification is exactly where in the spectrum of auxiliaries to assign *to*. It invariably selects a [VFORM *bare*] complement, exactly as do the modals. But all the modals are strictly finite, so that we would have the very odd situation of the one modal, *ought*, which selects an infinitive complement, taking as its complement a VP headed by another modal in, for example, *You really ought to do that*. This interaction strongly suggests that modals are not themselves a separate subcategory of verbs, but rather a set of auxiliaries which all share the property that they only have finite form. Since all but one of them selects a bare VP, it's natural to regard this as some kind of manifestation of group identity, but as *to* makes clear, finiteness on the one hand and selection of [VFORM bare] complements on the other are quite separate and in no way mutually dependent.

An independent set of questions arise in connection with the origin of *to* as an auxiliary: *have* and *be* have, of course, been obvious members of the category V for centuries, and modals such as *may*, *can*, *will*, and *ought* were originally full verbs in the ancestral common Germanic language. We still see evidence of this origin in the existence of the verbs *will* (as in to will something into being) and the archaic *ken*, German *können*. In other cases the origins are not so straightforward; *shall* originates as Anglo-Saxon *sceal*, meaning to owe, for example, incur a debt, hence take on an obligation, a sense still evident in the past form *should*, though somewhat concealed in the nonpast *shall*. In other cases, for example, *You better/best not (do that), I rather not (say)* adjectives and adverbs have been recruited to auxiliary status, and typically do not display the full set of NICE properties. In the case of *to*, the original source can be traced back to a Proto-Indo-European preposition, hence a form which never had any verbal morphology to begin with. We know that in the course of the past millenium, the modals lost much of the morphology that they shared with the class of 'normal' verbs to which they once belonged, so that the lack of morphological forms in the emerging class of auxiliaries would have been, over time, less and less of a barrier to treating *to* in a manner parallel to the modals. It seems likely that at some point in the past which we cannot at the moment identify, *to* took on the status of a head in the VPs to which it belonged, automatically assigning it the status of a verb – but one far more like the modals than any other kind of verb. At that point, the modern avatar of an ancient preposition became part of the grammar of English with the status of an auxiliary.

What is important for the picture of English syntax which has emerged in the preceding discussion, however, is the way in which a diverse set of syntactic patterns take on an orderly and even prosaic character once we make the seemingly radical move of assigning the morphologically frozen, preposition-like infinitive 'particle' *to* to the class of modal auxiliary verbs. Given that *to* is an auxiliary, for example, we can be assured that it equates its own subject with that of its VP complement along the characteristic lines of the other auxiliaries, allowing us to revisit and flesh out our earlier analyses of (11) and (13), which were given prior to our determination that *to* is indeed a verb with the raising (subject-sharing) property discussed at length in Chapter 3. Furthermore, as a verb, it must be given a VFORM value, one which distinguishes the peculiar distributional properties of the VPs it heads from those displayed by those headed by all other types, since that distribution is unique. The only VPs allowed as complements to raising verbs such as *seem* and control verbs such as *try* and *expect* are those headed by *to*, whereas infinitival VPs may *not* appear as complements to auxiliaries apart from *ought*, or verbs of sense perception (as in, e.g., *saw John (*to) leave the house*, etc.). We therefore assign the type *inf* as the value specified for the VFORM value specified for *to*, and enumerate the lexicon so that no other verb bears the specification [VFORM *inf*].

Problem

We have the following data:

i.   *I heard John to leave the house.

ii.   John was heard to leave the house.

How is it possible to have such a mismatch between the active and passive forms. Write lexical entries for both the finite past and the passive forms of *hear* and explain the relationship between them.

Armed with our new understanding of *to*'s behavior as a member in good standing of the class of verbs sharing the description [AUX +, COMPS ⟨VP[VFORM *bare*]⟩], we can now account completely for sentences such as (10) whose analysis was sketched earlier in (11) and (13):

(57)

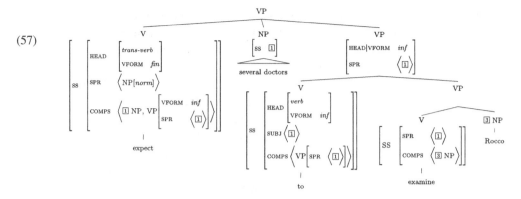

Given the SPR specifications that all auxiliaries share, *to* behaves in exactly the same way as the other [AUX +] verbs with respect to the SUBJ specifications of its VP complement, making this value available to higher predicates which select an infinitival VP in a fashion completely parallel to the selectional transparency induced by the auxiliaries considered in Chapter 3, so that little more needs to be said at this point about the internal structure of infinitival VPs. On the other hand, we still have a somewhat tricky set of facts to account for as we consider the full range of heads which *select* such VPs.

5.3   Raising Verbs, Continued

As discussed at length above, verbs such as *expect, believe, imagine,* and many others require identity between the SPR specifications of their VP complements and their NP complements, while denying those NP complements any kind of semantic role. This doesn't mean that these complements bear no semantic role at all, only that the roles they do bear are not in any way determined by the verbs that select them, but rather by their VP sisters, along the lines discussed above. As we saw in the previous discussion, this analysis has several important consequences – perhaps most dramatically, the semantic identity between clauses headed by raising verbs with nonpassive VP complements and passive VPs (as long as the direct object NP within the VP in the first case is the same as the NP selected by the raising verb in the second). This pattern contrasts with the behavior of *persuade*, which 'cares' very much about whether its complement is the subject of an active (*I persuaded the doctors to examine Rocco*) or of a passive *I persuaded Rocco to be examined by the doctors.* Verbs such as *believe*, which are often labeled *raising* verbs, thus impose very different semantic requirements on their complements from *control* verbs, such as *persuade*.

But we've only told half the story about the raising vs control distinction. Raising verbs such as *expect* equate the SYNSEM values of their NP complements with the SPR values of their VP complements, but it would be equally plausible to find that there are verbs which impose identity between the SPR values of their VP complements and their *own* SPR values. We've already seen that English auxiliaries have exactly this property, but it turns out that there are predicates in English which are not auxiliaries but which impose the same identity. For example, consider the verb *seem* in the examples in (58)–(60):

(58) a. $\left\{\begin{array}{l} \text{It} \\ \text{*There} \\ \text{Terry} \end{array}\right\}$ is raining.

      b. $\left\{\begin{array}{l} \text{It} \\ \text{*There} \\ \text{Terry} \end{array}\right\}$ seems to be raining.

(59) a. $\left\{\begin{array}{l} \text{It} \\ \text{*There} \\ \text{Terry} \end{array}\right\}$ is a lion in the garage.

      b. $\left\{\begin{array}{l} \text{There} \\ \text{*It} \\ \text{*Terry} \end{array}\right\}$ seems to be a lion in the garage.

(60) a. $\left\{\begin{array}{l} \text{Terry} \\ \text{*It} \\ \text{*There} \end{array}\right\}$ likes traveling.

      b. $\left\{\begin{array}{l} \text{Terry} \\ \text{*It} \\ \text{*There} \end{array}\right\}$ seems to like traveling.

This pattern is identical to what we've seen for auxiliaries in Chapter 3, but *seems* displays none of the NICE properties that define the class of [AUX +] verbs:

(61) a.   Rocco seems not to want to go. (Neg, wide-scope reading)
      b.   *Seems Rocco to want to go? (Inv)
      c.   *Rocco seemn't to want to go. (Contraction)
      d.   *Leslie doesn't want to go, but Rocco seems ∅. (Ellipsis)

Apart from the first of these, all the examples in (61) unequivocally contradict the expected behavior of auxiliaries. The first example is problematic, since it is not possible to distinguish the [$_{VP}$ V *not* [$_{VP}$ ...]] structure from the [$_{VP}$ V [$_{VP}$ *not* [$_{VP}$ ...]]] on the basis of meaning differences. We can see this clearly in the case of the finite complement version of *seem*, which is semantically identical to the one illustrated in (58)–(61):

(62) a.   It doesn't seem (to me) that Rocco wants to go.
      b.   It seems (to me) that Rocco doesn't want to go.

In one case, *not* occurs outside the complement to *seem*, and in the other case inside that complement, the same structural contrast that is possible with the string *Rocco seems not to want to go*. There is a small potential difference in meaning – in (62)a, one might be able to infer that what the speaker is denying is having a strong impression that Rocco wants to go, vs (62)b, where the speaker is asserting a strong impression that Rocco doesn't want to go. A parallel distinction can be faintly drawn out in the case of *Rocco seems not to want to go*, but the judgment, though it parallels (62)b (and thus points to the position of *not* 'inside' an infinitive VP complement *not to want to go*) is rather delicate for many speakers. Unfortunately, we cannot use displacement tests, as we have in previous cases, to determine whether or not *not want to go* is a constituent in (61)a, because the infinitive complements to *seems* do not displace: *Rocco seems to want to go/. . .*(and to want to go, Rocco seems)* – a fact which falls out of the analysis of *to* as an auxiliary, since, as we saw in Chapter 3, VP complements headed by auxiliaries do not displace (**. . . and have gotten the job, Rocco may __.*).

There is, however, another test which shows quite unequivocally that *seem* and similar verbs cannot be plausibly treated as auxiliaries. The auxiliary verb *do*, as we noted in Chapter 3, has the unique property that its VP complement must not contain an auxiliary head. Recall that strings such as those in (63) are all forbidden in English:

(63) a.   *I didn't have been studying.
      b.   *Did you be studying?
      c.   *Didn't she have studied?

Modals, of course, are excluded in principle from any VP complement to any auxiliary, since the heads of such complements are nonfinite, while modals are invariably finite; but both *have* and *be* would be eligible to head a VP selected by *do*, since both possess bare forms. Thus, the problem with (63) must be taken to be an effect induced by the selectional properties of *do* itself – in particular, the requirement stated in Chapter 3 that the COMPS list specification for *do* excludes complements of the form VP[AUX +]. It follows that any verb which can appear in place of the auxiliaries in (63) to yield well-formed results cannot be an auxiliary, and the results for *seem* indeed yield this conclusion:

(64) a.   She didn't seem to be studying.
      b.   Did she seem to be studying?
      c.   Didn't she seem to be studying?

A final test may be applied: the distribution of so-called rejoinder *so* parallels that of *not*:

(65) a.   A: She $\left\{\begin{array}{l}\text{should}\\\text{must}\\\text{will}\end{array}\right\}$ not do that.

            B: She $\left\{\begin{array}{l}\text{should}\\\text{must}\\\text{will}\end{array}\right\}$ so do that!

      b.   A: She has not done that.
            B: She has so done that!

      c.   A: She is not doing that.
            B: She is so doing that!

Unlike *not*, however, *so* does not seem to be able to attach to VPs as an adjunct on its own (*... *and so do that, she can!*. Thus, its appearance is dependent on an auxiliary to select (or at least 'host') it. Taking *seem* to not be an auxiliary entails that it cannot appear with rejoinder *so*, and indeed we observe exactly this restriction:

(66)   A: Rocco seems not to like Terry.
          B: *Rocco seems so to like Terry!

Since *not* and rejoinder *so* elsewhere parallel each other, the failure of *so* to appear following *seems* strongly suggests that the *not* following *seems* in the exchange is located within the VP complement, rather than as a sister to *seems*; since *so* (in contrast to *not*) never has adjunct status in VPs, it cannot appear preceding *to like Terry* with this status either, and hence is correctly ruled out from appearing in such cases at all, on the assumption that *seem* is not an auxiliary. Finally, while not is itself decisive, the fact that *seem* and other such raising verbs have a full or nearly full range of inflected forms paralleling those for other ordinary nonauxiliary verbs (*I seem/she seemed, Rocco has seemed*) is strongly consistent with the conclusion supported by the distributional evidence just given that *seem* is [AUX −].

These considerations force the conclusion that SPR value identity between a head and its VP complement is not a diagnostic feature for auxiliaries. Similarly, the parallelisms in (67)–(68) suggest that there are certain purely semantic properties the raising verbs have in common with auxiliaries, without belonging to the latter class:

(67) a.   A doctor $\left\{ \begin{array}{c} \text{may} \\ \text{seems to} \end{array} \right\}$ have examined Rocco.

     b.   Rocco $\left\{ \begin{array}{c} \text{may} \\ \text{seems to} \end{array} \right\}$ have been examined by a doctor.

(68) a.   The fur flew at the meeting.

     b.   The fur $\left\{ \begin{array}{c} \text{must} \\ \text{seems to} \end{array} \right\}$ really fly at those meetings.

The meaning identity of active/passive pairs is preserved 'across' an intervening raising verb, just as it is across an intervening auxiliary, and a similar parallelism holds for the preservation of idiomatic interpretation. Both phenomena point to a peculiar mismatch between the syntax and the semantics as a common property of the two different verb classes: in both cases, the verb fails to have a semantic relationship to its own subject. Instead, it in effect combines the latter's meaning with that of the VP complement, to yield an assertion of some sort, and then registers its own 'assessment' on that assertion. So, for example, in (67), *may* applies the meaning attached to *have examined Rocco* to *a doctor*, to give us a statement identifying a particular relationship between Rocco and some unspecified doctor – that the two are in an 'examine relationship' which is now completed at the time of the utterance – and then indicates that the status of this scenario is, 'possibly true.' *Seems*, as independently shown in *It seems that a doctor examined Rocco*, denotes something like 'gives the impression of being true.' Just like *may*, *seems* combines the meaning of its VP complement with that of its subject, to yield the same 'examine' scenario, but unlike *may*, which is somewhat noncommital, *seems* identifies the status of this scenario as 'has the appearance of being true.' Similar considerations apply to the case of idiom identity in (68).

These conclusions are, of course, analogous to our findings above in connection with *expect* and similar verbs. In both cases, there is a valent of the verb which plays no role in the relationship that corresponds to the verb's meaning. Rather, the verb combines that valent with one of its other valents to form a particular meaning, and only then does its own meaning apply to the result. In both cases, the failure of the verb to interact directly with the valent in question means, among other things, that the difference between active and passive VPs selected by the verb winds up having no semantic consequences, and that dummy pronouns and idiom chunks, as in (67)–(68), can be syntactic arguments of raising verbs, although they receive no semantic interpretation with respect to such verbs.

In the case of *expect*, we noted that in all the respects just reviewed, there is a contrasting class of verbs, for example, *persuade*, which seems to have a similar syntax, selecting NP and infinitival VP complements, but in which none of the transparency effects associated with the raising class hold. It is natural to ask if a similar class of verbs exists which contrasts in the same way with *seem*. What we are looking for are verbs which select an infinitival VP complement, but where the subject as well as the VP plays a semantic role with respect to the verb. Given that situation, we predict the following array of properties for such verbs:

- Semantically empty elements will not be able to appear as subjects. Having no semantic content, they cannot play the role of participants in the situation that the verb identifies.

- The passive invariance that is reflected in, for example, (67), and in the behavior of auxiliaries, will not hold. When the VP is passive, and the subject corresponds to the object of the active, the role the verb assigns to the subject will be different from the role assigned to it when it appears inside the VP as the direct object.

- Idiom invariance will fail. The assignment of a role to the subject means that it cannot interact with the rest of the idiom in the VP in the way that parts of idiomatic expressions do, because the assignment of a role to it by the selecting verb forces it to have a literal meaning that can play the part assigned to that role.

Consider, in view of this profile, the following data (where a superscripted # indicates an example which is syntactically well-formed but semantically highly anomalous):

(69) a.   *There $\left\{\begin{array}{c}\text{tried}\\\text{hoped}\\\text{wanted}\end{array}\right\}$ to be a lion in the closet.

b.   *It $\left\{\begin{array}{c}\text{tried}\\\text{hoped}\\\text{wanted}\end{array}\right\}$ to bother Leslie that Rocco spied for the Ostrogoths.

(70) a.   An officer $\left\{\begin{array}{c}\text{tried}\\\text{hoped}\\\text{wanted}\end{array}\right\}$ to identify Rocco.

b.   Rocco $\left\{\begin{array}{c}\text{tried}\\\text{hoped}\\\text{wanted}\end{array}\right\}$ to be identified by an officer.

(71) a.   The fur $^\#\left\{\begin{array}{c}\text{tried}\\\text{hoped}\\\text{wanted}\end{array}\right\}$ to fly.

b.   The cat $^\#\left\{\begin{array}{c}\text{tried}\\\text{hoped}\\\text{wanted}\end{array}\right\}$ to be out of the bag.

Every one of the predictions for the hypothetical class of verbs in question – which for historical reasons are referred to as control verbs – is satisfied for these three lexical items, on the single assumption that they each assign a semantic role to their subject. Is this assumption plausible? Consider *try*, which clearly posits some effort on the part of the subject. It's certainly true that in this case, and the others, the subject has a semantic role with respect to the situation denoted by the VP as well, but that is irrelevant so far as (69)–(71) is concerned. What counts is that *try*, *hope*, and *want* require there to be some individual who tries, who hopes and who wants respectively. This fact alone is sufficient to produce a radically different distributional pattern from that displayed by the raising verbs.

What still needs to be addressed, however, is exactly how the linkage between the subject and the VP is to be implemented in the case of control. We've been taking the key identity in the case of auxiliaries and *seems*-type raising verbs to hold between the SYNSEM values of the verb's own SPR feature and the VP's SPR specification, but so far have not really argued that this is the right way to do things; possibly it is, and should be the treatment also of control verbs, and possibly not – and perhaps one approach is better for the raising verbs and a different approach for the control verbs. But at the moment, the detailed argumentation that the reader should expect before accepting any solution has not been provided.

It's worth stopping for a moment to assess just what the equality of SYNSEM values solution commits us to, if we adopt it for any particular class of phenomena. The SYNSEM specification is where all grammatical information about the morphosyntactic, syntactic, and discourse-context pragmatic properties of linguistic signs is provided. Sharing SYNSEM values therefore entails that not only the meaning of the linguistic sign, but also the purely formal aspects of that sign's feature description are shared. This includes information about, for example, case, lexical category type, auxiliary status, and so on. None of this kind of information is retrievable from knowing the meaning of a linguistic expression: the difference between *I* and *me* is not a semantic difference, nor can we tell on the basis of the meaning of *seem* and *must* whether one or the other or both are auxiliaries. Sharing of SYNSEM values between two (or more) signs thus entails that any purely formal features, independent of meaning, will be shared, entailing that both signs appear in grammatical contexts compatible with those feature specifications.

Unfortunately, in order to test out this expectation in a straightforward way, it is necessary that the shared SYNSEM values have the desired grammatical effect in *both* contexts affected by this feature identity – both in the position where the overt subject appears in raising and in the VP whose SPR value is equated with that of the selecting head. This is a rather difficult matter to arrange, in English at any rate, because the purely formal properties of the complement VP's SPR value, such as AGR specifications, only register in any evident way with verbs which are finite, which neither auxiliary VP nor raising verb VP complements ever are. To determine whether or not SYNSEM identity is the right formal tool for the uses to which we've put it, we need to find some strictly formal property whose effects are transmitted through one or more raising or auxiliary verbs, and observe whether those formal properties have to be identical between the two signs.

An argument along these lines can indeed be found by examining the category of the complements which are interpreted semantically in a way parallel to a clausal subject:

(72) a.   I signaled [PP to Luanne] to get herself out of there as soon as possible.
     b.   The company relies [PP on Rocco] to handle its most sensitive legal issues.
     c.   I requested [PP of him] to forward the contract to our partners.

The head of the PP in all of these cases is essentially empty; as we've seen in many previous examples, it serves only a kind of 'case-marking' function, establishing a relationship between the subject, the object of the preposition, and the infinitival clause. We can substitute *prompt*, one of whose senses is something like 'display a gesture of some kind to indicate a course of action', and obtain *The director prompted Terry to move directly to the center of the stage*, with essentially the same semantics as conveyed by *signaled to Terry*. In effect, then, the meaning of the PP in this kind of construction is identical to the meaning of the prepositional object. But in terms of their categorial descriptions, the former is a projection of *prep* and the latter of *noun*, and the SPR value of all of the infinitive VPs in (72) are lexically specified as NPs, not PPs. Hence, none of the PPs in these examples can share its SYNSEM value with the infinitive VP's SPR value. But if the PP's meaning is taken to be the same individual as its head daughter's NP complement picks out, then that denotation can be shared with the meaning component of the VP's SPR value. Critically, we are not equating SYNSEM values between the PP complement and the infinitive VP complement, but only a subset of the semantic information – and therefore there will be no clash in morphosyntactic information (i.e., between the SYNSEM value of the PP, whose head is typed *preposition*, and that of the SPR value of the VP *to get herself out of there as soon as possible*, which must be typed *noun*).

When we look at verbs such as *believe*, *expect*, *assume*, and others that have the characteristic raising signature, we find that unlike the verbs in (72), there are none that have a PP VP complement structure, *unless* the VP is one which can have a PP subject:

(73) a.   Under the bed is a strange place to keep your beer.

  b.   I consider under the bed to be a strange place to keep your beer.

The fact that there are no raising verbs in English which take both a non-NP complement on the one hand and a VP complement which requires an NP SPR specification on the other – as vs verbs such as those in (72), which lack the raising profile and which do select such nonnominal complements – is extremely suggestive. In principle, of course, it could be a complete accident. But such a coincidence is improbable in the extreme. If verbs which have the raising property require the complete sharing of their direct object's SYNSEM values with the SPR value of their VP complement (including of course part-of-speech information located in HEAD), while control verbs such as *force*, *convince*, and *signal* only impose sharing of semantic information between their NP or PP complements and their VP complement's SPR value, then the pattern noted follows immediately.

Practice Exercise

Determine whether the predicates of English boldfaced in the following examples are raising or control verbs. You will have to construct appropriate sentences, along the lines illustrated in this chapter (e.g., using a range of types of subject or objects, as the case may be) in order to determine their status. Consult your own intuitions, but ask other native speakers to give you their judgments as well on the test sentences you come up with, and you should also do some searches on the internet to see if forms that you don't find acceptable are viewed by others as well-formed.

  i.   John **tends** to be a bit overbearing.
  ii.   The crisis **threatened** to spill over into the tense neighboring border areas.
  iii. Mary **offered** to help with the arrangements.
  iv.   The twins **turned out** to be real con artists.
  v.   The promises they gave us **failed** to be convincing enough to make us change our minds.
  vi.   My cousin is **prone** to be disastrously overconfident.

vii.   The board requires applicants to take a drugs test before they're interviewed.

viii.   I imagine Terrence to have spent a lot of time living by himself.

Present the evidence you've gathered to come to your conclusions, and explain just how the facts you present support those conclusions.

5.4   'Super-Raising': The French Tense Auxiliaries

The key to a straightforward treatment of both English auxiliaries and raising phenomena is, as per the preceding discussion, the direct identification of SYNSEM values between one of its valents and the SPR specification of another. Nothing other than this identification is needed to supply the semantics of these verbs with the information necessary to ensure the appropriate interpretations of sentences containing these elements. But there are phenomena which superficially seem to resemble the auxiliary/raising data in English, but where a major extension of SYNSEM value identification appears to be required. The French tense auxiliaries are one such phenomenon (see especially Abeillé and Godard (2002), on which the following discussion is based).

The formation of the most common past tense construction in French, the so-called passé composé, requires an appropriately inflected form of one of two auxiliaries, *avoir* 'have' and *être* 'be,' and a past tense participle, consisting of a specific morphological form of some verb, followed by that verb's complements:

(74) a.   Jean a **mangé** du saumon. 'Jean ate salmon.'

b.   Marie a **donné** [$_{NP}$ un livre] [$_{PP}$ à Olivier]. 'Mary gave a book to Olivier.'

c.   Etienne a **discuté** [$_{PP}$ avec Daniel] [$_{PP}$ au sujet de la politique]. 'Etienne argued with Daniel about politics.'

d.   Luc est **venu** [$_{PP}$ à la réunion hier]. 'Luc came to the meeting yesterday.'

e.   Claire est **arrivée** [$_{PP}$ à son hôtel]. 'Claire arrived at her hotel.'

In each case, the material following the past participle form of the verb in boldface in (74) realizes the COMPS requirements of that verb. For example, *donner*, the verb in (74)b, requires an NP and a PP[PFORM *á*]. This is of course essentially the same pattern we find in English: the *verb* heads of auxiliaries' VP complements display the VFORM properties the auxiliary has selected, and are followed by those phrases the complement heads themselves have selected. And just as this pattern for auxiliary + complement also holds for raising and control verbs in English, the same appears to hold in French as well.

(75) a.   Jean veut manger du saumon. 'Jean wants to eat salmon.'

b.   Etienne $\left\{ \begin{array}{c} \text{ose} \\ \text{peut} \end{array} \right\}$ discuter avec Daniel au sujet de la politique.

'Etienne $\left\{ \begin{array}{c} \text{dares to} \\ \text{can} \end{array} \right\}$ argue with Daniel about politics.'

Here, the verbs are not auxiliaries, but the control verbs *vouloir* 'to want' and *oser* 'to dare,' and the raising verb *pouvoir* 'be able (to).' These facts are parallel to the English pattern: *Rocco has/should/seemed to/wants to bet $10 with Leslie that the game will be a tie* display exactly the same combinatorial possibilities for *bet* as in *Rocco bet $10 with Leslie that the game would be a tie* – a sequence of NP, PP, and S. This distribution is exactly what we expect on the assumptions (i) that *bet $10 with Leslie that the game would be a tie* is a VP constituent and (ii) that auxiliaries, raising and control verbs, among others, take VPs as complements. In the same way, if we assume that *avoir, être, vouloir, oser*, and *semble* all have VP valents, with the VP consisting of the morphologically appropriate form of some verb and its complements, then all of the data in (74)–(75) falls into place: French auxiliaries, raising and control verbs mirror the properties of their English counterparts, at least in terms of the phenomena surveyed so far, and the natural explanation for the French facts can be captured in the same way as the English facts, by assuming that these classes of verbs in French, as in English, select VP complements which can only be formed by combinations of a lexical head and a sequence of elements satisfying the valence requirements of that head. It follows that if we can find tests for French constituency comparable to the constituency tests we applied in Chapters 2 and 3 on the basis of English data, we would expect to find that the strings of elements following the heads of French auxiliaries etc. will pass these tests with flying colors.

As it happens, we can find several such tests in French. Just as in English, we have proforms for VPs, but unlike *do so*, the proforms are actually *pronouns*, the ordinary clitics that appear in sentences such as *Elle l'aime*, 'She likes him,' the pronominal analogue of the sentence *Elle aime ce type* 'She likes that guy.' Unlike English, the proform notated *l'*, a contraction of *le* when it occurs before a vowel, does not appear in the same position as a corresponding full NP; rather, it precedes the verb which selects it as a valent, and sequences of such complement proforms appear as well, for example, *Les juges le lui a donée* 'The judges gave it to him', where both *le* '3rd person masculine' and *lui* 'to him' precede *donée*. In French, a pronoun can refer to a VP; thus, whereas in English the form ??*Rocco wants to catch an early plane and I want it too* is highly questionable at best, the French analogue is standard. We find this pattern in (76):

(76) a. Jean veut manger du saumon, et je le veut aussi. 'Jean wants to eat salmon, and I want to (eat salmon) also.'

b. Etienne $\left\{ \begin{array}{c} \text{ose} \\ \text{peut} \end{array} \right\}$ discuter avec Daniel au sujet de la politique, mais vous ne $\left\{ \begin{array}{c} \text{l'osez} \\ \textbf{le } \text{pouvez} \end{array} \right\}$ pas. 'Etienne $\left\{ \begin{array}{c} \text{dares to} \\ \text{can} \end{array} \right\}$ argue with Daniel about politics, but you $\left\{ \begin{array}{c} \text{don't dare to} \\ \text{can't} \end{array} \right\}$,

Such examples, in which the boldfaced *l(e)* forms consistently replace the strings following the raising and control verbs, strongly suggest that these strings must be reckoned as constituents, using precisely the same line of reasoning laid out in Chapter 1. Given the apparent parallelism the forms in (73) display with respect to the forms in (76), we would expect parallel behavior from the former according to the pronominalization. But what we find is exactly the contrary:

(77) a.   Jean n'est pas venu hier au rendez vous(*, mais Marie l'est). [**intended:** 'Jean has not come to the meeting yesterday, but Marie has.']

b.   Jean croyait avoir compris son erreur(*, mail il ne l'avait pas). [**intended:** 'Jean thought he had understood his mistake, but he hadn't.']

In the case of (77)a, the failure of the pronominalization option with *l'est* shows that *venu hier au rendez-vous* is not analyzed as a constituent so far as the pronominalization test is concerned, and similarly with the sequence *compris son erreur* corresponding to *l'avait* in (77)b. In spite of the parallel behavior of the tense auxiliaries vis-à-vis the raising and control verbs in the data in (73)– (74) – the fact that the verbal head following these verbs is always itself followed by exactly the right valent elements – there seems to be a major break between the auxiliaries on the one hand and all other verbs on the other.

The reader might well feel, at this point, that we don't yet know enough to come to a conclusion one way or the other, and that conclusion would indeed be the right one. It's possible that there is some particular property of tense auxiliaries that precludes their playing host, so to speak, to these preposed pronominals. If other tests for constituency diverge from the pattern in (77), that will help us determine whether the pattern suggested in those examples is representative or merely a syntactic idiosyncrasy.

In the first place, French displays a counterpart to the same fronting possibility that we applied in English in Chapter 1 to identify certain substrings of a sentence as VP constituents. In particular, the French fronting rule serves as a test for constituency, and gives positive results for the case of verbs such as *vouloir* and the other.

(78)   ... et discuter avec Daniel au sujet de la politique, Etienne $\left\{\begin{array}{c} \text{osait} \\ \text{voudrait bien} \\ \text{pouvait} \end{array}\right\}$.

'... and argue with Daniel about politics, Etienne $\left\{\begin{array}{c} \text{would dare to} \\ \text{would really like to} \\ \text{could} \end{array}\right\}$

—.

But again, we get a negative result when this test is applied to parallel constructions involving the French tense auxiliaries.

(79) a.   *... et discuté avec Daniel au sujet de la politique, Etienne a __

b.   *... arrivée à son hotel, Claire est __.

where the intended readings are those of (74)d and e.

Yet another test which distinguishes the tense auxiliaries from both raising and control verbs is VP ellipsis, examples of which in English were given in Chapter 3 and earlier in this chapter. We find the following contrasts in French:

(80)   Jean $\left\{\begin{array}{l}\text{voudrait}\\\text{oserait}\\\text{pouvait}\end{array}\right\}$ discuter avec Daniel au sujet de la politique, mais je

$\left\{\begin{array}{l}\text{ee veut}\\\text{n'oserait}\\\text{pouvait}\end{array}\right\}$ pas.

'Jean $\left\{\begin{array}{l}\text{would like}\\\text{would dare}\\\text{could}\end{array}\right\}$ argue   with   Daniel   about   politics,   but   I

$\left\{\begin{array}{l}\text{wouldn't like to}\\\text{wouldn't dare to}\\\text{couldn't}\end{array}\right\}$.

(81)   a.   Jean a eu l'intention de discuter avec Daniel au sujet de la politique(*, mais il n'a pas).

b.   Jean a pensé que Claire est arrivé à son hôtel à sept heures(*, mais elle n'est pas).

The asymmetry between raising/control verbs and the tense auxiliaries thus appears to be a persistent property of the grammar of French.

It appears that we have reason to reject the constituency of the V + XP ... ZP sequences following tense-marking *avoir* and *être*. But caution is advised here; after all, we've already seen, in Chapter 3, that there seems to be some prohibition on both fronting and *do so* replacement of auxiliary-headed VPs, even though much other evidence confirms the constituency of the strings involved. So while the burden of proof has definitely shifted to the proponent of the view that French tense auxiliaries take VP complements, we do not yet have a decisive refutation of that view, because no matter how much evidence accumulates that the complement structure of these auxiliaries does not behave the way we expect a constituent to behave, there is always the possibility that the divergence between the two classes of verb is due to something other than the (non)constituency of the complements associated with the tense auxiliaries. What would be decisive is the converse of the pattern we've been observing: rather than a set of facts which are merely compatible with the nonconstituency of tense auxiliary complementation, we need a pattern in the data which is *in*compatible with the *constituency* of this complementation. And, very fortunately, there is one more relevant test in French which is of just this latter sort, and which we can apply to the two different classes of verbs to obtain a decisive result.

Our diagnostic tool in this case is the French analogue of the *tough* construction in English exemplified by, for example, *Rocco is tough to please __*, which will be examined in detail in Chapter 7. The English version of this construction links a subject in the position of *Rocco* with a position from which it appears to be missing over a syntactic depth of (in principle) unlimited size: *This new kind of box was difficult to persuade Luanne to retool her factory to produce __*, where the underline indicates the seemingly missing material as in previous chapters, is an acceptable paraphrase of *It was difficult to persuade Luanne to retool her factory to produce this new kind of box*. The bracketing in (82) makes clear the number of structural levels involved in the relationship between the subject and the position following *produce*:

(82)   [$_{NP}$ this new kind of box] [$_{VP}$ was [$_{AP}$ difficult [$_{VP}$ to $_{VP}$ persuade Luanne [$_{VP}$ to [$_{VP}$ retool her factory [$_{VP}$ to [$_{VP}$ produce __]]]]]]]]

The linkage between the subject and the gap into which it is interpreted holds over seven structural generations (where each branch point along the path between *this new kind of box* and the gap following *produce* defines a generation). Such a structure is ruled out in French; dependencies of this sort are, for most speakers, sharply restricted to a complement position of the particular verb whose VP mother is selected by whichever adjective corresponds to *difficult* in (82). In effect, French speakers accept *This new kind of box was difficult to produce __* but not *This new kind of box was difficult to convince Luanne to produce __*, so that we have

(83)   Cette chanson sera difficile (*à réussir) à apprendre en un jour.

         'This song would be difficult to (succeed in being able to) learn __ in one day.'

When an extra layer of VP structure is added by making *apprendre en un jour* a complement of *réussir* 'succeed', the result is bad. In contrast, when there is no gap following *apprendre*, so that we have the French analogue of *It would be easy to succeed in learning this song*, we have no problem:

(84)   Il serait difficile à (réussir à) apprendre cette chanson en un jour.

         'It would be difficult to (succeed in being able to) learn this song in one day.'

It follows that the problem with (83) is strictly determined by the existence of too much structure between the subject and the position with respect to which it is semantically interpreted. The strict condition on this connection that there can be at most one intervening VP structure separating the subject from the gap site leads us to predict that when any raising/control verb intervenes between the subject and the verb whose complement is, in effect, the gap itself, we will get an ill-formed result, just as we do with the control verb *réussir*, and this prediction is confirmed:

(85)   Cette chanson sera impossible à $\left(* \left\{ \begin{array}{c} \text{réussir à} \\ \text{pouvoir} \end{array} \right\} \right)$ apprendre en un jour.

         'This song would be impossible to $\left\{ \begin{array}{c} \text{*succeed in learning} \\ \text{*be able to learn} \\ \text{learn} \end{array} \right\}$ in one day.'

But what happens when a tense auxiliary appears in place of *réussir* or *pouvoir*? The results turn out to be strikingly different:

(86)   Le programme sera difficile à **avoir** maîtrisé au moment de l'examen.
           'The content would be difficult to have mastered by the time of the exam.'

(87)   C'est le genre d'auteur utiles à s'**être** attaché dès son premier livre.
           'They're the kind of author useful to have hired from their first book.'

These examples are perfectly well-formed, and provide us with convincing evidence that the material following the tense auxiliaries *avoir* and *être* – shown in boldface in the two preceding examples – must indeed be treated as *not* constituting a single VP node, for if they did, we would have the structure for, for example, (86) given in (88):

(88)

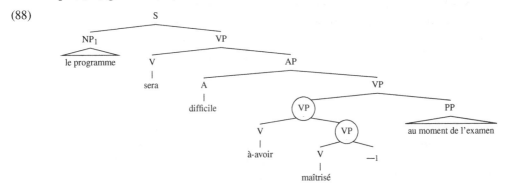

In this structure, there are two lexically headed VP nodes (circled in (88)) intervening between the gap (labeled __₁) and the adjective within whose VP complement the gap linked to the subject (labeled NP₁) occurs. Given the behavior of raising/control verbs in these constructions, such a structure should be ill-formed, for the gap would *not* be associated with the verb which projected to the VP complement of *difficile*. That verb would, in this scenario, be *avoir*, whose presence would constitute a barrier to the linkage between *le programme* and the gap following *maîtrisé*, just as impenetrable as that created by the presence of *réussir* or *pouvoir* in (85). Taking both this positive piece of evidence and the negative evidence that tense auxiliaries fail to license several independent constituency-sensitive constructions, we have overwhelming justification in taking the structure of (86)a to be, rather,

(89)

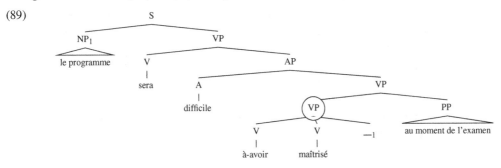

This tree, in which the material following *avoir* has a flat structure rather than forming a constituent, accounts directly for the contrast between (85) and (86)–(87); it also illustrates the kind of structure that makes pronominalization, VP fronting, and VP ellipsis impossible for sequences following the tense auxiliaries. Since a sequence *a discuté avec Daniel au sujet de la politique* will, on this 'flat' analysis, have the form

(90)

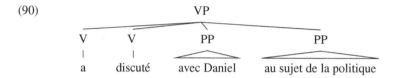

it follows that *a discuté avec Daniel au sujet de la politique* will not be eligible to appear in any constructions which require this sequence to constitute a VP.

But while this analysis provides a satisfying, economical solution to the problem posed by the raising/control verb vs tense auxiliary pattern, it creates an analytic dilemma, for we now have no obvious account for the fact that, in the examples for which (90) is a correct representation, the PPs following *a discuté* are exactly the complements which *discuté* requires in order to form a VP – even though, in the case of (90), it isn't actually forming a VP. And this pattern is completely general: the verb following a tense auxiliary is itself always accompanied by constituents of just the sort that it specifies on its COMPS list. Since it is the formation of a phrase around a head that, via the Head-complement Rule, forces the appearance of just those sisters for the head that the head demands, and since exactly these sisters appear in tense auxiliary constructions in spite of the fact that they do *not* form a constituent with the verb that normally selects them, we appear to have a major problem with our descriptive framework.

But the difficulty is only apparent. If we accept the correctness of our analyses to this point, then we must accept (90), along with several independent tests for headship which clearly identify *a* in the examples corresponding to (90) as the head of the VP. This can only mean that it is the COMPS list of *a*, not *discuter*, and of the tense auxiliaries generally, which is satisfied by the constituents which appear. This conclusion entails that in each case, *avoir* and *être* 'know' what the COMPS requirements of the verb that follows it are. More explicitly, the tense auxiliaries must be able to cross-reference the COMPS values of the nonauxiliary verb which follows them and ensure that the COMPS list of the latter is a sublist of their own valents. This sharing of information can be implemented if we assume that the auxiliary selects the nonauxiliary verb itself; the COMPS specifications of the latter will, in that case, be visible to the auxiliary, and all the latter need do is specify a portion of its COMPS list as identical to the COMPS list of the verb it selects. In effect, the auxiliary selects a verb as a complement and thereby gets to inherit the syntactic arguments of that verb as additional arguments of its own.

But there's more to this 'argument inheritance' relationship than just what happens with complements. Compare the following sentences:

(91)   Il me tracasse que Jean est un espion.
         'It bothers me that Jean is a spy.'

(92)   Il m'a tracassé que Jean était un espion.
         'It bothered me that Jean was a spy.'

We see from the first of these that the verb, *tracasser* 'bother', has a similar
argument structure to its English counterpart: it selects a dummy pronoun *il* 'it'
as its subject and an object NP (expressed prosodically by a clitic) and a finite
clause as complements. The key point is that this same dummy subject is required
in the passé composé: *avoir*, the head of the clausal VP, which means that the SPR
information provided by *tracasser* must be shared with the top-level VP. This of
course is exactly what we concluded in Chapter 3 for auxiliaries, and in this
chapter for raising predicates. We conclude then that *avoir* and *être* work the
same way, and that in addition, they share the COMPS specifications of the lexical
verb they select as well. When these tense auxiliaries take a verb as a complement
which requires a noncanonical subject, as does *tracasser*, they select that subject
themselves, and when their lexical V complement requires a normal subject, they
follow suit.

   The crucial aspect of this solution is that it does not require us to do anything
qualitatively different from the way we handle the transparency of subject
selection in the case of English auxiliaries and raising predicates, and we can
use essentially the same approach. Instead of simply equating SPR list values,
and stopping there, however, we also need to in effect build a new COMPS list
for the tense auxiliaries, based on which particular verb they combine with: the
tense auxiliary will take a description corresponding to that verb as one of its
complements, and will combine the latter with the COMPS list this verb specifies,
as well as mirroring this verb's SPR value. All morphological variants of the tense
auxiliaries then will share the following partial description:

(93)
$$
\begin{bmatrix}
\text{SPR} & \boxed{1} \\
\text{COMPS} & \left\langle \begin{bmatrix} verb \\ \text{SPR} & \boxed{1} \\ \text{COMPS} & \boxed{2} \end{bmatrix} \right\rangle \oplus \boxed{2}
\end{bmatrix}
$$

The verb *tracasser* 'bother' will be partially specified in the lexicon as (94):

(94)
$$
\begin{bmatrix}
\text{SPR} & \left\langle \text{NP}\begin{bmatrix}\text{NFORM} & il\end{bmatrix}\right\rangle \\
\text{COMPS} & \left\langle \text{NP}, \text{S}[que]\right\rangle
\end{bmatrix}
$$

We can, on the basis of these lexical entries, provide a tree for the French
sentence *Il a tracassé Jean que Luc est un espion* 'It bothered Jean that Luc
is a spy.'

(95)

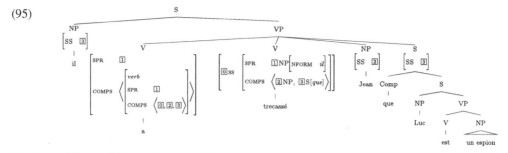

Avoir combines with a verb and with that verb's own valents: it takes over the verb's subject and its COMPS specifications, adding the verb itself at the top of its own COMPS list. The result is the flat structure illustrated in (95).

We can see the specification for the tense auxiliaries in (93) as a kind of logical extreme of the way raising works in English and many other languages: not only the subject, but *everything* is appropriated from a complement of the head. *Avoir* and *être* are total chameleons, with essentially *all* of their valence properties determined by a kind of mimicry of certain complements. What is particularly striking is the ease with which the architecture of the framework we have been developing captures this kind of somewhat unusual complementation pattern, in which a totally flat phrase structure disguises itself in the appearance of familiar hierarchical configuration. Further instances of the same sort of argument inheritance can be found in other Romance languages, in Germanic languages and in Korean, among others.

5.5   What Comes Next?

This brief survey of various kinds of nonfinite complementation patterns reinforces and further illustrates how straightforwardly grammatical patterns of some apparent complexity can be captured by fairly simple lexical specifications relating the valence specifications of various classes of words to each other. In this way, the selectional affinities of lexical heads, the auxiliary dependency, local relational dependencies and raising, control and argument inheritance phenomena can all be seen as a variation on a single basic grammatical theme. Lexical items express combinatorial requirements, and these requirements in entire classes of lexical items are related to those of other classes in completely systematic ways, giving rise to specific structural parallelisms between the constructions projected from members of these respective classes.

But there are other dependencies that do not conform to this tidy picture. By their very nature, valence-based dependencies are strictly local. The 'reach' of COMPS and SPR selection is confined to the mothers and sisters of lexical heads. Strictly speaking, this holds for SPR as well, but because, by the Head-complement Rule and the Head-adjunct Rule, SPR specifications are preserved even after COMPS specifications are canceled, it follows that a head which selects a nearly saturated phrasal category may be specified in such a way that it can access the information about its complement's SPR value, and in that way link that value to valence specifications higher up in the structure. We thus find examples such as *I believe there to have been thought to have been Vikings in pre-Columbian America*, which, though quite cumbersome, seems acceptably interpretable, where *there* in the object position of *believe* is linked to the lower instance of *been*, whose subject valent it is, by virtue of the lexical specifications of *believe, to, have, been*, and *thought*. But since this extended reach for SPR specifications depends entirely on the particular properties of auxiliaries and raising verbs, we find distant connections of this sort only in sentences where specific classes of words occur whose valence specifications allow them to mediate dependencies between constituents and their distant selectors.

There are, however, dependencies which hold over arbitrary syntactic depths and depend on no particular class of words. We have actually encountered these dependencies already; in fact, we have continually appealed to them as one of our two 'gold standard' tests for constituency. The phenomenon in question is displacement, whose own syntax we have deliberately overlooked up to this point, relying instead on the versatility and wide applicability of displacement constructions to shed light on the internal hierarchical organization of clauses. But obviously, the possibility of displacing a constituent over an indefinite structural distance while maintaining its connection to the location where it would normally appear reflects a critically important set of possibilities made available by natural language grammars. What properties must these grammars have in order that the displacement phenomenon is possible at all? In the next chapter, we provide a canonical instance of this phenomenon and show that the valence mechanism sufficient for all of the dependencies introduced up to the present cannot on its own account for the facts. A new formalism which can mediate these nonlexical dependencies is therefore necessary.

6 The Limits of Valence: Topicalization

6.1   Beyond Valence: Data

In the course of the preceding chapters, we've noted a diverse and interesting collection of grammatical dependencies and found that we can account for all of them through the simple mechanism of valence. The combinatorial possibilities of verbal heads are given in their COMPS and SPR/SPR values; to account for various morphosyntactic dependencies, or seemingly more complex 'relational' dependencies, all that is necessary is to ensure that heads with certain properties select valents with other properties corresponding to the specific dependency. But apparently this cannot be the whole story, in view of facts such as those in (1)–(4):

(1) a.   I like John.
     b.   John, I like __.
     c.   *I like.

(2) a.   *I like about John.
     b.   *About John, I like__.

(3) a.   I won't speak to John.
     b.   John, I *won't* speak to __.

(4) a.   I doubt $\left\{ \begin{array}{c} \text{John} \\ \text{*there} \end{array} \right\}$ became a spy.

     b. $\left\{ \begin{array}{c} \text{John} \\ \text{*There} \end{array} \right\}$ I *doubt* __became a spy.

Something unexpected is in evidence here: *like*, an obligatorily transitive verb (as shown in (1)c) can appear with no direct object in (1)b, as long as a potential valent appears *outside* the sentence of which *like* is the lexical head. And as (4) shows, it isn't only complements which exhibit this peculiar behavior; subject specifications seem to be satisfiable outside the clause of the selecting head as well – and, just as a normal NP but not dummy *there* can locally meet the SPR requirements imposed by *became*, a normal NP but not *there* can meet those requirements somewhat nonlocally. The fact that the same valence restrictions that we would independently posit for the SPR specifications associated with *became* are evident in the case of (4)b makes it *seem* indisputable that what we're observing here is a kind of delayed valence satisfaction possibility: the verb's SPR or COMPS value must be saturated by some actual constituent in the structure which conforms in all respects to the specifications which appear on that list – *like* requires an NP complement ((1)), not a PP ((3)); *became a spy* requires a normal subject, not a dummy element ((4)), and this must be what accounts for the parallels between (i) what can appear in the ordinary position where a head finds its valents and (ii) the displaced position where the distant valent somehow combines with the head to saturate whichever valence feature is involved. Following our practice in previous chapters in which we used displacement as evidence for constituency, we refer to the material which supplies this delayed valence satisfaction as the filler, and the structural position with respect to which the filler is displaced as the gap. Our concern now, however, is not displacement as a probe for structure, but rather as a phenomenon in its own right, and how to provide an account of it with the broadest possible empirical coverage.

6.2   Beyond Valence: Structure

Before we can attempt an analysis of this filler/gap construction, we need to determine just what the structure is that we're trying to relate to the construction's observed behavior – that is, where the filler's structural position actually *is*. As always, it is a mistake to simply assume in advance that some given configuration corresponds to the correct general characterization of a particular class of sentences; typically, there are several possibilities, and we need to find evidence that bears on which of these we have reason to support as the best fit to the data. In the case of the displacement construction illustrated in (1)–(4), the question of the filler's location boils down to two possibilities: if we say that S_0 is the clause dominating the gap site whose subject is to the immediate right of the filler, is the filler a sister to that subject, that is, does it occur *under* S_0, or is it a *sister* to S_0 itself? That is, which of the two possibilities in (5) is the correct description?

(5)

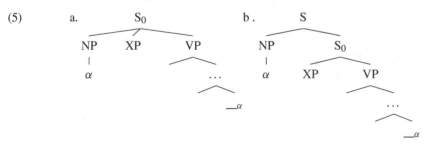

In considering what means we have available to choose between the alternatives in (5), it will be helpful to recall that we addressed a similar problem earlier, in connection with the syntactic position of complementizers, using several distributional properties of filler/gap constructions to develop an argument that these morphemes are markers attaching to entire clauses, rather than occurring as a sister to the subject within those clauses. It turns out that we can use the same kind of evidence to shed light on the issues in question, where the alternatives are parallel to those we considered in connection with *that*. Again, coordination plays a significant role in the argument, in particular, data of the sort shown in (6):

(6)   I know that *those* people, John likes __and Mary dislikes __.

In terms of the alternatives in (5), we need to choose between the following:

(7) a.

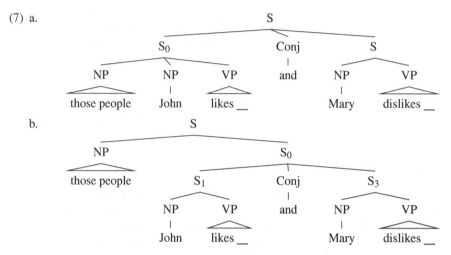

These rival structures help us pinpoint the kind of facts that will enable us to decide between them. In the case of (7)a, we are positing a filler inside one clause which fills a gap inside that clause, but also plays the role of the filler in the second clause. In the structure in (7)b, on the other hand, a filler stands outside a conjunction of clauses and the filler/gap relationship in the two conjuncts will be mirror images. To resolve the matter, we need to see what happens in a structurally parallel situation in which it's clear that a filler is inside one clause, and take note of whether or not a linkage to the gap site in the other clause is possible. The trick, of course, is to find such a structure.

   We have in fact seen just such a structure in our discussion of markers in Chapter 2, where a number of arguments were given providing substantial support for clausal structures of the form [s Complementizer S], and where we noted displacement constructions of the form *I know that John, no one really likes* __, unequivocally locating the fronted NP *John* within S. Suppose we conjoin another clause to this one whose syntax clearly puts it outside the first clause. This can be done quite simply, as in (8):

(8)   I know [s that [s John, Terrence really likes __]] but [s that [s Mary DETESTS John]].

If the scenario in (7)a were correct, then a displaced element internal to the first conjunct would still be interpretable as the filler of the gap in the second conjunct. It follows that it should be possible to omit *John* in the second conjunct in (8), since we would then expect that, just as in (7)a, the NP internal to the first clause on the left edge could be interpreted as the filler for the gap in the second conjunct. The result would be the example exhibited in (9):

(9)   *I know [$_s$ that [$_s$ John, Terrence really likes __]] but [$_s$ that [$_s$ Mary DETESTS __]].

But this example is clearly ill-formed. There is something missing after *detests*, and it is simply not possible to 'interpret in' the filler *John* from the first clause. Thus the prediction implicit in (7)a fails. The results are, however, exactly what we would expect on the basis of (7)b: the filler is external to both of the clauses that contain gaps, and the structural relationship between the filler and these two clauses is completely parallel, and so a constituent which can be interpreted as distantly 'filling' a gap in one of these conjuncts should be able, by whatever mechanism is taken to be sufficient for that case, to also fill a gap in the second conjunct – as long as that constituent is outside *both* conjuncts.

We therefore take it as given henceforth that a filler belonging to any category appears in a configuration instantiating the schematic structure in (5)b. Our next task is to identify the precise form of this mechanism. Clearly, there must be some connection between what is on some particular valence list for a given head and what kind of filler element winds up actually satisfying that selectional requirement. But is that requirement met in exactly the same way, whether or not the actual sign appearing in the structure occurs in the usual place as a sister, or outside the clause itself, in some kind of 'satellite' position as characterized by (5)b?

On the basis of our experience with auxiliaries and raising predicates, we might be tempted to reply in the affirmative. After all, in both cases, while the 'raised' subject at the top of the dependency literally satisfies the SPR valence requirements of its VP sister, it also, through the subject-sharing property of auxiliaries and raising predicates, simultaneously identifies the grammatical properties of the SPR specifications all the way down the chain of VPs between the finite VP at the top and the VP whose head does the actual selection of the subject at the bottom. Since it's usually a sound strategy to stick with what has already been shown to work, we might visualize something like the situation in (10) as a way to arrange for this delayed satisfaction of valence requirements:

(10)

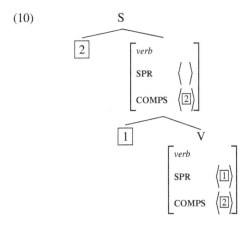

If we adopt (10) as the basis for displacement, then in, for example, (11), the verb *dislikes* will 'pass' an unsaturated direct object NP valence requirement up to its VP mother, and then in turn to the latter's clausal projection, where it will ultimately be saturated by the filler daughter of the root S.

(11)   Rocco, [$_s$ Luanne [$_{vp}$ dislikes __]]

That is, we have in (10) a structure in which the COMPS value is not satisfied locally, but instead shares that value with its phrasal mother. In this account, the head combines with its subject valent first, yielding a category which we have not previously encountered: a head saturated for its subject but not its complement(s). This category is obviously not an S, which is saturated for all arguments; nor is it a VP, which is saturated for all complements but not for its subject valent. Clearly a new pair of schematic rules will have to be introduced – one to allow a selecting head to combine with its subject argument first and only then with a complement, and one to combine a complement argument with the result of the previous combination (for, as things stand, there is no mechanism in place that ensures the sharing of the material labeled by $\boxed{2}$ between the filler and the COMPS value of the lower verb). All of this seems a very unwelcome complication of the normal valence-satisfaction apparatus of the framework, even if not undoable in principle.

In fact, however, matters are a good deal worse than (10). Consider the data in (12)–(14):

(12) a.   *I dislike __.

   b.   *Luanne believes that I dislike __.

   c.   *Those people are sure that Luanne believes that I dislike __.

(13) a.   Luanne thinks that I dislike $\left(* \left\{ \begin{matrix} \text{at} \\ \text{of} \\ \text{about} \\ \text{with} \\ \text{to} \end{matrix} \right\} \right)$ Rocco.

   b. $\left(* \left\{ \begin{matrix} \text{At} \\ \text{Of} \\ \text{About} \\ \text{With} \\ \text{To} \end{matrix} \right\} \right)$ Rocco, Mary thinks that I dislike __.

(14) a.   Those people are sure that Mary believes I dislike $\left(* \left\{ \begin{matrix} \text{at} \\ \text{of} \\ \text{about} \\ \text{with} \\ \text{to} \end{matrix} \right\} \right)$ John.

   b. $\left(* \left\{ \begin{matrix} \text{At} \\ \text{Of} \\ \text{About} \\ \text{With} \\ \text{To} \end{matrix} \right\} \right)$ John, those people are sure that Mary thinks I dislike __.

As we would expect, the failure to match a head's complement requirement is not forgiven no matter how many levels of structure are constructed 'on top of' it, either omitting any complement at all ((12) or by supplying the wrong kind of complement (13)a, (14)a). But attempting the same 'direct saturation' approach embodied in (10) to explain (13)b encounters the fundamental obstacle illustrated in (15):

(15)

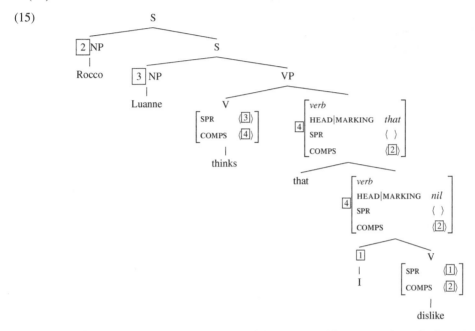

The structure in (15) should be understood as a graphic expression of the connectivity that would have to be established between the filler, *Rocco*, and *dislike*'s direct object position, the corresponding gap site – what we need, but not what we actually have – in order to obtain a well-formed result. How does *dislike* get its complement valence satisfied in this structure? The new schema necessary to account for (10), apart from adding a rather complex piece of machinery to our setup, won't help at all with (15) as things stand, because the 'missing piece,' *Rocco*, doesn't correspond to an argument of *thinks*, but rather of the verb *dislike* heading the VP that *thinks* selects as its complement. The problem is obvious: there is no way to transfer the missing NP COMPS specification of *dislikes* to *thinks*, because the latter has no NP complement value. *Thinks* selects only a verbal category – and, under the scenario we're considering, quite a strange one: *think* must have a special entry in the lexicon so that it can select a complement which is, as already noted, saturated for its SPR specification but not for its COMPS value. As a very rough first approximation we might propose (16):

(16)

$$\begin{bmatrix} \text{PHON} & \text{thinks} \\ \text{SS|VAL|COMPS} & \langle \text{S} \begin{bmatrix} verb \\ \text{MARKING} & that \\ \text{SPR} & \langle \ \rangle \\ \text{COMPS} & \langle \text{NP} \rangle \end{bmatrix} \rangle \end{bmatrix}$$

But this entry is clearly inadequate. The problem is that once *thinks* as per (16) combines with the odd complement whose properties are summarized in this lexical entry, it is saturated so far as its *own* COMPS value is concerned. So how can the unsaturated COMPS specification for *dislikes* get 'cashed out' at the top of the structure by the missing valent? The only way to implement the idea that fillers of gaps are just distantly positioned syntactic arguments satisfying the valence requirements of some selecting head is to assume that *think* itself inherits the unsaturated COMPS requirement of *dislikes*. That is, we would need an alternative lexical entry for *believes* along the following lines:

(17)

$$\begin{bmatrix} \text{PHON} & \text{thinks} \\ \\ \text{SS|VAL|COMPS} & \left\langle \boxed{1}, \text{S} \begin{bmatrix} verb \\ \text{MARKING} & that \\ \text{COMPS} & \langle \dots, \boxed{1}, \dots \rangle \\ \text{SPR} & \langle\ \rangle \end{bmatrix} \right\rangle \end{bmatrix}$$

This revision of the entry for *believes* in (16) introduces an NP valent identical to some unsaturated NP valent in the verb's complement clause. If this added complement itself is left unsaturated at the level of the VP headed by *thinks*, then it will indeed pass up to the clausal sister of the filler by whatever hypothetical mechanism we've assumed in the case of simpler examples such as (11).

Again, this strategy – which seems unavoidable if we assume that displacement phenomena are just another form of valence satisfaction – represents an enormous complication of the essentially simple notion of the combinatoric theory presented in Chapter 2. The unsaturated [COMPS ⟨NP⟩] value which *thinks* on this scenario has to share with its clausal complement must in turn be passed up to the VP *believe* heads, and then to the S that this VP heads, and only then can it be canceled out by the filler sister to that S. A narrative along these lines is necessary, since HPSG's principles operate strictly locally, and it therefore is crucial that the COMPS value of the gap be available in some part of the phrase structure which is locally connected to the filler, that is, the topmost verbal projection, the filler's sister. But were we to try to implement it, it would quite obviously necessitate a fairly complete revision of the Chapter 2 formulation of how syntax is projected from valence.

Considerable extra complexity is, however, the least of our worries with the revisions in question, for it turns out that the strategy is not just excessively complex but empirically untenable. As things stand, we have hypothetically committed ourselves to a view of valence saturation in which satisfaction of some selectional requirement(s) can be deferred, as long as the valence specification corresponding to that requirement is passed up to the next local level of structure as an 'add-on.' But what if we decide to saturate that requirement as a valent of the verb *thinks* immediately? On the analysis we're experimenting with, valence requirements can be freely transferred to higher levels of structure if they aren't saturated at the level of the head which introduces them lexically (e.g., *dislike*'s lexical requirement of a direct object NP). But there is nothing which actually *requires* us to defer this satisfaction of valence; if we supply *dislike* with an NP object sister, the result will be *Mary thinks that I dislike Rocco*. What happens if instead of appealing to some valence-sharing possibility to 'pass up' the NP complement, we simply allow it be 'cashed out' by supplying an NP sister for *thinks*? This is, after all, the canonical way to discharge selectional requirements. If filler/gap connectivity is supposed to be an instance of valence satisfaction, our default assumption must be that local resolution of such requirements is a robust possibility – and indeed, nothing we've seen or said to this point blocks that possibility. But the result of this exercise is anything but encouraging, so far as the approach embodied in (10) is concerned:

(18)   *I think Rocco that Luanne dislikes __.

where we assume the otherwise universal ordering in English whereby NPs precede clausal sisters. The example in (18) is irredeemably ill-formed, contrary to our expectations. There is no sentence of English which has the pronunciation corresponding to this example and which means the same thing as *I think that Luanne dislikes Rocco*.

We therefore must give up the analysis embodied in (10), or add a number of new principles, lexical entries and/or mechanisms to the already greatly overcomplicated inventory that, as we've already noted, (10) requires of us – and the latter is a risky strategy to follow. Each increase in the complexity of an analysis typically multiplies the number of unforeseen consequences which follow from that analysis, almost always guarantees serious problems of overgeneration, undergeneration, or both, and hence should be avoided. In effect, (18) is telling us that somewhere or other we've taken a wrong path in attempting to account for displacement and its connections with valence, and need to do some serious backtracking.

Our difficulties began when we tried to expand the mechanisms we've employed for ordinary valence satisfaction to encompass displacement effects, and that, presumably, is the move we need to rethink. The right strategy here is probably to simply accept that the phenomenon in question isn't an instance of valence satisfaction – though the latter clearly must play a role in the larger picture. After all, we've seen some evidence that displaced elements must conform to the valence specifications of the head whose selectional requirements haven't been locally met, for example, *like* in (1)–(2) and *became* in (4). At this point, there are a number of ways to proceed, but what they have in common is that none of them corresponds to anything like normal valence. And there's still more evidence along those lines:

(19) a.   I very much doubt John and Pat $\left\{ \begin{matrix} \text{are} \\ \text{*is} \end{matrix} \right\}$ spies.

b.   John and Pat I very much doubt __ $\left\{ \begin{matrix} \text{are} \\ \text{*is} \end{matrix} \right\}$ spies.

(20) a.   I very much doubt John $\left\{ \begin{array}{c} \text{is} \\ \text{*are} \end{array} \right\}$ a spy.

b.   John I very much $\left\{ \begin{array}{c} \text{is} \\ \text{*are} \end{array} \right\}$ a spy.

As discussed earlier in connection with agreement, there is good evidence that a language-specific rule holds in English which requires identity between the AGR specifications on the selecting head and those of the AGR specification given for its SPR list value. Agreement therefore implicates the valence properties of a head. The fact that agreement requirements are preserved between the position in the structure from which the subject is missing and the position in the structure where we actually find this missing subject can thus be taken as a clear indication of the role played by valence properties in the syntax of these displacement phenomena. Since the preceding discussion undercuts the possibility that displacement is nothing other than ordinary valence saturation, we need to work out a different approach in which information about selectional restrictions holding at the gap site is 'transmitted,' as it were, over the syntactic distance between the gap site and the constituent which in effect fills the gap.

The scare quotes here should be taken seriously. As usual, we are not supposing that this information, however it is encoded, in effect starts at one point in the structure and gradually spreads from node to node till it winds up at its destination. Rather, the connection is implemented between the gap site in the structure and the filler site, it holds simultaneously at all points, via the kinds of feature matching requirements evident in, say, (21):

(21) a.   John seems to have been telling the truth.

b.

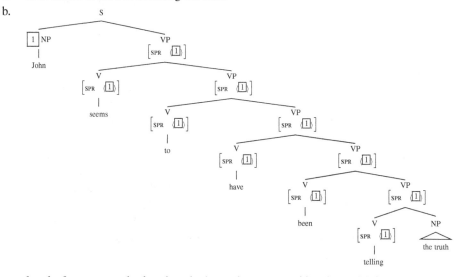

At every level of structure, the head verb shares its SPR specification with its VP complement as part of satisfying a lexically imposed feature equality which is a precondition for the appearance of both the V and the VP in the structure in the first place; the appearance of this SPR value on the VP mother is at each point in the structure determined by the Head-complement Rule; and the appearance of *John* as the NP constituent satisfying the valence requirements of the selecting head *seems* is determined by the Head-subject Rule. There is no sense of the value of SPR 'working its way up' from *telling* or 'working its way down' from *John*; rather, the entire structure exists as a whole – a network of feature identities which simultaneously satisfies at every point the constraint system constituting our theory of English. It's important to bear this perspective in mind, because, as per our earlier speculations, there are obvious connections between valence and the phenomenon of displacement illustrated in the preceding example, even though the latter cannot be reduced to the former.

Imagine, for example, that we had not a restricted set of lexical items with the raising property – the equality between SUBJ and complement VP[SPR] values that auxiliaries and a small number of nonauxiliary English verbs manifest – but a large number of such verbs, at least some of which could reappear at different points in the structure an arbitrary number of times. In that case, it's evident that we would be able to license trees with the general appearance of (21) which had no upper bound to the number of intermediate trees between *John* and *telling the truth*. But what has been said about the simultaneous constraint satisfaction that determines the well-formedness of (21) would apply equally to all such trees. The information that the subject of *telling the truth* must be a nondummy NP, for example, would be realized simultaneously in every tree in the structure, so that there would be a genuinely unbounded dependency holding between the lowest VP in the structure and the NP subject daughter at the very top. As already briefly noted, this kind of unbounded dependency would in a sense be an accident of the lexical properties of particular heads and the mechanism of valence satisfaction, with the 'raising property' essentially a kind of odd wrinkle of the lexicon that permitted this sort of arbitrarily long-distance linkage. But in the cases of actual displacement given above, where valence satisfaction is not involved, whatever mechanism we find optimal will necessarily work the same way: there will be some kind of locally satisfiable constraint mechanism at work, and it will hold at all points along the structural route between the gap site and the filler. The crux of the matter is, what should this mechanism consist of?

6.3   Beyond Valence: Mechanism

A successful account of the specific phenomenon illustrated in, for example, (14) requires three components:

i.   A means of linking the particular properties of the displaced constituent – the filler – to the rest of the structure.
ii.   A way to ensure a set of feature identities within that structure.
iii.   A mechanism to connect those identities to the specific valence requirements which must be satisfied at the gap site.

These are rather general and programmatic descriptions, but they're a useful starting point for working our way gradually toward a solution.

Consider, for example, the desideratum (iii), which will bear the burden of ensuring that, for example, in (19)–(20), number and person agreement imposed at the gap site by valence requirements, as noted above, are made available to be preserved across the syntactic domain separating the gap site from the filler. Here we are only speaking of connecting valence at the gap site to the rest of the structure, without worrying specifically about what happens in the rest of the structure as a result of that connection. The question is quite specific: *how* is valence to be translated into a form which is in principle 'portable' throughout a syntactic domain with no restrictions on size?

An important clue is available to us on the basis of the previous discussion in which it became clear that filler/gap linkages do not involve the saturation of a valence specification by anything like the mechanisms we developed in Chapter 2. On the other hand, in for example (10), either *dislike*'s COMPS value is saturated or it is not, and if it is not, then it is not possible to compose a VP on the basis of a head plus its complements, and therefore not possible to compose a sentence from a VP plus its subject, and so on. Therefore, we have to conclude that this COMPS requirement is indeed saturated, in spite of the fact that there is no sister to the head corresponding to the COMPS specification evident in the form of the sentence. If we cannot 'see' the material which saturates this requirement, then we can conclude, provisionally, that that material corresponds to an inaudible constituent – syntactically present, but unpronounced. The valence satisfaction mechanism involved here would simply be the usual analysis imposed by the Head-complement Rule. But what is left for us to do at this point is to determine how this inaudible constituent 'connects' with the distant filler at the very top of the filler/gap dependency.

One thing that the linkage mechanism we seek must account for, most immediately, is the fact that the existences of the filler and of the gap are mutually dependent. As (1)c illustrates, a gap without a filler leads to ill-formedness, and, as we see in (22), the same holds of examples in which we have a filler but no gap:

(22) a.   *John, I like Chris. [nonvocative]
     b.   *John, Mary believes that I like Chris.
     c.   *John, those people are sure that Mary believes that I like Chris.

This mutual dependence clearly points to a mechanism linking a filler to a gap and vice versa; but since on the reasoning above the gap is actually 'filled' by an inaudible element, the linkage must be between the filler and the form of that null element. A critical aspect of this seemingly tiny wrinkle is that any null element which actually saturates a given valence requirement necessarily satisfies all requirements holding an *overt* constituent in the structural position occupied by the gap site. We therefore have a significant clue about what (iii) above consists of: it must be a mechanism which in some way delivers the features of the null element at the gap site to whatever principle(s) in (ii) in the list above might be involved in enforcing the necessary feature identities through the structure to the point where they meet up with the filler. The point of this mechanism is to specify just what the necessary feature properties of the invisible constituent at the gap site are, but, as the above discussion of the 'direct saturation' approach shows, we have in our current feature inventory none which are suitable for this task.

We therefore need a new feature which can serve as the packaging, so to speak, for the array of features whose identity throughout the structure must be imposed. We can call this feature anything we like; the critical empirical question is, what portion of the total information that linguistic signs consist of does this feature need to include?

6.3.1   Is Constituent Structure Shared between Filler and Gap?

One very important bit of information that must *not* be part of the package is the PHON specification. After all, the filler is phonetically realized, while the constituent at the gap site, with which the filler must be completely consistent, is inaudible. Less obvious is whether or not all other information, for example, constituent structure, must be shared between the filler and the gap site. Consider, another kind of displacement, involving an interrogative *wh*-phrase as in (23):

(23) a. $\left\{ \begin{array}{c} \text{Who} \\ \text{Which friends of those people} \end{array} \right\}$ were you talking to about that?

b. You were talking to $\left\{ \begin{array}{c} \text{who} \\ \text{which friends of those people} \end{array} \right\}$ about that?

Both ways of posing the question are used in English, although the discourse circumstances are somewhat different: (23)a is more or less the default way to query the addressee, while (23)b – which, when the *wh*-word is given high-pitch intonation, usually indicates that the speaker missed part of the speaker's previous utterance and wants it repeated – can also, when the *wh*-word is stressed, be used without high pitch or rising intonation as part of a 'cross-examination' kind of discourse. In the latter circumstance, the question is evoking a narrative of events from the persons questioned, and the lack of inversion seems connected to an effort to underscore the key points of the hearer's testimony while prompting them to continue with the narrative. But such pairs are not always possible:

(24) a.   What the hell were you thinking of when you did that?
     b.   *You were thinking of what the hell when you did that?

(25) a.   How in the world did you figure the solution out?
     b.   *You figured out the solution how in the world?

Evidently, there are displaced elements which can *only* appear as displaced elements.

Another piece of evidence, of a rather different kind, involves the modal auxiliary *need*, which takes a bare-form VP complement and which, like certain other modals, does not inflect for *any* grammatical features:

(26) a.   We need(*ed) not listen to them.

    b.   ??*I didn't think we need(ed) listen to them.

If *need* actually had a past tense inflection, even if not morphologically marked, then (26)b would be well-formed on the suffixless option, parallel to *I don't think that they hit any target/I didn't think that they hit any targets*. The curious and useful property of this *need* is that it belongs to the class of negative polarity items mentioned briefly in Chapter 3:

(27) a.   We need *(not) listen to them.

    b.   I *(don't) think we need listen to them.

Need, like other NPIs, must be semantically affected by negation, but unlike many others, that negation can be syntactically rather distant, applying not only from a higher position, as in (27), but also from a lower:

(28)   You need worry about none of these possibilities.

On the assumption that displacement involves a precise mirroring of the phrase structure of the filler at the gap site, we would expect that in a case such as (29)a, we would have a phrase structure along the lines of (29)b:

(29) a.   John predicts I'll worry about only three of these things, and worry about only three of them I probably WILL.

    b.

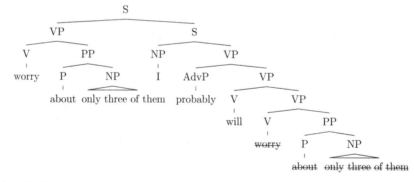

All that is missing at the gap site, on this general approach, is the actual pronunciation; the whole constituent hierarchy of the filler, with the lexical items at the bottom, is present. Yet in the corresponding case with *need* in place of *will*, the example is completely ill-formed:

(30)   *John insists I need worry about only three of these things, and worry about only three of them I probably need.

The assumption that a complete copy of the filler is present at the gap site makes the failure of the NPI *need* in the second conjunct, where displacement has occurred, utterly mysterious. A similar pattern arises in cases such as (27)b, which is fine when the negative is present in the higher clause as long as the VP *listen to them* is in its normal position. But when fronted, the result is spectacularly bad, as in (31)a, as vs (31)b:

(31) a.   ... and I don't think we need listen to them.

b.   *... and listen to them, I don't think we need.

c.   ... and listen to them, I think we need NOT.

The explanation for this difference is not one that we can address at this point, but for our purposes, the crucial point is that, if the structure were what the 'complete copy' hypothesis about the gap site dictated, we would have a structure along the lines of (32) – the same structure which underlies the impeccable (31)a.

(32)

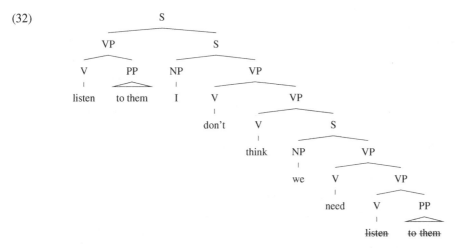

Since the syntactic/semantic conditions on modal *need* are met in (31)a–b, they are, on the 'complete copy' analysis, predicted to have the same (well-formed) status. The striking difference between them therefore shifts the burden of proof heavily onto the 'complete copy' analysis.

On balance, then, the analytic decision to treat the relationship between gap sites and fillers as one in which neither phonology nor constituency is shared seems not only well motivated, but also in a sense follows as the null hypothesis on the version of the phrase structure framework presented in this book, because the internal structure of signs is nowhere mentioned among their feature specifications; hence, it would involve a tremendous complication of the grammar if we were to attempt to communicate information about this internal structure to some other part of the tree. It still leaves us with the problem of deciding just what portion of the filler's sign description *is* shared with the gap site, but here we have certain clues, some of which have already been alluded to.

6.3.2   Filler/Gap Linkage Via SLASH

6.3.2.1   SLASH at the Bottom of the Dependency

Let's start with what we have reason to believe *doesn't* have a role in the linkage between the filler and the gap: phonology and the internal constituent structure of the filler (contrary to the 'complete copy' hypothesis) – just what we expect if the information shared between the top and bottom of the extraction dependency is a SYNSEM value. So what we are looking for is a way to ensure the identity of the SYNSEM values of the filler and of the gap site. SYNSEM gives both morphosyntactic information and a representation of the meaning of the sign, which appears to be correct. Without going into detail at this point, there are a number of indicators which make it clear that the semantic interpretation of the filler must be available at the gap site. The most obvious is the fact that we interpret normal undisplaced constituents and topicalized constituents exactly the same with respect to the head whose valence element they correspond to: *I like John* and *John, I like* both assert a relation corresponding to *like* which holds between the speaker and some individual named *John*. That meaning is, moreover, available for interpretation with respect to any other head in the structure which has a valent specified as identical to the SYNSEM of the displaced constituent; for example, we see that in *Who do you believe to have forged those documents?* the SPR specification of the VP *to have forged those documents*, whose interpretation depends on that of the direct object of *believe*, is immediately understood as being determined by the meaning of *who*, just as in the undisplaced version *You believe WHO to have forged those documents?* The same holds in the case of idiomatic interpretation: *We need to keep HOW close tabs on the Committee's membership/How close tabs do we need to keep on the Committee's membership?* At the same time, we've seen, via data such as (19)–(20), that agreement phenomena, which reflect part of a sign's SYN specification, are also part of the shared information which must be mediated between the filler and its matching null category at the gap site. So both parts of the SYNSEM that we've referred to – the SYN and SEM components – must be included in the package that carries the shared information across the syntactic distance separating the two ends of the filler/gap pathway, and apparently nothing else.

Let's assume for the moment, then, that it is the SYNSEM value alone of the filler which is shared with the hypothesized null complement in gap position. Again, this looks tantalizingly like an instance of ordinary valence satisfaction, because SYNSEM values are exactly the kinds of data structures which appear on the valences lists of the selecting head – but as we've already discussed at length, filler/gap linkage (or 'connectivity,' as it is often called) cannot be a matter of direct valence saturation, because the conditions which have to be met in the general case of displacement are at severe cross-purposes with the conditions which apply to valence saturation. Whatever means we employ to package the specifications which must be shared between the filler and the gap will therefore not be part of the valence mechanism, that is, will not be the COMPS or SPR feature. But it *can* involve a feature of some other kind, subject to its own set of constraints and requirements. Having decided that the SYNSEM value of the filler is what is shared with the gap site, and that we need a new feature to 'carry' this information, we can now work out a concrete proposal for exactly what happens at the gap site to produce the gap itself.

The approach taken and motivated earlier calls for the gap site to be occupied by a phonologically null category, one which – as is typical of lexical entries – lacks internal structure. Since the fronted material is a phrasal category (even if, as in *Magazines, I really have no use for __*, it takes the form of only a single word), we would, on this approach, have an instance of a phrasal-type lexical item, similar to names such as *Rocco* and proforms such as *her, this* etc. Critically, however, we only get such items appearing when there is a matching filler at the 'top' of the relevant structure – no gaps without a filler, as we've observed – so whatever feature we choose to package the filler and gap's SYNSEM specifications must be reserved for filler/gap connectivity *exclusively*. What distinguishes this lexical item from all others will be the fact that it has an empty PHON specification. If the only lexical item with a null phonology is specified so that its own SYNSEM value is identical to that of the 'packaging' feature – whatever that value is – then, indirectly, the SYNSEM of the empty category and that of the filler, which *also* matches that of the 'packaging' feature, will be identical, just as we want. Graphically, the picture we're looking for is like the following, where F is the as-yet unnamed packaging feature:

(33)

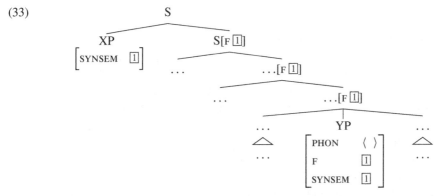

If we build into the grammar the exclusive correlation of an empty PHON specification with the identity of F's value and that of YP's SYNSEM value, then we will only find gaps where there are fillers. Precisely how to arrange this will be discussed below, but at this point, we at least know in relatively specific terms what formal outcome we need to ensure.

Let's start with the easiest part of the analytic problem here: naming F. For historical reasons, this feature is generally referred to as SLASH – although some sources use the term GAP, a practice which has not been adopted very widely. The term was introduced in the early 1980s in the theoretical framework directly ancestral to the one we've been developing in this book, and originates in the fact that in that earlier approach, a category XP containing a gap of category YP was written XP/YP – a notation which originates in a rather different grammatical theory, but with a somewhat similar significance. (The convenient availability of a standard-keyboard character to indicate the presence of a gap doubtless played a role in its adoption as well.) In the earlier approach, / was not the name of a feature, but was later reinterpreted as one, at which point / was replaced in the formalism by the name of the character, SLASH, although the / notation was and is still used as a kind of shorthand. The category at the gap site will now have the form

(34)
$$
\begin{bmatrix}
\text{PHON} & \langle\ \rangle \\
\text{SLASH} & \boxed{1} \\
\text{SYNSEM} & \boxed{1}
\end{bmatrix}
$$

We refer to a prosodically empty constituent with the specification in (34) as a *trace*. The identity of the SLASH and SYNSEM values in this lexical entry guarantee that any category whose SYNSEM value matches the [SLASH $\boxed{1}$] specification in (34) will necessarily have the same morphosyntactic properties that hold at the gap site.

This picture will be revised in important ways in the discussion below, but for the moment is close enough to where we need to end up that it's practical to switch our attention to desideratum (ii) in the list given above, the nature of the mechanism which licenses a pathway of shared information between the bottom of the filler/gap structure and the top.

6.3.2.2   SLASH between the Gap and the Filler

The obvious challenge in bridging the structural separation between the gap and the filler is that that structural separation cannot be specified in advance; the size of the set of possible intervening nodes between the two has, strictly speaking, nonfinite cardinality – essentially, it is the size of the set of integers, since for any number of intervening two-generation trees in the structure which lies between the filler and the gap, another can always be added to yield a grammatical result. This is not a mathematical property of the grammar itself, but rather a fact about natural languages as objects, and therefore no rigorous proof of the claim can be given. But consider a situation in which a VP occurs between the filler and the gap, so that we have the following situation:

(35)

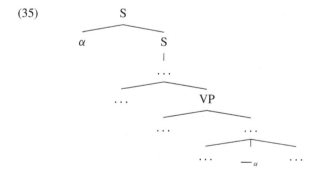

where __$_\alpha$ indicates the position of the gap corresponding, more formally, to the filler category in (34). Without exception, VPs can be modified by adjuncts, with the well-formedness of a VP dominating a gap site uncompromised by the presence of a (semantically compatible) adjunct. We have, for example,

(36) a.   Who did you [$_{VP}$ meet __for lunch]?

b.   Who did you [$_{VP}$ [$_{VP}$ __meet for lunch yesterday]]?

c.   Who did you [$_{VP}$ [$_{VP}$ [$_{VP}$ meet __for lunch] yesterday] near the park]?

d.   Who did you [$_{VP}$ [$_{VP}$ [$_{VP}$ [$_{VP}$ meet __for lunch] yesterday] near the park] in that little restaurant]?

e.   Who did you [$_{VP}$ [$_{VP}$ [$_{VP}$ [$_{VP}$ [$_{VP}$ meet __for lunch] yesterday] near the park] in that little restaurant] to talk about the lawsuit]?

f.   Who did you [$_{VP}$ [$_{VP}$ [$_{VP}$ [$_{VP}$ [$_{VP}$ [$_{VP}$ meet __for lunch] yesterday] near the park] in that little restaurant] to talk about the lawsuit] after contacting the Committee's attorneys]?

The connection between the gap and *who* seems impervious to the massive proliferation of intervening VP nodes, although presumably a point will come when neither the speaker uttering such sentences nor anyone else will be able to make total sense of the utterance, due to their sheer length and the limitations of memory that are inherent in any data storage system, biological or artificial. There are many other such illustrations of the fact that, so far as we can tell, there is no way to impose an upper limit on the number of nodes in a filler/gap pathway – a fact which any effort to link the SLASH specifications of the gap to the SYNSEM value of the filler must take into account.

There is, however, no need for the grammar itself to make reference to the unboundedness of the potential distance between the polar positions in the displacement dependency. In order to ensure that the necessary information bridges the syntactic distance involved in any given case, all that is required is that a mother category and at least one daughter category share SLASH specifications:

(37)

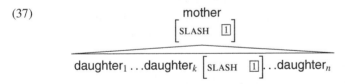

There are two possibilities: either (i) k is the gap site itself, or (ii) k is on a filler/gap pathway and is not itself the gap site, which it must dominate, thus entailing that it dominates at least one daughter itself. Thus k is not only a daughter of the upper local tree, but also the mother of the lower local tree:

(38)

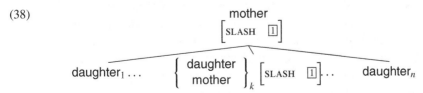

For concreteness, let's assume that k branches. Then we will have a structural object which can be schematically represented as in (39):

(39)

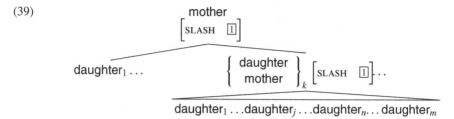

Since we are, however, requiring that the mother and at least one daughter share SLASH values, the structure in (39) is not yet compliant with the proposed grammar: it must rather take the form in (40):

(40)

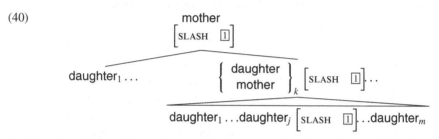

At this point, the careful reader may have noticed that the particular formulation suggested – that 'the mother and at least one daughter share any given SLASH values' – guarantees that if there is a SLASH value in any daughter, it must be shared with the mother, to exactly the degree that a SLASH value borne by the mother must be shared with some daughter. In effect, neither the mother's nor daughter's SLASH value is primary: if there is a SLASH value in one, the same SLASH value is found in the other, and if one of them bears no given SLASH value, the other must not as well – double or nothing, as it were. But this is just the beginning: it turns out that we can have multiple fillers, linked to different gap sites, as well, whose different SLASH values must share at least certain parts of the same structural pathway. For example, consider the sentence in (41):

(41) a.   John is someone who I'm never sure what to say to.

     b.   John is someone who$_2$ I'm never sure what$_1$ [$_{vp}$ to say __$_1$ to __$_2$].

There are two gaps in the VP *to say to*, which means that two distinct SLASH values must be connected to the two distinct fillers subscripted as 1 and 2 respectively. Evidently, then, the value of SLASH must be an object which can contain multiple SYNSEM specifications. There are various types of data structures which could be recruited for use as the value for a packaging feature carrying information about multiple objects; the simplest one, in terms of the use we will be making of it, is the set, and we will henceforth treat SLASH as a set-valued feature, whose members will, for the time being, be taken to be the kinds of objects that are specified as values of the SYNSEM feature.

The use of a set-valued feature allows a very compact, even elegant formulation of the principle which was suggested quite informally in connection with (37)–(40):

> **Slash Principle (preliminary version):** the SLASH value of a phrase is the union of the SLASH values of its daughters.

Suppose there is no displacement. Then in every VP in the structure, the SLASH value of the daughters will be the empty set; hence, the SLASH value of the mother will be the union of empty sets, that is, the empty set. Suppose again that there is a single gap in one of the daughters. Then the union of the SYNSEM values of all the daughters will be the set containing that SLASH value, which by the Slash Principle will also appear as the mother's SLASH value.

But we still do not know exactly where in the sign description the feature SLASH 'lives.' In (34), for convenience, it was presented as a top-level category, but no evidence for this choice was given. In fact, it is very likely that this architecture is not correct. As we will see later in this chapter and in the next chapter, in certain cases a head will select a complement, or a marker must match the properties of a head, on the basis of whether or not that complement or head contains a gap – that is, bears SLASH. But since selection and matching situations in general make reference to the SYNSEM value of the complement or head respectively, we must conclude that SLASH 'lives' somewhere *inside* SYNSEM.

This conclusion in itself seems harmless enough – but it creates a major technical problem for us. Consider (42):

(42)
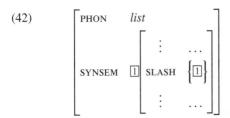

Here, a feature SYNSEM is specified for a different feature, SLASH whose value is that of the structure *containing* this second feature. A specification such as this corresponds to a situation in which the graphic object depicting the algebraic structure of a category has the property called *cyclicity*, which involves something like an infinite regress: SYNSEM contains a SLASH specification, whose value is that of the whole SYNSEM, which therefore contains the same SLASH value, whose value is that of the whole SYNSEM, which, and so on. This in itself is not nearly as problematic as it might seem; such structures are actually mathematically coherent and permitted by the logic which licenses the kind of representations we have been employing throughout this book. The actual difficulty is an empirical byproduct of this cyclic property: the whole point of SLASH is that the gap must share SYNSEM values with the filler, but if they do so according to (42), the filler itself has a SYNSEM value, [1], which includes a nonempty SLASH value, and thus will *itself* have to dominate a gap! The tree in (43) will make the point clear:

(43)

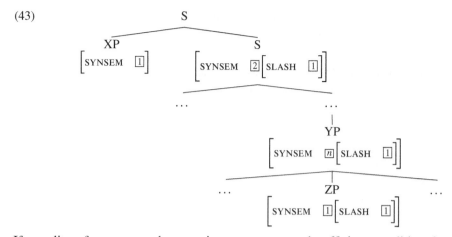

If equality of SYNSEM and SLASH is a necessary and sufficient condition for introducing a trace – an NP with a null phonology (notated [$_{NP}$ e]), and if the SLASH value reflects the SYNSEM value of the filler, it follows inexorably that in (43), the filler must actually take the form of the only item in the lexicon whose SLASH and SYNSEM values are identical – that is, the gap itself!

(44)

$$\begin{bmatrix} \text{PHON} & \langle\ \rangle \\ \text{SYNSEM} & \boxed{1}\!\left[\text{SLASH}\ \boxed{1}\right] \end{bmatrix}$$

It follows that on this analysis, there can never be an actual filler audibly present in a filler/gap construction.[1] *This* is the problem that (42) poses, and since on the face of it there are only two choices for our feature architecture here – either SLASH is part of SYNSEM or is not part of it – we seem to have arrived at a major impasse in our treatment of displacement phenomena.

But there is a way out, one which incurs very little additional complexity in the machinery of the grammar. Suppose we 'segregate' SLASH from the rest of the SYNSEM value, the truly local part, and say that what must be identified are the *local* parts of the filler's syntactic and semantic information, on the one hand, and the *local* part of the empty category's syntactic and semantic information, on the other. The crucial material – things such as part of speech, number, and person agreement values, and meanings – will equate, on this approach, but the filler's SLASH value and that of the gap category itself can freely differ. We therefore replace the feature geometry we've been assuming up to this point with the following:

---

[1] This is a slight oversimplification of the possibilities; conceivably the filler could branch, and [SLASH ①] would then have to propagate down to the filler's descendents. But at some point, the SLASH feature would have to come to rest (or we'd never have a sentence), and the only way to 'cash out' that SLASH value would be a descendent of the filler constituent which was in effect the same as its ancestor – an impossible situation. Immediately or at some later point, then, the same problems will arise on the analysis we're considering.

(45)

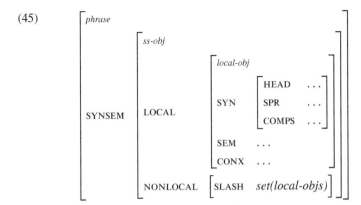

where *ss-obj* and *local-obj* identify the type of objects that values for SYNSEM and *local* must be, respectively, that is, what combinations of features must have their values specified in order for these combinations to be the values of these two features. We explicitly identify the type of the objects which can be values of SLASH as sets of LOCAL values, and now revise our definition of the empty category at the gap site accordingly:

(46)

$$\begin{bmatrix} \text{PHON} & \langle \ \rangle \\ \text{SYNSEM} & \begin{bmatrix} \text{LOCAL} & \boxed{1} \\ \text{NONLOCAL|SLASH} & \{\boxed{1}\} \end{bmatrix} \end{bmatrix}$$

The SLASH principle will force a SLASH value carrying the LOCAL specifications of the filler to appear throughout the structure at whose top the filler appears and at the bottom of which the gap appears.

At this point, then, we have some reason to believe we've identified the way to account for the bottom of the filler/gap dependency (via the feature geometry summarized in (46)) and the middle of the dependency (via some suitably revised version of the Slash Principle). In order to complete the analysis, we must ensure that, at the very top of the dependency, the LOCAL specification of the filler appears in the SLASH set of some constituent *C* dominating the gap site. Since there is in principle no necessity within the current framework for anything corresponding to extraction – an empirically desirable aspect of our approach, since not all languages exhibit long-distance displacement phenomena – it will be necessary to state a kind of rule schema that establishes the legality of both the displacement phrase structure and the necessary feature identities. These identities must, *ipso facto*, be stated at a point in the structure where the relevant features of the filler – the ones that will be represented throughout the pathway between that constituent and the gap site – are 'visible,' so to speak, to the SLASH specification at the very top of this pathway. There is only one place where we find this visibility: in the structure in (47), where both the LOCAL information carried by the filler and the SLASH specifications that capture that information, and link it to the empty category at the gap site, are represented in a single two-generation tree:

(47)

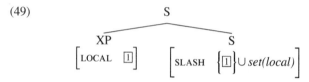

We must therefore formulate a separate Head-filler Rule whose effect is both to license the structure in (47) and to enforce identity between the XP's LOCAL value and the SLASH value of its clausal sister:

(48)   **Head-filler Rule (preliminary version):** A completely saturated phrase of type *verb* whose MARKING specification is *nil* may be specified for a FILLER-DTR with a LOCAL value $\boxed{1}$ which is a member of the head daughter's SLASH set value.

Thus, if we have the structure (47) at all, it must have the form

(49)

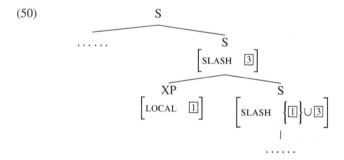

The point of (49) is that, as observed above, (48) could possibly apply not at the root level but at a lower level point in the structure, dominating multiple gaps, some of whose fillers occur higher up in that structure. In that case, the mother's SLASH value will not be an empty set, but will rather contain the LOCAL values of one or more fillers which appear higher in the structure:

(50)

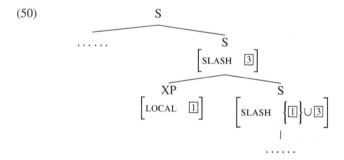

The Head-filler Rule requires only that the LOCAL information for the filler introduced at any given point in the structure is added to whatever *other* information appears on the filler's sister as a result of fillers still higher in the structure. If there are no other such fillers, as in the cases we've seen so far, then the filler in (49) will contribute the *only* SLASH set value that appears on the head daughter, that is, $\boxed{3}=\varnothing$, and we have

(51)

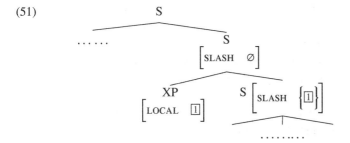

This analysis thus accounts for the top of the filler/gap pathway.

If we put together the conclusions we've come to about the nature of the gap site as per (46) and the propagation of information along the filler/gap pathway via the Slash Principle with those determining the syntax of the top (embodied in the Head-filler Rule), we have an explicit account of every phase of the linkage between the gap and the filler in topicalization, illustrated in the following section with concrete examples.

6.3.3   Connectivity via SLASH: The Complete Picture

We can connect the dots in our account of the long distance dependency represented by topicalization in the following schematic display integrating the three components of that dependency – the top (determined by the HEAD-FILLER RULE), the arbitrarily deep intervening structure (governed by the SLASH Principle), and the gap site (defined by the lexical entry (46)) – in a single-tree format for the simplest case of displacement, that is, the situation in which there is only a single filler and a single gap:

(52)

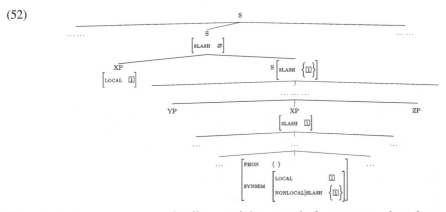

There is, however, one more detail to straighten out before we can show how actual instances of the topicalization phenomenon fall out from the proposals introduced so far. The Slash Principle requires phrases and at least one daughter to share SLASH specifications. But the situation depicted in (52) appears to contain a violation of that requirement: the S node immediately dominating the filler has an empty SLASH value, but its head daughter has a nonempty SLASH value as per the Head-filler Rule. The Slash Principle mandates the sharing of SLASH values between a phrase and its daughters, which therefore appears to rule out the situation just identified in the structure (52); and since this structure is a schematic representation of the distribution of SLASH values in all instances of topicalization, we appear to have arrived at a contradiction within our own analysis.

To eliminate this inconsistency, it will be necessary to modify *something* in the formal machinery we've introduced up to this point. One possibility is to allow the head daughter's SLASH specification to appear on the node labeled by the filler's mother – but this cannot be right, since it entails that in sentences such as *John, I really like*, there is an unfilled gap. To see this, consider the ill-formed example in (53)a, with the structure in (53)b:

(53) a.   *I really like.

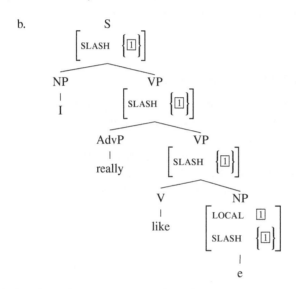

Obviously such structures must be ruled out, but the only practical way to do so is to impose, as a language-specific condition on English, a restriction on root sentences which requires them to bear empty SLASH values. The problem is that if *John, I really like* has a nonempty SLASH at its root node, it too will be ruled out – obviously not what we want. What's needed is some way of exempting the mother in (52)b from the requirements that are otherwise imposed by the Slash Principle. At the same time, any modifications of our analytic framework to this point must ensure that (53) still violates the relevant requirement on root sentence and is hence correctly ruled out. This outcome could conceivably be effected by exempting the S sister of the filler and its root node mother (but no other descendents) from the Slash Principle, so that the SLASH on the latter would not necessarily pass up to the root. The trick here is to carry out this exemption in a general way, rather than simply positing it as an add-on stipulation in the statement of the Slash Principle.

The approach actually taken in HPSG involves a bit more finesse. Along with the actual SLASH value that is shared between the filler's sister and the latter's LOCAL value, we associate another kind of SLASH feature, whose value is a singleton set, and which is part of the specification given for another feature, called TO-BIND. To distinguish the two kinds of SLASH value, we posit the feature organization in (54):

(54)

$$\left[\text{SYNSEM}\left[\begin{array}{ll}\text{LOCAL} & \ldots \\ \text{NONLOCAL}\left[\begin{array}{ll}\text{INHERITED} & \left[\text{SLASH} \quad \ldots\right] \\ \text{TO-BIND} & \left[\text{SLASH} \quad \ldots\right]\end{array}\right]\end{array}\right]\right]$$

All phrase structure schemata whose head daughters are of type *phrase*, except for the Head-filler Rule, will specify that their head daughters have a TO-BIND|SLASH value of ∅, and all lexical items, apart from a particular subset discussed in some detail in the next chapter, will similarly have an empty TO-BIND value. The Head-filler Rule, however, will impose on the phrasal head daughter a nonempty TO-BIND|SLASH, and the Slash Principle will be revised to take advantage of this property. In particular, we restate both of these syntactic conditions as follows:

(55)   **Slash Principle (final version):** the SLASH value of a phrase is the union of the SLASH values of its daughters minus the TO-BIND value of its head daughter.

(56)   **Head-filler Rule**

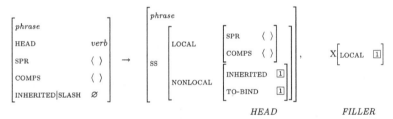

Our linear ordering restrictions will for the most part locate the filler to the left of the clausal head, but there is one situation which will presumably call for a separate statement (whose form we needn't worry about here): when a clause itself is the filler (as in, e.g., *That John will be proven innocent, we can only hope*), it must precede the clause from out of which it has been displaced. The role these revisions place will emerge in the following section, illustrating a complete filler/gap pathway via a concrete example.

6.3.4   Connectivity: A Case Study

The effect of the system developed in the preceding discussion can be clearly exhibited in the licensing of the sentence in (57):

(57)

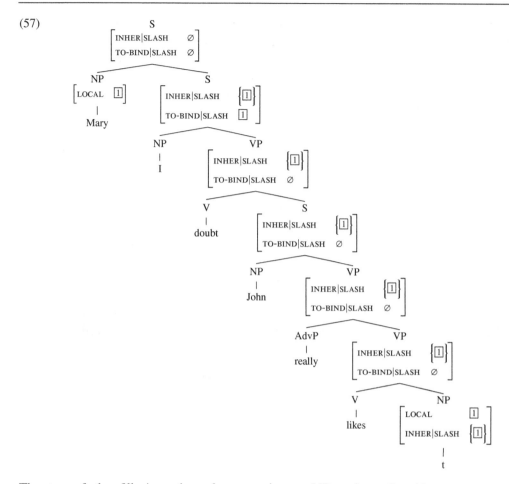

The top of the filler/gap dependency posits an NP and an S with an INHERITED|SLASH specification whose set value matches the LOCAL feature value of its NP sister. At least one daughter of S must display the same SLASH specification; the tree just given represents one of the possibilities, but in principle there's no reason why this SLASH value could not instead – or in addition, as will be discussed in detail in the following chapter – be an attribute of the NP daughter, in which case we would ultimately wind up with a sentence displaying either a gap in subject position or a subject properly containing a gap. A gap in highest subject position would not be recognizable under ordinary circumstances, of course, since the filler would appear immediately to the left of the subject gap, with no way to distinguish this 'string-vacuous' displacement configuration from an ordinary in-situ subject. But in embedded position we would recognize the gap following the embedding verb, for example, *John I very much doubt __wants anything to do with Mary*, where the SLASH value has been realized as identical to the LOCAL value of the NP subject. In the case of (57), a different possible satisfaction of the Slash Principle is exhibited; here SLASH is shared between S and its phrasal head, the root VP. This constituent in turn shares SLASH with its clausal daughter, the complement of the head *doubt*, and with the VP head of that clause, its own VP daughter, and, finally the NP complement of this VP's head daughter.

At every stage of this chain of identities, the value that SLASH bears constitutes the morphosyntactic profile of the filler. But at the very bottom, this SLASH specification is in effect equated, via its identity with the LOCAL specification of the NP, with the morphosyntactic inventory of the gap site. Thus, the gap and the filler are, in all but their phonology and their specification for SLASH itself, the identical category. It follows that whatever conditions apply at the gap site will only be satisfied if the distant filler's properties are in compliance with those conditions. The impact of this linkage is clear enough in the case of a nonsentence such as

(58)   *Mary I very much doubt __are in favor of John.

Mary is a singular NP, and the English agreement pattern, which we briefly touched on in Chapter 4, does require third person singular NPs to match up with a specific form of each verb. The gap will mirror the morphosyntactic properties of the name *Mary*, along the lines just illustrated – but those will be the wrong properties in terms of the conditions at the gap site, where an in situ NP would have to be specified with a plural number value in the AGR feature. We can change *Mary* to *Mary and Terrence*, or we can change *are* to *is*, but the structure in (58) represents an unacceptable conflict between the properties of the filler and the properties the trace at the gap site must embody. Thus the SLASH mechanism, in completely local fashion, propagates a connectivity relationship over arbitrary syntactic depths and distances.

6.4   Cross-linguistic Evidence for the Locality of Extraction

Although it may not be apparent, the locality of this connectivity linkage makes an important prediction. We note to begin with that it is inherent in the very architecture of the HPSG framework developed in this book that all nonlocal dependencies must ultimately turn out to arise from an assembled set of local dependencies. For instance, structure sharing of SPR values allows subject selectional transparency to extend only as far within a structure as it's possible to supply lexical items, such as auxiliaries and raising verbs, bearing the right SPR identities. Structure sharing of SLASH values makes this kind of dependency possible in a way completely independent of the lexical properties of particular vocabulary items – but this unlimited reach for morphosyntactic dependencies can still only be implemented in HPSG by iterated local identities. Unlike transformational rules, the licensing schemata and constraints in HPSG cannot refer to anything except mothers and daughters in phrasal representations; the theory is, in a very real sense, a system of restrictions on statements about what mother/daughter configurations can look like, and the strong hypothesis of the framework is that all natural language dependencies can be shown to follow, in a general and concise fashion, from statements of this kind. This position is not just a theoretical axiom; it also entails a very specific consequence – that every mother/daughter structure on the filler/gap pathway necessarily contains a record, in the form of a SLASH specification, of the connection between the distant filler and the distant gap site. Hence, it follows as a direct consequence of HPSG's foundational assumptions that there could in principle be phenomena whose occurrence hinges on the presence of a nonempty SLASH specification, and which therefore can only occur on the filler/gap pathway.

In contrast, various forms of transformational grammar *impose* a certain locality, by stipulated conditions on how far an extracted constituent can legally displace on each move. But these conditions are simply add-ons, falling out of nothing inherent in the theory architecture. They were originally stipulated in order to motivate syntactically certain apparent restrictions on filler/gap linkages which now appear very strongly to be due to nonsyntactic factors (as discussed in detail in the following chapter), and it would therefore be quite defensible to argue that transformational frameworks now no longer have *independent* motivation for these locality stipulations on movement operations. That cannot be true in HPSG; as a theory of possible two-generation tree structures, the locality it posits is in a sense part of the *definition* of the framework. It is therefore particularly noteworthy that filler/gap-pathway-dependent phenomena of the sort noted above as logical possibilities inherent in the organization of HPSG turn out to exist. We offer a brief survey from a sample of these languages to show the diversity of the grammatical phenomena whose privileges of occurrence are confined to syntactic domains characterized by nonempty SLASH specifications.

6.4.1   French

Inversion in French is a much more general phenomenon than it is in English. Interrogatives allow finite nonauxiliaries to invert freely; so we have *Jean, veut-il boire de vin ou de bière?* 'Does Jean want to drink wine or beer?' with the third person singular form of *vouloir* 'want' to precede the subject *Jean*. But this 'plain vanilla' invertibility is still specific to interrogation, and it is still restricted to pronouns outside extremely formal or reported speech. Thus, in contrast to the preceding example, **Veut Jean boire de vin or de bière* is unacceptable as an alternative posing of the same question. But there is an interesting class of exceptions, shown in the contrast between (59) and (60)(the data in this section is taken from Kayne and Pollock 1978):

(59) a.   Le fait que cette fille t'a communiqué ne nous intéresse pas.

b.   Le fait que t'a communiqué cette fille ne nous intéresse pas.

'The fact that this girl told you about does not interest us.'

(60) a.   Le fait que cette fille t'a parlé ne nous intèresse pas.

     b.   *Le fait que t'a parlé cette fille ne nous intèresse pas.

            'The fact that this girl spoke to you does not interest us.'

In the a examples, we see the canonical word order in French, a fairly orthodox SVO language. In (59)b, an alternative, completely normal and stylistically high-register order is presented, in which *cette fille* appears to have been postposed with respect to the VP *t'a communiqué* 'told you about.' This is an unusual word order for a Romance language, and it does not appear to be possible in the seemingly quite parallel example in (60). The difference in the two sentences corresponds quite closely to the difference in the English translations, and hinges on the fact that there is a gap following the transitive verb *communiqué* 'communicated [something]' as vs the intransitive *parlé* 'spoke.' In (59) is an instance of a filler/gap construction, where *le fait* is interpreted into the gap site via the relative pronoun *que*, which is the syntactic filler. In the case of (60), there is no gap, and *que* is rather a French analogue of *that*, a finite clause marker. The real difference between the two structures can be represented as follows:

(61)

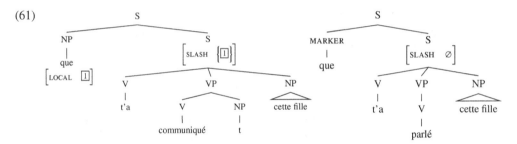

It is the presence of non-empty SLASH in the mother's specification which licenses the appearance of the post-VP subject.

This generalization entails two consequences: on the one hand, *any* clause that intervenes between the appearance of a filler and a gap site should license this unusual inversion pattern, and on the other, we should find that where displacement is absent, the inversion pattern cannot occur, even when the interpretations in such cases are parallel to those in which displacement occurs. There is a problem with obtaining data bearing on the first point, however: extraction from a finite clause precludes inversion in any higher clause; although such examples have been reported in the literature, their status is too problematic to serve as a confirmation of the first of these predictions (in contrast to Irish, where the same prediction is verified by robust data). The second prediction is, however, supported by all available evidence. The contrast between (62)–(64) and (65)–(66) is completely representative:

(62)   **Quand** [ₛ partira ton ami **t**]?

         'When will your friend leave?'

(63)   **Avec qui** [$_s$ jouaient tes enfants **t**]?
         With whom were your children playing?

(64)   Oú [$_s$ espèraient dîner tes amis **t**]?
         'Where did your friends hope to dine?'

(65) a. Ton ami partira quand? 'Your friend will go when?'
     b. Ton ami partira où? 'Your friend will go where?'

(66) a. *Partira ton ami quand?
     b. *Partira quand ton ami?
     c. *Partira ton ami où?
     d. *Partira où ton ami?

These examples do not merely establish the dependence of the NP-inversion pattern on the presence of a nonempty SLASH specification in the clause; they also make it clear that the appearance in a fronted position of a *wh*-like element such as *quand* 'when', *ou* 'where,' and similar forms – whose relationship to the head V is that of adjunct rather than valent – are nonetheless to be interpreted as instances of extraction, in spite of the fact that by their very nature, adjuncts, being optional in the first place, do not leave 'visible' gaps. This characteristic of their distribution has led to suggestions in the past that adjuncts by their very nature as unselected constituents are ineligible to participate in filler/gap linkages in a manner parallel to syntactic arguments. The data in (62)–(66) show, however, that such proposals are untenable, because the appearance of French adjuncts in fronted position in these data is associated with exactly the same inversion possibilities as is the displacement of material linked to overt gap sites.

It is important to understand exactly how the French evidence presented above, as well as the cross-linguistic data given below, provide evidence for the locality of displacement. Suppose we tried to capture the conditions licensing extraction-triggered inversion according to the global condition on the form of trees, stated in (67), making no reference to SLASH:

(67)   Full NP inversion is possible only in clauses whose S node dominates a gap site.

Assuming (67), we could have a filler in one position, a gap site somewhere lower down, and then inspect the full tree structure to see if (67) were satisfied. Local propagation of a SLASH feature would not be necessary. This formulation is empirically incorrect, however, since a clause might dominate not only a gap site but its filler, as in (68):

(68)   Les femmes se demandent à qui Jean a donné à ce livre.
         Les femmes se demandent **à qui** [$_s$ Jean a donné **t** à ce livre]
         'The women wonder to whom Jean gave that book.'

The structure of the sentence *Je me demand à qui Jean a donné à ce livre* is exhibited in the second line: it is clear that in this structure, we would be allowed to invert *les femmes* and *se demandent*. But in French, a subject/verb sequence higher in the structure than the filler of a gap does not license inversion: *Les femmes se demandent à qui pour parler* 'The women wonder who to speak to' does not have an inverted version in which *les femmes* follows *parler*. To get the facts right, we would have to frame the condition as follows:

(69)   Full NP inversion is possible only in clauses whose S node dominates a gap site but not the filler associated with that gap site.

This formulation works, but notice that it is substantially more complicated than (67), and no simpler than a hypothetical rule, corresponding to no actually observed phenomenon in any language, along the lines of (70):

(70)   Full NP inversion is possible only in clauses whose S node is a sister to a gap site.

or indeed, than the similarly unobserved pattern captured by (71):

(71)   Full NP inversion is possible only in clauses whose S node is a sister to a clause dominating a gap site.

The point is that the notion, 'occur on a filler/gap pathway not including the filler,' has no special status as a simple condition on whole trees; it involves just one of a very large number of possible structures involving configurations within which a gap might occur, without any kind of default status, naturalness, or simplicity in terms of the formal description of trees. Being on a filler/gap pathway reflects no more of a unique grammatical property than being a sister to a node which dominates a filler/gap pathway, or any of various other configurational possibilities one might imagine. In effect, such a 'global' approach to the kind of phenomenon that French displays makes the special status of clauses between the filler and the gap a kind of arbitrary accident. To put it slightly differently, we have, on the global, whole-tree approach, no *particular* reason to anticipate that any language would use a morphological, syntactic or prosodic marking mechanism to set off this one particular kind of nonlocal relationship across a very diverse range of languages. None of the hypothetical proposals in (69)–(71) corresponds to any kind of independently justified mechanism of the grammar which leaves its own 'footprints' over the class of sentences which, under each of these counterfactual conditions, would be marked by the NP inversion option. The condition in (69) would simply be one of a number of possibilities, with no obvious explanation for the fact that none of those other possibilities have ever been observed.

On the other hand, if the syntactic distance between the filler and the gap site is mediated by a feature-sharing relationship which, as it were, leaves a clear set of footprints between the gap site and the filler that traverses all and only the intervening clauses, then we have a simple, natural basis for this specific kind of NP inversion: inversion possibilities are defined by a nonempty SLASH value, and hence confined to just those clauses on a filler/gap pathway. Thus, the local interpretation of the French NP inversion facts makes sense of the distribution of clauses permitting such inversion – by correlating this distribution in one-to-one fashion with a distinct grammatical property that is only available *if* one assumes a mechanism for filler/gap connectivity operating locally, one two-generation tree at a time, in effect. It is therefore a significant advantage of the framework developed in this book that the very definition of the framework as a system defining possible two-generation trees allows, by its very nature, such connectivity *only* via such local mediation (as opposed to having this locality imposed from outside, as in frameworks operating with structure-changing rules which are inherently defined over arbitrarily large syntactic objects).

An interesting empirical consequence of the conditions on NP inversion in French is that the appearance of this inversion enables speakers to (at least partially) eliminate ambiguities potentially arising from the lack of evidence about which syntactic domain a fronted modifier is supposed to apply to. Such ambiguity doesn't arise in all cases; in (72), for example, it's entirely clear that *avec qui* 'with whom?' is being asked in connection with Marie's dining, rather than someone else's thinking:

(72)   Avec qui croit-elle qu'a soupé Marie?

       'With whom does she think that Marie has dined?'

But this unambiguousness is an accidental outcome of the kind of activity which thinking consists of. In other situations, there is more than one way to connect an adjunct to the rest of the S in a way which makes sense of the modification. So in English, a sentence such as *When did Mary say that Paul had died?* permits two readings: one in which *when* is understood as a query about the time of death, and another in which the temporal adverb is understood as eliciting information about the time of Mary's utterance. By and large, context will make it clear which of these is intended, but a certain amount of guesswork is still involved. In French, this source of ambiguity is considerably reduced. In general, if an *où* 'where?' or *quand* 'when?' modifier corresponds to a gap site in a structure $[_{S_1}$ NP V $\ldots [_{S_2}$ NP V $\ldots]]$ in S_1 but not S_2, we expect to find that NP inversion is not possible in S_2, whereas if the gap site is located within S_2, then NP inversion will be possible. In the case of adjuncts, this means that if the adjunct modifies the meaning of the higher clause, the lower clause will not allow inversion, so that the existence of inverted structure in S_2 makes it immediately clear that the adjunct meaning applies to the meaning conveyed in the lower clause (since that is where the filler must be linked to in order for S_2 to qualify for exercise of the inversion option). And this is indeed the case: (73) is still ambiguous, because NP inversion is optional and we don't know if it can or cannot apply to S_2.

(73)   Où/Quand Marie a-t-elle déclaré que Paul était mort?

       'Where/when did Marie declare that Paul had died?'

But (74) is completely explicit: the gap must be in S_2, because otherwise we would not have the inversion option. Hence the question must be about the time or place of death, rather than the time or place of Marie's statement.

(74)   Où/Quand Marie a-t-elle déclaré qu'était mort Paul?
         'Where/when did Marie declare that Paul had died?'

The occurrence of NP inversion in a clause in which a gap may or may not be present is thus a decisive indication that a filler is indeed linked by SLASH connectivity to that clause.

6.4.2   Irish

We find in Irish a pattern of connectivity marking which has a radically different appearance from French, but which is strikingly parallel in making overt the linkage between local trees which mediate the syntactic domain of a filler/gap connection. In the following examples, the *g-* and *a-* forms are characterized as complementizers in the theoretical literature on Irish, and are in strict complementary distribution: the *g-* complementizers mark clauses which do not contain a gap, and the *a-* forms mark clauses which do. Unlike the situation in French, moreover, there is no independent bar to the appearance of *a-* series complementizers in intermediate position on the linked pathways between the filler and the gap. (The data in this section is taken from McCloskey (1979).) In (75), we have the normal case of a clausal complement in which all syntactic constituents appear 'in situ':

(75)   Shíl   mé **goN**   mbeadh sé ann.
         thought I   COMP would-be he there
         'I thought that he would be there.'

In (76), we see multiple instances of *g-* complementizers, as is appropriate to a series of clauses in which all valence requirements are locally satisfied by overt constituents. In (77), however, while the lower clause contains no gap sites and is appropriately marked with a *g-* complementizer, the upper clause, which is missing its subject (as indicated by the gap marker __), is identified via an *a-* form.

(76)   Dúirt mé **gurL**   shíl   me **goN** mbeadh sé ann.
         said I   **goN**+PAST thought I   **goN** would-be he there
         'I said that I thought that he would be there.'

(77)   an fear   **aL**   shíl   __ **goN**   mbeadh sé ann
         [the man]$_j$ COMP thought e$_j$ COMP would-be he there
         'the man that thought he would be there'

Since Irish is a VSO language, the lack of an NP following *shíl* in (77) is a clear sign that some distant element must be interpreted 'into' the position where the subject normally appears – in this case, *an fear* 'the man'. On the other hand,

the Irish clause corresponding to the complement of *shíl* is complete in terms
of overt elements, hence has the same general structure as (75), and requires
a *g*-class complementizer. The structure of (77) is depicted in (78), where the
subscripted $\boxed{1}$ denotes (some component of) the CONT value of the nominal
head:

(78)

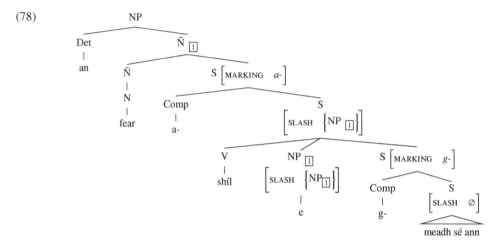

The implementation of the distributional pattern displayed by the Irish complementizers is quite straightforward; as members of the category type *marker*,
complementizers bear a feature SPEC which determines the kinds of heads they
can co-occur with. Note that this requirement is completely independent of the
Irish data; recall that in English, we rely on SPEC values to correlate *that* with
finite clauses and *for* with infinitive clauses, as per our discussion in Chapter 2,
where the following lexical descriptions are given:

(79)   a. $\begin{bmatrix} \text{PHON} & \text{that} \\ \text{SS} & \begin{bmatrix} \text{MARKING} & \textit{that} \\ \text{SPEC} & \begin{bmatrix} \text{VFORM} & \textit{fin} \\ \text{SPR} & \langle \ \rangle \\ \text{COMPS} & \langle \ \rangle \end{bmatrix} \end{bmatrix} \end{bmatrix}$ b. $\begin{bmatrix} \text{PHON} & \text{for} \\ \text{SS} & \begin{bmatrix} \text{MARKING} & \textit{for} \\ \text{SPEC} & \begin{bmatrix} \text{VFORM} & \textit{inf} \\ \text{SPR} & \langle \ \rangle \\ \text{COMPS} & \langle \ \rangle \end{bmatrix} \end{bmatrix} \end{bmatrix}$

Using these entries as a model, we can capture the Irish facts quite simply along
the lines in (80):

(80)   a. $\begin{bmatrix} \text{PHON} & \text{a-} \\ \text{SS} & \begin{bmatrix} \text{MARKING} & \textit{a-} \\ \text{SPEC} & \begin{bmatrix} \text{LOC} \begin{bmatrix} \text{VFORM} & \textit{verb} \\ \text{SPR} & \langle \ \rangle \\ \text{COMPS} & \langle \ \rangle \end{bmatrix} \\ \text{NONLOC|INHER|SLASH} & \{ \ldots \} \end{bmatrix} \end{bmatrix} \end{bmatrix}$

b.
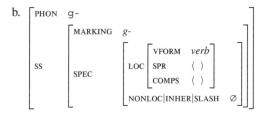

No greater complexity is required to specify the distribution of the Irish complementizers in terms of the gaps which (don't) occur within the clauses they mark than what is needed to account for the distribution of *that* and *for* in English. No formally arbitrary concept such as 'lies on a filler/gap pathway' is required. Instead, the simple lexical descriptions in (80), imposing a specific form of the complementizer depending on the content of a clause's SLASH specification, guarantee that *a*- complementizers will appear always and only on clauses which dominate gaps, just in case these clauses occur *below* the point where a filler is specified which satisfies the gap. In the case of (78), it is evident that the rule which introduces a relative clause adjunct to the nominal head will impose a TO-BIND|SLASH specification corresponding to the INHER|SLASH specification, on the clause which is the sister to the nominal modified by the relative clause. Hence, assuming that the only gap in a sentence containing the NP in (78) is the one within the relative clause, all S node dominating this NP will have *g*- complementizers, not *a*- complementizers.

It follows immediately from the specifications in (80) that every clause in an extraction dependency dominating the gap site, but occurring below the point where the extracted filler is introduced in the structure, will be marked with an *a*- complementizer, since each such clause will display a nonempty SLASH specification. We see exactly this predicted pattern in (81)–(82):

(81)   an   fear **aL**   shíl mé   **aL**   bheadh __   ann
        [the man]$_j$ COMP thought I   COMP would-be e$_j$ there
        'the man that I thought would be there'

(82)   an fear   **aL**   dúirt mé **aL**   shíl   mé **aL**   bheadh   __ ann
        [the man]$_j$ COMP said   I   COMP thought I   COMP would-be e$_j$ there
        'The man that I said I thought would be there'

Moreover, regardless of the depth of the extraction, as soon as we identify the gap site, where the SLASH feature is 'cashed out' as a prosodically silent constituent, we know that all lower clauses which themselves are not associated with an extraction will be marked by *g*- class complementizers, a point illustrated in (77) and at still greater structural depth in (83):

(83)   an fear   **aL**   dúirt sé **aL** shíl __   **goN** mbeadh sé   ann
        [the man]$_j$ COMP said he COMP thought e$_j$ COMP   would-be he   there
        'the man that he said thought he would be there'

And apart from its inherent interest as a convincing demonstration of the local nature of information sharing in extraction dependencies, the grammatical

marking of extraction pathways in Irish provides further corroboration of the
convergence between valent and adjunct extraction. In Irish, just as in French,
we find the morphosyntactic diagnostic for filler/gap linkages only in contexts
where there is a genuine displacement, a fact which establishes conclusively
that the displacement of adjuncts is mediated by the same mechanism as the
displacement of material selected by a head:

(84)   I mBetlehem **aL**   dúirt na targaireachtaí **aL**   béarfaí
        [in Bethlehem]$_j$ COMP said the prophecies   COMP would-be-born

        an Slánaitheoir __.
        the Saviour   e$_j$
        'It was in Bethlehem that the prophecies said the Saviour would be born.'

(85)   an lá   **aL**   bhí muid i nDoire __
        [the day]$_j$ COMP were we   in Derry e$_j$
        'the day we were in Derry'

(86)   Cén uair   **aL**   tháinig siad ńa bhaile __
        [which time]$_j$ COMP came   they home   e$_j$
        'What time did they come home?'

Neither the copula in Irish nor *tháinig* selects a constituent corresponding to a
temporal description, nor does *béarfaí* select a constituent indicating location.
But in all these cases we find a fronting of these modificatory phrases associated
with one or more *a-* series complementizers. The structural probe that extraction
pathway marking adds to our analytic toolkit thus attests in the most direct
fashion that extraction is formally independent of valence.

6.4.3   Icelandic

In Icelandic, as in a number of Germanic languages, basic clause
structure in finite clauses is characterized by so-called V2 structure. Unlike
English, whose long close contact with French is nearly a millenium old, most
Germanic languages are characterized by basic word order possibilities in which
the subject can, but need not, precede the verb; the one requirement in such
sentences is that the verb appears second. For example, we have a typical German
sentence:

(87)   Die Zwillinge spielen die Violine an der Schule
        det twins   play   det violin at det school
        'The twins play the violin at school.'

But we also find the word orders in (88):

(88)   { Die Violine spielen die Zwillinge an der Schule } 'The twins play the
        { An der Schule spielden die Zwillinge die violin }
        violin at school.'

The one constant in these various permutations is the appearance of the verb *spielen* in second position. There is a somewhat different sense associated with each of these possibilities with respect to the others: whichever constituent precedes the verb is interpreted as, in some sense, what the sentence is contributing information about. But in terms of truth conditions, all of the interpretations are the same. This array of facts is reminiscent of the topicalization construction we've been examining in detail in this chapter, with one extremely important caveat: English structure is relentlessly SVO, so that when a constituent is fronted, the subject remains in position preceding the verb. In German, the subject has no special claim on pre-V position, and will readily appear following the verb, if some other constituent (which is then interpreted as the topic of the sentence) precedes the verb.

Icelandic is a typical Germanic language in displaying this same V2 phenomenon. This V2 grammatical pattern interacts with the distribution of a dummy pronoun *það*, 'there/it,' which appears, along with V2 clause structure, as the subject of (i) passive forms of intransitive verbs, as in (89) and (ii) an active form of the verb, with postverbal subject structure, exemplified in (90) (all Icelandic data taken from Zaenen 1983 except where noted):

(89)   það var dansað í gær.
         there was danced yesterday
         'People danced yesterday.'

(90)   það drekka margir vín   á Íslandi
         there drink   many wine in Iceland
         'Many people drink wine in Iceland.'

There are specific restrictions on the appearance of *það*. It may not precede the tensed component of the verbal complex if other material precedes the latter as well; conversely, if all the major constituents of the sentence follow the verb, then *það* MUST precede the verb – except under one condition: when a clause falls on a filler/gap pathway, then *það* may not appear under any circumstances. Either some other component of the clause must precede the verb, or if the subject is indefinite or the verb is an 'impersonal passive' form (which would otherwise require *það*), then, and only then, can the verb appear as the first element of the clause.

To get a sense of how these restrictions interact, consider the examples in (91) and (92):

(91) a.   Hann spurþi, hvaþ drekki margt fólk   á Íslandi.
           he   asked what drink many people in Iceland
           'He asked what many people drink in Iceland.'

     b.   *Hann spurði, hvað það drekki margt margt fólk á Íslandi.

(92) a.   Vodka veit   ég að   er talið að   drekki margt fólk   á Íslandi.
           Vodka know I   that is said that drink   many people in Iceland
           'I know it is said that many people in Iceland drink vodka.'

   b.   *Vodka veit ég að það   er talið að drekki margt fólk á Íslandi.

   c.   *Vodka veit ég að það er talið að það drekki margt fólk á Íslandi.

In (91)a, the clause over which the extraction dependency holds has an indefinite subject (*margt fólk* 'many people'); hence, as noted *það* must not appear (hence the ill-formedness of (91)b; the clause reveals verb-first (V1) form, and so is good. In (92), the verb which heads the clause which is the site of the extraction is an impersonal passive (*er talið* 'is said'), and therefore in (92)a, we again find V1 form with no appearance by *það*. The examples in (92)b and c, on the other hand, are ill-formed, because in these forms the expletive pronoun appears, contrary to the requirement that it be omitted in a configuration on a filler/gap pathway.

Consider now the problem in (93):

(93)   *Í Rússlandi sagði hann að   drekka margt vodka á   Íslandi.
           In Russia   said he   that drink   many vodka in Iceland
           'In Russia he said that many people drink vodka in Iceland.'

Here we've omitted the expletive – illegally, because there's no extraction pathway involved. *Í Rússlandi* is understood to be a description of the context for the root clause ('he said. . .'); it cannot be interpreted as applying to the lower clause, hence is not interpretable as part of an extraction dependency. To ensure well-formedness in this kind of structure, the expletive must appear, as in (94):

(94)   Í   Rússlandi sagði hann að   það   drekka margt vodka á Íslandi.
           In Russia   said he   that there drink   many vodka in Iceland
           'In Russia he said that many people drink vodka in Iceland.'

Moreover, just as in French and Irish, the pattern works the same for adjuncts as for complements.

(95) a.   Hann spurði, hvar   væri dansað
           he   asked where was danced.
           'He asked where people danced.'

   b.   *Hann spurði, hvar *það* væri dansað

(96) a.   Hann spurði, hvenær væri dansað
           he   asked when   was danced
           'He asked when people danced.'

   b.   *Hann spurði, hvenær það væri dansað

In both examples, *það* is forbidden; instead, the V1 pattern is forced. Finally, we see the effect of adjunct extraction over two clauses (data from H. Thainsson, p.c.):

(97)   Á Íslandi sagði hann að drykkaju   margir vodka __ .
          In Iceland said he   that drink(past subj.) many vodka
          'In Iceland he said that many people drink vodka.'

(98)   ?Á Íslandi sagði hann að það drykkaju   margir vodka (*__).
          In Iceland said he   that there drink(past subj.) many vodka
          'In Iceland he said that many people drink vodka.'

In (97), the example is well-formed under the interpretation in which the comment reported refers to Icelanders' drinking preferences. In (98), the example is reasonable (although stylistically somewhat infelicitous) as long as *á Íslandi* is understood to refer to the speaker's location. But the sentence cannot be interpreted as a report on what Icelanders habitually drink, since *á Íslandi* would then have to scope within the embedded clause and hence link to a gap there, which rules out the appearance of *það* in subject location in that clause.

Here again, we see a morphosyntactic effect which is exclusively associated with clauses on filler/gap pathways, and which holds over extraction domain beyond a single S node. The Icelandic case is more complex to state than the parallel effects in French and Irish, and utilizes quite different morphosyntactic resources, but the effect is the same: a clear flagging of extraction pathways over multiple levels of clausal structure, arguing again for the local registration of extraction dependencies – an automatic consequence, as we've seen, of the connectivity mechanism based on SLASH that HPSG uses to account for these dependencies.

6.4.4   Yiddish

The Germanic language Yiddish contains several different inversion constructions; here we're concerned with the particular variety which is triggered by extraction. In Yiddish displacement constructions, inversion is in complementary distribution with complementizers; thus, in (99), the first two examples are good, because we either have inversion in the subordinate clause or a complementizer, but not both, whereas the c. example is bad because it *does* have both. If the complementizer is omitted, then inversion must occur at all nodes along the filler/gap pathway. If the complementizer is included, then inversion is proscribed – all the way along the extraction pathway, except in the root clause. This pattern is restricted to filler/gap linkages, again, including adjunct extraction (data from Diesing 1990).

(99) a.   Vos hot er nit gevolt **az** mir zoln   leyenen?
          what has he not wanted that we should read
          'What did he not want us to read?'

     b.   Vos hot er nit gevolt zoln   mir leyenen?
          what has he not wanted should we read
          'What did he not want us to read?

c. *Vos hot er nit gevolt **az** zoln mir   leyenen
what has he not wanted that we   should read

d. ?Vos hot er nit gevolt **az** es zoln   mir leyenen
what has he not wanted that es should we read
'What did he not wanted us to read?'

e. *Vos hot er nit gevolt mir zoln   leyenen
what has he not wanted we should read

The starred examples are bad because they either contain both extraction registration phenomena (as in (c)) or neither (as in (e)). Again, we see exactly the same effect with adjuncts as with complements:

(100) a. Ven   hastu   gezogt **az** Max hot geleyent dos bukh t?
when have-you said   that Max has read   the book
'When did you say that Max read the book?'

b. Ven   hastu   gezogt hot Max geleyent dos bukh t?
when have-you said   has Max read   the book
'When did you say that Max read the book?'

(101) a. *Ven hastu gezogt Max hot geleyent dos bukh t
when have-you said Max has read the book

b. * Ven hastu gezogt **az** hot Max geleyent dos bukh t
when have-you said that has Max read the book

6.4.5   Welsh

Finally, we consider an example of this connectivity-marking phenomenon from Welsh which has only come to light in the past few years (in contrast to the other examples given, which have been known since the late 1970s; see Borsley 2010). The verb 'be' has two extra tenses which ordinary verbs don't have, generally called present and imperfect. (Ordinary verbs do not have a present tense, just something known as a present-future.) The present tense and for some speakers the imperfect tense as well cannot appear in affirmative complements, though their occurrence in negative complements is acceptable (data from Robert Borsley, p.c.).

(102)   *Mae   John yn   meddwl [mae   Mair yn   licio rhywun]
be.PRES.3sg John PROG think   PRES.3sg Mair PROG like someone
Intended: 'John thinks Mair likes someone.'

Instead of the present tense, what looks like the infinitive appears:

(103)   Mae   John yn   meddwl [bod Mair yn   licio rhywun]
be.PRES.3sg John PROG think   be   Mair PROG like someone
'John thinks Mair likes someone.'

But, crucially, the ordinary present tense is fine in an affirmative complement if the latter is part of an unbounded dependency pathway.

(104)   Beth mae   John yn   meddwl [mae   Mair yn   licio __]
          what be.PRES.3sg John PROG think   PRES.3sg Mair PROG like   __
          'What does John think Mair likes?'

Information about this phenomenon is still scarce, but it appears to be the case that this dispensation is available for the normal present tense within clauses at all points within an extraction dependency.

6.5   What Comes Next?

The discovery of the grammatical phenomenon described above must count as one of the most striking empirical confirmations of a theoretical architecture in the history of the field. As stressed above, only a framework in which all grammatical dependencies are, by necessity, mediated by restrictions on information sharing stated over locally defined objects (such as phrasal signs and their daughters) can be said to *entail* the possibility of extraction pathway marking, in the sense that in order to establish an extraction dependency, an object must be licensed which corresponds exactly to the domain which displays the grammatical 'footprints' of the dependency – a set of structures each point of which displays the information that a gap will have to be licensed in the larger structure to which each of the local objects belongs, somewhere structurally below each of those objects.

It is of course true that operations whose domain of application is arbitrarily large can still have local conditions imposed on them to restrict those domains in a way that makes available data structures adequate to state principles for extraction pathway marking. Since the early 1970s, transformations have been heavily constrained so that they can only operate what is (very roughly) statable as a clause-by-clause basis. There is no inherent limit on the size of the syntactic structures which may be mapped to other structures by a transformational operation, so that this locality is a very different kind of restriction from the *inherent* locality of restrictions in HPSG – but one might claim that the empirical landscape which motivated the 'localization' of transformational operations wound up configuring the latter in exactly the right way to account for the extraction pathways marking facts we examined in the foregoing. From this point of view, transformations as local structure-changing operations were motivated by one set of data and vindicated by a logically quite different set of data. We've seen the latter, but what were the phenomena which induced the reduction of transformations to clausal domains in the first place?

The next chapter is devoted to an overview of these phenomena, which have come to be known as 'island effects.' Syntactic islandhood refers to structural contexts from out of which extraction is difficult or impossible, that is, fillers cannot be linked to gaps within those contexts. The formulation of constraints on transformations which had the effect of reducing their scope of operation to a one-clause-at-a-time basis was motivated by the need to give an account of these island effects, and restrictions on the 'reach' of transformational rules turned out to support the local marking of extraction pathways discussed above.

But further investigations have suggested very strongly that syntactic islands are not syntactic in nature at all, but rather represent a convergence of *functional* effects – restrictions on working memory, requirements imposed by the need for discourse to be coherent, and so on. It follows that syntactic transformations do not actually appear to require the kind of local formulation of movement possibilities that were believed necessary in the syntax itself, and therefore, as we will see in the following chapter, there are no compelling grounds for supposing that empirical requirements, if not framework design conditions themselves, yield the locality of displacement that extraction path marking seems to demand. We now turn to a detailed discussion of these issues in the final chapter of this textbook.

7   Epilogue: Unbounded Dependencies and the Limits of Syntax

The topicalization construction discussed in some detail in the previous chapter is only one of a wide variety of unbounded dependency phenomena in which a filler must be linked to a gap site. One can cluster these phenomena into two major groups, on grounds we discuss below, with a third group falling somewhere between the two, showing certain properties of both. For several decades all of these constructions linking fillers to gap site have been regarded as embodiments of a single connectivity mechanism – a view allowing a considerable simplification in syntacticians' picture of the licensing conditions on natural language grammars. But what is the basis for this assumption?

The very earliest form taken by the argument for a unitary filler/gap mechanism shared by all unbounded dependencies was based on a particular set of constraints, or restrictions, to which all constructions embodying that mechanism were sensitive. In a very influential paper, Chomsky (1977) argued along these lines for an approach in which a single movement operation underlay all types of extraction phenomena. In the previous chapter, we've seen some instances of these constructions and noted that in certain languages they all display the same grammatical behavior in marking the intermediate substructures between fillers and gap sites in some special manner. We now look more systematically at the form of these various constructions, prior to a survey of the supposed syntactic constraints that they were thought to obey. The theoretical development of this set of constraints, and the attempt to derive them as effects from ever more abstract and general principles, is arguably the driving force behind most of the developments in syntactic theory from the mid-1970s on. We conclude with a review of the empirical status of the constraints themselves, and consequences of more recent research in this domain for syntax as a field of inquiry and as a component of the grammars of human languages.

7.1   Extraction Constructions in English

7.1.1   Fillers in Topic Position

The constructions we consider in this section are similar to topicalization in a crucial respect: they display a constituent at the left edge of the clause which is linked to an arbitrarily distant gap site. In this respect they replicate the structure we derived for filler/gap linkages in the preceding chapter. There are a variety of such constructions, involving both finite clauses and nonfinite VPs.

7.1.1.1 *Wh*-Questions and Relative Clauses

The examples in (1) display typical *wh*-questions, while relative clauses appear in (2):

(1) a.   **What/Which plates** did John put on the table?

b.   I wonder **what/which plates** John put t on the table.

(2) a.   This is the book **which** John wrote t.

b.   I visited the cathedral **which** John had described t to us.

In the examples in (1), a *wh*-word, or phrase containing a *wh*-word, appears in the filler position. Leaving aside the cases of inverted word order, a topic constituent could replace the filler in the embedded clause in (1)a (*Those plates, John (definitely) put on the table*). In the case of (1)b, the clause with a *wh*-filler is embedded within a sentence headed by a verb belonging to a particular class, which requires a *wh*-filler to appear in the clause it selects. Such questions, while they don't have inverted form, must be understood as interrogatives on the basis of data such as (3), where the negative polarity item *ever*, of the sort discussed earlier in Chapter 3, is acceptable and must therefore be in the semantic environment of a polarity trigger. This trigger can, roughly speaking, only be either negation (of which there is no evidence here) or an interrogative operator, as in (3)a–b. When no interrogative is present, as in the c example, the example is anomalous. The evidence is good, therefore, that embedded *wh*-clauses are indeed questions.

(3) a.   What did John ever put on that table?

b.   Did John ever put anything on that table?

c.   *John ever put something on that table.

d.   I wonder what John ever put on that table.

The semantics of questions are complex and difficult, but it seems clear that the contribution of the *wh*-filler is information, interpreted at the gap site, about properties of the set of possible objects that could be answers to the question. In, for example, *Which Italian sports cars does John like to race?*, the speaker is in effect asking the hearer to enumerate one or more objects X, Y, ... such that *John likes to race X, John likes to race Y* and so on are all true statements, where X, Y... all satisfy the description 'is an Italian sports car.' This is rather different, of course, from what we find with topicalization, where the interpretation of the topicalized sentence and its untopicalized, 'in situ' analogue are the same; in the case of questions, the meaning of the *wh*-phrase is not an ordinary name or identifying description (*John, that white cat, my cousin from Seattle*) but a more complex kind of object. The effect of the *wh*-extraction, however, is to link the semantic operation of this filler to the gap site, with the result that the question is taken as a request for identification of the set of objects which could be interpreted into the gap site to yield a true statement. For example, *Who did John criticize?* will be interpreted as a request to enumerate the set *A* of individuals such that for any member *x* of *A*, the statement *John criticized x* is true.

It is worth noting in passing that *wh*-questions and relatives display an interesting property whereby a *wh*-word can 'carry' certain other elements with which it is syntactically linked, although to a somewhat limited degree. We have

(4) a.   Who were you talking [$_{PP}$ to t]?

  b.   [$_{PP}$ To whom] were you talking t?

This pattern is usually referred to as 'pied piping': not only the *wh*-word, but the PP whose head selects the *wh*-word appears in the fronted position.

Relative clauses, in contrast, are a class of adjunct which attach to the head of an NP, and which attribute a property to that head, much as adjectives do:

(5) a.   This is clearly a cat **who** is hungry.

  b.   Rocco is the professor **who(m)** Terrence sold a Lamborghini to t.

  c.   Tuesday is a day **when** Mary can finally relax t.

The sentence in (5)a supplies a double description of a certain animal, both of which must be satisfied for the sentence, understood in a particular context of utterance, to be true: the creature in question must be both a cat and be hungry, making the sentence effectively synonymous with *This is a hungry cat*. The sentence in (5)b likewise identifies Rocco as having two properties: being a professor and having purchased a Lamborghini from Terrence. The sentence in (5)c asserts that Tuesday is a day with the property that there is some point during that day when Mary can finally relax. In general, the filler in the relative links the head NP to the gap site (Rocco, a person, is identified with the gap site via *who*, while Tuesday, an abstract temporal object, is associated with the gap site via *when*). The effect of the relative clause adjunct on the nominal head it attaches to is thus to create a pair of properties both of which hold of the object denoted by the NP containing the relative clause, and multiple relative clauses supply more descriptions which must be satisfied, just as multiple adjective modifiers do: *This is a hungry fat cat/This is a cat who is hungry who is fat*. Again, in terms of the syntax, the filler/gap structure is essentially the same as in the topicalization construction, although the interpretation is quite different. As we would expect from this parallel between *wh*-questions and relatives on the one hand and topicalization on the other, the distance between the filler and the gap site proves open-ended:

(6) a.   Which Italian towns did you talk to Rocco about getting some suggestions from Luanne about us visiting t?

  b.   Perugia was one of the Italian towns which I talked to Rocco about getting some suggestions from Luanne about us visiting t.

Relatives display pied-piping in which, as opposed to *wh*-questions, the *wh*-word is far more embedded than is possible in questions:

(7)   There are certain senior faculty and administrators, answers to questions about the academic integrity of whom many of us are very anxious to hear t.

The *wh*-word by itself can be extracted: *There are certain senior faculty and administrators whom many of us are very anxious to hear answers to questions about the academic integrity of t*. We cannot in a limited space address how it is that the *wh*-property of relative clause *wh*-words in effect diffuses through larger and larger phrases of which those words are elements, giving very large constituents the same displacement privileges as the *wh*-words themselves, but it represents an important species of unbounded dependencies which is formally independent of extraction.

We also note cases of relative clauses which do not display overt fillers. One such class of data comprises so-called *that*-relatives:

(8) a.   John is the person that Mary likes.
   b.   John is the person that likes Mary.
   c.   Joe is the guy that I believe Terrence assumes Anne likes.
   d.   I read a book that you'd really like.
   e.   There's only one day that we can get together likes.

One suggestion intended to unify examples of this is that *that* is actually a *wh*-proform in disguise. A major objection to this suggestion is the pattern displayed in (9):

(9) a.   John is the person to whom/*that I gave the book.
   b.   John is the person whose/*thats book I gave to Mary.
   c.   John is someone even to see whom/*that makes me irritable.

The counterargument to the objection based on (9) is that such data only challenge the pronominal analysis of *that* if the latter is taken to potentially instantiate accusative case, like *which* or *who*. If, however, we restrict relative *that* to nominative case, then it is barred from ever appearing in object position. While this analysis works so far as (9) is concerned, it has its own questionable aspects. In particular, nominative case has a very confined distribution in English, restricted to pronouns either occupying or linked by SLASH connectivity to finite clauses subject position, suggesting that in some sense accusative case is the default in English. It therefore would seemingly be a somewhat eccentric property of the grammar to license a variant-pronunciation *wh*-element that was exclusively nominative. And this kind of reservation about the nominative proform analysis of *that* receives strong confirmation from the fact, noted in Pullum and Huddleston (2002), that relative clause *that* would be serving as a proform across a wider range of anaphoric uses than any other proform in the language:

(10) a.   They gave the prize to the **girl** that/who spoke first.

  b.   Have you seen the **book** that/which she was reading?

  c.   He was due to leave the **day** that/when she arrived.

  d.   He followed her to every **town** that/where she went.

  e.   That's not the **reason** that/why she resigned.

  f.   I was impressed by the **way** that/*how she controlled the crowd.

  g.   It wasn't **to you** that/*who/*. . . I was referring.

  h.   She to be the **happiest** that/*how/*. . . she has ever been.

Not only does the distribution of *that* range over that of nominal *wh*-proforms *who, which, when, why* (where temporal expressions such as *Tuesday, that day* are clearly nominal, though functioning as modifying adjunct phrases, and likewise for, for example, *that way*), it covers the full spectrum of nonnominal cases (e.g., (10); cf. *She resigned *(for) that reason*) and the cases in (10)g and h for which there is no *wh*-form. And beyond Pullum and Huddleston's distributional argument, a still more dubious aspect of the nominative proform analysis emerges when we look at a significant subset of the *that* tokens in (10): arguably, for example, in the case of (10)d, *that* does not correspond to a nominal anaphor since *went* does not take an NP complement, nor can a locative NP serve as an adjunct:

(11)   She went *(to) that town.

Here again, the overt relative proform *where* must be a *wh*-analogue of *there*, that is, a pro-PP form, and likewise for the *that* which shows up in (10)d. Given that the instances of *that* in at least (10)d, f, g, and h are clearly not nominal, one has to ask just how sensible it is to ascribe case – which otherwise appears in English, as well as many other languages, *exclusively* on nominal categories – to *that*. Given the rather far-fetched extension of case specifications on the basis of a hypothesis about the distribution of exactly one lexical item in English which itself manifests no morphological inflectional properties at all, it seems far more likely that the failure of *that* to sponsor pied-piping is due to the fact that it is not a pronoun at all, but rather something for which we have independent motivation, namely the finite clausal complementizer.

  A further major break with between the distribution of *that* and *wh* in relatives involves so-called headless relatives. We have the data array in (12):

(12) a.   Have you got a copy of **what** she was reading?

  b.   He was due to leave **when** she arrived.

  c.   They accompanied her to **where** she had to go and then said goodbye.

  d.   I wasn't happy with **why** he did it, but at least he did it.

  e.   I wasn't impressed with **how** he did it.

Headless relative clauses have received a variety of analyses over the years, but one aspect of their behavior independent of any particular treatment of them is the fact that in not one of the cases in (12) can we replace the *wh*-form with *that* and have a well-formed sentence at all, let alone an alternative version of a headless relative construction: **They accompanied her to that she had to go and then said goodbye*, etc. Given the distributional ubiquity of *that* in standard relative clauses as per (10), this is a remarkable lacuna, but if the 'pivot' of headless relative clauses must actually be a relative proform, the ill-formedness of a clause with a finite complementizer rather than such a proform is exactly what is predicted, and requires no further modification or ad hoc restriction imposed on *that*.

Similar considerations constitute the second of Pullum and Huddleston's observations about the distributional dichotomy between *wh*-proforms and relative clause *that*: the lack of a genitive form for an hypothetical nominative version of the latter (e.g., **...the woman whose/*that's turn it was*). This morphological possibility is covered under the stipulation that *that* is exclusively nominative – but it falls out as an *automatic* consequence of we take *that* to be a complementizer, since markers do not have any case assignment in the first place. The authors note that

> there are non-standard regional dialects of English in which *that's* does occur, as in *the man that's leg was broken*. We certainly do not believe that such examples necessitate a pronoun analysis for the dialects concerned, and certainly they do not establish this analysis as valid for all dialects.   (2002: 1057)

We can actually go a bit further than Pullum and Huddleston's point here, for if *that's* indeed *were* a genitive relative pronoun, we should see completely parallelism in critical cases of pied-piping, where genitives can indeed appear following pronouns:

(13)   Rocco sent some money to someone's needy parents, but I don't know to
$\left\{ \begin{array}{c} \text{whose} \\ \text{that's} \end{array} \right\}$.

Do the dialects in question support this kind of pied-piping? If not, the existence of such forms lends no credibility at all to the suggestion that *that* is a relative pronoun, since, contrary to the simple kind of case cited by Pullum and Huddleston, the behavior of these 'genitive' forms fails to follow a significant distributional generalization holding of unequivocally genitive forms in English.

Pullum and Huddleston's third point is that *that* can be omitted in relative clauses in a way largely (although not completely) parallel to its apparent optionality in finite clauses. As they note, these omissibility conditions 'have it in common that they are related to the need to mark explicitly the beginning of a subordinate clause under certain structural conditions. And in both cases, ... *that* is more readily omitted in simple structures than in complex ones. There is no pro-form in English that is systematically omissible under remotely similar conditions' (2002: 1057).

The only actual piece of evidence which appears to support relative pronominal *that* is the fact that when *that* occurs in what appears to be relative clause subject position, it does not trigger the same kind of ill-formedness that we find when a subject has been displaced following a complementizer:

(14)   I saw a sign that really confused me.

(15) a.   I said that John really confused me.

    b.   Who did you say (*that)__really confused you?

If *that* is a complementizer, then there must be a gap in subject position preceding *really confused me* in (14), since no other NP occupies that position. But where we know that *that* is unquestionably a complementizer, as in the case of (15), we find that a gap directly following the complementizer gives rise to a markedly unacceptable form. Why then is (14) completely well-formed?

We will in fact return to this phenomenon below, and briefly resume the discussion of relative clauses in connection with the contrast between subject gaps in declarative clausal complements and presumed subject gaps in *that*-complementized relatives. The crucial point which will emerge is that, contrary to much theoretical analysis during the 1980s and 1990s, the contrast in question now appears to be most plausibly explained as a prosodic, not syntactic effect, and the key to the difference between (14) and (15) is likely to be found, ultimately, in details of the differing phonologies of these classes of constructions.

7.1.1.2   *Wh*-clefts

Wh-clefts have a very distinctive appearance: an expletive *it* subject appears along with the copula *be*, followed by a clause with a *wh*-filler which resembles a relative clause but differs from them in being able to take names and pronouns as their predicates:

(16) a.   It was $\left\{ \begin{array}{c} \text{Rocco} \\ \text{me} \end{array} \right\}$ who Terrence complained about.

    b.   *If Luanne says one more nasty thing to [$_{NP}$ me who Terrence complained about], I'm going to say something I'll probably regret.

Clefts typically identify the post-copula constituent as the object that uniquely has the property defined by the *wh*-clause. In (16)a, for example, *John* is identified as satisfying the description 'the one person Terrence complained about.' Again, clefts are completely unbounded: *It was Sue who Terrence told Patricia to make sure Christopher remembered to invite t to the book club meeting on Friday*. They too display pied-piping:

(17)   It was ROCCO pictures of whom appear on post office walls last Friday afternoon.

7.1.2   Fillers in Argument Positions

The overt *wh*-fillers in questions, relatives, and clefts can all be assigned the same configurational position as the fronted elements in topicalizations, and the analysis in each case carries over in essentially the same way from the treatment of auxiliaries in the previous chapter. But there is a class of unbounded dependencies in which no actual filler can be identified. The gap is rather interpreted in terms of some element in the sentence which satisfies one of the valence requirements of a selecting head. The most widely discussed of these dependencies is usually referred to as the *tough* construction, but there are a number of others which display most of the same properties, with some variation. What is particularly notable about this class of constructions is that they are tied to specific lexical items, in a way that the following data exemplify.

7.1.2.1   *Tough* Constructions

In this class of dependencies, a constituent which satisfies the SPR specification of an adjective is interpreted in gap position within a clause. The examples in (18) are representative of the possibilities associated with *tough* predicates.

(18) a.   This box was tough (for us) to produce t/*it.

   b.   This box was tough (for us) to persuade Luanne to produce t.

   c.   This new kind of box was tough to persuade Luanne to retool her factory to produce t.

There are many members of the subclass of *tough* predicates, but quite a few adjectives do not belong to this class:

(19)   *John would be { eager / reluctant / unlikely } to resolve { *t / the conflict }.

Note also *It's normal to find John in a bar* but **John is normal to find in a bar*, and further, that *unlikely* and *impossible*, seemingly separated semantically by nothing but degree of improbability, behave quite differently so far as the *tough* class properties are concerned: while *unlikely*, as (19) shows, does not qualify for membership in this class, *impossible* does: *This problem is impossible to solve in finite time.* There thus appears no general semantic characterization of which predicates are eligible to appear in *tough* contexts and which are not.

There is a common view that in examples such as *John is tough for us to please*, *tough* appears with a PP[*for*] complement and an infinitival VP complement containing a gap, which is somehow linked to the semantics of the NP complement of *for*. Examples such as (20), however, show that this is an incorrect analysis.

(20)   How easy is John [$_s$for you to please]?

This appears to be a version of a kind of extraposition construction illustrated by *How interested is John in early Western music?* However this linkage is established – and it is far from clear what the right analysis here is – it appears to be possible for complements and adjuncts linked to a phrase with a displaced head to appear to the right of verb heading the clause from which the AP is extracted. The issues involved in working out the right analysis here are deep and complex, but fortunately we don't need to resolve them to be able to work out a motivated representation for *tough* filler/gap structures. Examples such as (18) show that the linkage between the filler and the gap site is indeed unbounded, so that the SLASH mechanism is called for. At the same time, it's clear that the complete LOCAL value of the filler cannot be shared with the gap site, because in typical cases such as (18), the CASE specification of the subject interpreted into the gap site is nominative, while the CASE value of the gap is accusative. We therefore must impose a much more limited sharing of values on the gap site. Suppose that there is a feature – part of the SEM value of the subject – which corresponds to the particular semantic identity of the subject, as is often assumed to be specified for every linguistic sign. Call this feature IDEN(TITY). Then all that SLASH need transmit to the gap site is the subject's IDENTITY feature value, and nothing further is needed. The *tough* adjective will select an infinitival phrase of category *verb* specified as containing a gap via a SLASH value, a value moreover whose IDENTITY feature is fixed in the lexicon as identical to that of the adjective's SPR value:

(21)

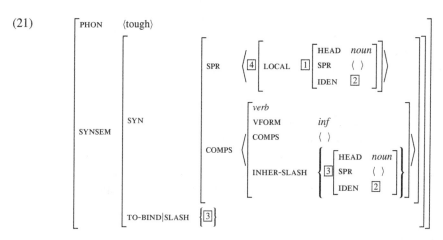

Note that while the subject of *tough* LOCAL value differs from the LOCAL value of *tough*'s infinitive complement, the IDENTITY specifications of the two LOCAL values must be the same. Therefore the potential difference in CASE values of the subject and the gap site, which 'realizes' the inherited SLASH value borne by the selected complement, is irrelevant; there is nothing which requires them to be the same. The linkage between the *tough* subject and the gap site can be graphically depicted as in (22), where, to save space, the feature specification for *tough* in (21) is abbreviated as Γ:

(22)

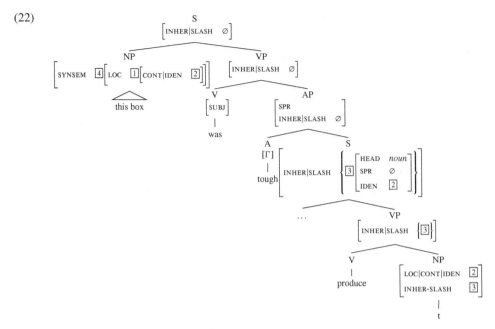

The NP at the gap site must, in order to cash out as a trace, have a LOCAL value ③ identical to the SLASH value introduced by *tough* as part of its COMPS specification. But that LOCAL value will be in principle different from the LOCAL value of the subject *this box*, so that the subject and the silent NP at the gap site can differ in CASE (and possibly other) values without penalty. Critically, however, *tough* ensures that the IDENTITY specification of its own subject, as given in its SPR value, is identical to the IDENTITY value carried in the SLASH specification it introduces via its COMPS element. Hence, the empty category at the gap site will be interpreted with the same denotation as the subject *this box*. Note that the TO-BIND|SLASH feature specified on the head of the AP as part of its lexical entry (and, more generally, of all members of this class of adjectives) will block the sharing of INHER|SLASH values higher up the tree, just as in the case of structures licensed under the Head-filler Rule discussed in the previous chapter.

In fact, the treatment for *tough* dependencies just outlined is insufficiently general, because the *tough* subject need not be nominal. Consider the following data:

(23) a.   Doing that willingly seems very strange.

b.   Does doing that willingly seem all that strange?

c.   Doing that willingly seems hard to imagine.

(24) a.   Under the bed would seem to be a strange place to store your beer.

b.   Would under the bed seem to be such a strange place to store your beer?

c.   Under the bed is hard for me to picture as the best place to store your beer.

In such examples (which can be replicated for still other constituent types), we have non-NPs which, by virtue of their eligibility for inversion, are clearly subjects. Such non-NPs can also appear as *tough* subjects, as the c examples show. Hence, the lexical specification in (21) must be modified to take account of such examples, though the emendations necessary are quite straightforward.

It is sometimes claimed that the subjects of *tough* predicates do not have a semantic relationship to what is denoted by the adjective itself: that such adjectives, rather, specify relations between some individual and some event involving that individual. Thus, in *Anne is difficult for Terrence to please*, the assumption in such claims is that this sentence posits a particular relationship between Terrence and the situation of Terrence pleasing Anne, that Anne only figures in the semantics as part of the pleasing relationship, and that this example is representative of the class of *tough* predicates generally. On this account, *It is difficult for Terrence to please Anne* provides a more transparent documentation of the semantic representations involved, and this view has been, from early days in modern syntactic theory, so widespread that it was considered the default analysis up through the early 1970s to take *it*-subject versions of the *tough* construction, of the kind just mentioned, as the structural source of the filler/gap version, with the subject being a true filler, extracted from its object position following *please* and inserted into subject position, replacing *it*. Later versions of the analysis took the *tough* subject to be in situ, where *easy, tough, difficult,* and so on denied their subjects any semantic status. Such status was due entirely to the interpretation of those subjects according to their identification with the trace in *object* position within the infinitive. But there is good reason to question this general characterization of the *tough* subject. Note, for example, cases such as (25):

(25) a.   It's obnoxious to try to talk to Mary. [E.g., because a dozen hostile Rottweilers live with her in her office.]
  b.   Mary is obnoxious to try to talk to.
  c.   It's obnoxious to try to talk to Mary, though she herself is quite nice to talk to.
  d.   #Mary is obnoxious to try to talk to, though she herself is quite nice to talk to.

The point is that in some cases, the *tough* predicate has to be construed as a relationship between some individual and, roughly speaking, a state of affairs, and in other cases, as with *obnoxious*, it denotes a relationship between some individual (here, the implicit *infinitive* subject), a state of affairs, and another individual, some property of whom or which is implicated in the relationship. The lack of a semantic role for the *tough* subject suggested by standard textbook instances of the construction is thus not a central property of the construction itself – an important conclusion, in view of the fact that a number of influential analyses of *tough* have hinged in part on the lack of a semantic role for the *tough* subject.

7.1.2.2   Too/Enough Constructions

Tough predicates are far from the only class of forms linking an argument of some head (typically, but not necessarily, a subject) to a gap position within a complement of that head. Virtually any adjective can be part of such an expression when preceded or followed by the degree modifiers *too* and *enough* respectively. This pattern of behavior is exemplified in (26)–(28).

(26) a.   John is too stubborn for me to argue with.
    b.   John is too stubborn for me to argue with him.
    c.   John is too stubborn to argue with.
    d.   *John is too stubborn to argue with him. (with *him* taken to identify *John*)

(27) a.   John is stubborn enough for me to argue with.
    b.   John is stubborn enough for me to argue with him.
    c.   John is stubborn enough to argue with.
    d.   *John is stubborn enough to argue with him. (with *her* taken to identify *John*)

(28) a.   */??John is too stubborn for me to believe that Mary would argue with.
    b.   */?? John is stubborn enough for me to believe that Mary would argue with.

(29)   John is $\left\{ \begin{array}{l} \text{too stubborn} \\ \text{stubborn enough} \end{array} \right\}$ for us to regard as worth persuading Terrence to include on the list of potential adjudicators.

For most speakers, the complement to the *too/enough* adjective must be some nonfinite projection of the verb, as is also the case with *tough* predicates, with no finite clauses intervening between the infinitive and the gap site. But the two construction types diverge so far as the occupant of the gap site is concerned: *John is easy for us to talk to him* is clearly defective, while *John is relaxed enough for us to talk to him* is unexceptionable. This possibility, however, only arises when the complement to the *too/enough* adjective is clausal; when it is a VP, that interpretation is unavailable (*John is relaxed enough to talk to him* must be about John talking to someone else, not about people in general talking to John). This behavior is quite mysterious, and no satisfying account of it is available, although it has been noted repeatedly in the literature on so-called 'missing object constructions', as the general class of dependencies including *tough*, *too/enough*, and others discussed in the following subsections used to be labeled.

Regardless of the source of these complications, however, the extraction possibilities manifested by *too/enough* adjectives can be handled the same way, though the mechanics are somewhat tricky. If we take *too* and *enough* to be adjuncts, we have the rather peculiar situation of a modifying element changing the valence possibilities of the head targeted by the adjunct's MOD value. A separate rule could be stated, something one might think of as 'the Head-*too/enough* rule,' which specifies that an AP may consist of a head with a preceding *too* or a following *enough*, along with a verbal complement saturated for COMPS and possibly specified for a nonempty SLASH value sharing IDEN values with the subject of the adjective – but a rule as specialized as this in its coverage seems like massive overkill.

Probably the best way to handle the problems posed by *too* and *enough* is take a different view of the infinitival complements: they should be seen, not as complements of the adjectival head, but as (optional) valents of the degree adverbials themselves. Thus, we will have a phrasal category along the lines displayed in (30):

(30)   [$_{DegP}$ too [$_{S/XP\ or\ VP/XP}$ ...]]

The linear ordering of these adjunct elements so that *too* is separated by the head from its infinitive complement, while *enough* follows the head and is adjacent to its SLASHed valent, is determined by a *linearization* mechanism which we have not introduced in this textbook, but which is independently motivated by a wide range of facts about languages with much freer constituent order than English. This mechanism – which may also be responsible for cases such as *an easy man to please* and *a good friend to have at your side in a tense situation* – determines a left-to-right order of elements in which material belonging to different constituents is nonetheless 'shuffled' together in the phonological yield of the signs in which those constituents serve as subcomponents. Thus, *too* and *enough* are both the heads of adverbial phrases which select gap-licensing infinitive VP complements. They then combine with an adjective via the Head-adjunct Rule, yielding a *too/enough* predicate which links the value of the SLASH feature to the SPR specification of the adjective – but where the adjective, in the case of *too*, separates the degree adverbial and its VP complement. In this approach, the linear order of words is not determined by the phrase structure hierarchical relations within a sentence, but by the interaction of a number of different conditions, some of which may be prosodic. The details of this technology go well beyond the scope of the current discussion, but the approach to linear order briefly outlined here does seem to be a viable strategy for handling the cases under discussion.

7.1.2.3   Cost/take

The lexical items *cost* and *take* have rather idiosyncratic properties among English verbs: they follow the pattern of *tough* insofar as they have both *it*-subject and filler/gap versions.

(31) a.   It cost me a lot of money to finish the upstairs.
    b.   The upstairs cost me a lot of money to finish.
    c.   *I cost a lot of money to finish the upstairs.

(32) a.   It took me ten hours to finish the upstairs.
    b.   The upstairs took me ten hours to finish.
    c.   I took ten hours to finish the upstairs.

(33) a.   This project took me a lot of time to work out a strategy about how to finish t.

b.   This project cost me a lot of effort to assemble the resources to complete.

These two verbs differ somewhat in behavior: *take* (unlike *cost*), allows two different arguments of the verb to appear as subject, in addition to *it* (although there is a plausible alternative possibility that there are actually three verbs *take*, one of which takes an *it* subject and has no gaps in its complement, one of which takes a subject (e.g., *I*), whose semantic role corresponds to the post-verb NP of the first *take* (i.e., *me*), and also has no gaps, and one in which one of the arguments in the infinitival complements is represented by a gap, linked to the subject (e.g., *the upstairs*) by a SLASH pathway. Here again, the proposal summarised in (21) will handle these data, giving us the unbounded scope of the dependency as per (33).

7.1.2.4   Purpose Clauses

Finally, we have the case of purpose clauses. These are exemplified in (34), where there appears to be an interesting difference in status between the example with *persuade* as an intermediate verb and the example with *give*.

(34) a.   I brought these books for you to read on the train.

b.   ?I brought these books for you to persuade John to read t on the train.

c.   I brought these books for you to give to John to read t on the train.

There is a subtle but clear difference in the meaning here that corresponds to a difference in the expectations that an object will be entrusted to someone responsible for donating it to a third person, as vs to someone responsible for convincing someone else to do something with it. When this sort of independent semantic factor is taken into account, it's clear that purpose clauses have the key property of unboundedness in the linkage between the object interpreted into a gap site and that gap site itself.

There is a certain temptation to identify such clauses as infinitival relatives; one has examples such as *A book for you to read on the train is the one thing I forgot all about, dammit!* It is straightforward to show that the infinitive in this latter case is a constituent of the subject NP, whose gap is identified with the subject, hence a relative clause. But we can find contexts which clearly distinguish purpose clauses from relatives, as in (35):

(35) a.   This is a book for you read t on the train.

b.   *This is it for you to read t on the train.

c.   I brought it (for you) to read t on the train.

While relative clauses generally resist adjunction to names or proforms, this aversion is particularly strong in the case of the *it* personal pronoun. In the clear case of a relative clause, as in (35)a, *it* cannot replace *a book*, since in relative clauses the head of NP and its adjunct are themselves a constituent. But in the case of purpose clauses, where the evidence strongly supports an analysis of such clauses as VP adjuncts, there is no problem with an NP *inside* the VP modified by the adjunct taking the form of a pronoun. Here, too, the unbounded depth of the gap site within the adjunct can be neatly captured by an analysis similar to that offered earlier for *tough* constructions, though the particular mechanisms which are involved in identifying the 'target' of the purpose clause and making it available for identification with the contents of that clause's SLASH feature involve technical issues that we are not able to explore here.

7.2 'Syntactic' Restrictions on Filler/Gap Linkages: An Incomplete Survey

7.2.1 The Complex NP Constraint

The first detailed consideration of supposed syntactic conditions on extraction phenomena – and arguably one of the three most important pieces of syntactic research in the past fifty years – was Ross' 1967 MIT doctoral dissertation, *Constraints on Variables in Syntax*. In the core chapter of his dissertation, Ross listed a number of specific phrase structure configurations which appear to break the connection between displaced material and the gap sites originally occupied by that material (where transformational grammar assumed that a special movement operation was responsible for the displacement phenomenon). Such configurations are often referred to as 'islands'; constituents stranded in island configurations have no way to leave them. So, for example, we find many cases such as the following:

(36) a. I never saw the car which John sold to those people.
     b. *Which people did you never see the car which John sold to __?

(37) a. You accepted John's offer to insult who?
     b. *Who did you accept John's offer to insult __?
     c. *Mary was the critic who I accepted John's offer to insult.

(38) a. I became aware of the rumor that John had worked for Mary.
     b. *Who did you become aware of the rumor that John had worked for __?
     c. *The critic who I became aware of the rumor that Mary had challenged to a duel entered the room.

Note that this restriction applies across the whole range of filler/gap dependencies. *Tough* constructions and their relatives are equally sensitive to it:

(39) a. It wouldn't be hard to justify our plan to attack Ostrogothia.
     b. Our plan to attack Ostrogothia wouldn't be hard to justify t.
     c. ??*Ostrogothia wouldn't be hard to justify our plan to attack t.

It has long been assumed in transformational grammar that the structure of infinitival complements as in (37) and (39) is

(40)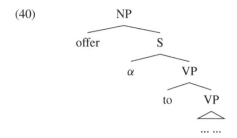

where α corresponds to some NP which is unpronounced, either as a result of deletion under identity or because it has a null phonology. In either case, the point is that infinitival VPs are actually the surface yield of underlying clausal structures. Against this background, and on the basis of facts such as (36)–(38), Ross formulated the restriction summarized in (41).

(41)   **Complex NP Constraint**
        Nothing can be extracted out of an NP where the gap site is under S in the configuration

Readers may notice that these examples are not completely parallel semantically. The first two are relative clauses, finite and infinitival respectively, in which the NP containing the relative clause represents the intersection of the properties corresponding to the head of the NP (*car* in (36), e.g.) with the property corresponding to the relative clause ('the property of having been sold by John to those people' in (36)). But the case of (38) is somewhat different: here, the clause *that John had worked for Mary* does not seem to modify anything – that is, it does not appear possible to identify an object which possesses both the property of being a rumor and some other property that is designated by 'that John worked for Mary.' The latter is not a property (in the sense that being green, or being heavier than water, or being the last person who saw Terrence alive is). Rather, it is a statement about the world, which is either true or false. The relationship between 'rumor' and 'that John had worked for Mary' thus seems to be more along the lines of the semantic connection between *student* and *of chemistry* in *John is a student of chemistry*: just as *student* entails the existence of a particular domain of knowledge (i.e., the domain which John is studying and by virtue of which s/he is a student), *rumor* entails the existence of some particular proposition – that is, some potentially true depiction of a certain state of affairs – whose possible but not verified reality merits the description of the status of this proposition as a rumor. The clause associated with *rumor* in this example seems to display semantics we would associate with a complement, rather than with an adjunct.

This impression is reinforced by the ordinary *one* replacement test discussed at length in earlier chapters. We find the following:

(42) a.   The $\left\{\begin{array}{l} \text{fact} \\ \text{belief} \\ \text{rumor} \end{array}\right\}$ that the twins worry about__excessively is far less disturb-

ing than the one they routinely laugh at__.

   b.   ??*The $\left\{\begin{array}{l} \text{fact} \\ \text{belief} \\ \text{rumor} \end{array}\right\}$ that the twins worry about everything excessively is far

less disturbing than the one that they routinely feast on haggis.

There can be little doubt that in these and similar cases, the clausal complements of noun heads such as *fact* and *rumor* behave radically differently with respect to dependents that contain a gap and can be construed as modifiers (as in (42)a) than they do in cases where the dependent is not construable as a modifying property, but rather as specifying the content of a background assumption associated with nominals that describe the status of propositions (such as *fact*, *belief*, *rumor*, *claim*, etc.). Putting it another way, clausal dependents which display the syntactic properties of complements seem to mean quite different things than those which look more like adjuncts.

These facts appear to confirm the correctness of Ross' conclusion that the phenomenon exhibited in (36)–(42) reflects a configurational property of a certain set of Engish examples, rather than some semantic property of that set. The only remaining issue *seems* to be whether or not Ross' formulation is sufficiently general. For much of the history of modern syntax, the 'default' position has in fact been that it is not, and that the facts motivating the Complex NP Constraint (CNPC) can be shown to fall out from a more general condition called Subjacency, which encompasses a number of phenomena that Ross treated separately from the CNPC, or did not address at all.

7.2.2   *Wh*-Islands

The empirical domain that has most generally been taken to bear on the adequacy of the CNPC as Ross formulated it is often referred to as '*wh*-island' phenomena. Examples are given in (43):

(43) a.   I wondered who I should ask to frame the question more politely.
   b.   *How much more politely did you wonder who you should ask to frame the question__?

(44) a.   I wondered who John said was dancing under the bridge at Avignon.
   b.   *Where did you wonder who John said was dancing __?

(45) a.   I wonder what Mary gave to John
   b.   *Who do you wonder what Mary gave to__

There is no complex NP here. Nonetheless, the b examples are uniformly defective in a way that seems not unrelated to the cases of CNPC violation displayed earlier. Such data is said to exhibit *wh*-island effects, where the abstract *wh*-island configuration can be depicted as follows:

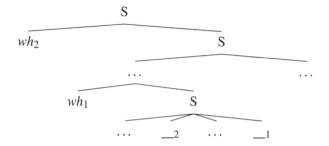

7.2.2.1   Subjacency

Uniting Subjacency and the *wh*-island effect under a single generalization represented a natural move in the late 1970s, once a consensus had
been reached that it should be possible to deduce the range of descriptive
generalizations that Ross and others had discovered in the domain of island
phenomena from more general (and necessarily more abstract) restrictions. One
version of what became the 'touchstone' for the theory of island in a certain style
of syntax can be stated as follows:

> No single movement operation may relate positions separated by more than
> one *bounding* node, where for English the bounding nodes in a tree are (on
> some analyses) those labeled NP, S and S̄ (where S̄ was taken to be a clausal
> constituent with a sister complementizer position, of the form [ₛComp S],
> whether or not the complementizer position was filled with any actual lexical
> material).

There were actually many variants of this restriction, and the set of 'bounding
nodes' – category labels that counted in determining when a movement operation
had carried a filler too far up the tree – were believed to vary from language to
language. This range of possibilities was said to reflect parametric variation: the
restriction was invariant, presumably a part of the linguistic knowledge shared
by all members of the human species, but the operation of the restriction was
relativized to particular category choices made for each language.

To see how Subjacency worked, imagine that we have the structure (46)
corresponding to (47):

(46)

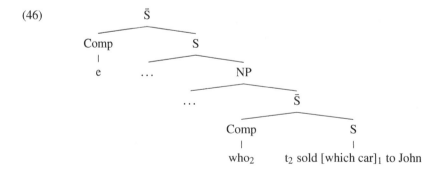

(47) a.   You met the guy who sold *which* car to John?

     b.   *Which car did you meet the guy who sold __to John?

Who has moved to its 'safe' position in Comp. Only one bounding node, S, has been crossed, so the structure is legal so far. But by this move, Comp has been removed as a landing site for the next move, by *which car*. The latter can only move to a Comp node, however, and there is only one available – at the very top of the structure. If *which car* moves, however, it will cross three bounding nodes in a single move: the S which immediately dominates it, the NP within which it is contained, and the highest S node directly under the root $\bar{S}$. This is more than enough to yield the massive ill-formedness, achieving actual uninterpretability, that (47) appears to display.

Consider now (45). The first movement of *what* deprives *who* of a landing site within its own $\bar{S}$ clause. It must therefore move to the Comp of the root clause, crossing the lower $\bar{S}$ and the highest S node, again violating Subjacency. Again, the result is unintelligible.

Finally, consider another of Ross' constraints, the Sentential Subject Constraint. The point of this constraint was to block movement of a *wh*-phrase from a clause in subject position, as in (48):

(48) a. $[_{\bar{S}}[_{\bar{S}}$ [$_{\bar{S}}$That [$_{S}$ John spied for *who*]] disturbed you greatly]]?

     b.   *I wonder $[_{\bar{S}}$who$_1$ [$_{S}$ t$_1$ [$_{\bar{S}}$t$_1$ that [spied for t$_1$]] disturbed you greatly.]]

When *who* moves out of the embedded clause in subject position (call it S_0), it passes up to the Comp node occupied by *that*. To reach the next Comp node, the one for the whole sentence of which it's the subject, it must pass in one movement past an $\bar{S}$ node and then the S node above that, a path notated by subscripted traces in (48). Again, Subjacency blocks the final structure, an ostensibly correct result.

The extensive 'reach' of the Subjacency condition, its apparent ability to rule out a large range of structures which required separate stipulation in Ross' thesis, gave one specific constraint a descriptive track record seemingly unparalleled in the history of work on filler/gap phenomena. It was therefore regarded as a signal triumph of syntax in the tradition inaugurated by Chomsky in 1957. But there were additional reasons, discussed in the final section of this chapter, for the satisfaction that theorists took in Subjacency, making it something like the jewel in the crown of grammatical theory. Nonetheless, other phenomena were known that it provided no account for, and these required separate treatment.

7.2.2.2   The Coordinate Structure Constraint

The second major island constraint that Ross proposed concerned a curious property of coordinate structures which appear in extraction contexts. The kind of facts that caught Ross' attention appear in (49)–(51):

(49) a.   I play cards with the gang and go to night classes on alternate Thursdays.

b.   ??/* Who do you play cards with _ and go to night classes on alternate Thursdays?

c.   ??/*What do you play cars with the gang and go to _ on alternate Thursdays.

(50) a.   Florence is the city that I visited _ last year and would like to return to _ in the near future.

b.   To whom have you presented your plans – or shown your prospectus –?

c.   Visit Paris, John definitely will _ this summer and I really should _ sometime next year.

(51) a.   I like raspberries and papayas in fruit salad.

b.   *What do you like raspberries and – in fruit salad?

c.   *What do you like – and papayas in fruit salad?

(52)   *What do you like _ and _ ?

In (49)a, we have a VP which is composed of two finite VPs:

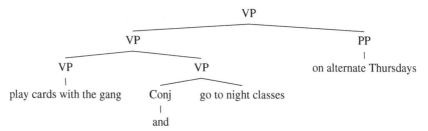

The two remaining examples in (49) display a gap in one or the other conjunct, and both are markedly unacceptable. Ross took the ill-formedness of this particular distribution of gaps in conjunctions as representative, and observed that, as in (49)b–c, the effect held regardless of which extraction construction was implicated in the extraction: in (49)b, we have a wh-question and in (49)c, a relative clause. Such examples contrast dramatically with the status of (50), where we find a single filler linked to gaps in both conjuncts. In (51), we again see evidence that extraction from only one of two conjuncts yields ill-formed results – but the pattern is different in these two cases: in (52), extraction from both conjuncts is just as bad as the asymmetrical extraction in (51).

Just as with the CNPC, the CSC applies not only to wh-filler and related constructions, such as topicalization, but also to tough-type constructions:

(53) a.   It is easy (for us) to please John and offend Mary.

b.   John and Mary are easy (for us) to please and to offend, respectively.

c.   *John is easy (for us) to please t and offend Mary.

d.   *John is easy (for us) to please Mary and offend t.

as well as relatives and clefts without *that* or *wh*:

(54) a.   *That's the church I greatly admired Rheims cathedral and studied t.

b.   *It was THAT church I greatly admired t and studied Rheims cathedral.

Ross took the patterns exhibited in (49)–(53) to indicate that two separate constraints were involved: (51)–(52) show that extraction *of* conjuncts is strictly forbidden (the Conjunct Constraint), while (49)–(50) illustrate what he called the Element Constraint. Together, these make up the Coordinate Structure Constraint.

(55)   **C(oordinate) S(tructure) C(onstraint):**
i.   **Conjunct Constraint:** Conjuncts may not be extracted.
ii.   **Element Constraint:** No element may be extracted from a proper subset of the conjuncts in a coordination.

The Element Constraint, it will be noted, does not forbid extraction from a conjunct; it only rules out extractions which apply to some but not all of the coordinated constituents. The restriction imposed in (55) is often referred to as the 'across the board' (ATB) condition: a gap in a coordinate structure anywhere entails that an extraction dependency holds in *every* conjunct in the coordination, regardless of the category of the mother. In the examples of the CSC given above, the conjuncts were all VPs. But note cases such as (56):

(56) a.   Who did you read John [$_{NP}$ [$_{NP}$ a story about] and [$_{NP}$ a poem by (*Shelley)]]?

b.   John is someone whom I'm not [$_{AP}$ [$_{AP}$ worried about or much interested in (*Terrence)]].

c.   Which shelf should I stack these books [$_{PP}$ [$_{PP}$ on top of (*the piano)] or [$_{PP}$ next to]]?

d.   That guy you were talking to, [$_{S}$ [$_{S}$ most of us don't trust] and [$_{S}$ few of us like (*Terrence)]]

Coordinations of NP, AP, PP, and S display exactly the same pattern as VP coordinations, giving the CSC a high degree of generality. The independence of this condition from the others observed by Ross is self-evident – in all of the above cases, an extraction is present that would be legal if the structure involved were not a coordination – giving it a *sui generis* status as a primitive constraint that simply had to be posited for English (and for many other languages, as subsequent research seemed to indicate).

7.2.3   *That*-Trace Effect

Shortly after Ross' dissertation appeared, work by Joan Bresnan (1977) revealed another perplexing restriction on English extraction. Bresnan's examples consisted of data such as (57):

(57) a.   I insisted (that) John was a spy.

b.   Who did you insist (*that) t was a spy?

There is no general problem with extraction from a clause with a *that* complementizer:

(58)   What do you think that we should do about all this nonsense?

And there is no problem with extraction of subjects, as (57) itself makes quite clear. The problem arises when the filler is linked to a subject gap position following a complementizer, yielding a result which speakers almost invariably find severely defective. This phenomenon was widely known (and is still typically referred to) as the *that*-trace effect, although it also arises when subjects following *if* and *whether* are displaced (**Who did you wonder if/whether __would get the job?*). For at least a decade after it was discovered, the *that*-t effect was taken in much influential work to be yet another primitive condition, a kind of 'surface filter' on extraction which just had to be assumed as part of the grammar of English, with no obvious deeper source.

A line of thinking which began in the early 1980s seemed to suggest, however, that such a source might well exist. The details are complex, but the general idea was that a trace cannot just appear anywhere. It has to occur in a context in which it has a particular relationship to a selecting head, or, as a secondary possibility, in a configuration which *resembles* head-selection contexts in the right way. So, for example, in a structure such as

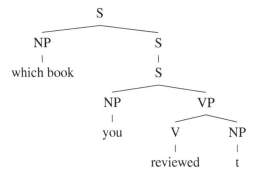

which will be part of the representation of the sentence *I wonder which book you reviewed*, the head V is in the right position, as the left sister, to be a lexical selector of an NP complement. Whether or not this selection actually takes place, the 'left sister' configuration was taken to correspond to special licensing properties that made the appearance of a following trace legal. But literal sisterhood wasn't necessary. For various reasons, it was assumed at this time that the following configurations defining structural relations between X and YP were at some abstract level equivalent, under the right circumstances:

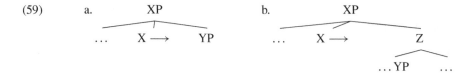

depending on what Z is. The fact that the complement of *expect* followed by what is assumed to be an infinitive clause contains an accusative subject, as is [s *her* [vp *to get the job*]] in *I expected her to get the job* under standard transformational assumptions, shows that the subject of such clauses is in a parallel relationship to YP in (59)a, since in, for example, *I expected her at 9a.m.*, accusative case also appears. It was understood that accusative case assignment was determined by a lexical head in a privileged configuration, with both cases in (59) as subspecies of the same general privileged configuration.

Approaches which sought an account of the *that*-t effect at a deeper level than the simple surface filter account assumed through the late 1970s started from the premise that one or the other of these configurations had to hold if YP were a trace. So in, for example, *Which of these people did you expect* t *to get the job*, the trace is in the same privileged configuration that *her* is in *I expected her to get the job*:

(60)

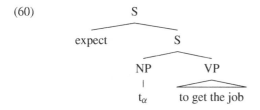

In this position, extracting [α *which of these people*] might be seen as unproblematic because the extracted constituent, while not lexically selected, is still in the privileged configuration (59)b, so that we would expect to get *Which of those people do you expect* t *to get the job?* There's a problem with this approach, however: it's clear that the subject position of *finite* clauses does not satisfy the restrictions on Z in (59)b. We do not, for example, get *I expected him would get the job.* Yet extraction from finite subject position, as we've seen in (57), is unproblematic as long as *that* is not present. Hence, examples such as *Which of these people did you expect to get the job* are actually misleading; if being in the privileged configuration is necessary for traces to appear, simply being in the position of YP (59)b may not capture the necessary notion of 'privilege.'

Transformational theorists working in this early to mid-1980s framework therefore made a further assumption. In the kind of analysis of filler/gap linkage they favored, a constituent in a certain position moves in a series of steps, always upward and to the left, appearing in some 'protected' position on the periphery of the clause and then moving up/left-ward again, leaving a trace behind. The result is a chain of movements from one protected position to a higher protected position, and the typical structure of filler-trace/linked traces along this chain is displayed in (61):

(61)

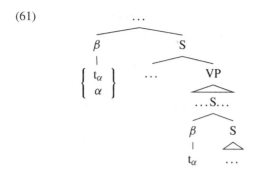

The idea is that this configuration bears *some* relation to the configuration in (59)b, enough that it can be seen, at a quite abstract level, as an instance of the same tree-geometric relation. And, just as in the case of (59)b, much depends on just what intervenes between the lower trace and the structure higher up. In particular, if the 'landing site' for the movement leaves the trace in a position where a complementizer is present, the lower trace is separated from the upper trace by a barrier which nullifies the connection between the two traces, and the movement fails. Hence, when the subject of the clause moves into the special protected position within its own clause, and then further up the tree, the privileges associated with the configuration in (61) fail. If this rather elaborate story were correct, then we would have an account of why the structure in (57)b is ill-formed when *that* is present: the configuration in this case would be as in (62), an instance of a failed linkage in (61):

(62)

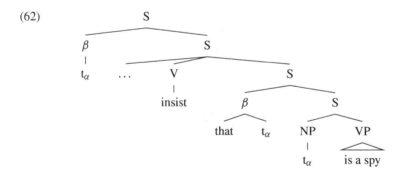

The presence of *that* was assumed to interrupt the connection between the filler and the trace, with the resulting configuration failing the requirement that the special structural relationship must hold between traces and either the filler or a higher trace left by the filler on its upward movement path.

    Readers may be wondering whether, apart from the seemingly quite contrived nature of this kind of account, it incurs a serious misprediction. If a chain of filler/trace or trace/trace linkages is broken by an intervening complementizer, do we not also rule out data such as (63), where the filler and the gap are separated by an arbitrary number of clauses displaying an overt complementizer?

(63) a.   Who does John think that Terrence should hire t?

    b.   Who did Mary assume that John thought that Terrence should hire t?

    c.   Who did Chris say that Mary assumed that John thought that Terrence should hire?

There is no question that these examples degrade as the number of *that*s increases, and can be improved by omitting the complementizer. But the degradation is gradual, not immediate and decisive as in the case of (57). If we take this steady decrease in felicitousness to reflect something about the way we process such sentences in real time, then the conclusion must be that the structures themselves are legal, in spite of the fact that the connectivity chains involved are not instances of the privileged configuration.

Crucially, however, in each of these cases the lowest trace *does* occur in the privileged configuration *with respect to its lexical selector*. At the point in the series of derivational steps where the lowest trace is checked for compliance with the 'privileged configuration' requirement, it will get a pass. The same is true for the example in (57)b in which the complementizer is missing, since there will be no barrier separating the trace from the filler. Thus, the well-formed cases will be licensed and the unacceptable instance of (57) will be blocked.

But now a new problem arises: adjunct fillers can freely move through higher clauses to fillers, even when a clause marked with *that* intervenes:

(64) a.   When [$_s$ do you suppose [$_s$ that **t** John will leave **t** on his next trip?]]

    b.   How fast [$_s$ would you say [$_s$ that **t** Mary can expect to run 100 meters **t**?]]

    c.   Tuesday, [$_s$ I don't think [$_s$ that **t** we're doing very much of anything **t**.]]

In all of these cases, the movement chain of the fronted filler passes safely through a complementizer-marked clause, yet the examples are good. The reason cannot involve licensing in the structure (59)a, since adjuncts do not appear as selected elements. These data appear to be clear counterexamples to the 'privileged configuration' explanation.

To circumvent this difficulty, theorists added a further wrinkle to the system, consisting of two parts: in the first place, the stage at which adjuncts are licensed by filler/gap chains occurs later than the point at which arguments of the verb are licensed, and in the second place *that* is 'edited out,' for purposes of chain licensing, before this later stage (but not until argument licensing has been determined). It follows that at the stage where the status of the adjunct chain is determined, the structure of (64)a will look like (65):

(65)   When [$_s$ do you suppose [$_s$ ~~that~~ **t** John will [$_{vp}$ [$_{vp}$ [$_{vp}$ leave] **t**] on his next trip?]]]

At this point, although *that* is present in the phonological representation, it is no longer visible at the particular syntactic where adjunct traces are checked in terms of whether they satisfy the privileged-configuration criterion. Various versions of this by now extraordinarily complex and only rather vaguely spelled out scenario appeared during the later 1980s and early 1990s, but the essential features of the approach sketched in this section are preserved in later variants.

7.3   Rethinking the Status of 'Syntactic' Constraints

Within the past decade and a half, a fundamental shift in perspective has begun to permeate thinking about constraints of the kind discussed above. This increasingly held view breaks decisively with the assumption, widely maintained in the three decades following the appearance of Ross' thesis, that the prohibitions on filler/gap connectivity sketched above are syntactic in nature – that is, that they arise from restrictions explicitly stated on syntactic objects which restrict the yield of the grammar to a subset of those otherwise licensed. On this more recently developed approach to the data cited earlier in this chapter, the unacceptable (and sometimes uninterpretable) sentences are syntactically well-formed. That is, nothing is *structurally* deficient about them. The problems that arise are due to independent (but occasionally interacting) sources that either violate restrictions imposed by some nonsyntactic part of the grammar, or incur costs that have little to do with the grammar directly, but rather with the nature of psychological mechanisms (depending, e.g., on certain kinds of memory) required to process linguistic information in real time. Such processing events are easily derailed – possibly to the point of failure – by certain kinds of interference and complexity. The latter factors, rather than any kind of prohibitions on structures, which give rise to the ill-formedness previously attributed to configuration-based constraints.

The key evidence that the factors responsible for supposedly structural ill-formedness are in fact *non*syntactic is that it is possible to find sentences which in the relevant respects display exactly the same structures as those taken to be blocked by the syntactic constraints assumed, but which are markedly better – even completely acceptable. Small adjustments in certain directions make the result better or worse, and, starting from the best-formed structural versions of these supposedly inadmissible structures, one can construct progressively less well-formed versions by adjusting certain factors that have little or nothing to do with structure in the relevant sense. This line of research was pioneered by Robert Kluender, a syntactician and psycholinguist, at the very end of the twentieth century, and gradually it has come to represent the default hypothesis about 'island' and related effects.

Kluender's major impact was in the domain of the CNPC and related effects – those phenomena in which the abstract geometrical account of filler/gap linkage possibilities was previously held to have achieved its greatest success. Subsequent investigators, borrowing heavily from his insights and methodology, have pursued work on other island phenomena that we have not discussed, successfully extending his processing-based account to this domain as well. In still other species of defective phenomena, however, pragmatic factors, as in the case of the CSC effects, rather than real-time processing obstacles, seem to be responsible for the difficulty. And in still others (e.g., the *that*-t facts), the culprit seems likely to turn out to be phonological. Thus, island constraints do not only seem likely to be nonsyntactic in nature, they apparently do not seem to constitute a unitary class of *any* kind.

7.3.1   CNCP and Related Phenomena

Kluender's innovation takes as its point of departure a well-known effect arising from the repetition of specific structures underlying the form of a certain kind of relative clause, the so-called 'center-embedded' type, illustrated in (66).

(66)   The man [$_s$ the host knew __] left the room.

Clearly, there's nothing wrong with this structure (whose name comes from the fact that the relative clause is embedded after the nominal subject head and before the VP); it's altogether unexceptionable, and apparently not even noteworthy. But when this structure is iterated – that is, when the relative clause subject itself contains an identical structure – things get bad very quickly. Thus, a traditional display of the accumulation of comprehension difficulties to the point of failure would take the following form:

(67) a.   The man left the room.
     b.   The man the host knew left the room.
     c.   The man the host the intelligence people investigated knew left the room.
     d.   The man the host the intelligence people the reporter interviewed investigated knew left the room.

English speakers generally agree that the rot sets in in (67)c, which is markedly difficult to process without a very deliberate use of intonation to make clear the intended structure; and (67)d is still worse. Such examples were known at a very early stage of syntactic research, and became a clichéd piece of evidence that whether or not some string of words was acceptable only indirectly implicated its status as a possible output of the rules of the grammar. The assumption for many years has been that there is something about the nature of center-embedded structures which taxes the very short-term memory resources available to keep track of linguistic structures. In the case of (67), these effects make it difficult for the hearer to link particular nominal structures in the string preceding the verbs to the verb whose gap the nominal needs to be associated with. The particular configuration in (67)d requires a certain correspondence pattern between the nominal heads and their respective correlated verbs and gaps which is known, in other contexts, to yield strings which are difficult or impossible to sort out.

All this was old news even in the 1970s. But Kluender's remarkable results during the 1990s made it clear that much of the thinking about center-embedding constructions had missed possibly the most important point: these structures

could be improved significantly by certain purely lexical adjustments. A hierarchy of intelligibility follows directly:

(68) a.   The woman [the man [the host knew __] brought __] left
     b.   < The woman [that man [the host knew __] brought __] left.
     c.   < The woman [a man [the host knew __] brought __] left.
     d.   < The woman [someone [the host knew __] brought __] left.
     e.   < The woman [someone [he knew __] brought __] left.
           (Kluender 1998: 254)

where we follow Kluender's usage in notating relative acceptability with inequal-
ity markers. The improvement between the first and the last of these examples is
quite striking. Yet nothing about the structure has changed. What has happened
to yield this unexpected improvement?

   In passing from (68)a to (68)c, note the progressive reduction in the definiteness of the NP subject in the highest relative clause. *The man* conveys uniqueness
more strongly than *that man*, while *a man* indicates no uniqueness at all. In (68)d,
we find a completely indefinite NP, *someone*, from which all we can infer is that
an unspecified human being is being referred to. Finally, in the final example,
the subject of the lower relative clause is replaced by a pronoun *he*, carrying far
less information than the definite NP *the host*. Cumulatively, what has happened
is that the intermediate NPs between the highest NP and the lowest gap site,
into which this NP must be interpreted, have been in some sense diminished in
terms of their information content, in particular, their referential specificity. This
reduction has the concomittant effect, of course, of increasing the referential
specificity of the filler which has to go the furthest distance to find its gap
site, relative to intermediate fillers occupying positions at clause boundaries
along the way. Apparently, then, the problem with center-embedded relatives
is not structural in essence; while there are structural aspects to it, such as the
location of clause boundaries in relation to where the various NPs occur, these
structural facts do not determine the difficulty of psychologically processing such
relatives successfully. Rather, they only create the possibility for a high degree
of difficulty in that task, depending on what else is going on, and it's that 'what
else' that turns out to play the critical role. The determining factor seems to be
the degree to which the hearer, trying to link a filler to an increasingly deeply
embedded gap site, encounters processing tasks along the way which have to
be solved first, and which thereby lead the speaker to in effect lose track of the
filler in topmost position. Linkage of fillers to gap sites, in the case of center-
embedded relatives, is thus more successful to the degree that the filler can be
made more informative and its intervening NP competitors made less so.

   Readers need to keep clearly in mind that from the outset, as already noted, the
diminished acceptability/intelligibility effects in center-embedding constructions
were taken to reflect facts about the mechanism by which speakers establish
the relationships among parts of the sentence required for interpretation, rather
than whether or not such relatives were sanctioned as legal by the grammar.

Kluender's discoveries about the improvements in comprehensibility in these constructions was therefore altogether plausible, even expected, *if* we make certain specific assumptions. We can say in advance that the 'repair' strategy exhibited in (68) makes sense on the assumption that judgments of a legal structure which is psychologically difficult to process in real time can be dramatically improved through means which have nothing to do with structural factors. But the corollary is that if we do see such improvement, that constitutes strong evidence that the problem with these constructions is not structural in origin, but something much more like the case of center-embedded relatives. In other words, *wherever* we find marked incremental improvement along these lines – including phenomena long thought to be strictly structural – we have reason to doubt that the data in question really are ruled out by the grammar. For if that were the case, no manipulations which leave the offending structure intact should lead to any improvement, let alone a significant one. Conversely, the prediction is that if the CNPC effects are syntactic in origin – that is, if the grammar actually does not license sentences displaying these effects, due to the violations of a purely structural constraint they display – then what worked to improve center-embedded relatives should have no significant effect on the status of filler/gap constructions containing these violations.

So the evidence that Kluender offered in support of his claim that we see exactly such improvement is quite telling, particularly because the factors which lead to this improvement are *the very same ones* that yield the successful examples of center-embedding in cases such as (68). In particular, his data include examples such as (69)–(70):

(69) a.   John, I can't think of anyone [who likes __] >
     b.   John, I can't think of a random assortment of tradespeople [friends of whom] like __].

(70) a.   What do you need to find the professor who can translate?
     b.   < What do you need to find a professor who can translate?
     c.   < What do you need to find someone [who can understand __].
     d.   < Which article do you need to find someone [who can translate __?]
     e.   < Which article do you need to find someone [to translate __]?
            (Based on Kluender (1998): ex.(12))

In the case of (69), increasing the complexity of intervening NPs on the boundary of the lower clause (*anyone* → *a random assortment of tradespeople, whom* → *friends of whom*) leads to a distinct reduction in the status of a structure which is unproblematic in the first example. In (70), we see the opposite: starting from e, working our way back to a, a highly acceptable example of an extraction from a relative clause diminishes in status when the same lexical items occur in corresponding places but the relative clause is finite rather than infinitive. And the result gets still worse, when the filler is made less referentially specific, until we get to the barely comprehensible question in a.

We actually don't need to look very far to find perfectly well-formed sentences which flagrantly violate Ross' CNCP, and every subsequent reformulation of the CNCP in more abstract terms. So consider (71):

(71)   Euthanasia is a topic which$_2$ I can never find anyone who$_1$ I can argue with t$_1$ about t$_2$

This sentence is already good enough that most speakers regard it as quite acceptable. Removing either of the *wh*-words improves it even more, and removing both of them makes it still better. Finally, changing the 'definite' finite tense to the 'indefinite' infinitive yields the best case of all:

(72)   Euthanasia is a topic$_2$ I can never find anyone$_1$ to argue with t$_1$ about t$_2$.

Note that the 'base case' here in (71) is already acceptable to start with, an indication not only that the CNCP is empirically dubious to begin with, but also that the factors which ameliorate ill-formed cases have a positive effect on already good examples. Since in the latter situation there is nothing perceived to be wrong with the 'unimproved' example, the improvements added by the various techniques noted by Kluender – minimizing the informativeness of the intermediate NPs, maximizing the informativeness of the filler, eliminating the verbal analogue of nominal definiteness by using infinitive rather than finite tense/aspect marking – must have a strictly processing-based effect. It follows that the CNPC fits the profile not of a structural condition (blocking the licensing of word strings which violate that condition) but of a performance effect which inhibits the processing of a legal sentence (reducing its comprehensibility by interfering with the identification and retention of possible reference targets, and preventing the latter from surviving long enough in the processing task to be linked to the filler).

But the explanatory reach of these discoveries extends well beyond the CNPC and its latter-day reformulations. Let's reconsider the *wh*-island cases from earlier. For example, few would argue that (73) is an acceptable example:

(73)   Who did you wonder what Mary said to t ?

We modify the form of the example, without changing the structure, by replacing the finite with an infinitive form:

(74)   Who did you wonder what to say to t ?

This datum is indeed markedly better than (73). But we can make it better still, by 'beefing up' the content of the filler:

(75)   Which of the people at the party did you wonder what to say to t ?

Almost magically, the barely comprehensible (73) has been made not just comprehensible, but eminently acceptable. Still better examples can be constructed:

(76)   John is someone who$_2$ I never know what$_1$ to say t$_1$ to t$_2$.

Recall that the unified explanation for both the CNCP and the *wh*-island effect posited a necessary condition on movement of fillers whereby some constituent C can only be displaced to specific open positions on the left of the nearest clausal node, thereby blocking the possibility of extraction in cases where such a position (i) is not available, or (ii) is available but is already filled, leaving the only possible movement site for C too far away to be accessible. But given that we can find examples which are entirely acceptable but where the same 'offending' structures are involved, the whole somewhat baroque edifice of the purely syntactic constraint system which has emerged since Ross' thesis appeared seems increasingly dubious. Rather, the phenomena supposedly captured by these constraints are much better fits for a nonsyntactic description as performance effects. Under that view, the one supported by the kinds of data surveyed above, the nontrivial burden of keeping one or more fillers in memory long enough is defeated by competing demands on memory, attention, and similar aspects of psychological performance.

7.3.2   The Coordinate Structure Constraint Reexamined

Can we extend the kind of analysis for the CNPC/*wh*-island effects to the Coordinate Structure Constraint? The prospects are bleak: none of the issues that yield the predictively successful account of former classes of data hold for the CSC. There is no difference at all between the good and the bad cases of extraction from coordinate structures apart from the number of conjuncts the gap appears in. Consider, for example, our earlier datum *Who do you play cards with _ and go to night classes on alternate Thursdays?* There is no problem at all with *Who do you play cards with _ (every Thursday)?*, nor with *Do you go to night classes on alternate Thursdays?* What kind of processing effect would punish a filler/gap linkage into an otherwise legal clausal structure when the latter is conjoined with an equally legal nonextraction construction?

Framing things in this way is just the beginning, however. The probable nonexistence of a viable processing account of the CSC facts does not mean that the syntactic explanation is vindicated. It only means that nonprocessing explanations must now be considered. And the fact that such an account may well be preferable to a syntactic account along Ross' lines gets a major boost from the existence of coordinate structures, discovered in the mid-1980s, supporting extractions which fail to apply to all the conjuncts in a coordination. Consider, for example, the following cases:

(77) a.   This is the house that I plan to dress up as a water use inspector and break into t.

   b.   How many political debates can you listen to t and not become completely cynical?

   c.   This is the cereal that I plan to eat t for breakfast every morning and live to be 100.

These data were discovered in the mid-1980s (see Goldsmith 1985, Lakoff 1986), a long time before a coherent proposal appeared which made sense of why cases such as (49)b are ill-formed, but not (77). The proposal, offered by Andrew Kehler (2002), explains a number of surprising and seemingly counterintuitive patterns in the interaction of coordination and extraction.

Kehler's account starts by asking what the discourse effect of extraction is. Almost invariably, extraction has the effect of converting a constituent which is just another element in the clause into what we might informally call the topic of interest in the sentence. Hence, it is quite reasonable to take the extracted constituent to be, in some subtle and elusive sense, more prominent than other components of the clause.

Consider, for example, (77)a. The topic of the discourse is clearly *the house*. One could say, in place of this example, *Speaking of houses, I plan to dress up as a water use inspector and break into one*, where the locution *Speaking of X* serves to identify what it is that the speaker is isolating as that about which subsequent information will be supplied. The fact that *house* is fronted is, Kehler argues, doing the same work as *Speaking of...*, and one can see how both can be used in the same sentence, as in (78)a. But if one tries to apply the *Speaking of* test to one constituent and extraction to a different constituent, as in (78)b, the result is clearly anomalous.

(78) a.   Speaking of houses, this is the one that I plan to dress up as a water use inspector and break into t.

 b.   #Speaking of water use inspectors, this is the house that I plan to dress up as one and break into t.

The sentence in (78)a is fine, as predicted by Kehler's analysis of *Speaking of* and extraction as doing the same work. But for that same reason, (78)b is predicted – correctly – to be distinctly strange, even unacceptable, because the *Speaking of* test is identifying water use inspectors as the topic – that about which subsequent information will be supplied – whereas *houses* is identified as the topic by its role as filler of the gap. It thus makes sense to take extraction to have, as one of its pragmatic consequences, the role of identifying the discourse topic. If then in (77) *the house* is the discourse topic, linking this NP to a gap position is completely consonant with the sense of this sentence, in which the information in the first conjunct is clearly subordinate and secondary to that of the second conjunct. The coordination in effect establishes not just an order of events, but an order of importance: the first conjunct essentially tells us the 'how' of the action (at least in part), but the second tells us the 'what'. In a way, the sentence as a whole sketches a complex event in which we learn first the means, and then the goal. There is thus a significant asymmetry, in terms of what is contributed to the meaning, between the two conjuncts. And, crucially, this asymmetry is perfectly compatible with a syntactic structure whereby an NP from the second conjunct appears in a position where it will automatically be interpreted with the status of a discourse topic, since the discourse topic, the house, is what the goal (breaking into a house) is all about.

What about (77)b? Here, the meanings involved are seemingly quite different: the first identifies something like the cause of the event in the second. Cause and effect are quite different from means and ends, but again, there is a significant asymmetry between the two, one which we would expect to tolerate an operation on only one of the coordinated VPs, giving its meaning special prominence with respect to the other. We might also expect that an extraction from only the second clause, corresponding to the effect of the first, would be acceptable, as is indeed the case:

(79)   That's the guy that John went ballistic and got into a slugging match with t.

Such examples are acceptable, but seem a bit less natural than the cases where the gap is in the first VP. Here the kind of processing facts already discussed may play a role: we have to retain the filler *guy* in the place in our 'grammatical memory' for an extra length of time, and do not know until the very end what the connection is between the filler and the situation reported in the conjunct on the left.

The third example in (77) seems to correspond to something which has both means/end and cause/effect semantics. And again, an extraction from only one of the clauses is altogether unproblematic. The corresponding second-conjunct type of extraction, *One hundred years – that's the advanced age I plan to eat this cereal every morning and live to* t – again seems well-formed (though possibly slightly less felicitous than (77)c). These judgments are difficult to reconcile with the notion of the CSC as a hard restriction on possible syntactic structure, but makes perfect sense as the outcome of an interaction of discourse interpretation factors.

Why then are the examples in (56) bad when the relevant option is taken in each case to include the NP in the second conjunct? Consider the unextracted version of (56)d:

(80)   Most of us don't trust that guy and few of us like Terrence.

The relationship between the two clauses here is fundamentally different from any of those in (77). The two clauses can be reversed in order with no change in the sense of the sentence, unlike, for example, (77)a, where inverting the conjoined VPs changes not only the temporal order of the events depicted, but also their means/ends relationship: now the point of dressing up as a water use inspector is no longer the way to achieve the main objective (breaking into the house), but is itself the main objective, and breaking into the house is somehow a part of achieving that objective (perhaps a fake water use inspector uniform is available inside). Similar changes occur when the precedence relations between the coordinated constituents in the other sentences are changed. But nothing of the sort happens in (80). The relationship between the meanings of the two coordinated clauses is strictly parallel: neither has priority over the other, and the message makes sense only when understood as a presentation of attitudes that in some sense are mirror images of each other.

Given this parallelism, the effect of topicalizing a constituent from only one of the conjoined clauses will be intrinsically contradictory. The basis for what Kehler calls the *coherence* of sentences such as (80) is, as just observed, the juxtaposition of two situations which are presented as matching each other in crucial ways. For purposes of establishing such coherence it is essential that there be no asymmetry between the clauses. But since extraction establishes the topic status of the displaced element, the effect of fronting from only one of those conjuncts, but not the other, is to introduce a marked mismatch between the clauses: one of them is in effect what the whole coordination is about, and the other one is therefore necessarily secondary to that. The coherence of the sentence is there lost, because it is only by virtue of the parallelism that the two clauses have anything in particular to do with each other. Thus the conditions for a coherent interpretation and the effect of fronting from only one conjunct grind against each other, making it impossible for the speakers to know what to do with such sentences.

A strong prediction follows from this account: extraction should be possible if the parallelism between the two sentences can be maintained. But this will only be possible if the extraction favors neither conjunct in terms of some kind of central, favored or prominent status, such as supplying the information about the sentence topic. The only way that an extraction which elevates a constituent *C* to topichood (and thus identifies the clause from which *C* was extracted as the critical information carried by the sentence) is for the extraction to link *C* to *both* conjuncts (or, more generally, all of the conjuncts in a coordination based on parallelism). It follows that to maintain coherent interpretation, filler/gap relations into a coordinated structure with a parallel interpretation must apply across the board.

There is a corollary to this story: if a coordination imposes a parallel interpretation, non-ATB extraction will be blocked, but any nonstructural change which alters the interpretation possibilities so that a means/end, cause/effect or some similar nonsymmetrical interpretation is possible will allow the same structure to support non-ATB extraction. Thus, compare

(81) a.   I caught the bus last week and attended a lecture this morning.
     b.   ??*Which lecture did you catch the bus last week and attend t this morning?

with

(82) a.   I caught the bus and attended a lecture this morning.
     b.   Which lecture did you catch the bus and _ attend this morning?

The improvement from (81)b to (82)b is dramatic, to put it mildly. Yet the only change is the suppression of the first conjunct's temporal adjunct *last week*. By removing this adjunct, it becomes possible to plausibly construe the VP *catch the bus* as identifying an event which is something like the means to the end of attending the lecture, corresponding to the second conjunct VP. Without removing this adjunct, the split in timing between when the bus was caught and when the lecture was intended makes this construal prohibitively unlikely, in which case the only coherent interpretation is that *catch the bus* and *attend the lecture* are being presented as parallel activities.

A further prediction follows. Since what non-ATB extraction hinges on is (non)parallelism in the semantic relations between the coordinated constituents, rather than the particular meaning of the coordinating particle, we would expect to see the same correlation between parallel readings and ATB extraction, and between nonparallel readings/non-ATB extractions in the case of other conjunct particles that we've documented for *and*. In fact, both *or* and *but* display the same range of possibilities for symmetrical and asymmetrical interpretations as *and*, for example

(83) a.   John will go to Seattle this week or visit Chicago next week. (parallel/alternatives)

  b.   Chris will be polite to the guests or face a stern talking-to (non/parallel/cause-and-effect).

Just as with *and*, we find extraction from *or* coordinations ill-formed under a symmetrical reading:

(84)   ??*Which city will John go to Seattle this week or visit t next week?

And again, non-ATB extraction becomes completely acceptable when the intended reading is based on an asymmetrical semantic relationship between the conjuncts. Two nice examples from actual text are the following:

(85)   [He] regards the limitless abundance of language as its most important property, one that any theory of language must account for t or be discarded. (Campbell 1982: 183)

(86)   Penitence abroad is little worth. There where we live lie the temptations we must defeat t, or perish. (Reade 1869)

These examples are just as good as any of the similar cause/effect or means/end examples we've seen with *and*, and it is straightforward to construct others which are equally well-formed. And the same pattern holds for *but*:

(87) a.   ??*What did John have t for lunch but ate soup for dinner? [symmetric]
  b.   ??*Who did John vote for t but Mary voted for Obama? [symmetric]

(88) a.   Aspirin … THAT's what I went to the store but forgot to buy! [asymmetric]
  b.   There's is the medicine that John took but got sick ill anyway. [asymmetric]

The contrast here between the symmetric non-ATB extraction in (87) and the symmetric ones in (88) is again striking. Readers should have no trouble ascertaining for themselves that the relatively rarely used conjunct marker *yet* behaves in a fashion exactly parallel to *but* and the other coordination particles.

The generality of this effect across the quite restricted class of conjunct mark-ers has a very important implication for our assessment of Kehler's nonsyntactic analysis. A syntactic counteranalysis has been proposed in certain quarters, in which there are two *and* particles, one of which is the 'true' conjunction marker, reflecting the parallel/contrast relationship between conjuncts, and the means/end, filler/gap, setting/event etc. asymmetrical marker, which is not a true coordination marker and whose behavior cannot therefore refute the syntactic basis for the ATB requirement assumed in Ross' and later work in theoretical syntax. Certainly, if this pattern were restricted to *and*, this analysis might have some plausibility, based as it would be on a single lexical item, in spite of the fact that by the very nature of Kehler's hypothesis, the pattern in question shouldn't depend on particular lexical items but rather on the relationship between the two conjoined clauses themselves. Conversely, however, what we find is *exactly* the latter pattern, which, if it were a matter of lexical accident, would entail that all of the English conjunct particles quite coincidentally 'split' into two homophonous lexical items, one of which denotes a parallel relationship and the other of which denotes a nonparallel relationship. But there is no limit to the number of ways two coordinated constituents can relate to each other. Why would this same *specific* split occur repeatedly through the class of conjunct particles? The massive appeal to coincidence on which this counter-analysis rests is extremely suspect, and rules out the latter as an alternative to Kehler's analysis at the threshold.

We therefore have a solid basis for taking the CSC to reflect the interaction of the pragmatic effect of extraction with the nature of the meaning relations in terms of which speakers relate the propositions expressed by sentences to each other. This is, again, not a configurational story but a *functional* account, based not on phrase structure hierarchical relations but rather on how speakers make sense of sets of propositions. The content differs from the functional account Kluender gives for various island constraints, but what the two analyses have in common is that the syntactic realm plays a distinctly secondary part in these restrictions on the speaker's judgments. The contrast between the two cases should alert us, however, that different realms of phenomena outside the syntax proper may be responsible for different specific effects which give us the false impression that a failure of grammaticality is involved. This important lesson has considerable relevance for our understanding of the *that*-trace effect introduced in the preceding section.

7.3.3   Where Does the *That*-Trace Effect Come from?

If any apparently syntactic restriction seems a poor candidate for a semantic or pragmatic explanation, it has to be the *that*-trace effect. The difference between the respective contexts in which subject extraction is possible and in which it fails has essentially no impact on meaning: *I don't believe John ever mentioned that fact to me* and *I don't believe that John ever mentioned that fact to me* are true or false under exactly the same conditions, and there do not appear to be any conditions on discourse that are sensitive to the presence or absence of *that*, such that, for example, extracting the subject and making it a topic, along the lines of Kehler's explanation for the CSC, will predictably lead to an interpretive roadblock. Obviously, extraction of nonsubjects from clauses preceded by *that* and other complementizers is perfectly legal, and it's difficult to envision a purely interpretive problem which hinges on the subject/object distinction. *John is someone who I can't believe that Inspector Lewis would arrest* has exactly the same truth conditions as **Inspector Lewis is someone who I can't believe that _ would arrest John*, but the difference is severe, and representative. And while there is a good deal of evidence, much of it due to subsequent work by Kluender, that subjects represent difficult domains from within which to extract material, there is no reason at all to believe that extraction *of* entire subjects themselves is a processing liability. The free extractability of subjects which are not in post-complementizer position is as convincing on this point as possible.

It is of course conceivable that some kind of processing difficulty arises as a result of the intervening *that* preceding a gap site, making it difficult to identify the point in the structure to which the filler in *that*-t violations must be linked. One might envision a scenario in which the presence of material between the higher selecting verb and the gap position of the selected clause conceals the latter from the processing routine seeking a position into which the filler can be interpreted. But this seems unlikely too, given the fact that data such as *Which person did you learn only* YESTERDAY *would be offered the job?* seem reasonably good, with appropriate intonation. Certainly nothing like the *that*-t effect is evident here. And, in contrast to the case of the CNPC and *wh*-island phenomena, there seems no psycholinguistic evidence favoring a processing account of the *that*-t effect. For decades, then, some syntactic account of this particular phenomenon seemed unavoidable. And the fact that the syntactic explanation sketched above – which emerged in the early 1980s under the label 'Empty Category Principle' (ECP) – became integral to many analyses of quite unrelated phenomena was a further incentive for theorists to avoid looking at it in any other terms.

It was therefore a bit of a shock for theorists to be reminded, in the mid-1980s, of a discovery a decade earlier by Joan Bresnan, who had first reported the *that*-t effect facts, of a set of conditions under which the effect disappears completely. Bresnan had offered the following data:

(89) a.   Who did she say that tomorrow would regret his words?
     b.   . . . an amendment which they say that tomorrow will be law.
     c.   Which doctor did you tell me that during an operation had had a heart attack?
            (Bresnan 1977: 194)

At the time, the *that*-t effect was something of a curiosity, without any theoretical gravitas; the ECP umbrella over a wide range of syntactic phenomena was years away. So Bresnan's examples didn't make much of an impact when they first appeared. But over time, they began to percolate into the active literature on extraction, until they became impossible to ignore.

The first responses to the kind of data Bresnan reported attempted to reconcile the facts with the ECP account, but these efforts were rather contrived and stipulative, and there was increasing skepticism about this direction of analysis. One basis for this skepticism was the range of somewhat tortured accounts of the smooth movement of unselected adverbs through the bottleneck of complementized clauses that was impassible for the unselected subjects. The empirical basis for these accounts was minimal, and an interest in alternative approaches which didn't implicate adjunct extraction in any way emerged and grew in the first decades of the twenty-first century. And the principal thrust of these alternative approaches was that the explanation for the *that*-t effect is evidence of a certain set of *phonological* facts.

A recent paper by Jason Kandybowicz (2006) is a good example. Kandybowicz points out a number of constructions, in addition to those noted by Bresnan, which seem to at least ameliorate the severity of the effect, in certain cases quite markedly, and several other subtle aspects of the effect which point to a solution in terms of intonation properties in the relevant data. His account can be roughly summarized as follows: complementizers and traces cannot be next to each other within a single unit of intonation, as the latter are understood in phonological theory, when the complementizer begins that intonational unit. A certain separation is necessary, and this separation can be achieved in various ways, each of which contributes to the reduction of the *that*-t effect's severity. (It is very tempting to speculate that there is a linkage between this proposal and the general approach taken by Kluender and those pursuing his research paradigm in terms of processing bottlenecks at the edges of clauses which can be ameliorated in various ways, and to see the source of the *that*-t problem as a difficulty that the close linkage of the complementizer and trace poses for recognition of the trace *as* a gap site. It seems likely that not only the kinds of factors noted by Kluender, but also various others are implicated in these effects. Matters of prosody, for example, almost certainly play a role in expediting or inhibiting the processing mechanism's efforts to connect the filler to a site within the structure where it can receive a coherent interpretation. And further work along the lines sketched here ultimately will surely lead to a far more general theory of filler/gap processing in which morphological, semantic, pragmatic, and prosodic factors play significant roles.)

A natural first reaction to the prosodic treatment of the *that*-t effect is that the decisive judgments of ill-formedness which speakers almost universally render on examples without any of the ameliorating properties surely cannot be just the result of 'sounding wrong,' which is what a phonological account might (mistakenly) be assumed to consist of. But there are precedents for just such a prosodic explanation masquerading as a syntactic effect. For a long time, the following kinds of data were taken to reflect a syntactic fact about the 'second object' position associated with verbs such as *tell*, *give*, and *show*, which take two NP complements. The second of these NPs cannot be a weak (i.e., necessarily unstressed) pronoun:

(90) a.   I told John the facts.

b.   *I told $\left\{ \begin{array}{c} \text{John} \\ \text{her} \end{array} \right\}$ them.

It has been assumed, in much literature over the forty years, that this pattern reflects a lexical property of such verbs ruling out pronouns from the second NP position, and some fairly intricate arguments have attempted to use this supposed fact about such verbs to construct claims about the nature of filler/gap dependencies. But in the mid-1980s, an unpublished paper by Arnold Zwicky circulated which demonstrated that the effect in (90) had a far simpler basis. As it happens, a number of other phenomena display patterns similar to the 'double object' construction exhibited in (90). What they all have in common are morphosyntactic properties that prevent the unstressed pronoun from attaching itself phonologically to a preceding or following lexical item. They must therefore stand on their own as independent intonational units. But such units necessarily contain a major stress. Since the second NP in double object constructions has the status of an intonational phrase, it follows that in the normal course of things, weak indefinite pronouns – so called because they cannot receive normal intonational stress – will not appear in this second object position.

Zwicky's solution is completely consonant with standard views of intonational phrasing, and eliminates what otherwise would be a very eccentric stipulative lexical restriction on a particular class of verbs. In purely scientific terms, it makes the most sense of any proposal about these strange cases. But the kinds of negative judgment this prosodic violation induces is much more like what one expects from syntactic ungrammaticality – illustrating the fact that a phonological source can have an effect indistinguishable from a syntactic failure.

A similar prosodic restriction is very likely the source of the constraint against extraction of one or more whole conjuncts discussed in connection with the CSC. Consider the following data:

(91) a.   I don't know where John, is, but I'm waiting $\left\{ \begin{array}{c} \text{for him} \\ \text{for'm} \end{array} \right\}$

b.   I don't want to hear John griping about my cooking $\left\{ \begin{array}{c} \text{or him} \\ \text{or'm} \end{array} \right\}$ pointing out to anyone who will listen that he'd really like to go out to dinner tonight.

These are examples of a familiar prosodic reduction of the pronoun *him*, attaching the final nasal residue of the reduction to the preceding word – in the cases in (91), the preposition *for* and conjunct particle *or* – to a single syllabic nasal, whose syllabicity is itself reducible almost to the point of disappearing. Both the full and the reduced form of *him* appear in the above examples, and readers should note that there is no problem with the reduced pronoun in (91)b. But the case of (7) is different:

(92)   I don't know what happened to John, but it's been years since I heard from
Mary $\left\{ \begin{array}{l} \text{or him} \\ \text{*or'm} \end{array} \right\}$

What's the difference? The simplest, most likely account of what's wrong with
the phonology in (92) is that each conjunct or disjunct in a coordination must
contain at least one stressed syllable. This generalization appears to hold over a
very wide range of cases. But if so, then nothing more need be said to rule out
extraction – either asymmetric or ATB – of whole conjuncts from coordination.
Extraction is prosodically realized as silence, and that entails, of course, that
there is nothing to bear stress. Hence, cases such as (51) follow directly, without
anything further needing to be said.

We are now in a better position to understand the difference between (14)
and (15) which constitutes the one substantial argument on behalf of the
relative pronoun *that* analysis we considered above. If the kind of evidence
that Kandybowicz offers for what used to be called ECP effects is sound, the
contrast between these two kinds of data reflects not a structural distinction but
a prosodic one. Kandybowicz's own explanation involves a number of technical
points about both syntactic structure and the relationship between this structure
and the phonological constituency which we cannot explore, but the gist of his
analysis is that an empty category may not appear on the left edge of a syntactic
constituent which corresponds to a phonological phrase.

In the African language Nupe, whose relative clauses behave in ways quite
parallel to those in English, clausal complementizers also block extractions
as in the ECP data displayed above, but there is a dedicated relative clause
complementizer which can appear in directly before a VP just as English *that*
can in (14). Kandybowicz demonstrates that this apparent exemption from
ECP effects is predicted on his account, because in Nupe, the relative clause
complementizer is *part of* the relevant phonological phrase that corresponds
to the syntactic clause from which the subject has been extracted. The subject
gap in the relative clause is not on the left edge of that phrase; instead, the
phonology of the relative complementizer begins that phrase, and the gap follows
it. Hence there is no 'missing' phonological material on the left edge of the
crucial phonological phrase, and the latter is well-formed. If something similar
were true in the case of English relative clauses, but not *that* complements, we
would get the discrepancy between the two that is at issue.

One highly suggestive fact which supports such a parallel analysis for English
is that both relative clause and the finite declarative complementizer with an in
situ subject are pronounced in normal-paced speech with a markedly reduced
vowel: [ðət] rather than [ðæt], suggesting that these markers have cliticized to
the following word, that is, have been integrated into the phonological phrase
corresponding to the clauses they mark.

(93) a.   Rocco's the guy that [ðət] was here yesterday evening.

     b.   I think [ðət] Rocco needs to get his story straight.

But when speakers attempt to pronounce sentences in which a subject gap in a clausal complement follows *that*, the pronunciation of the complementizer is typically the full [ðæt] form:

(94)   *Who do you think [ðæt] likes pizza?

The contrast indicates that the marker has failed to cliticize – that is, to attach itself, as a kind of prosodic dependent – to *likes*, and so remains outside the prosodic phrase – whose leftmost element will therefore be the phonologically null gap position, and hence ruled out.

Clearly, much more work is needed to explore this line of research, but it appears to be a very promising route to a full account of ECP effects cross-linguistically. On balance, it seems fair to say that the number of contraindications to the relative pronoun *that* hypothesis, combined with the success of the *that*-as-marker counteranalysis, gives the latter a decisive edge as a treatment of relative clauses. Beyond this conclusion, it is also a very effective illustration of how identifying the nonsyntactic origins of many phenomena previously assumed without question to reflect constraints on syntactic form makes it possible for us to find simpler analyses for a wide range of phenomena whose prior analysis depended, explicitly or implicitly, on assumptions involving the role of such constraints.

7.4   Conclusion: The Limits of Syntactic Explanation

Scholars who have spent any time investigating the history of modern linguistics are likely to come to the conclusion that social factors – in particular, what we might call wars of ideas – have played at least as much of a role in the direction taken by research in the field as an idealized disinterested curiosity. Human languages are unlike any other animal communication system, and seem to have a deeply intimate – if somewhat elusive – relationship to our ability to think, reason, and grasp a unitary picture of the world. Hence it is not surprising that language has been one of the main arenas in which different views of human nature and the mind have engaged in often ferocious intellectual combat, for what are arguably among the highest stakes imaginable: our own sense of our place in nature, and our relationship both to other animal species and to our information-processing creations, which in certain problem-solving domains, such as mastery of chess and other closed rule systems, have already surpassed our own abilities.

Contemporary linguistics benefited greatly from its emergence at a period when a certain view of psychology was dominant which the data of natural language could challenge very effectively. The behaviorist era, one of many expressions of positivist thinking that became increasingly influential during the 1930s, took the mind to be a learning device that in essence paired external stimuli – observable features of the environment that human senses are attuned to recognize – with certain behaviors that yielded positive outcomes as responses to those stimuli. Thoughts, as the internal cognitive states imagined in a naive 'common sense' kind of view, did not really exist in this positivist psychology; rather, thoughts were regarded as a sort of mental sensation accompanying stimulus/response habits. It follows from this general way of viewing the mind that essentially *any* behavior that is rewarded sufficiently will become established as normal, expected, and eventually unquestioned. After-the-fact psychological and emotional states are the organism's way of ensuring that positively reinforced behavior becomes automatic and something close to instinctive, but themselves have no causal independence so far as what individuals actually do. The picture which emerges is one of human beings as arbitrarily programmable automata, blank slates on which experience has inscribed certain patterns of action (and, secondarily, of thinking) in the face of various challenges and possibilities.

Cracks in this tidy picture began to appear with the work of the behavioral psychologist Karl Lashley, who showed that much of human thought and behavior is not a response to immediate events, but rather represents complex stored sequences of what can only be thought of as internal instructions, often representing strategies based on quite abstract pattern recognition that could not be directly inferred from what was actually present in the environment. The impact of Lashley's findings and those of the new generation of cognitive psychologists who followed him and greatly expanded the research program he initiated was dramatic, and created an intellectual opening for approaches to language that rejected the confines of behaviorist psychology. Early work in generative grammar could point to a wealth of interconnected facts that made the positivist view of the mind as a set of circumstantially advantageous conditioned reflexes extremely difficult to defend. Compare, for example, *There tended to continue to appear to be financial irregularities in the reports* vs *There tended to try to appear to be financial irregularities in the reports*. Facts of this sort could not in any remotely plausible way come from experience with the word strings in question, given that speakers need to be able to link dummy *there* to the SPR position of all of the verbs in the lower VPs connecting the matrix subject with *be*. And what kind of simple behavioral model could account for the fact that, if you know that *John knew that Mary was a spy* is true, you automatically know that *It was known by John that Mary was a spy* is a good sentence and that it means exactly the same thing? Knowledge of such relationships are difficult or impossible to reduce to stimulus/response arcs.

The progress of linguistic research in the early phase of modern linguistics revealed the existence of a vast web of such internal representations, representations which, moreover, implicated items to which a speaker had not been previously exposed, but on the basis of whose distribution in one context (taking a clausal complement *that* + S) a native speaker of English would immediately infer a form exactly corresponding to *It appears to have been known that* + S. The productivity of this cognitive system fell completely outside the predictive horizon of behaviorist psychology and helped discredit the latter as an even approximate theory of normal human psychological operation.

But by far the most effective of such weapons in the grammatical theorists' arguments against the simplistic behaviorist model of the mind was the nature of the constraints which supposedly regulated the linkage between fillers and gaps. The various developments of the notion of Subjacency intended to subsume both the CNPC and *wh*-island effects, or the characterization of the privileged configuration instantiated in (i) lexical selection of sisters, (ii) indirect 'government' of the daughter *C* of a sister with no barrier node separating the selecting head and *C*, and (iii) the relationship between linked traces in a chain of movement traces left behind by a constituent extracted in stages from an embedded position to the top of some tree. The very abstract structural relationships under which all of these different configurations become unitary would be virtually impossible to induce from any kind of simple stimulus/response model of learning. Such phenomena themselves represented a dazzlingly scaled-up version of the kind of evidence Lashly presented to argue that such models could not possibly capture human cognitive abilities, but rather that some kind of 'stored program' model had to be invoked to account for, in this case, speakers' virtually instantaneous sense that strings of words which contain violations of such island conditions do not constitute sentences of the language. Island effects, and the progressively more abstract accounts of them developed during the three decades after Ross' dissertation brought those effects to the attention of theorists, therefore became – along with a handful of similarly high-level structural conditions on what other parts of a sentence NPs can refer to – a touchstone in a war of ideas that has been, in some respects, constantly in the background of modern grammatical theory.

The impact of Kluender's work becomes evident in this connection when we consider the role that constraints on extraction played in various arguments theorists offered against the possibility of inducing such constraints from communicative functions or nongrammatical aspects of language use. Take as an example the following argument by the syntactician and historian of linguistics Frederick Newmeyer, who, after citing a number of Swedish sentences which legally violate the CNPC, comments that:

> [g]iven the assumption that Swedish speakers do not differ from speakers of English in their intrinsic capabilities to process discourse, one must wonder how contentful the claim is that the Complex Noun Phrase Constraint reflects (or is an artifact of) its discourse function to facilitate comprehension. It is quite clear that English and Swedish speakers learn different structural possibilities, which only indirectly reflect their discourse functions.   (1983: 106)

Newmeyer's discussion here and throughout his book is eminently reasonable, based on the understanding of the facts at the time. The crucial problem for such arguments, however, was the degree to which they underestimated the degree to which effects of the kind Newmeyer alludes to might not have a basis in either behaviorist-style conditioning *or* formal properties of some kind of genetically based 'stored program' reflecting linguistic knowledge. The impact of Kluender's findings in terms of this false dichotomy are spelled out in one of his seminal papers:

> apparent crosslinguistic differences have turned out to be not so different after all. There were several proposals in the 1970s and early 1980s on the basis of *wh*-island and complex NP island phenomena in Italian ... and the Scandinavian languages ... claiming that Subjacency must be defined differently in these languages. However, it has since been shown that English exhibits the same range of exceptions ... Moreover, Saah and Goodluck (1995) have demonstrated that even in a language which allows extraction from island contexts (Akan, a Kwa language spoken in Ghana), speakers will reject them for reasons of processing difficulty.   (Kluender 1998: 268)

The effect here is fairly devastating. It turns out that English and Swedish differ very little on the key point: the same kinds of violations of the CNPC occur in English and in Swedish, and in both languages, processing factors play a major role in determining what 'violations' will and will not be accepted among native speakers – and, critically, the ameliorating factors, as noted above, are precisely those which reduce the severity of the acknowledged processing failures accompanying center embedding. For this reason, it seems quite possible that the kind of results that Kluender and other psycholinguists have obtained is still unwelcome in certain quarters: the better established such results become, the weaker the argument that the abstractness and detachment from any functional basis of extraction constraints supports the separate, encapsulated module of dedicated linguistic knowledge that theorists have long sought to establish. But there is I believe a quite different view that can and should be held in this domain of research.

Suppose that as theorists gain greater knowledge of the specific psycholinguistic mechanisms that are in play during ordinary linguistic activity, facts from a variety of different extra-syntactic domains will come to be seen as playing the critical role in what have previously been taken to be syntactic phenomena. This trend, if it continues to unfold along the lines illustrated in this chapter, will in no way diminish the central claims of syntax to its place as the specification of sentence structure in human languages. On the contrary, by purging the data that syntax is responsible for of interference effects due to 'noise' from processing and performance issues, grammarians will have a much better chance of discovering a parsimonious, formally satisfying characterization of the 'modular' properties of our syntactic knowledge. Discovery of the system of constraints which cannot be attributed to functional factors will give us a much clearer window into the operations that must be in effect 'simulated' by real-time mental processes. A similar division of labor emerges as a conclusion in the work of the psychophysicist David Marr, who provided a mathematical characterization of the calculations somehow neurophysiologically embodied in the human visual system, yielding the information required by visual systems to deduce structures mirroring the properties of objects in the world. Marr's work in the 1970s and early 1980s revealed the kind of computations which the neural apparatus of the human visual system had to carry out on the primary data – levels of stimulation of light falling on the retina – received and operated on by that system. But it also made clear that those operations could not be directly modeled by any finite physiological apparatus, even in principle. The goal for vision research, as Marr defined it in his groundbreaking work, had to be the identification of complex routines built into the nervous system that *simulated* the calculations he and his associates had shown to be the right ones to yield the data structures whose expression in sensory form we call vision. Something very much like this relationship between the form of linguistic theory and the psychophysical architecture of the mind/brain seems to be emerging from the research on island effects reviewed in this chapter.

At present, it's an open and entirely empirical question as to what degree the neural architectures supporting linguistic knowledge and use are dedicated exclusively to language. But it seems indisputable that neither this question nor any of the others suggested by the preceding discussion will be successfully addressed until the irreducible core of our syntactic knowledge has been teased apart from the effect of other systems with which it interacts. Work in this direction, far from threatening to assimilate syntax to usage, contributes substantially to the identification of what is uniquely syntactic about human languages – and syntacticians, who overwhelmingly regard themselves as scientists, should welcome that outcome, whatever form it takes.

So it is, I think, appropriate to conclude this presentation of the tools of syntax, and the thinking behind their application, with a recognition that syntax itself has explanatory limits in characterizing the sentences that speakers accept as well-formed. Those limits are the complement to the insights that a restricted toolkit comprising formally well-defined concepts and precise definitions can yield over domains in which semantics, pragmatics, phonology, and psycholinguistics fail to capture the dependencies that we find in natural languages. Whether a given phenomenon belongs to one or the other domain of data is, again, an empirical question, and often the best approach is to pursue multiple lines of explanation at once. But when we find that our purely syntactic accounts are becoming convoluted and cumbersome, or require us to invoke only vaguely specified concepts and indulge in what is often called handwaving, then the time has probably come to recognize that the game isn't worth the candle, and to seek a solution in the interface between syntax and the many other domains which jointly enter into our judgment about whether a string of words is in fact a sentence of our language.

Suggestions for Further Reading

There is a vast literature on all of the topics discussed in the past seven chapters, much of it demanding a deeper technical background than I'm assuming for people using this textbook. The following sources should, however, be largely accessible to readers who've worked their way through all of the preceding material. The bibliographies of these sources will then offer further routes to still more advanced material. Full bibliographic details on all of these suggested readings are included in the list of references at the end of this volume.

Chapter 1

The material covered in the first chapter, which is intended to assist the reader in developing a sense of the critical patterns in data from the point of view of syntacticians, is more or less standard in syntax textbooks; a particularly nice example is Robert Borsley's *Syntactic Theory* (1993). But probably the most comprehensive explanation of what syntacticians are really after, and how they structure their inquiries to lead to the kind of elegant, far-reaching generalizations that constitute the Holy Grail of linguistics, is to be found in Andrew Radford's *Transformational Grammar: A First Course* (1988).

Chapter 2

The primary technical tools in this chapter are the decomposition of category labels into highly structured complex symbols utilizing feature names and values supplied for those names, and statements of constraints, using the format of context-free phrase structure rules, on the form of possible two-generation trees in terms of feature identities which must be satisfied in order for a given tree to be legal.

The treatment of categories as complex symbols was first introduced into theoretical discourse very early in an important but generally neglected paper by Gilbert Harman (1963), which provoked a rather hostile response by Chomsky (1964), who subsequently reintroduced the use of features without reference to Harman's prior work, first at the level of lexical categories (1965) and subsequently at the phrasal level (Chomsky 1970: 207–208), where the resistance to such treatment is attributed to the American structuralists of the 1940s and 1950s – despite the fact that the decomposition of phrasal categories into a category type and level of phrasal complexity, which anticipated Chomsky's own use of complex symbols in his 1970 paper, was first proposed by just such an American structuralist, Zelig Harris, in work published in the 1940s and early 1950s. Modern theoretical investigations of the formal status and empirical basis for the use of features include work by Steven Lapointe (1980), Granville Corbett (1981) and chapter 2 of the watershed monograph *Generalized Phrase Structure Grammar* by Gerald Gazdar, Ewan Klein, Geoffrey K. Pullum, and Ivan Sag (1985). An excellent summary of the state of the art in this domain is available at the Surrey Features Project www.surrey.ac.uk/LIS/SMG/morphosyntacticfeatures.html

The analysis of context-free rules in this chapter, and their suitability as a licensing device for constituency in natural language grammars, closely follows the analysis presented in Pullum (1982b) with much of the latter incorporated in Gazdar et al. (1985). Context-free PS rules are treated in a straightforward and fairly accessible way in Hopcroft and Ullman (1979), but probably will provide the reader interested in syntactic applications of computational rule formalisms with much more information than they want to know. A major discovery in the 1980s, by Stuart Shieber, was the existence of a language whose grammars require rules of mildly greater expressive power than context-free rules make available; see Shieber (1985) for the evidence and relevant analysis.

For the refinements of treatment of constituency in linguistic categories, particularly in NPs, Radford (1988) is once again invaluable.

Chapter 3

In the first era of modern linguistic theory, all auxiliaries were treated as *sui generis* objects unrelated to the class of lexical items introduced via the category V. *Can, should, will,* and so on were taken by Chomsky (1957) to be instances of a category Modal, while *have* and *be* weren't assigned a syntactic type at all, but were introduced syncategorematically – without benefit of a category label, that is – in the phrase structure rules for English VPs, with the auxiliary *do*, moreover, not even a full-fledged member of the English lexicon, but only brought into existence by a tranformational rule whose efficacy itself depends on a somewhat artificial use of diacritic notation. This treatment and its successors over the next decade – which missed significant generalizations, and made severe mispredictions – was first challenged in work by John R. Ross (1969). Chomsky (1972) dismissed this treatment as simply a revision of notation, but as noted by Huddleston (1974), the difference between Ross' proposal and the analysis of auxiliaries in *Syntactic Structures* is anything but notational; of Ross' original ten arguments for taking auxiliaries to be verbs selecting various VP complements, eight substantive challenges to Chomsky's 1957 analysis were completely unaffected by the reinterpretation of notation that Chomsky took to be the whole story of his 1972 paper. Huddleston adds further, quite persuasive evidence to Ross' reanalysis (some of which is cited in Chapter 3), and virtually all subsequent work outside of the transformationalist camp has followed the 'main verb' approach to auxiliaries. Perhaps the most comprehensive development of this analysis is to be found by Gazdar et al. (1982), whose basic ideas were carried over by Gazdar et al. in 1985, on which much of the analysis given in the text is based, and preserved largely unchanged by Pollard and Sag (1994). A particularly insightful critique of the way auxiliaries and other grammatical phenomena are treated in *Syntactic Structures*, from the technical perspective (but with important empirical fallout noted), is given by Pullum (2011).

Perhaps the most contentious issue in the material covered in Chapter 3 is the status of infinitival *to* as a morphologically defective member of the class of auxiliaries. A set of persuasive arguments to this effect are given by Pullum (1982a), whose conclusions are, however, vigorously opposed by Huddleston (2002), where an analysis of *to* as an infinitival marker is defended. Huddleston's arguments are themselves challenged by Levine (2012) on the basis of several of the arguments given in Chapter 3.

Chapter 4

The material in this chapter can be broadly characterized under the heading 'local dependencies,' and the main point of the chapter is that almost all of the dependencies discussed can be elegantly captured by valence specification on the relevant (class of) lexical heads. Agreement is the main exception, and presents an extremely varied and complex set of conditions which typically coexist in a single language. A number of arguments about agreement given in this chapter are due to Kathol (1999), whose importance would be difficult to overstate. The data on the Icelandic case come from Andrews (1982); an interesting take on the full case system, including some quite problematic-seeming patterns which are not discussed in Chapter 4, is given by Sag et al. (1992), and a somewhat different view by Bouma (1992). Work on the passive construction has been continuous since Chomsky's original discussion (1957); the earliest treatment in the context of an articulated modern theory of phrase structure is chapter 4 of Gazdar et al. (1985). Subsequent approaches in the same modern phrase structure traditions have in effect replicated the content of this analysis, though the formal objects that are systematically related to each other, as in the form of the lexical rule given here, roughly following Pollard and Sag (1987), are quite different.

The data from Chukchee are taken from Palmer (1994), who in turn cites them from Kozinsky et al. (1988).

What I've referred to as 'super-raising' – the selection of a lexical complement by some head, with all of the latter's valence specifications appearing as arguments of that head – reflects an analysis first worked out for German by

Erhard Hinrichs and Tsuneko Nakezawa (1989). Their analysis not only solved a number of perplexing problems involving the behavior of a certain class of verbs in German, but proved to be the key to understanding clause structure in many other languages, as noted in Chapter 4. The analysis for French given above is a simplified presentation of a much fuller analysis given by Abeillé and Godard (2002).

Chapter 5

In an earlier phase of grammatical theorizing, infinitival complements were taken to be derived from the same sources as finite complements, an approach that has persisted, if somewhat less directly, in more recent analyses. But in the late 1970s, a number of influential theorists began to see infinitival VPs as *sui generis* constructions, reflecting the combination of nonfinite forms of verbs directly with their complements, rather than the result of operations deriving them by a series of complex steps from full clauses. The implications of this reassessment, as noted by Brame (1976), turn out to entail nontransformational sources for all local dependencies: passive, extraposition, raising, and so on. Brame's proposals heralded a major break in the syntax research community between proponents of movement-based accounts and so-called 'monostratal' frameworks which now seems to be a permanent fixture of the field. The approach pursued in this chapter is based on Pollard and Sag (1991) and chapters 3 and 7 of Pollard and Sag (1994).

Chapter 6

For decades, nonlocal dependencies, in particular displacement, were taken to offer definitive proof that no system equivalent in expressive power to grammars defined by context-free rule systems could possibly offer an adequate account of natural language; a particularly clear example of the argumentation involved is available by Baker (1978). But in 1981, Gerald Gazdar (1981), in what could plausibly be argued to be the single most important paper on the syntax of extraction, demonstrated that arbitrarily deep linkages of fillers and corresponding gap sites can be established without using rule systems that transcend the power of context-free rules, and further, the possibility of linking a single filler to multiple gap sites – as well as the putative fact, universally accepted at that time, that extractions from coordinated phrases were syntactically constrained and apply 'across the board' as per Ross' Coordinate Structure Constraint – followed directly, without any additional machinery or stipulation, from his phrase-structure-theoretic formulation of displacement. Later versions of Generalized Phrase Structure Grammar, the framework which Gazdar and his associates were developing at the time, refined the mechanism of the 1981 paper by reinterpreting his solution as the propagation of a feature SLASH, which was incorporated into HPSG, as in chapter 4 of Pollard and Sag (1994), borrowing heavily from the system outlined in its theoretical ancestor Gazdar et al. (1985). The treatment of all displacement connectivity effects as manifestations of a single mechanism has been challenged at various times, even, to a small degree, in Pollard and Sag's assumption that the syntactic type of the gap in *tough*, *too/enough*, and related constructions is pronominal, as opposed to the status of gaps in topicalization and *wh*-extractions; this general position is examined at length by Levine and Hukari (2006) and found to lack sufficient support to lend it credibility as an alternative to the hypothesis of a uniform connectivity mechanism.

A further perspective on the French inversion data and its analytic consequences is developed by Bonami et al. (1999), and a detailed examination of the fit between the Irish complementizer data and the overall architecture of the framework for analyzing displacement developed in this chapter is given by Bouma et al. (2001).

Chapter 7

The literature on various kinds of 'unbounded connectivity' constructions runs to thousands of articles, book chapters, and monographs. In the aftermath of Ross' dissertation, theorists advanced a succession of progressively more abstract characterizations of the syntactic conditions on filler/gap linkages, a number of which can be fairly described as Byzantine in their complexity. The challenges by Kluender (1998), Kehler (2002), Kandybowicz (2006), and Kandybowicz (2009) strongly suggest that these efforts to capture extraction 'island effects' were fundamentally misguided, and additional corroboration for this position can be found in several important follow-up studies, for example, further support for Klueder's position is given by Hofmeister and Sag (2010), Hofmeister et al. (2013b), Hofmeister et al. (2013a), Hofmeister et al. (in press), and Chaves (2013), while Kehler's analysis of the Coordinate Structure Constraint receives both strong cross-linguistic and strong cross-constructional support from Kubota and Lee (2015).

References

Abeillé, Anne, and Danièle Godard. 2002. The syntactic structure of French auxiliaries. *Language* 78: 404–452.

American Heritage Dictionary, The. 2000. 4th edn. Boston, MA: Houghton Mifflin Harcourt.

Andrews, Avery. 1982. Case in modern Icelandic. In *The Mental Representation of Grammatical Relations*, ed. Joan Bresnan, pp. 427–503. Cambridge, MA: MIT Press.

Baker, C.L. 1978. *Introduction to Generative-Transformational Grammar*. New York: Prentice-Hall.

Bonami, Olivier, Danièle Godard, and Jean-Marie Marandin. 1999. Constituency and word order in French subject inversion. In *Constraints and Resources in Natural Language Syntax and Semantics*, ed. Gosse Bouma, Erhard Hinrichs, Geert-Jan M. Kruift, and Richard Oehrle, pp. 21–40. Stanford, CA: CSLI.

Borsley, Robert. 1992. More on the difference between English restrictive and non-restrictive relative clauses. *Journal of Linguistics* 28: 139–148.

1993. *Syntactic Theory: A Unified Approach*. London and New York: Edward Arnold.

2010. An HPSG approach to Welsh unbounded dependencies. In *Proceedings of the Seventeenth Conference on HPSG*, ed. Stefan Müller, pp. 80–100. Stanford, CA: CSLI.

Bouma, Gosse. 1992. A lexicalist account of Icelandic Case Marking. In *Proceedings of CoLing-92*, pp. 94–100. University of Nantes.

Bouma, Gosse, Rob Malouf, and Ivan Sag. 2001. Satisfying constraints on extraction and adjunction. *Natural Language and Linguistic Theory* 19: 1–65.

Brame, Michael. 1976. *Conjectures and Refutations in Syntax and Semantics*. New York: North-Holland.

Bresnan, Joan. 1977. Variables in the theory of transformations. In *Formal Syntax*, ed. Peter W. Culicover, Thomas Wasow, and Adrian Akmajian, pp. 157–196. New York: Academic Press.

Campbell, Jeremy. 1982. *Grammatical Man*. New York: Simon & Schuster.

Chaves, Rui. 2013. An expectation-based account of subject islands and parasitism. *Journal of Linguistics* 49: 285–327.

Chomsky, Noam. 1957. *Syntactic Structures*. The Hague: Mouton.

1964. *Current Issues in Linguistic Theory*. The Hague: Mouton.

1965. *Aspects of the Theory of Syntax*. Cambridge, MA: MIT Press.

1970. Remarks on nominalizations. In *Readings in English Transformational Grammar*, ed. Roderick Jacobs and Peter Rosenbaum, pp. 184–221. Waltham, MA: Ginn.

1972. Some empirical issues in the theory of transformational grammar. In *Goals of Linguistic Theory*, ed. Stanley Peters, pp. 63–130. Englewood Cliffs, NJ: Prentice Hall.

1977. On *Wh*–Movement. In *Formal Syntax*, ed. Peter Culicover, Thomas Wasow, and Adrian Akmajian, pp. 71–132. New York: Academic Press.

Corbett, Granville. 1981. Syntactic features. *Journal of Linguistics* 17: 55–76.

Delahunty, Gerald P. 1983. But sentential subjects do exist. *Linguistic Analysis* 12: 379–398.

Diesing, Molly. 1990. Verb movement and subject position in Yiddish. *Natural Language and Linguistic Theory* 8: 41–79.

Gazdar, Gerald. 1981. Unbounded dependencies and coordinate structure. *Linguistic Inquiry* 12: 155–184.

Gazdar, Gerald, Geoffrey Pullum, and Ivan Sag. 1982. Auxiliaries and related phenomena in a restrictive theory of grammar. *Language* 58: 591–638.

Gazdar, Gerald, Ewan Klein, Geoffrey K. Pullum, and Ivan Sag. 1985. *Generalized Phrase Structure Grammar*. Cambridge, MA: Harvard University Press.

Ginzburg, Jonathon, and Ivan Sag. 2000. *Interrogative Investigations: The Form, Meaning and Use of English Interrogatives*. Stanford, CA: Center for the Study of Language and Information.

Goldsmith, Jon. 1985. A principled exception to the Coordinate Structure Constraint. In *Proceedings of the Chicago Linguistic Society 21*, ed. Paul D. Kroeber, William H. Eilfort, and Karen L. Peterson, pp. 133–143. Chicago Linguistic Society.

Harman, Gilbert. 1963. Generative grammars without transformational rules: A defense of phrase structure. *Language* 39: 597–616.

Hinrichs, Erhard, and Tsuneko Nakezawa. 1989. Subcategorization and VP structure in German. In *Proceedings of the Third Symposium on Germanic Linguistics*, ed. Shaun Hughes and Joe Salmons, pp. 1–12. Amsterdam: John Benjamins.

Hofmeister, Philip, and Ivan Sag. 2010. Cognitive constraints and island effects. *Language* 86: 366–415.

Hofmeister, Philip, Laura Staum Casasanto, and Ivan Sag. 2013a. Islands in the grammar? Standards of evidence. In *Experimental Syntax and Island Effects*, ed. Jon Sprouse and Norbert Hornstein. Cambridge University Press.

Hofmeister, Philip, Peter Culicover, and Susan Winkler. in press. Effects of processing on the acceptability of 'frozen' extraposed constituents. *Syntax*.

Hofmeister, Philip, Florian Jaeger, Inbal Arnon, Ivan Sag, and Neal Snider. 2013b. The source ambiguity problem: Distinguishing effects of grammar and processing on acceptability judgments. *Language and Cognitive Processes* 28: 48–87.

Hopcroft, John, and James Ullman. 1979. *Introduction to Automata Theory, Languages and Computation*. Reading, MA: Addison-Wesley.

Huddleston, Rodney. 1974. Further remarks on the analysis of auxiliaries as main verbs. *Foundations of Language* 11: 215–229.

2002. Nonfinite and verbless complementation. In *The Cambridge Grammar of the English Language*, ed. Rodney Huddleston and Geoffrey K. Pullum. Cambridge University Press.

Huddleston, Rodney, and Geoffrey K. Pullum. 2002. *The Cambridge Grammar of the English Language*. Cambridge University Press.

Kandybowicz, Jason. 2006. *Comp-Trace* effects explained away. In *Proceedings of the 25th West Coast Conference on Formal Linguistics*, ed. Donald Baumer, David Montero, and Michael Scanlon, pp. 220–228. Somerville, MA: Cascadilla Proceedings Project.

2009. Embracing edges: Syntactic and phono-syntactic edge sensitivity in Nupe. *Natural Language and Linguistic Theory* 27: 305–344.

Kathol, Andreas. 1999. Agreement and the syntax–morphology interface in HPSG. In *Studies in Contemporary Phrase Structure Grammar*, ed. Robert Levine and Georgia M. Green, pp. 223–274. Cambridge University Press.

Kayne, Richard, and Jean-Yves Pollock. 1978. Stylistic inversion, successive cyclicity and move NP in French. *Linguistic Inquiry* 9: 595–621.

Kehler, Andrew. 2002. *Coherence, Reference and the Theory of Grammar*. Stanford, CA: Center for the Study of Language and Information.

Kluender, Robert. 1998. On the distinction between strong and weak islands: A processing perspective. In *The Limits of Syntax*, ed. Peter Culicover and Louise McNally, pp. 241–279. New York: Academic Press.

Kozinsky, I.Š., V.P. Nedjalkov, and M.S. Polinskaya. 1988. Antipassive in Chukchee: Oblique object, object incorporation, zero object. In *Passive and Voice*, ed. Masayoshi Shibatani, pp. 651–707. Amsterdam and Philadelphia: John Benjamins.

Kubota, Yusuke, and Jungmin Lee. 2015. The Coordinate Structure Constraint as a discourse-oriented principle: Further evidence from Japanese and Korea. *Language* 91: 642–675.

Lakoff, George. 1986. Frame Semantic Control of the Coordinate Structure Constraint. In *Proceedings of the Chicago Linguistic Society 22.2*, ed. Anne M. Farley, Peter T. Farley, and Timothy Stowell, pp. 152–167. Chicago Linguistic Society.

Lapointe, Steven G. 1980. A lexical analysis of the English auxiliary verb system. In *Lexical Grammar*, ed. Teun Hoekstra, Harry van der Hulst, and Michael Moortgat, pp. 215–254. Dordrecht: Foris.

Levine, Robert. 2012. Auxiliaries: *To*'s company. *Journal of Linguistics* 48: 187–203.

Levine, Robert, and Thomas Hukari. 2006. *The Unity of Unbounded Dependency Constructions*. Stanford, CA: Center for the Study of Language and Information.

McCloskey, James. 1979. *Model-Theoretic Semantics and Transformational Grammar*. Dordrecht: Reidel.

Newmeyer, Frederick J. 1983. *Grammatical Theory: Its Limits and Its Possibilities*. University of Chicago Press.

Palmer, Frank R. 1994. *Grammatical Roles and Relations*. Cambridge University Press.

Pollard, Carl J., and Ivan Sag. 1987. *Information-Based Syntax and Semantics*. Stanford, CA: Center for the Study of Language and Information.

1991. An integrated theory of complement control. *Language* 67: 63–113.

1994. *Head-Driven Phrase Structure Grammar*. University of Chicago Press.

Postal, Paul. 1972. The best theory. In *Goals of Linguistic Theory*, ed. Stanley Peters. Englewood Cliffs, NJ: Prentice-Hall.

Pullum, Geoffrey K. 1982a. Syncategorematicity and English infinitival *to*. *Glossa* 16: 181–215.

1982b. Free word order and phrase structure rules. *Proceedings of the Northeastern Linguistics Society* 12: 209–220.

2011. On the mathematical foundations of *Syntactic Structures*. *Journal of Logic, Language and Information* 20: 277–296.

Pullum, Geoffrey K., and Rodney Huddleston. 2002. Negation. In *The Cambridge Grammar of the English Language*, ed. Rodney Huddleston and Geoffrey K. Pullum. Cambridge University Press.

Radford, Andrew. 1988. *Transformational Grammar: A First Course*. Cambridge University Press.

Reade, Charles. 1869. *The Cloister and the Hearth*. Boston, MA: Fields, Osgood & Co.

Ross, John R. 1969. Auxiliaries as main verbs. *Studies in Philosophical Linguistics* 1: 77–102.

Sag, Ivan, Lauri Karttunen, and Jeffrey Goldberg. 1992. A lexical analysis of Icelandic case. In *Lexical Matters*, ed. Ivan Sag and Anna Szabolcsi, pp. 301–318. Stanford, CA: CSLI.

Shieber, Stuart. 1985. Evidence against the context-freeness of natural language. *Linguistics and Philosophy* 8: 333–344.

Zaenen, Annie. 1983. On syntactic binding. *Linguistic Inquiry* 14: 469–504.

Index

absolutes, 116–119

adjuncts, 54, 55, 74, 79–100, 132, 149, 155, 157, 167–169, 171, 182, 187, 191, 192, 206, 253, 266, 268, 272, 274, 276, 290, 292, 295

agreement, 65, 67, 83, 87, 93, 109, 140, 141, 146–151, 183–187, 244, 246, 250, 256, 263

antipassive, 189–192

argument inheritance, 226–234

auxiliaries, 14, 17, 66, 67, 101–141, 146, 150, 151, 167, 168, 178, 186, 187, 195, 196, 202, 207–218, 239, 245

auxiliary, 196

auxiliary dependency, 102–141

auxiliary inversion, 105–106, 108, 120, 136–141

behaviorist era in psychology, 319, 322

bounding nodes, 296–297

bracket notation, 10, 24–28, 38, 52, 79

case, 143–146

in Icelandic, 145–146

center embedding, 305–307, 322

Chukchee, 188–190

clausal subject inversion, 163–165

clefts, 285, 299

complementizers, 89–97, 159, 204–205, 237, 269, 272, 275–276, 283–285, 300

complements, 295

Complex NP Constraint, 293–295, 321

COMPS, 56–76, 82, 88–101

COMPS feature, 236, 237, 240–242, 246, 250

Conjunct Constraint, 299

constituency, 14–37, 57, 95, 101

containment relation, 25–29

context-free rules, 42, 47, 60

contraction, 106–107

control verbs, 217

Coordinate Structure Constraint (CSC), 297–299, 309–314

cost/take, 291, 292

deontic interpretation, 140

determiners, 76, 82–85, 95, 101, 146–149, 204

displacement, 8–24, 30–36, 92, 93, 97, 165, 236–278

test, 11, 12, 16, 21, 24, 37, 45, 46, 52, 58, 90, 98, 181, 182

do so, 13–32, 113, 114, 116, 168, 214, 227, 229

domination relation, 25–35, 42

Element Constraint, 299

ellipsis, 107–108, 140, 212–213

Empty Category Principle (ECP), 315

empty list, 60, 62, 70, 71, 74, 75

ergativity, 188–192

extraposition, 166–174, 202, 287

features, 56, 58

French, 148–151, 226–234, 264

grammar, 18, 33, 34, 36, 38, 42, 47, 55, 56, 58, 59, 65, 73, 85, 86, 94, 98, 99

Head Feature Principle, 66, 67, 69, 70, 74, 75, 82

HEAD features, 66–69

Head-adjunct Rule, 88–89, 234

Head-complement Rule, 69–76, 82, 85, 199, 232, 234, 245, 246

Head-filler Rule, 258–261

Head-marker Rule, 205

Head-specifier Rule, 84, 85, 194, 195, 197

Head-specifier-complement Rule, 137

Head-subject Rule, 73–76, 90, 245

Head-subject-complement Rule, 141

heavy NPs, 44, 152, 161, 181, 183, 195, 200

Icelandic, 272–275

immediate constituency, 25–26

immediate dominance, 26, 29, 61

immediate precedence, 35

infinitival complements, 94, 159–162, 194, 234

infinitival *to*, 202, 218

INV feature, 141

inversion, 207, 212, 247, 264

Irish, 269–272

island phenomena, 293–323

judicial sanction, 64, 65